COM+ Programming
with Visual Basic

COM+ Programming
with Visual Basic

Jose Mojica

O'REILLY®

Beijing · Cambridge · Farnham · Köln · Paris · Sebastopol · Taipei · Tokyo

COM+ Programming with Visual Basic
by Jose Mojica

Published by O'Reilly & Associates, Inc., 101 Morris Street, Sebastopol, CA 95472.

Editor: Ron Petrusha

Production Editor: Catherine Morris

Cover Designer: Pam Spremulli

Printing History:

> June 2001:   First Edition.

Library of Congress Cataloging-in-Publication Data

Mojica, Jose.
   COM+ programming with Visual Basic / Jose Mojica.
     p. cm.
   ISBN 1-56592-840-7
    1. COM (Computer architecture) 2. Computer programming 3. Microsoft Visual BASIC. I. Title.

QA76.9.A73 M65 2001
005.2'768--dc21   2001033137

[M]

Table of Contents

Preface

From 1992 to 1997, 95% of my development was done in Visual Basic, and about 5% of my development involved writing components for Visual Basic using the Microsoft Foundation Classes (MFC) in C++. Then, in 1998, I received an offer from a company to develop a set of COM components using a class library called the ActiveX Template Library (ATL) exclusively in C++. At the time I took the position, I thought I knew COM fairly well, and although I knew the C++ side of development would be a little difficult, I was convinced that within a few months I would be able to master it. Boy, was I in for a big surprise! After a few days, I realized that I knew very little about COM. In fact, I learned that, in many ways, Visual Basic shields us from knowing about COM. Part of me thought, "That's what VB is for—to hide you from the details of the technology so that you can be more productive."

After a few months at the job, I realized that, although the goal of Visual Basic is to hide the architecture so that we can be more productive, it turns out that there are many times in Visual Basic development when the technology sneaks out from under the covers. Once in a while, you will see options like DLL Base Address or Threading Model and wonder, "Should I turn that on?" "Should I change that number?" "What exactly does that mean?" The most frustrating thing is being faced with the technology and not knowing how to solve a simple problem only because VB has done such a good job at hiding things in the past. I also realized that had I known how things worked internally in the architecture, I would have done things completely differently on occasion. From then on, I was on a crusade to learn! I wanted to learn exactly how things worked not only in the component architecture but also at the operating system level.

Later, COM+ was released. Once again, Microsoft made it extremely easy for us to take COM components and make them part of a COM+ application and apply services to them. But then I would hear things like, "Make sure not to add all your components to it" or "Make sure not to turn on transactions for your components if you are using only one database." It is extremely frustrating to have to deal with the technology and be told not to do this and to do that and not really know what you are supposed to do. I found that learning the guts of the technology may be hard at first but that it makes it significantly easier later to make decisions about design, coding, and deployment.

Later this year, you are going to see a brand new component architecture from Microsoft called .NET. You may be wondering how .NET is going to change things for COM+. .NET is a completely new architecture resembling COM+ very little. However, let me assure you that COM+ is not going away any time soon. In fact, the Windows 2000 operating system is heavily dependent on COM+. What's more, it is going to be a while before the COM+ services work natively with .NET. But I do not want to sound like a salesperson here! Instead, I would like to tell you what I believe will happen next year to us VB developers.

My current job is teaching COM+ and Visual Basic .NET to different companies. When I teach Visual Basic .NET, students often come to me and say, "But what has happened to Visual Basic—it no longer hides any of the internals." Visual Basic .NET is a brand new language. It is going to radically change the expectations of VB developers. In many ways, the things you will have to know about the runtime and about the way the architecture works will be the same things that C++ developers programming in C# will have to know. By the end of next year, if Microsoft is successful with its deployment of .NET and your company adopts it, your programming job will be very different. It is my opinion that you should start learning things now. This book will help you with both the COM+ side and the transition to .NET.

What I have tried to do in this book is not to teach you every detail about COM+ services. My goal was rather to teach you how the architecture works. The services are arguably the icing on the cake. For example, this book does not cover COM+ events. Some of you may ask, "Why not?" Well, the services in COM+ may come and go; what's important for you to learn is how the architecture works internally. Then, you will be able to quickly figure out any of the services. I felt that it would be best to cover the services that have the biggest impact in your life: transactions and security. The rest of the COM+ coverage in the book focuses on how Microsoft is able to provide you with the services in the first place and how to interact with the environment.

Who This Book Is For

I often joke with my colleagues that the target audience for this book is VB developers who are tired of hearing that C++ developers know more than they do. If you are tired of not knowing how the technology works and why VB does things the way it does and if you are tired of wondering when to turn on this switch as opposed to this other switch, this book is for you.

Now, I felt compelled to tell you up front who this book is not for. If you are looking for a book that just tells you the basics of the technology with practical code that you can plug into your application and with the idea that you will learn how to create a three-tier database application, unfortunately, this book is not for you.

You do not have to be an advanced VB developer to pick up this book, but you do have to have the mindset that this book is about the guts of the technology. I want to stress that the sample code in this book is meant to illustrate how the architecture works and sometimes to stretch VB's capabilities. If you miss books like *Hardcore Visual Basic*, by Bruce McKinney, this book is for you.

This book is also for you if you are interested in learning the guts of .NET for VB developers. Granted, it is very difficult to explain everything about .NET in one chapter, but I believe the information in that last chapter will give you an appreciation for how the technology has changed internally and how beneficial the changes are.

How This Book Is Organized

The term COM+ is a marketing term and, as such, tends to confuse certain things. For example, people sometimes get confused about the distinction between the abbreviations COM, DCOM, MTS, and COM+. In reality, the term COM+ refers to two things. First, COM+ represents the integration of the COM model with the MTS services model. Second, COM+ refers to a series of services that Microsoft provides for you, like distributed transactioning, role-based security, easy deployment of your application, and so forth. The acronym COM in many ways sounds old in comparison to COM+, but this is just a side effect of the marketing effort. In reality, COM and COM+ are the same thing when it comes to how the components are made. COM+ components are COM components, and COM components are now called COM+ components.

With that in mind, the book is organized as follows:

Chapter 1, *COM+ Internals*

Explains the progression from COM to DCOM to MTS, COM+, and finally .NET. It is meant to provide you with an overview of what Microsoft has been trying to accomplish with component technology for the last eight years and where we are headed later this year and next year.

Chapter 2, *Interface-Based Programming*

Explains the benefits of using interfaces in your programming and shows how interfaces are crucial for versioning. It also explains why COM uses interfaces.

Chapter 3, *How Interfaces Work Internally*

Explains what interfaces look like at the memory level. The chapter is meant to expose you to how the VB compiler generates VB COM objects in memory. It also exposes you to the most widely used interfaces in COM, IUnknown and IDispatch.

Chapter 4, *In-Process Servers*

Discusses how ActiveX DLLs work. It discusses the difference between the *CreateObject* function and the New keyword. It also explains how objects are instantiated and examines the process of activation from the client to the server.

Chapter 5, *Out-of-Process Servers and COM's Remoting Architecture*

Explains how ActiveX EXEs work. It explains multithreading, including COM's apartment model. It also explains how COM makes it easy for a client to talk to a remote component, but at the cost of performance.

Chapter 6, *Versioning*

Explains how to go about creating new versions of your components that are compatible with old versions. This chapter explains the difference between binary compatibility, project compatibility, and no compatibility. Also, this chapter shows how to write interfaces in IDL.

Chapter 7, *COM+ Applications*

Explains what COM+ services are. It also explains how to create a COM+ application and add your components to it. This chapter shows how to deploy COM+ applications to client machines.

Chapter 8, *Writing and Debugging COM+ Code*

Shows how to write code that interacts with the COM+ services. This chapter also talks about the COM+ architecture and discusses various ways to debug your application.

Chapter 9, *Transaction Services*

First discusses transactions and record locking in general while focusing on SQL Server and Oracle. It then examines how to talk to the Distributed Transaction

Coordinator (DTC), which enables you to have multiple database systems involved in the same transaction. At the end of the chapter, you learn the effects of turning on transactioning services for your components.

Chapter 10, *COM+ Security*

Discusses how COM and COM+ security affects the communication between clients and servers. The chapter explains how COM+ security has its roots in RPC security and shows you how to make calls to the server—including requests over the Web—secure.

Chapter 11, *Introduction to .NET*

Covers the architecture of .NET and how compilers produce Intermediate Language (IL). This chapter also shows the new versioning scheme in .NET, as well as many of the other new features in VB.NET. Thereafter, the chapter shows how to mix both COM+ and .NET.

Obtaining The Sample Code

All of the example Visual Basic source code from *COM+ Programming with Visual Basic* is freely downloadable from the O'Reilly & Associates web site at *vb.oreilly.com*. Just follow the link to the book's title page, then click on the *Examples* link.

Conventions Used in This Book

Throughout this book, we have used the following typographic conventions:

`Constant width`

Indicates a language construct such as a language statement, a constant, or an expression. Interface names appear in constant width. Lines of code also appear in constant width, as do function and method prototypes.

Italic

Represents intrinsic and application-defined functions, the names of system elements such as directories and files, and Internet resources such as web documents. New terms are also italicized when they are first introduced.

`Constant width italic`

Indicates replaceable parameter names in prototypes or command syntax and indicates variable and parameter names in body text.

How to Contact Us

We have tested and verified all the information in this book to the best of our ability, but you may find that features have changed (or even that we have made mistakes!). Please let us know about any errors you find, as well as your suggestions for future editions, by writing to:

O'Reilly & Associates
101 Morris Street
Sebastopol, CA 95472
1-800-998-9938 (in the U.S. or Canada)
1-707-829-0515 (international/local)
1-707-829-0104 (fax)

You can also send messages electronically. To be put on our mailing list or to request a catalog, send email to:

nuts@oreilly.com

To ask technical questions or comment on the book, send email to:

bookquestions@oreilly.com

For technical information on Visual Basic programming, to participate in VB discussion forums, or to acquaint yourself with O'Reilly's line of Visual Basic books, you can access the O'Reilly Visual Basic web site at:

http://vb.oreilly.com

Acknowledgments

I would like to thank my editor and first tech reviewer, Ron Petrusha. Ron did a lot of work to make this book a reality. I would like to thank my colleagues at DevelopMentor who reviewed this book, including Ian Griffiths, who provided me with a lot of insight on the way that compilers work and the internals of interfaces; Bob Beauchemin, our database expert, who added valuable comments to my transactions/database chapter; and Keith Brown, from whom I learned everything I know about security through his book, *Programming Windows Security*, his articles, his comments on my security chapter, and his talks at DevelopMentor. These guys were directly involved in the tech review of this book. Also, I would like to honorably mention Timothy J. Ewald; among other things, he came up with the term *raw-configured components*, and he's directly responsible for my passion for topics such as context, activities, and JITA. I would also like to thank Daniel Creeron for doing a complete once-over on the book.

I know that technically my wife and kids did not do the writing for the book, but I would like to thank them for putting up with the many hours I had to invest in writing it. Thank you.

1

COM+ Internals

As Visual Basic developers, you and I love the fact that VB lets us create full applications in a relatively short amount of time. There is no doubt that, compared to other languages on the market, Visual Basic stands out as perhaps the leading rapid application development (RAD) language. One of the things that make Visual Basic so easy to use is that VB hides a lot of the details of the technology from us. In Visual Basic, for example, you could live a happy and fruitful life without knowing what a message loop is or learning anything about the types of messages that the OS sends to each window. (If you do not know how things are done at this level, then you are proof that the Visual Basic team has done its job correctly.)

COM+ is also an architecture that the Visual Basic team has decided to hide from you. The problem is that almost every aspect of what you can or cannot do with Visual Basic classes is governed by the rules of COM. You may ponder the fact that every "public" class you have in an ActiveX DLL or ActiveX EXE is a COM component, and you may decide that item of information is just an interesting piece of trivia. According to this view, in the real world it matters not whether you are writing COM components or Widgets—the only thing that matters is that they work correctly and that they deliver what they have promised. This is an interesting thought, because the real question then becomes: what do we gain from COM+? It seems fitting then to take some time to define the term and analyze some of the claims it has made.

What Is COM+?

COM+ is an interesting term. What makes COM+ a particularly interesting term is that it is used very frequently, yet very few people know what the term actually means. Most people think COM+ is the next version of COM. (The term *COM* refers to the Component Object Model—a specification Microsoft introduced in 1992.) Actually, COM has changed very little from its Windows NT 4.0 cycle to the introduction of COM+ in Windows 2000. It is fair to say that COM+ is actually more the next version of a Microsoft product named Microsoft Transaction Server (MTS), and it is even more exact to say that COM+ is actually the integration of the MTS service model with the COM APIs. To understand what all this means, let's talk about COM first, then MTS, then see why these two models were merged in COM+.

COM

As I mentioned earlier, *COM* stands for the Component Object Model. COM is one of those terms that sound old; in fact, the first specification came out around 1992. However, COM is still heavily used today; without COM there would be no COM+. In fact, without COM, VB classes and components would behave very differently.

COM is a specification, and it is also to some extent the implementation of the specification. The goals of COM are the following:

Interoperability between different languages
> Components from one language should communicate with components from another language. Also, a client program written in one language should be able to use a component written in a different language.

A standard for versioning
> *Versioning* is a big word, but it means that existing client programs should work with newer versions of the component. Actually, the versioning scheme dictates that new versions of the client should work with old versions of the component as well. They may decide to display a message telling the user to upgrade the component, but the program should not crash.

Environment for components with different threading requirements
> COM is a technology for interoperability between components that have high thread affinity and those that have low thread affinity or no thread affinity. *High thread affinity* means that certain components can get calls from only one thread. Visual Basic components have high thread affinity. *Low thread affinity* means that the component may have a group of threads making calls into its methods. *No thread affinity* means that the component may receive calls from any thread. COM was designed to enable communication between all these types of components.

Location transparency
> *Location transparency* is the idea that you should be able to write a client program in such a way that the code works when the component is on the same thread, a different thread in the same process, a different process on the same machine, or even a different process on a different machine. There should be

no difference in the way you write code to use that component. There may be a difference in how you design the methods for the component. For example, if you know a component is going to be used remotely, you may design the methods to minimize the round-trips around the network, but the bottom line is that a client will use the same method calls when the component is local as when the component is deployed remotely.

One of the main aspects of the COM specification is the definition of what a COM interface is and what those interfaces look like in memory. COM is therefore a specification for compiler makers for how COM objects should behave and how their interfaces should look in memory. The specification also discusses how COM components are packaged into COM servers. In the VB world, we know those packages as ActiveX DLLs or ActiveX EXEs.

COM is more than a specification. Microsoft also ships COM libraries that have APIs for creating instances of COM objects. COM also includes a loader that uses the registry to find the ActiveX DLL or ActiveX EXE hosting the components.

The architecture of COM and its promises have not changed very much in the transition to COM+—COM+ components are really COM with a different name. What has changed to some degree is the way that the APIs work and the loader (the things Microsoft ships with the OS). The main difference in the APIs is that they have knowledge of the MTS model. To understand that statement better, let's talk about MTS.

Microsoft Transaction Server (MTS)

MTS was originally a separate product that worked with Windows NT 4.0 and was part of the NT Option Pack 4.0. It was meant to serve as an *object broker*—a server product that manages instances of objects. It was also meant to be a piece of software that would interact with and drive the Distributed Transaction Coordinator (DTC). The DTC is a service that manages transactions that involve more than one database (or other resource managers) at the same time. Transactions that involve more than one resource manager are hard to manage; they involve the use of a protocol known as the two-phase commit protocol. Also, MTS introduced a way to better manage the security of the components at a method level. MTS uses a model called role-based security, in which you can define groups of users and grant them access to different parts of the component.

What makes MTS an interesting product is that in order to offer services such as an ability to drive the DTC, to support role-based security, and even to some extent to control the lifetime of objects, MTS uses a model known as interception. *Interception* means that, when the client creates an instance of your component, MTS intercepts the request and hands you an object that looks just like the object you requested. Internally, MTS then creates an instance of the true object the client requested. The idea is that every time you make a method call, the call actually goes through the impostor MTS-provided object first before reaching the true object. By intercepting each call, MTS can provide services that do their job before and after each method call.

The problem facing the MTS team was that they did not want to add their code directly to the COM APIs in the first release. For example, it is a lot easier to intercept a call to create a component if the API calls in COM are MTS-aware to begin with. However, if you do not want to change the way the APIs work, then you have to resort to other techniques of interception that could be considered "hacks." When you specify that you would like your component to be an MTS component (and this is done by adding your component to an MTS package through an administration program), MTS changes some registry keys. The changes it makes to the registry tell the COM APIs that the ActiveX EXE containing your component is actually *MTX.EXE*, an MTS server, instead of your server. This little trick makes it possible for MTS to inject its code before creating an instance of your COM component. As a result, in Windows NT 4.0, COM and MTS work together but are not integrated.

The problem with this lack of integration is that at times you have to code your COM component in such a way that you will not break the relationship between the impostor component and your component. It is very easy to do things that can make the client retrieve a reference to your component instead of to the MTS impostor component, and the result is that the services stop working correctly. The full integration of the COM architecture with the MTS mode is known as COM+, and it is available only in Windows 2000.

COM+

COM+ is the next version of MTS. It is the next version in the sense that it relies on the MTS model of interception and also adds a few new services. If you know how to write code that interacts with the MTS services, then you know how to interact with the COM+ services—the functions are practically identical, and all the old functions work in COM+. One big improvement is that when you specify that a COM component is part of a COM+ application (MTS packages have been renamed to COM+ applications), the system does not rely on registry hacks to provide you with services. The COM APIs have been rewritten to detect that the COM component has been marked as a COM+ component and to provide the client with the impostor object instead of a direct reference to the true object.

Therefore, be aware that the COM architecture itself has not changed much. A few concepts have been added in COM, such as a new boundary called *context* that you will learn about in this book. The main thing to realize is that the literature on COM+ sometimes refers to the architecture of the components (which in reality is just COM, just as it was before), and sometimes it refers to the new services (or really the new version of MTS).

COM and COM+

In this book, you are going to learn how COM technology works and how to interact with the services. The reason we refer to things as COM in the first half of the book instead of COM+ is that, in reality, COM+ is COM with a few enhancements. At the end of the day, what you are really writing are COM components that work in COM+ applications. The book also shows you how some of the most interesting services work internally. This leads us to another question—in the world of Visual Basic, why do we need to know how things work internally?

Knowing the Internals

If we are VB developers and the goal of VB is to hide the COM+ architecture, why do we need to know things at a low level? Well, it turns out that VB is good about hiding 90% of the technology. The problem is that the other 10% makes life very difficult. A number of topics can be mastered only if you understand how the architecture works internally. It becomes a lot easier to solve those problems if you have a good grasp of the architecture than if you don't; in fact, in some cases, it becomes possible for you to solve those problems, whereas it remains impossible without some knowledge of the internals.

It would be easy for me to just tell you to stay away from this or that feature or to turn on this option in x situation and to turn it off in y situation (and in fact a lot of authors do just that). I felt that, as a VB developer, I'd had enough of not knowing why some things work the way they do; life gets a lot easier when you know exactly what's happening. It turns out that with some knowledge of the internals, you can also stretch VB farther than you could imagine. Let's take a look at some of the topics in the troublesome 10% of COM/COM+ technology.

One of the most frustrating things in Visual Basic is versioning. The problem with versioning is that VB tries to hide too much from you. You may have had, for example, the situation in which you recompile your ActiveX DLL or ActiveX EXE and then find that the client program using it stops working. Some developers end up rebuilding every component and every client every time a little change is made. However, it turns out that one of the reasons VB uses COM as its core technology is to prevent the situation in which you have to distribute everything again to the client.

The problem is that VB components use COM interfaces to group their methods, and these interfaces have a globally unique identifier (GUID) number assigned to them. The client uses GUIDs to tell COM what interface and what component it wants to create. C++ developers have full control of how the GUIDs are generated and when they are changed—they work with GUIDs directly. VB developers do not look at GUIDs directly; the compiler and debugger generate the numbers automatically as needed. By default, the compiler assigns a new GUID each time you compile the project. When you compile the client using that interface, the client code becomes dependent on the GUID for that interface. Since the default in VB is to generate new ones, each time you re-compile the component's project, you end up with a new GUID, and the existing clients stop working.

If you are an experienced VB developer, you may be thinking, "That's not a problem—all you have to know is how to set the Version Compatibility options in Project Properties." It turns out, though, that those settings work well only part of the time. Those options are meant to instruct VB when to keep GUIDs the same as before and when to generate new ones. However, sometimes even a small change to one class is enough to force VB to change the GUIDs for every class in the project.

The versioning problem is easier to master if you use interface-based programming, understand the COM activation sequence, understand how GUIDs are assigned to each part of your component, understand the difference between the **New** operator and the *CreateObject* function in VB, and understand the difference between the versioning options. To make it even easier to master, however, you could take full control over interface declarations by creating your own type libraries. A *type library* is a binary file that describes the interfaces and components in an ActiveX DLL or ActiveX EXE. VB automatically creates a type library and embeds it as part of the ActiveX DLL or ActiveX EXE. In extreme cases, it turns out that you could even replace the type library VB creates with one you create.

You can, of course, develop components and COM+ applications without knowing about any of these disparate topics and techniques, but, sooner or later, you're going to run into versioning problems. And quite possibly, others may suspect that the versioning problems resulted from your breaking the "COM contract." Armed with knowledge of these topics, you're much less likely to run into versioning problems. As a result, you'll be able to create much more sophisticated COM+ applications that at the same time are far more robust and require far less maintenance.

The second aspect of COM programming that seems to surface before long is threading. It's true that as a VB developer you do not have to create your own threads, or even worry about multiple threads making calls into your methods at the same time. However, knowing about threading can sometimes save you a lot of problems. The first evidence that the VB team could not hide threading issues altogether is in Project Properties, where there is a setting for ActiveX DLLs called Threading Model. How can anyone choose the value for this option without understanding what a threading model is in the first place? To make matters worse, there are settings like Unattended Execution and Retained in Memory that complicate things a little.

The way in which VB manages variables and objects like the App object and the Err object when your objects work in different threads also makes threading knowledge necessary. It turns out that global variables (and we can discuss the merits of using them in the first place in a later discussion) stop being global when your components run in different threads. You have to keep in mind that even though your component code may not be creating multiple threads, COM+ will be creating multiple threads and managing instances of your components, sometimes in different threads and sometimes in the same thread. So data that your application treats as global is suddenly not so global anymore.

Finally, there are a number of services in COM+ that are not available to VB developers solely because of our threading model, and there are some services that were designed to accommodate VB's threading models. What makes things more difficult is that it is very easy to break the COM safety for VB objects and in some cases cause deadlocks if you do not understand how COM's threading mechanism works.

The third issue that quickly comes into play is the myth of *location transparency*. The problem with location transparency is that COM has taught us that components should work equally well when they are on the same thread as when they are in a different process on a different machine. The problem is that round-trips along the network or the Internet take a lot longer than direct calls to a component on the same thread. Thus, this is another area in which knowing what is happening internally, and especially knowing how to adjust settings in COM+ services, can greatly increase your performance.

Some developers make the mistake of putting a component in a COM+ application and leaving the settings with the default values. It turns out that the defaults are there for backward compatibility with MTS. By turning off about five features, you gain lots of performance benefits and consume a lot less memory.

The fourth aspect of programming that requires a low-level knowledge is transactions. Nearly every database application in COM+ eventually deals with the transactions. Many developers make the mistake of turning on transactioning support for their components just because they want to use transactions in their code. In Chapter 9, you will learn everything that happens when you turn on transactioning support in COM+ applications.

Finally, there is the issue of security. VB has absolutely nothing for adjusting security in COM components. This is one of the aspects of the architecture that is just not addressed with high-level features on the Visual Basic side. As a result, it is very difficult for VB developers to readily understand how to ensure that information is transmitted in a secure fashion between the client program and the server program. It is also very difficult to understand how security in Internet Information Server (IIS) affects your COM+ applications.

Introduction to .NET

By the time this book hits the streets, you likely will have heard about a new technology coming from Microsoft called Microsoft .NET (.NET for short). The question in a lot of developer's minds is "How does .NET interact with COM+?" Well, the bad news is that .NET has very little to do with COM. Microsoft has decided in many ways to abandon the existing COM architecture for developing components and is investing instead in a brand new technology called .NET. That does not mean that COM+ is dead; in fact, for the first version of .NET, if you are planning on using COM+ services, it makes a lot more sense to develop COM+ components than .NET components. Also, the current versions of the OS and the upcoming version, Windows XP, are all built to use COM+ natively. It will be a couple of years before the COM+ services are changed to .NET services.

However, Microsoft is making it possible to use .NET components in COM+ through a COM callable wrapper. The idea is that the .NET execution engine, the software responsible for loading and executing .NET components, will also act as a COM server. Thus, .NET components will use the same principles as MTS in which the calls to them from COM clients will go through yet another impostor object that will do the job of translating calls from COM (now referred to as unmanaged space) to .NET (referred to as managed space). It is possible through wrappers for .NET components to make calls to COM components and for COM components to make calls to .NET components. In Chapter 11, you will learn the details of this brand new architecture and how to make the two architectures interoperate.

All the major compilers (VB included) have been rewritten to emit a high-level form of assembly language called Intermediate Language (or IL). This means that VB will no longer compile code to native code that the processor can understand. Instead, VB compiles code to IL, and a Just-in-Time compiler at runtime (or at deployment time) changes the IL code to native code. The concept is similar to the way Java programs execute. Because the compilers have been changed to emit IL, a number of features have been added or changed to conform to the IL specification. In many ways, VB.NET is a brand new language—with a lot of exciting enhancements. In Chapter 11 you will also learn about IL, the .NET architecture, and the new features in VB.NET.

2

Interface-Based Programming

In this chapter, you will learn the basics of interface-based programming. Although this may seem like review to some Visual Basic developers, the truth is that—from my experience teaching at various companies—very few developers understand how interfaces work in Visual Basic, and those who do, do not employ interface programming in their projects.

Interfaces are the primary building blocks of COM+. What's more, even if it may have been possible to avoid interface-based programming with Visual Basic altogether in previous versions of COM and Windows, this is no longer possible with COM+ and Windows 2000. To take advantage of the new features of COM+, you must understand interface-based programming and write your code in such a way that it utilizes interfaces as much as possible. Interface-based programming is not only necessary to take advantage of new features in COM+, but it also provides us with a mechanism for upgrading our components. Furthermore, interface-based programming makes it possible for us to use a feature in object-oriented programming known as *polymorphism*. Polymorphism is a loaded term in the object-oriented world. One definition is that multiple classes may have the same method with the same signature (input and output parameters) but have slightly different semantics. For example, classes like CChecking and CSavings may each have a MakeDeposit method, and even though the overall intent of the methods may be the same (to add money to the account's balance), it may be that each implementation is slightly different. With polymorphism, it is possible to write a global function that takes as a parameter either of these classes and calls the appropriate implementation of the MakeDeposit method depending on the object type that the caller sent in. Another definition is that a component can act as if it were a collection of multiple components. If you create an instance of the component, it may be used with a function that works with type A components, or it may be used with another function that expects B components. A component that can act as many different components is said to be *polymorphic*. You'll learn more about these two aspects of polymorphism later.

After you learn the basics of interface-based programming, you will learn about some standard interfaces that are available in COM+. VB hides the use of these standard interfaces from developers. However, to truly understand COM+, you are going to examine the inner workings of VB objects and discover how VB uses these standard interfaces behind the scenes.

But before you learn the principles of interface-based programming, you may want to examine why you want to bother with it at all.

Why Interface-Based Programming?

In the "good old days" of Basic programming, software was built using line numbers, GoTos, GoSubs, and Returns. A program would normally start at line 100 and continue linearly through lines of code numbered at intervals of 10. Many times, a portion of the code needed to be used from more than one place in the program. In those instances, programmers would place the code in line 1000, for example, and call it from wherever it was needed by issuing the command `GoSub 1000`. The code at line 1000 would then execute and, after it was done, it would issue the `Return` command. So programmers would end up with code such as the following:

```
100 REM This is my GWBasic program
110 Dim A As Integer, VL As Integer, VH As Integer, bC As Integer
120 Print "Welcome to Widgets USA Order System"
130 Print "Select from the menu options below..."
140 Print "1. Enter Order"
150 Print "2. List Orders"
160 Print "3. Delete Order"
170 Print ""
180 Input "Enter number 1-3",A
190 REM Let's check that the input was valid
200 VL = 1 : VH = 3: Gosub 1000
210 If bC = 1 Then Goto 500
220 Print "Incorrect menu option, please try again"
230 Goto 180
500 REM Continue executing program
999 END
1000 REM This piece of code checks that we have a valid entry
1010 If A >=VL or A<=VH Then bC=1 Else bC = 0
1020 Return
```

Lines 1000 through 1020 check the validity of a menu entry. They assume that VL was set to the lowest valid entry and VH was set to the highest valid entry prior to executing the code. The code also assumes that the entry number the user selected is stored in the A variable. This piece of code returns bC = 1 if the entry was valid or bC = 0 if the entry was invalid.

Except for the very few developers who are still using DOS and GWBASIC and refuse to upgrade their 286 machines, the majority of Basic developers would agree that the preceding code listing is very difficult to maintain and upgrade. Suppose, for example, that you were asked to pull the code that verifies the validity of a menu choice from the program and insert it into another project. You cannot use the code in lines 1000 through 1020 without also importing the line that declares the necessary variables (line 110). You also need to make sure the values of VL and VH are set before calling the code (line 200), not to mention that the user's menu choice must be stored in variable A (line 180). Then, you must make sure that the menu-display code uses the variable bC to determine whether to continue with the program or ask the user to reenter his choice (line 210). All this, and this is only a 19-line program!

A step in the right direction was the introduction of subroutines and functions in Quick Basic. This made it possible to create a *VerifyMenuChoice* subroutine from the code in lines 1000 to 1020, as follows:

```
Function VerifyMenuChoice(Choice As Integer, LowVal As Integer, _
                    HighVal As Integer) As Integer
    'This piece of code checks that we have a valid entry

    If Choice>=LowVal And MenuChoice<=HighVal Then
       VerifyMenuChoice = -1
    Else
        VerifyMenuChoice = 0
    End If

End Function
```

The menu code could then be rewritten to use the code in the subroutine:

```
100 REM This is my QuickBasic program
110 Dim A As Integer
120 Print "Welcome to Widgets USA Order System"
130 Print "Select from the menu options below..."
140 Print "1. Enter Order"
150 Print "2. List Orders"
160 Print "3. Delete Order"
170 Print ""
180 Input "Enter number 1-3",A
190 REM Let's check that the input was valid
210 If VerifyMenuChoice(A, 1, 3) = -1 Then Goto 500
220 Print "Incorrect menu option, please try again"
230 Goto 180
500 REM Continue executing program
999 END
```

We could go a step farther and place the code that displays the menu itself into a function as follows:

```
Function DisplayMainMenu() As Boolean
    Dim A As Integer
    Print "Welcome to Widgets USA Order System"
    Print "Select from the menu options below..."
    Print "1. Enter Order"
    Print "2. List Orders"
    Print "3. Delete Order"
    Print ""
    Input "Enter number 1-3",A
    DisplayMainMenu = A
End Function
```

Then with the aid of the **Do While...Loop** language enhancements, we could get rid of line numbers altogether and rewrite the code as follows:

```
'This is my Quick Basic Program
Dim A As Integer

A = DisplayMainMenu()

Do While VerifyMenuChoice(A, 1, 3) = 0
    Print "Incorrect menu option, please try again"
    A = DisplayMainMenu()
Loop

'Continue executing program
END
```

Not only is the preceding code easier to read, it also is easier to reuse. You may, for example, use the *DisplayMainMenu* and *VerifyMenuChoice* functions in other projects without needing to make modifications to them.

Subroutines enable us to reuse code and to maintain it. However, they do nothing to facilitate code distribution. The previous code would most likely have been distributed as part of one executable. If there had been a bug in the *DisplayMainMenu* function, the company would have had to ship a new copy of the executable. What's more, if multiple executables were using the same code, the company would have had to ship a number of executables just because of a bug fix in one function. Also, if the code had been enhanced to display a fancier menu, each executable would have to be rebuilt to take advantage of the new features. One danger was that some executables could have been missed, and thus some of the programs would have displayed the old version of the menu while others displayed the new version. But that never happened, right?

What we need is a way to reuse code, not at a source level but at a binary level. Windows was built from the ground up to address the issue of code distribution. It did this by introducing Dynamic Link Libraries (DLLs). DLLs provide us with precompiled libraries of functions. Multiple programs can bind to a DLL and call the functions in it. In the Windows equivalent of the previous example, *DisplayMainMenu* and *VerifyMenuChoice* would be exported functions of a DLL (*funcs.dll*, for example). The code that uses those functions would have been part of an executable that binds to that DLL. To access the DLL, a VB developer would have to add a declaration for each function of the DLL, as follows:

```
Declare Function DisplayMainMenu Lib "funcs.dll" () As Integer
Declare Function VerifyMenuChoice Lib "funcs.dll" (MenuChoice As Integer, _
        LowValue As Integer, HighValue As Integer) As Boolean
```

This was definitely of great advantage in the areas of code maintenance and reuse. It was good for code maintenance because if multiple programs used the *DisplayMainMenu* function and a bug needed to be fixed in the function, it would have been possible to simply send customers a new version of the *funcs.dll* library without recompiling the executables. Likewise, if the *DisplayMainMenu* function had been enhanced, programs using the function would automatically use the new version of the function as soon as the old version of the DLL was replaced by the new version. DLLs were also good for code reuse because multiple executables could use the same set of functions in the DLL.

Another paradigm that has influenced software development is *abstraction*. We live in an object-oriented world. Nearly everything we interact with can be thought of as an object. Consider, for example, your VCR interacting with your TV, both of them sitting on a table. Each of these objects has properties. You do not have to know how they work; they just work. You only have to know how to connect them together. If you want to upgrade your TV, you can simply buy a new one and plug the old VCR into it—it is that simple.

Developers like to represent programming tasks as objects—this is known as abstraction. In a bank application, a developer may begin writing software by first defining components, which may include an Account component. The Account component may have a property for the account balance, and it may have functionality attached to it, such as the ability to deposit and withdraw money.

Function-based programming with DLLs does not support abstraction and therefore does not support object-oriented programming. DLLs serve as a library of functions only and therefore lack object qualities.

The need for abstraction and for object-oriented paradigms led developers to more object-oriented languages, such as C++ and Smalltalk. The need for object-oriented paradigms has also influenced Visual Basic. In Visual Basic 4.0, Microsoft introduced a new type of code module known as the class module. With the class module, VB developers were for the first time able to build an application using abstraction. Developers create objects by first defining a template (or class) using the class module. The template is built by adding public and private members (variables, functions, or properties). For example, an account class named CAccount, which other programs may use as part of a COM DLL, might be defined as follows:

```
' Class CAccount

Private m_dBalance As Currency

Public Property Get Balance() As Currency
    Balance = m_dBalance
End Property

Public Sub MakeDeposit(ByVal Amount As Currency)
    m_dBalance = m_dBalance + Amount
End Sub
```

The preceding example has a private field (a private member variable) called *m_dBalance*. It stores the actual balance in the account. The class contains two public members, one property and one function. The Balance Property Get member returns the value of the private field. The MakeDeposit function (or method) increases the balance by a certain amount.

Clients use the class by first creating an instance of the class. To create an instance of the class, a client first declares a variable to hold a reference to the class, then invokes the **New** keyword to tell VB to create an instance of the component in memory, as follows:

```
Dim Acct1 As CAccount
Set Acct1 = New Account
```

 It is possible to use the notation `Dim Acct1 As New CAccount`; however, in this case, the object will not be allocated until the program reaches a line of code that uses the object, such as `Acct1.MakeDeposit(400)`.

After creating an instance of the class, the developer will most likely invoke methods and use the properties that the class designer has made available. For example, the developer may wish to make a deposit to the account by calling the MakeDeposit method:

```
Call Acct1.MakeDeposit(1.99)
```

As you can see, the client program uses the public properties and methods of the class and thus depends on these methods to continue having the same names, the same parameters (or method signature), and the same *semantics*. Having the same semantics means that the MakeDeposit method cannot suddenly reformat the drive in the next release instead of depositing money into an account.

COM developers often use the term *method signature* to refer to the number of parameters, the parameter types, and the return value type of a function. COM rules state that method signatures should not change from one release to the next.

What happens when the designer of the class is asked by management to change the method signature of the MakeDeposit subroutine to include an additional parameter, like *Available* As Currency? The *Available* parameter tells the class what amount of the deposit is available immediately. Therefore, the signature of the subroutine needs to change as follows:

```
Public Sub MakeDeposit(ByVal Amount As Currency, ByVal Available As Currency)
'...
End Sub
```

This type of change presents a problem. A client program already exists that has a dependency on the previous version of MakeDeposit. If the subroutine is changed, the change will prevent the client from functioning. However, the subroutine needs to change.

One solution to the problem is to make a new class called CAccount2 and include the new version of the function in this class. Client code that was using the CAccount class would be left intact, and new code would use the new CAccount2 class. Other languages facilitate the creation of classes that closely resemble an existing class by enabling the developer to use inheritance. *Inheritance* is the ability to create a child class (also known as the derived class) from an existing class (also known as the base class); the child class adopts as much functionality as it requires from the base class. Inheritance may be available at different levels. Visual Basic 6 only supports what is known as *interface inheritance*; this term will be explained in detail later. For now, it is sufficient to know that in VB 6 a class may adopt another class' method signatures and not their functionality. What use is it to adopt the signatures without the actual functionality behind the methods, you may ask? The answer is coming shortly.

Visual C++, Java, C#, and VB.NET enable a developer to use *code inheritance*. This means that a child class inherits both the method signatures and their functionality (although these languages enable developers to use interface inheritance only if they so desire, and it turns out to be a better solution in a number of cases).

The following code shows an example of code inheritance using VB.NET:

```
Class CAccount 'The CAccount class serves as the base class

    Protected m_dBalance As Decimal
```

```
    Public ReadOnly Property Balance() As Decimal
        Get
            return m_dBalance
        End Get
    End Property

    Public Sub MakeDeposit(ByVal Amount As Decimal)
        m_dBalance = m_dBalance + Amount
    End Sub

End Class

Class CAccount2 : Inherits CAccount
    Private m_dAvailable As Decimal

    Public Sub Overloads MakeDeposit(ByVal Amount As Decimal, _
                             ByVal Available As Decimal)
        m_dBalance += Amount
        m_dAvailable += Available
    End Sub

    Public ReadOnly Property AvailableBalance() As Decimal
        Get
            return m_dAvailable
        End Get
    End Property

End Class
```

You are going to learn more about .NET in Chapter 11; for now, let's talk about the inheritance feature. In the previous example, CAccount2 acquires all the functionality of CAccount. That means that if a client creates an instance of CAccount2, it can call all the methods of CAccount, because a CAccount2 object is a CAccount object as well. The definition of CAccount2 contains only the things that are different between the two classes. For example, the code in CAccount2 defines a new version of the MakeDeposit method, one that has two parameters. The method declaration uses the keyword **Overloads**, which tells the compiler that there is more than one version of the MakeDeposit method. (You will learn more about method overloading in Chapter 10.) The definition of CAccount2 also extends the class with a new property, AvailableBalance.

Because VB 6 does not support code inheritance, you would have to create a new class module and use the clipboard to copy as much code as needed from the old version of the class to the new version of the class. The new version of the class would have the new version of the MakeDeposit function as follows:

```
Public Sub MakeDeposit(ByVal Amount As Currency, ByVal Available As Currency)
    '...
End Sub
```

This approach has two problems. First, every change requires that you create a new class and duplicate the code for all the functions that remain intact. Second, your program may have general functions located in code modules or forms that depend on a particular class. For instance, take the following *CalculateInterest* function:

```
' Module General.bas

Public Function CalculateInterest(ByVal Acct As CAccount) As Currency
End Function
```

Notice that the *CalculateInterest* function requires a parameter of type CAccount. However, the new version of the class is named CAccount2. With this approach, you must change the function to receive a class of type CAccount2. An "ugly" workaround to avoid having to make these types of changes is to use Variants for all your input and output parameters to begin with, but this means that you lose all the type safety features of the language. By making all your parameters Variants you are telling a client that it is perfectly legal to send a string value or even a user-defined type (UDT) such as a rectangle to the *CalculateInterest* function. The same would be true if you used the word Object, but in this case you are telling the client that any object would do. Clearly the function can work only with classes that are of type CAccount or CAccount2.

It is precisely these two issues that interface-based programming addresses. Interface-based programming gives us a mechanism by which we can upgrade method signatures easily.

Defining Interfaces in Visual Basic

What keeps us from upgrading the CAccount class is that the client has a dependency on the first version of the public members of the class. There is no problem with changing private members, since they're completely transparent to the client, but you cannot change public members. There is a one-to-one relationship between the class itself and the public members of the class. If the public members were not part of the CAccount class, then the client would not have dependencies on the class, and the class could be changed without problems. Therefore, we must dissociate the public member declarations from their implementation. To do this, a new entity known as an *interface* is built. The simplest definition of an interface is that it is a class with public properties and methods but without any code. The class serves as a definition of methods, a protocol that a client will use to communicate with the class. In Chapter 3, you are going to learn a more concrete definition. However, for now it is sufficient to think of an interface as a class with declarations but without code. For example, let's return to the CAccount class. Instead of adding public members directly to this class, let's create a second class and call it IAccount. The IAccount class will have the following code:

```
' Class IAccount

Public Property Get Balance() As Currency
End Property

Public Sub MakeDeposit(ByVal Amount As Currency)
End Sub
```

As you can see from the definition, there are no private members defined for the class, only public members: the Balance property and the MakeDeposit method. This class defines an interface. Just as a class module defines a template for creating objects, an interface is a template for creating other class modules. The interface class is not meant to be a creatable entity, which is why it is a good idea to change the Instancing property of the class to 2 - PublicNotCreatable. (The Instancing property is available only when creating an ActiveX EXE, ActiveX DLL, or ActiveX Control project).

 You should set the Instancing property of interface classes to 2 - PublicNotCreatable. This setting prevents Visual Basic clients outside of the project in which the class is defined from creating an instance of the class.

The interface is useless by itself, since it contains only public members that have no code and therefore no functionality. Once the interface has been designed, you must provide an implementation of the members in the interface. To do so, you must create another class. For instance, to continue our IAccount example, we might create a second class named CChecking that provides an implementation of the IAccount interface. It does this by including the statement Implements IAccount in the code for the class, as follows:

```
'Class CChecking

Implements IAccount
```

Once you enter the statement Implements IAccount, the object drop-down box on the top left side of the code window will list the IAccount class, as shown in Figure 2-1. The function drop-down box on the top righthand side of the code window will list all the properties and functions of the IAccount class, as shown in Figure 2-2.

Note that you must add the property and method declarations to the CChecking class by selecting each IAccount entry from the drop-down list. You must

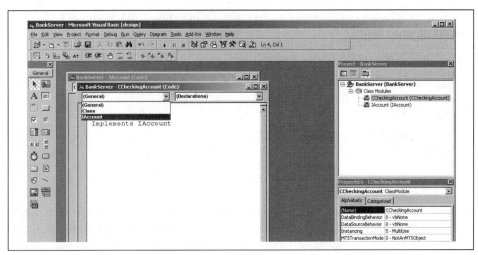

Figure 2-1. The IAccount interface entry

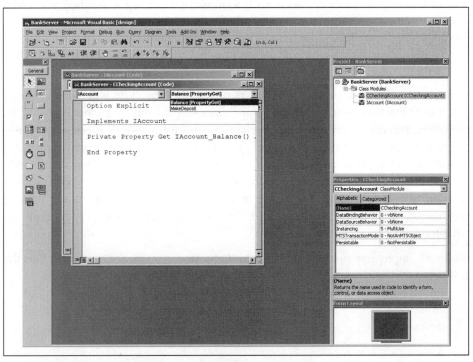

Figure 2-2. The IAccount properties and methods

implement all the functions in IAccount, even if the implementation is to do nothing. In other words, you must at a minimum add function stubs for each member in IAccount. Otherwise, VB will give you a compile-time error. Implementing an interface means that you agree to support *all* the routines of the interface. The end result will be that the CChecking class will have the following definitions:

```
' Class CChecking

Option Explicit

Implements IAccount

Private Property Get IAccount_Balance() As Currency
End Property

Private Sub IAccount_MakeDeposit(ByVal Amount As Currency)
End Sub
```

Notice that both of these functions are marked as private. They are not public functions of the CChecking class, but they are implementations of the function definitions of IAccount. (It is a little confusing that they are marked as private, because you can still reach them, only not through CChecking directly.) A good way of thinking about these functions is to think of what happens when you add a CommandButton to a form and write code for the Click event as follows:

```
Private Sub Command1_Click()
    MsgBox "Hello"
End Sub
```

The Command1_Click event is marked as private, but the code will still execute; it just means that code outside of the form cannot call the function directly. It will be executed through a VB internal mechanism—the form listens for window messages from the operating system and fires an event when the operating system reports a button click action. This is similar to what happens when using interfaces. Although the internal mechanism is different for control events and for interface method notifications, the principle is the same. You will learn the internal mechanism that triggers the private interface implementation functions in Chapter 3.

To finish implementing the functions in IAccount, you may enter code like the following:

```
' Class CChecking

Option Explicit

Implements IAccount

Private m_cBalance As Currency

Private Property Get IAccount_Balance() As Currency
    IAccount_Balance = m_cBalance
End Property
```

```
Private Sub IAccount_MakeDeposit(ByVal Amount As Currency)
    m_cBalance = m_cBalance + Amount
End Sub
```

Using a Class Through an Interface

Now, let's look at how the client may use the class through the interface. The first step is for the client to declare a variable of the type of the interface as follows:

```
Dim Acct As IAccount
```

What exactly happens when you declare a variable such as in the preceding line of code? Visual Basic allocates some memory (4 bytes) to hold a memory address for the object. VB does not actually create the object in memory until it is told to do so. However, it does allocate a container known as Acct to hold the memory address of the object once it is created. The Acct container will hold the memory address &H00000000 (that is, a null pointer) when the variable is declared. Figure 2-3 shows a representation of the Acct memory variable.

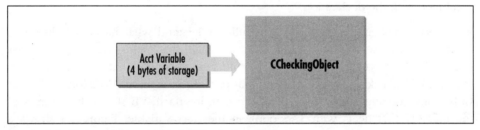

Figure 2-3. Memory representation of the Acct variable

If you are an experienced C++ developer, you may find it interesting to examine the layout of VB objects in memory. VB provides several undocumented functions to enable you to obtain the memory address of an object. These functions are: *VarPtr*, *ObjPtr*, and *StrPtr*. *VarPtr* returns the address of a variable. *ObjPtr* returns the address of an object. Therefore, if Acct were the variable, you could ask VB to report the address of the variable itself with the *VarPtr* function, or you could ask VB to report the address of the object that Acct is pointing to with *ObjPtr*. The function *StrPtr* returns the address of a string. Again, you could ask VB to report the address of the variable that points to a string or the address of the memory where the string buffer is allocated.

Remember that the class **IAccount** does not implement the functions Balance and MakeDeposit. It simply provides a definition for the functions. Therefore, we must set the Acct variable to point to an object that implements the functions of **IAccount**.

To create an object that implements the IAccount interface, you must create an instance of the CChecking class as follows:

```
Set Acct = New CChecking
```

Notice that for this mechanism to work, you must use the New operator in a separate line from the declaration. It is possible in Visual Basic to combine the New operator with the declaration of the variable, as follows:

```
Dim Acct As New CChecking
```

In this case, the object is not allocated at the time it is declared; it is allocated whenever subsequent code tries to use the variable Acct. However, in this type of declaration, the variable type and the type of the object created must be the same. Therefore, to use the interface style of programming, you must separate the declaration from the allocation. It turns out that the preferred method of allocating an object is to use the New operator in a separate line, because it provides us with knowledge of when that object is created in memory and when that object is destroyed. It is more difficult to know this when using the form of New that is combined with the declaration.

A lot more explanation is required to fully understand what happens when you create an instance of the object with the line that reads Set Acct = New CChecking. However, for now it is sufficient to know that VB allocates an instance of CChecking in memory and that part of the memory VB allocates for the CChecking contains support for the IAccount interface. VB stores the address of the memory that deals with IAccount in the Acct variable. Figure 2-4 shows a pseudomemory layout of a VB object when it is allocated. The figure will be expanded as the chapter continues.

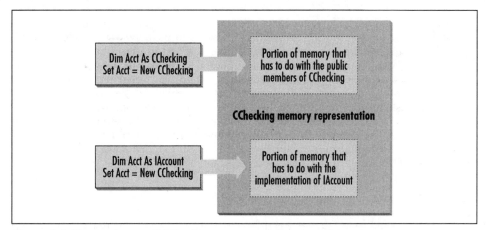

Figure 2-4. Memory layout of CChecking

Notice from Figure 2-4 that if we had declared the Acct variable as type CChecking (`Dim Acct As CChecking`), the Acct variable would store the memory address that represents the public members of the CChecking component. However, because we asked for `IAccount`, we are given a different memory address. Nonetheless, realize that when we ask for VB to create an instance of the CChecking class (regardless of what we are asking for in the `Dim` statement), VB allocates an object that in a sense contains two subobjects. (Whether these subobjects are really objects in OOP modeling terms is irrelevant to the discussion.) Both subobjects are in memory—the object that deals with the CChecking part of the object and the memory that deals with the `IAccount` interface part of the object—and these two subobjects act as a unit to represent the entire object. This will be explained in more detail in Chapter 3.

The end result is that now the client code may call on methods for the `IAccount` interface as follows:

```
Dim balance as Currency

balance = Acct.Balance
```

In summary, the client code would look like the following:

```
Dim Acct As IAccount
Set Acct = New CChecking
Dim balance As Currency
balance = Acct.Balance
```

Notice that the only way to use the Balance property is through the interface `IAccount`. For example, the following code will result in a compile error:

```
' Bad code
Dim Acct As CChecking
Set Acct = New CChecking
Dim balance As Currency
balance = Acct.Balance
```

The preceding code is incorrect because Balance is not a property of CChecking. Before examining in more detail how it is that VB enables us to switch from one interface to another, let's get a feeling for how interfaces work at a higher level by creating another object that implements the same interface.

Polymorphism I (Multiple Components— Single Interface)

The term *polymorphism* refers to many different things in object-oriented lingo. One aspect of polymorphism is that two classes may share a single interface but implement the methods in the interface slightly differently. To illustrate this meaning of polymorphism, let's suppose we add a CSavings class to the project:

```
' Class CSavings

Option Explicit

Implements IAccount

Private m_cBalance As Currency
Private m_dInterest As Double

Private Property Get IAccount_Balance() As Currency
    IAccount_Balance = m_cBalance
End Property

Private Sub IAccount_MakeDeposit(ByVal Amount As Currency)
    m_cBalance = m_cBalance + Amount + (Amount * m_dInterest)
End Sub
```

Notice that the preceding code is very similar to that of the CChecking class, except that the MakeDeposit subroutine actually adds some interest to the *Amount* sent it (this is a very good savings account). This shows that the definition of the interface tells the implementer nothing about how the code for the function is to be written. Each class may have a different interpretation of the MakeDeposit routine. (Later, you will see that this is especially good for polymorphism.) The only requirement is that they have similar semantics—in other words, that the two implementations do roughly the same thing with slight variations; MakeDeposit in CSavings does not remove money from an account, for example.

At this point, our project has two implementation classes, CChecking and CSavings, and one interface class, **IAccount**. Both the CChecking class and the CSavings classes implement the **IAccount** interface. What may not be readily apparent is that to use the CSavings class, all you need to do is change the line that creates an instance of the object, as follows:

```
Dim Acct As IAccount
Set Acct = New CSavings
Dim balance As Currency
balance = Acct.Balance
```

The client code is identical except that instead of creating an instance of the CChecking class, the code creates an instance of the CSavings class. Both of these classes implement the **IAccount** interface. Because the code is written to call methods through the interface, the code is identical. In fact, the following code would also work:

```
Dim Acct As IAccount
Set Acct = New CSavings
Dim balSavings As Currency
balSavings = Acct.Balance
Set Acct = New CChecking
Dim balChecking As Currency
balChecking = Acct.Balance
```

We could take this a step further and write a function that reports the balance for any account that implements the `IAccount` interface:

```
Public Sub ReportBalance(ByVal Acct As IAccount)
    MsgBox "Balance = " & Acct.Balance
End Sub
```

Notice that it is possible to send to this function an instance of either the CSavings class or the CChecking class. If the code were not using the interface programming style, it would be difficult to write a function like *ReportBalance*. You would have to define the *Acct* parameter as type Object or Variant. This means that a developer using the function may send any object to the *ReportBalance* function. This would not exclude a developer from creating a class of type CDog and passing it to the *ReportBalance* function. The function would then have to attempt to call the Balance property and catch the error if the object did not have the appropriate property. You would have to make sure that every class that is going to be passed to the *ReportBalance* function has a Balance property. Not only does every class require a Balance property, but also, without using an interface, one cannot assume that a class that has a Balance property also has the MakeDeposit method. So each function would have to check for the existence of this method in functions that require it as well.

Using interfaces, the function will accept only classes that implement the `IAccount` interface, which by definition must have an implementation for all the functions in `IAccount`. If you attempt to send in a class like CDog that does not implement the interface, VB will respond with runtime error 13, "Type Mismatch."

Polymorphism II (Single Component— Multiple Interfaces)

The second meaning of the term *polymorphism* is the ability of a component to act as many different types of components. It can do this by implementing multiple interfaces. To illustrate, let's define a second interface called `ISaveToDisk`. The purpose of this second interface is to save the balance information to a file. To define this new interface, you would add another class to your project and name it `ISaveToDisk`. Then you would change the instancing property of this class to 2 - `PublicNotCreatable` and add a function to your class without any code, as follows:

```
' Class ISaveToDisk

Option Explicit

Public Sub Save()
End Sub
```

Once the interface is defined, you must implement it. Suppose for the sake of argument that only the CChecking class implemented the interface. In other words, only instances of CChecking could save the balance to disk (no wonder the bank can afford to give such generous interest on savings accounts). The CChecking class would then be modified as follows:

```
' Class CChecking

Option Explicit

Implements IAccount
Implements ISaveToDisk

Private m_cBalance As Currency

Private Property Get IAccount_Balance() As Currency
    IAccount_Balance = m_cBalance
End Property

Private Sub IAccount_MakeDeposit(ByVal Amount As Currency)
    m_cBalance = m_cBalance + Amount
End Sub

Private Sub ISaveToDisk_Save()
    'the implementation of this function is left as an exercise
    'for the reader
End Sub
```

Suppose that management has asked you to modify the *ReportBalance* function to save the balance of the account if it supports the ISaveToDisk interface. Because the function accepts any class that implements IAccount, there is no guarantee that the developer using the function will send in a class that supports both the IAccount interface and the ISaveToDisk interface. VB provides an operator—TypeOf...Is—to test whether the object supports an interface. You use the TypeOf...Is operator in an If statement as follows:

```
If TypeOf [object] Is [interface] Then
End If
```

With this operator, it is possible for the *ReportBalance* function to test whether the object that was sent in also supports the ISaveToDisk interface, as shown:

```
Public Sub ReportBalance(ByVal Acct As IAccount)
    MsgBox "Balance = " & Acct.Balance

    If TypeOf Acct Is ISaveToDisk Then
        Dim Persist As ISaveToDisk
        Set Persist = Acct
        Call Persist.Save
        MsgBox "The Account information was saved to disk"
    Else
```

```
        MsgBox "The account object cannot be saved to disk"
    End If

End Sub
```

If you examine the preceding code, you will see that the function now tests whether the object that *Acct* points to supports the `ISaveToDisk` interface. Notice that it is not possible to simply call methods of the `ISaveToDisk` interface through the `IAccount` interface, so you must obtain a reference to the `ISaveToDisk` interface before calling the Save method. This is an example of polymorphism. The lines of code that accomplish polymorphism are the following:

```
Dim Persist As ISaveToDisk
Set Persist = Acct
```

At a high level, you started with an object of type `IAccount`, and now you have an object of type `ISaveToDisk`. The same object was morphed from one type to another. This happens through a COM mechanism that you will learn later. The important thing is that by implementing multiple interfaces, it is possible to switch the personality of an object.

Using Polymorphism to Upgrade Classes

Earlier in the chapter, you learned that interface-based programming offers a way to easily upgrade classes. Polymorphism is the mechanism that enables us to make the upgrading process possible.

You may recall that we started with one definition of the MakeDeposit subroutine:

```
Public Sub MakeDeposit(ByVal Amount As Currency)
End Sub
```

Then we wanted to modify it as follows:

```
Public Sub MakeDeposit(ByVal Amount As Currency, ByVal Available As Currency)
End Sub
```

The MakeDeposit definition is now part of the `IAccount` interface. You are not able to change the signature of a function (the parameter types, the number of parameters, or the return type). If you did, existing clients that expect a certain signature would no longer work.

Instead, now that the client code is designed to use interfaces, it is possible to create a second interface, `IAccount2`, that contains the new definition. This means that you would add another class to your project as follows:

```
' Class IAccount2

Public Property Get Balance() As Currency
End Property
```

```
Public Sub MakeDeposit(ByVal Amount As Currency, ByVal Available As Currency)
End Sub
```

CChecking can now implement both the `IAccount` interface and the `IAccount2` interface. Old client programs that were compiled to use the old version of CChecking expect the class to support the `IAccount` interface. Now, even though there is a new version of CChecking, because the new version still implements the `IAccount` interface with the same definition, these clients will continue to work. New clients can be written to use the new interface, `IAccount2`.

For example, suppose an old version of the client code used the `IAccount` interface to make a call to the MakeDeposit method as follows:

```
Dim Acct As IAccount
Set Acct = new CChecking
Call Acct.MakeDeposit(5000)
```

The new version of the client can be written as shown:

```
Dim Acct As IAccount
Set Acct = New CChecking

If TypeOf Acct Is IAccount2 Then
    Dim Acct2 As IAccount2
    Set Acct2 = Acct
    Call Acct2.MakeDeposit(5000,2000)
Else
    Call Acct.MakeDeposit(5000)
End If
```

Why write the client code to first use `IAccount` instead of going directly to `IAccount2`? In other words, why not do the following:

```
Dim Acct As IAccount2
Set Acct = New CChecking
```

The preceding code assumes that you are always working with the new version of CChecking. The first version of the code makes no assumptions. When defining the *Acct* object variable, it first asks for the `IAccount` interface. Both the old version of the class and the new version of the class support this interface. Then the code asks if the object supports the new interface. If it does, the code uses the new version of the MakeDeposit routine. Otherwise, the code falls back on the old version of MakeDeposit. This means that if the CChecking class were being exposed through a DLL (say *Account.dll*), the new client (say *Banking.exe* Version 2.0) could work with Version 1.0 of *Account.dll* or with Version 2.0 of *Account.dll*. What's more, *Banking.exe* Version 1.0 would also work with *Account. dll* 1.0 and with *Account.dll* 2.0. How can the old version of *Banking.exe* work with the new version of *Account.dll*? It can because *Banking.exe* 1.0 was designed to use the `IAccount` interface. It will not, of course, use the new functionality in CChecking, but it will use the old functionality. Because every new version of

CChecking will continue to support the IAccount interface, there is no danger of it breaking old clients.

Review

I made the point at the beginning of the chapter that interface-based programming provides us with a mechanism to upgrade classes. To use interface-based programming, you must first define an interface in the server code. We refer to the entity that provides the class or interface definition as the *server.* (Do not worry at this time about how the server is packaged—you will learn more about that in later chapters.) To define an interface, you must add a class to your project and add public properties and methods (subroutines or functions) without any code. Remember that the interface is not meant to be a creatable class; it is only meant to provide the definition of functions. This is why it is a good idea to mark its instancing property as PublicNotCreatable.

Once you have defined the interface, you must implement it in a class. To do so, you simply create a new class and use the Implements statement. Once you have used the Implements statement, the code window will list the interface class as an object in the object drop-down list. Select it and then select each function of the interface in the function list drop-down. Once you have added each property and function in the interface to your implementation class, then you write code for each of the methods of the interface. This is all that needs to be done by the server.

To use the implementation class through the interface definition, you declare a variable of the interface type, then set the variable to a new instance of the implementation class. You can also use the TypeOf...Is operator to find out if a class supports a certain interface.

If you need to change a method definition in an interface, you simply create a new version of the interface, *Interface2*. Then, you implement both the old version of the interface and the new version of the interface.

This book is a lot about what happens underneath—what VB is really doing behind the scenes. Therefore, in the next chapter, you are going to look beyond the high-level mechanism of interface-based programming and find out exactly how interfaces work internally and why it is that we can switch from one interface to another.

3

How Interfaces Work Internally

In the last chapter, you learned the benefit of interfaces at the user level. You learned why we need interfaces conceptually and how to define and use them. In this chapter, you are going to learn what interfaces really are at the memory level. In so doing, you are going to learn some of the core rules of COM. You are going to see the problems that existed before COM and how the COM rules make it possible to overcome those problems.

 This chapter is not for the weak of heart. If you do not want to know how interfaces work internally, feel free to skip this chapter for now and revisit it later.

Life Without Interfaces

Let's try to imagine life before COM and also life without classes. That would mean that you have user-defined types (UDTs) that represent components and code modules that have global functions. This is not much different than life with VB 3. Also, imagine that the latest version of VB did allow you to create DLLs.

Now suppose that you are designing a banking application. Understanding the benefit of separating code that will be shared among several applications, you define a UDT inside the DLL to represent an account:

```
Enum AccountTypeConstants
    Checking = 1
    Savings = 2
End Enum
```

```
Type Account
    AccountType As AccountTypeConstants
    Active As Boolean
    Balance As Currency
End Type
```

The UDT has three data members: AccountType, Active, and Balance. The AccountType member in the structure refers to an enumerated type, **AccountTypeConstants**, defined above the UDT. To use this UDT, all that a user has to do is use the **Dim** statement and then set the members of the UDT, as shown in the following code fragment:

```
Dim Acct As Account
Acct.AccountType = Checking
Acct.Active = True
Acct.Balance = 1000
```

Notice that to use a UDT, you do not have to include the **New** keyword. This is because VB allocates the memory for the UDT at the time that it encounters the **Dim** statement.

How much memory does VB allocate? You can use the *Len* function in VB to find out how much memory VB allocated for the structure. In this case **Len(Acct)** returns 14 bytes. The 14 bytes come from 4 bytes for the AccountType member, 2 bytes for the Active member, and 8 bytes for the Balance member. However, because of VB's 4-byte alignment, we need to adjust the Active member to 4 bytes (each member needs to occupy memory in multiples of 4 bytes). This means that the structure really requires 16 bytes of memory. In fact, VB's *LenB* function returns the exact number of bytes (16) that the UDT requires.

If the previous client code were in a separate program, a standard EXE, for example, then VB would have to know at compile time how much memory to allocate (16 bytes), and it would have to know that AccountType was held in offsets 0 through 3, that the Active member was held in offsets 4 through 7, and that Balance was held in offsets 8 through 15. Figure 3-1 shows a diagram of the memory representation of the UDT.

After VB compiles the program, it doesn't really know about the Account datatype; it only knows about memory sizes and offsets. The machine code that's generated after the program is built is roughly equivalent to the following code in VB terms:

```
Private Declare Function GetProcessHeap Lib "kernel32" () As Long
Private Declare Function HeapAlloc Lib "kernel32" (ByVal hHeap As Long, _
                ByVal dwFlags As Long, ByVal dwBytes As Long) As Long
Private Declare Function HeapFree Lib "kernel32" (ByVal hHeap As Long, _
                ByVal dwFlags As Long, ByVal lpMem As Long) As Long
Private Declare Sub CopyMemory Lib "kernel32" Alias "RtlMoveMemory" ( _
                ByVal Destination As Long, ByVal Source As Long, _
                ByVal Length As Long)
```

```
Private Sub Form_Load()
    'get a pointer to the process' heap space
    Dim hHeap As Long
    hHeap = GetProcessHeap

    'allocate memory for the structure on the heap
    'notice that this function uses the number of bytes required for
    'the structure. The structure requires 16 bytes
    Dim pointer As Long
    pointer = HeapAlloc(hHeap, 0, 16)

    'set the AcctType data member, we load the value into a variable
    'then we copy the value to the first 4 bytes in the structure
    Dim AcctType As Long
    AcctType = Checking
    Call CopyMemory(pointer, VarPtr(AcctType), 4)

    'set the active data member
    Dim Active As Boolean
    Active = True
    Call CopyMemory(pointer + 4, VarPtr(Active), 2)

    'set the account balance data member
    Dim Balance As Currency
    Balance = 1000
    Call CopyMemory(pointer + 8, VarPtr(Balance), 8)

    'when we are done we clear the memory
    Call HeapFree(hHeap, 0, pointer)
End Sub
```

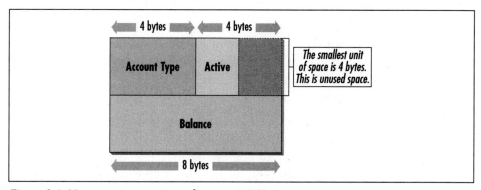

Figure 3-1. Memory representation of Account UDT

The code generated as the result of compiling the client program has a lot of
dependencies on memory offsets, and this presents a number of problems. For
example, what happens if we change the size of the structure in the DLL code
without recompiling the EXE? In other words, what would happen if we changed
the data structure to the following (the new member is shown in boldface)?

```
Type Account
    AccountType As AccountTypeConstants
    Active As Boolean
    Balance As Currency
    AvailableBalance As Currency
End Type
```

If you were to look only at the client code before compilation, you would think that nothing needed to change, because in reality all we have done is add a data member. Since the old data members are still available, the client code should be able to find the members correctly. But if you were to look at the previous pseudocompiled code, you would definitely see some flaws with our approach. Clearly the size of the structure has changed; now it requires 24 bytes of memory. The compiled image of the EXE allocates only 16 bytes. The client program may continue to work correctly with the 16 bytes allocated for the structure. After all, the only members in the structure that it refers to in its code are the first three members, which reside within the 16 bytes of memory allocated. But what if the client program passes a pointer to the structure to a function in the DLL? The DLL code may try to address the *AvailableBalance* member in the structure. The offset for the member is beyond the 16 bytes allocated. The DLL code would then either read an invalid value from memory or write to a location that was not allocated for the structure, normally resulting in a crash of the application sometime during its execution.

Therefore, it does not make sense to make changes to the structure on the DLL side and allocate the memory for the structure in the client code, since the DLL code may change. The alternative is to always allocate memory on the DLL side, which is precisely what COM does.

COM Rule #1: Memory for an object is always allocated by the COM server (ActiveX DLL or ActiveX EXE).

If you are an experienced VB developer, you may be wondering what this means, since you clearly call **New** on the client side. I promise that we will address this later; for now, let me inform you that **New** is just a wrapper for a COM call that VB has to make. The purpose of the COM call is to make the server code allocate the memory for the object. It is simply a trick that VB does for you.

Continuing with our UDT example, if the server rather than the client is to be responsible for memory allocation, it would be necessary for the DLL side to have a function by which the client code can create an instance of an Account structure. If

we were to represent this function in terms of pseudocompiled code, it would look
something like the following:

```
Public Function CreateAccount(ByVal AccountType As AccountTypeConstants) As Long
    'get a pointer to the process' heap space
    Dim hHeap As Long
    hHeap = GetProcessHeap

    'allocate memory for the structure and return address to client
    Dim pointer As Long
    CreateAccount = HeapAlloc(hHeap, 0, 24)

End Function
```

Now the allocation has been moved to the DLL side and, since the structure is
defined on the DLL side, any time we change the structure and recompile the DLL,
the compiler will adjust the *HeapAlloc* line to reflect the correct number of bytes.
That solves part of the problem with distributing the DLL. The other problems are
the offsets of the data members. If you look at the original client pseudocompiled
code, any time we set a member in the structure, such as `Acct.Available =
1000`, VB compiles that line into a *CopyMemory* operation into a certain offset of
memory. The offsets are calculated at compile time and are not changed dynamically at runtime. This is OK as long as we add data members to the end of the
data structure, but what happens if we remove a member from the data structure
or if we insert a member into it? Then our offsets would be wrong, and the client
program would write to the incorrect place in memory.

This problem would be solved if the dependency on the offsets were also moved
to the DLL side. One way to do that is for the DLL to provide functions to read the
values and set the values of the data structure. Then the client would have a
dependency on the functions and not on particular offsets in memory. For
example, the DLL could have a function like the following in pseudocompiled
code:

```
Public Function GetAccountActive(ByVal PointerToAcct As Long) As Boolean
    Dim Active As Boolean
    Call CopyMemory(VarPtr(Active), pointer + 4, 2)
    GetAccountActive = Active
End Function
```

In the preceding code, when the client wants to read the value of the Active
member in the Account data structure, it does not access the data member directly,
because, as you saw, this would mean that the client would have to know the
offset in memory for the data member. Instead, the client calls the
GetAccountActive function. This function on the DLL side extracts the data from
the correct offset. If the data structure changes, the DLL needs to be recompiled,
and the act of recompiling causes the compiler to recalculate the offsets. This
means that the function will always return the appropriate value. The same type of

function would have to be added for setting the Active data member, as well as for getting and setting all other data members. This leads us to the next rule of COM.

 COM Rule #2: A client accesses data members in an object through functions.

Again, this rule may be harder to understand if you are already an experienced VB developer. If you are an experienced VB developer, you may be wondering why you can declare a public data member such as the following:

```
'Class CAccount
Public Active As Boolean        ' Note that this is the public variable of a class
```

then be able to access it in a client program with the following code:

```
Dim Acct As CAccount
Set Acct = New CAccount
Call Acct.Active = True
```

Doesn't that mean that we are accessing data members directly? The answer is, "No." This is another time that VB plays a trick to give the illusion of having classes as opposed to building COM classes. Whenever you declare a data member as public, VB in reality exposes two functions to the client, one to read the value and one to set the value. The client code then calls the get or the set function accordingly whenever you get or set the value of the data member.

Now that the DLL exposes functions to get and set the various data members within the structure, we have solved most of the problems that kept us from simply upgrading the DLL without having to recompile the client. While there are other problems that we will talk about in the next chapter, let's focus on the possibility of storing server code in an EXE instead of a DLL. If we had exposed the structure through an ActiveX EXE, we would have another problem: a pointer in one process is meaningless in another process, so our *CreateAccount* function (which simply returns a pointer to the client) would fail.

There is yet another problem, but it is more of an object-oriented issue than a problem. The issue is that there are now potentially a lot of functions in the DLL. The Account structure is meant to work for both checking accounts and savings accounts. The client simply sets the AccountType data member in the structure to specify the type of account. The DLL may have functions like *SetAccountActive* that work equally well for both types of accounts. But what if we had functions like *CalculateInterest* or *OrderChecks*? It is difficult to see whether these functions work equally well for both types of accounts. There is nothing to keep the client code honest.

Thus, we need to have different groupings of functions in the DLL. It would be nicer, for example, if we had all the functions that worked for both accounts in one group, all the functions that were specific to checking accounts in another group, and all the functions that had to do with savings accounts in another group. This is the purpose of interfaces. An interface is simply a grouping of functions. The real purpose of the interface is to turn a set of functions into a type. In our case, we would most likely have three interfaces: `IAccount`, `IChecking`, and `ISavings`.

Memory Layout of Interfaces

You know that the interface is just a group of functions, but what is it really in terms of memory? Well, to understand interfaces, you have to know how a client binds to functions in a DLL.

Whenever you load a program, the code for the program is mapped into virtual memory. The program uses a CPU register known as the instruction pointer that tells it in essence what line of code to execute next (in reality it stores the memory location of what machine instruction to execute next). Whenever the program encounters a call to a function or a subroutine, the machine code simply tells the instruction pointer to jump to the place in memory where the function resides.

Thus, any time you make a method call, all that you are doing is changing the instruction pointer to point to a different piece of code. This is often referred to as making a "jump." The address of the next instruction after the jump instruction (the address that would have come next if we had not made the jump, often called the *return address*) is saved. When the program is done executing the functions, it issues a "return." The return simply sets the instruction pointer to the return address. (Granted, this is a simplified view, but this is in essence what happens.)

DLLs contain a number of exported functions. Since making method calls is simply jumping to a particular place in memory, this means the client code needs to know where the code for the functions in the DLL resides. However, the code for these functions is not available to the client code at compile time; only the definition of the functions is available.

Since the code is not available, it is impossible for the compiler to know where exactly in memory the code for the function resides. What the compiler does instead of writing the exact jump address at compile time is to build an *import table*. The import table is an array of memory addresses to the functions in the DLL. The import table has an exact location in memory at compile time. The compiler then generates code to use the addresses in the import table whenever your code makes a call to one of the imported functions. In essence, this means that if the DLL has a function like *OrderChecks*, the compiler code for the client uses the import table to find out where the *OrderChecks* function resides. Since the compiler knows where the import table resides in memory, it can write an actual memory address in the compiled code. When the OS loader loads the DLL and maps the functions of the DLL into virtual memory, the table is filled with the actual memory addresses of each function. Thus, the client program code jumps to the import table address, which then jumps to the actual function in the DLL.

For the compiler to build the import table, it must have the name of the DLL and the names of each of the functions in the DLL at compile time. This is certainly possible for the most part, but it is a very limiting proposition. What if we wanted to choose programmatically at runtime which DLL to load? Suppose that there were two versions of *BankServer.DLL*, one that was meant for English-speaking countries and one for Spanish-speaking countries? We do not want to compile the client EXE with a dependency on both DLLs; we just want to load the correct one at runtime.

Windows provides a mechanism for binding to a DLL dynamically at runtime; this is done using two functions, *LoadLibrary* and *GetProcAddress. LoadLibrary* loads the DLL code into memory given the name of the DLL; *GetProcAddress* returns the address in memory of a function given its name. Languages like C++ then allow you to make a jump to the address returned by *GetProcAddress*. If you had a different DLL for each language supported by your application, the code could simply check a flag for language and call either `LoadLibrary("BankEnglish.DLL")` or `LoadLibrary("BankSpanish.DLL")`, then call `GetProcAddress("OrderChecks")` and jump to the function. However, all we have now is a mechanism for loading DLLs and executing functions at runtime; we still have a bunch of functions without groupings.

There is a third mechanism, and this is the mechanism that COM uses; it is called the *virtual function table*. This mechanism for determining function addresses is for the client code to ask the DLL for the addresses to its functions at runtime; this is the *virtual function* method. The client code still needs to know something at compile time, because, after all, the client code will be calling a certain function, and the compiler must write in an address to jump to. With the virtual function mechanism, the client code uses a lookup table. The client obtains an address for a group of functions at runtime. The compiler writes code to jump to a particular entry in the table based on the position of the function within the table and the address it obtained from the DLL code. The group of functions is known as a *virtual table*. If, for example, the DLL had two functions like *OrderChecks* and *StopCheckPayment*, the developer could specify that these two functions be part of the same virtual function table. And in fact, the developer of the DLL would have to specify that *OrderChecks* is the first function in the table and that *StopCheckPayment* is the second. The client code then asks the DLL for a pointer to this virtual function table and uses the table to know which function to call. When the compiler compiles the client code and encounters a line of code such as `Acct.OrderChecks`, all the compiler does is write code to jump to a calculated address. The address is calculated from a statement that reads "get a virtual function table from the DLL and jump to the address specified in the first entry of the table." Along the same lines, a call to `Acct.StopCheckPayment` would translate to "get a virtual function table from the DLL and jump to the address specified in the second entry of the table."

The following assembly code (ASM) shows what the actual client-side compiled code looks like:

```
Call Acct.MakeDeposit
00401B20    mov        eax,dword ptr [acct] ;the address of the object
00401B23    mov        eax,dword ptr [eax]  ;find the lookup table
00401B25    push       dword ptr [acct]     ;pass the address as a parameter
00401B28    call       dword ptr [eax+1Ch]  ;call function
```

Notice that the client obtains a pointer stored in the Acct variable that is going to be used in calculating the address of the function to which the client code will jump. Figure 3-2 illustrates how the preceding ASM code works.

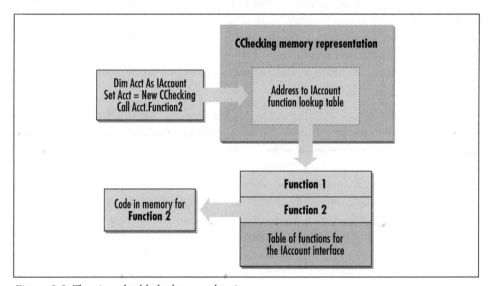

Figure 3-2. The virtual table lookup mechanism

The ASM code takes the address in Acct to find the address to a lookup table (that is the purpose of the first two lines of ASM). Once we have a lookup table, we are going to make a call into a function within the lookup table. The last line of the preceding ASM says "jump to address [acct...address of lookup table...lookup table] + 1Ch and save the return address," which translates to function number 8 in the lookup table (1C = 28 decimal; if you consider that the first function is at offset 0 and that entries are 4 bytes apart, then the functions would be at 0,4,8,12,16,20,24,28, and 28 is therefore function number 8).

The virtual function mechanism gives us the best solution to our problems:

- It gives the sense of types or groupings. This is because now the writer of the DLL can create one virtual function table for each group of functions. For example, a developer might have one virtual function table for functions that were in common for checking and savings accounts, another table for functions specific to checking accounts, and another for those specific to savings accounts.

- By using the virtual function mechanism, we can uphold the rule to always access the object through functions instead of having dependencies on the data members themselves.

This leads us to the definition of an interface. An *interface* is a pointer to a virtual function table (or a vptr to a virtual function table, or vtable). COM developers always say that an interface is a vptr to a vtable. In summary, the virtual function table is an array of function pointers, and an interface is a pointer to the location of this table in memory that is provided at runtime by the DLL. Now that we have interfaces defined, we can modify the second rule of COM.

 COM Rule #2 (revised): A client accesses a COM object through interfaces.

Notice that the client code jumps to an address that is mostly calculated but also has a fixed offset to a particular function. The compiled code for the client has a dependency on the location of the function within the table. In other words, if the compiled image says to jump to function number 8 in the table, it will jump to the eighth function even if it gets a different table from what it expects. This means that if we ever change the layout of this table in any way, we would break existing client code. This leads us to the third COM rule.

COM Rule #3: Interfaces are immutable. That means that once a client has been released to the general public, it cannot be changed. If we were to remove functions, or even change the order of the functions, we would break existing clients. Again, if you are an experienced VB developer, you may be thinking that of course you can change the order of the functions and existing clients continue to work—you guessed it, another trick VB does for you. In reality, VB keeps the same order of the functions if you compile your project with the correct attributes; more on this in Chapter 6.

COM as a Binary Standard

The rules of COM state that for a client to communicate with a COM object, the COM server must allocate the memory for the object, and all access to the object must occur through a COM interface. COM is said to be a binary standard because it further defines the memory layout of interfaces. An interface is a pointer to a lookup table of functions. The pointer is known as a *vptr*, and the lookup table of functions is known as a *vtable*. Thankfully, we do not work with interfaces at the vptr and vtable level. If you were working in C (not C++), you would have to code a vptr and a vtable by hand, because the language does not offer any natural mappings of these structures to high-level language features. C++ and Visual Basic, however, do map interfaces to classes.

Interface Mappings In C++

When a C++ developer marks a function as virtual in a class and creates an instance of the class or creates an instance of a class that derives from a class with virtual functions, the C++ compiler creates a virtual function table (vtable) to represent the virtual functions of the class. Remember, the vtable is an array of pointers to functions. To each class that has virtual functions or derives from a class that has virtual functions, the C++ compiler adds a hidden data member known as a vtable pointer (or vptr). This hidden member is a long integer (4 bytes) that stores the address of the vtable array that corresponds to the class. The first 4 bytes of an object in memory will therefore be the vptr.

An interface in C++ is a class that has only pure virtual functions. Pure virtual functions are virtual functions that do not have an implementation. A class that has pure virtual functions cannot be created directly—it must be implemented in another class. A C++ developer normally creates a concrete class to implement the interfaces class. The standard mechanism for doing so is to derive the concrete classes from the interface classes you wish to implement.

Figure 3-3 shows you the relationship between a C++ class, a vtable, a vptr, and a member variable in memory for a class that uses multiple inheritance to implement interfaces. Notice from Figure 3-3 that the first 8 bytes in the memory representation of the object store the addresses of two vtables containing pointers to the functions of each interface.

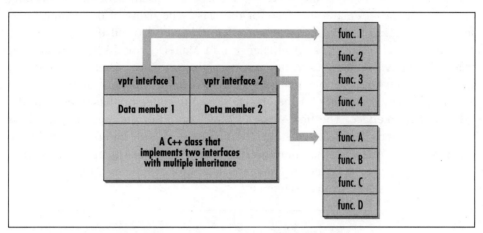

Figure 3-3. The memory layout of a C++ object with virtual functions

Interface Mappings in Visual Basic

VB uses a similar memory representation for objects defined in Visual Basic. Let's look at code from both the VB server and the client. The following code defines a class called CChecking and shows how the client code uses it:

```
'***Server Code***
' Class CChecking

Option Explicit

Private m_cBalance As Currency
Public Active As Boolean

Public Property Get Balance() As Currency
    Balance = m_cBalance
End Property

Public Sub MakeDeposit(ByVal Amount As Currency)
    m_cBalance = m_cBalance + Amount
End Sub

'***Client Code***
'This line tells the compiler to allocate 4 bytes to store a pointer
'to the default interface for the CChecking
Dim Acct As CChecking
```

```
'Allocates object on the server side
Set Acct = New CChecking

'Makes a call through a vtable
Call Acct.MakeDeposit(5000)
```

When the client requests the server to allocate an instance of the CChecking class, VB defines a default interface for the class. The name of the default interface is _CChecking. This default interface is composed of all the public members of the CChecking class (GetBalance and MakeDeposit). VB then builds a vtable (an array of addresses to functions) for that interface, where each entry in the array points to the implementation of the public functions of the class. Then VB allocates some memory for the object. Part of this memory has to do with the _CChecking interface. The first 4 bytes in the portion of the memory that deals with the _CChecking interface store a vptr for the default interface. Part of the memory VB allocates for the entire object is for storing data members defined in the class. Figure 3-4 illustrates the memory layout of a VB object that has public members and no **Implements** statements.

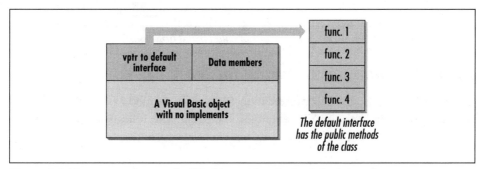

Figure 3-4. The memory layout of a VB object with only the default interface

The client code first allocates 4 bytes to hold the address of the _CChecking interface. Then it tells the server to allocate an object of type CChecking. The server hands the client the memory address of the portion of the total memory it allocated that stores the vptr to the _CChecking interface. The address is stored in the Acct variable. The line that calls the *MakeDeposit* function (Acct.MakeDeposit(5000)) represents a call into a vtable function. The compiler has to know that Acct refers to the _CChecking interface, and therefore it knows that the memory address it holds points first to the memory location of a vtable of the variable type. The compiler also knows from the definition of the _CChecking interface that the *MakeDeposit* function is the second function in the vtable, so it finds the address of the second function in the vtable and calls it. It finds the vtable from the vptr that the variable Acct points to.

As you can see, the memory layout of the C++ object and the memory layout of the VB object are similar. Both store a vptr, or a pointer to a vtable. A vtable is simply an array of pointers to functions. This means that any language that can create a UDT or an array of long integers to hold addresses of functions can create a vtable. The only thing the language compiler has to know is that, when it asks for an interface from the server, the first 4 bytes of the memory address the server returns will be an address to a vtable (a vptr). This also means that any client from any language that knows the layout in memory of COM interfaces can communicate with any language that can create objects with interfaces that use the same layout.

Consider, for example, a C++ client that uses the CChecking class in a VB server. The C++ code would be the following:

```
class _CChecking
{
public:
    virtual CURRENCY Get_Balance()=0;
    virtual void MakeDeposit(CURRENCY Amount)=0;
};

_CChecking *Acct;
//this is a pseudo function to illustrate that the C++ client
//must also let the creation occur on the server code.
CreateAccount(&Acct,Checking);
Acct->MakeDeposit(5000);
```

When the client code executes the *CreateCheckingAccount* function, the VB client allocates memory for the CChecking class. Part of this memory represents the default interface for the CChecking class: **_CChecking**. The first 4 bytes of this memory contain a vptr. The C++ pointer variable Acct is assigned a pointer to the vptr that points to the **_CChecking** vtable. The C++ compiler converts calls to interface functions to code that calculates the address of a function based on a vptr and a function offset. To C++ developers, it looks as if they are making a method call, when in reality the compiler code has to calculate the address of the function. Each call in the C++ side to an interface method directly translates to a call on the VB side, as shown in Table 3-1. Notice that the pointers to functions in the C++ structure are mapped in memory to the address of the VB functions. That is because the memory layouts of the vptrs and vtables are identical.

Table 3-1. How C++ members are mapped to VB members

C++ struct	VB object
Vptr	Vptr
vtable[0]	AddressOf Property GetBalance
vtable[1]	AddressOf Sub MakeDeposit

When the C++ client executes the code `Acct->MakeDeposit();` the compiler translates that call to the following:

```
//Acct->MakeDeposit
Acct->vptr->vtable[2](5000);
```

Notice that the C++ compiler uses the vtable to determine which function to call. This pointer points to the address of a VB function, so the code executes on the VB server object.

In conclusion, COM defines a memory layout by which all interfaces must abide. The first 4 bytes of any memory that refers to an interface is a pointer to a vtable (a vptr).

Type Libraries

It's time to leave the pre-COM era behind. Let's look at the server and client code the way that it exists today using COM. It makes sense at this point to look at each line of a client program and study what VB is doing for us.

Suppose that we start with the CChecking class defined in the following code:

```
' Class CChecking

Option Explicit

Private m_cBalance As Currency

Public Property Get Balance() As Currency
    Balance = m_cBalance
End Property

Public Sub MakeDeposit(ByVal Amount As Currency)
    m_cBalance = m_cBalance + Amount
End Sub
```

The VB client code to use this class is the following:

```
Dim Acct As CChecking
Set Acct = New CChecking
Call Acct.MakeDeposit(5000)
Set Acct = Nothing
```

In the preceding client code, VB first allocates 4 bytes of memory to hold the address of an object. It does this in the declaration of Acct: `Dim Acct As CChecking`. In the next line, VB does a couple of things. Although it appears that the `New` keyword causes VB to allocate the memory for the object on the client side, you have learned that this is not the case with the COM mechanism (in fact, this is not a good technique when it comes to upgrading objects where there might be two different definitions, one in the client and one in the server). Therefore, this code causes the server to allocate memory for the object. At that point, VB creates a vtable for the CChecking class. The entries in the vtable are pointers to the public functions of the class. The memory layout of the _CChecking interface contains the vptr in the first 4 bytes, which tells the object where in memory the vtable exists. The memory address of the object itself is saved in the 4 bytes allocated for the Acct variable. At this point, the Acct variable points to the _CChecking interface in memory. The VB compiler knows that the Acct variable refers to a COM object and that, therefore, the variable points to a vptr to a vtable.

When the client code executes the **Acct.MakeDeposit** line, VB looks in the vtable for the memory address that corresponds to the *MakeDeposit* function. It does this by looking at the definition of the interface when it is compiled. It knows that *MakeDeposit* is the eighth function in the vtable, so it looks in the vtable at entry number 8 and uses that address for making the call. Notice how important it is for the client and the server to agree on the signatures and the order of the functions in the interface definition.

How does the client know the definition of the interface? VB generates a type library when you compile your ActiveX DLL or ActiveX EXE. A *type library* is a binary file (or a Windows resource) in a Microsoft private format—that is, the layout of the binary file is undocumented and accessible only through a set of functions that Microsoft provides. The type library file contains the definition of the interfaces that a COM server provides. It also defines the classes that provide implementation for those interfaces. The VB compiler creates a type library file automatically whenever you compile your COM server.

You use a type library file when you are building a client. To specify that you want to use a type library file, you use the References dialog box, available from the Project → References menu option (more about this in the next chapter). Type library files generally have a *TLB* extension. You may, however, never have seen a *TLB* file because the COM spec says that the *TLB* file may also be incorporated directly into the *DLL* file or the *EXE* file for the server as a Windows resource. This is exactly what VB does—it includes the type library as a resource file inside the ActiveX DLL or ActiveX EXE.

The Visual Basic team invented type libraries; languages like C++ do not have to use them. In fact, the preferred way to define interfaces in C++ is to use the Interface Definition Language (IDL). IDL is not a programming language in itself, and it is not even Microsoft's language, although Microsoft has extended IDL to include COM. IDL was introduced by the Open Software Foundation (OSF) when they published a specification document called *The Distributed Computing Environment (DCE) Remote Procedure Calls (RPC)*. It was a specification for how clients were to communicate to remote objects through the network using interfaces. The language is used to define the interfaces themselves; you do not write loops or

error-trapping code in IDL. Microsoft used IDL for its implementation of the specification known as MSRPC and later expanded IDL to include definitions for COM
interfaces as well as type libraries. A C++ developer normally defines interfaces in
IDL and runs the IDL source through *MIDL.EXE* (Microsoft's IDL compiler). MIDL
can output various files, including header files for C++ developers to use when
accessing an object or implementing an object, a type library file for Visual Basic
developers to use, and code for DCOM's remoting architecture (more in the next
chapter).

Though IDL is a lot like C, one of the main differences is that parameters in function declarations have attributes. These attributes tell the developer and the
remoting layer the direction in which the parameters are meant to flow. Something that is difficult to tell from C is whether parameters are meant to be **in**
parameters, **out** parameters, or **in-out** parameters. Attributes in IDL makes this
very clear. You will learn more about writing IDL source files in Chapter 6.

COM Standard Interfaces: IUnknown and IDispatch

So far you have seen how interfaces are represented in memory and what an
object like CChecking looks like in memory when it has a single interface, the
default interface. Let's shift now to the case in which a developer adds functionality to the CChecking class by defining another interface, **IAccount**, and implementing the interface in the object. The following code shows how a developer
might do this:

```
' Class IAccount

Option Explicit

Public Property Get Balance() As Currency
End Property

Public Sub MakeDeposit(ByVal Amount As Currency)
End Sub

' Class CChecking
Option Explicit
Implements IAccount

Private m_cBalance As Currency

Private Property Get IAccount_Balance() As Currency
    Balance = m_cBalance
End Property
```

```
Private Sub IAccount_MakeDeposit(ByVal Amount As Currency)
    m_cBalance = m_cBalance + Amount
End Sub
```

The client code using this code would look like the following:

```
Dim Acct As IAccount
Set Acct = new CChecking
Call Acct.MakeDeposit(5000)
Set Acct = Nothing
```

What VB does in this case is a little different. When the object is allocated in memory on the server side, VB builds two vtables. One vtable contains the public members of the _CChecking default interface. As it is right now, there are no public functions in CChecking. Nonetheless, if there were, then they would be part of a vtable. When VB sees the **Implements** statement in the server code, VB allocates a separate vtable to contain the public functions for the **IAccount** interface. This is the vtable that has the *Balance* and *MakeDeposit* function entries. The addresses of the functions in this vtable point (in essence) to the implementation code in the CChecking class. There are now two vptrs floating around in memory: one for the _CChecking vtable and one for the **IAccount** vtable. Now it is not so simple to map the client variable to the correct vtable. It takes a little teamwork.

It appears from studying the memory layout of VB objects that when VB allocates memory for the CChecking class, it creates two subobjects, one whose layout starts with a vptr to the _CChecking interface and one whose layout starts with a vptr to the **IAccount** interface. Both of these objects are in memory. The client's job is to tell the server which of the two subobjects it needs (i.e., which vtable it needs). The job of the server is to hand to the client the address of the little object with the correct vptr. How does it do this? The compiler adds a hidden function called *QueryInterface* to the server object. This function has two parameters. The first parameter is the name of the interface the client is requesting. This is an **in** parameter; that is, the client supplies this value as an argument when it calls *QueryInterface* on the server.

 In the next chapter, you will learn that the true name of an interface is not a string name like "IAccount"—if it were, two companies might come up with the same name for two different interface definitions. Instead, COM uses long numbers that are guaranteed to be unique. These numbers are called GUIDs, or globally unique identifiers. GUIDs were created by the Open Software Foundation (more on this in the next chapter). The first parameter in *QueryInterface* is the GUID (or unique number name) of the interface.

The second parameter is the address that will hold the requested vptr. This is an out parameter for the client; that is, the parameter's value is provided by the server and returned to the client when the function finishes execution. So the statement `Set Acct = New CChecking` does more than tell the server to create an instance of the object—it also asks the object to provide it with a certain vptr. In this case, because the Acct variable was declared as type `IAccount`, VB calls *QueryInterface* asking for the `IAccount` interface. The compiler built vtables for each interface supported in CChecking. At runtime, the server then allocates memory for the entire object and within the object creates what appear to be two subobjects, each of which holds the vptrs for each vtable supported. Then the *QueryInterface* function is called on the server side, and VB examines the requested interface parameter and hands the correct subobject back to the client.

What happens if the object implements multiple interfaces, as when a second interface called `ISaveToDisk` is implemented in the CChecking class? When VB allocates memory for the CChecking class, it creates three vtables: one vtable for the _CChecking public members (the default interface), one for the `IAccount` interface, and one for the `ISaveToDisk` interface. Then, it appears to create three subobjects in memory. Each of these subobjects has a memory layout that begins with the vptr of the corresponding vtable. If the client code now uses both interfaces, let's see what would happen. Consider the following client code:

```
Dim Acct As IAccount
Set Acct = New CChecking
Dim SD As ISaveToDisk
Set SD = Acct
Set Acct = Nothing
Set SD = Nothing
```

Notice how polymorphism is achieved through the *QueryInterface* function. Recall that when VB executes the line that reads `Set Acct = New CChecking`, VB also calls the *QueryInterface* function to request from the server the object with the correct vptr. When the code executes the line that reads `Set SD = Acct`, all VB does is call *QueryInterface* again and ask now for the memory address of the object with a vptr to the `ISaveToDisk` interface.

What happens when VB encounters the line `Set Acct = Nothing`? Just as the server code allocates the memory for the object, under COM rules the server code must also deallocate the memory. Deallocating memory is an operation that depends on the memory representation of the object. Thus, it makes sense that calling `Set Acct = Nothing` would make the server side delete the object from memory. However, notice that two variables require this memory to exist. VB cannot simply delete the entire object from memory when it encounters the first `Set Acct = Nothing`—the developer may still want to use it through SD. It must not destroy the object until it encounters the second `Nothing` (`Set SD = Nothing`). This means that VB will need to keep track of how many variables are pointing to the object. VB does this by adding two other hidden functions to the server object: *AddRef* and *Release*. The server object keeps a counter of how many variables are using the object memory. When the client requests another interface through *QueryInterface*, the *QueryInterface* function calls the *AddRef* function in the object, and this function tells the object to increase its internal count. The client code `Set Acct = Nothing` in the client code is translated to `[Obj].Release`. The *Release* function tells the object to decrease the counter by 1. When the internal reference counter for the object reaches 0, then the object will release itself from memory. Therefore, in the previous client code, the two calls to *QueryInterface*, one in the `New` and the second in the `Set SD = Acct`, tell the object to increase the count by 2. When the code executes the two = `Nothing` lines, *Release* is called twice and the count goes down to 0, telling the object to destroy itself from memory. This means that every COM object needs to have at least three functions—*QueryInterface*, *AddRef*, and *Release*—to work with clients. Because every object needs to have those three functions in some way, Microsoft grouped the functions into a separate interface known as `IUnknown`.

IUnknown

The `IUnknown` interface is the most important interface in COM. An object is not considered a COM object unless it implements this interface. In fact, the COM rules state that every interface definition must be derived from `IUnknown`. This means that the first three entries in every vtable are pointers to the *QueryInterface*, *AddRef,* and *Release* functions. For an object to implement the `IUnknown` interface, it must maintain a variable to hold a reference count. It must add 1 to this variable when *AddRef* is called; it must decrease this variable by 1 when *Release* is called; and it must hand out the correct memory address for the requested vtable in the *QueryInterface* function.

The reason you may have been doing COM objects in VB for years without knowing about `IUnknown` is that VB hides the implementation of `IUnknown`. In other words, you never have to add a statement like `Implements IUnknown`. Now that you know that every object must implement the `IUnknown` interface and that every interface must derive from `IUnknown`, let's see what this means about how VB objects are implemented.

Studying the memory layout of VB objects with the C++ debugger, you can derive a likely scenario for how VB COM objects are constructed. Figure 3-5 shows you a likely representation of the memory layout of VB objects.

When VB allocates memory for the CChecking class, it allocates a vtable for each interface that is implemented in the object. This means that, using our last version

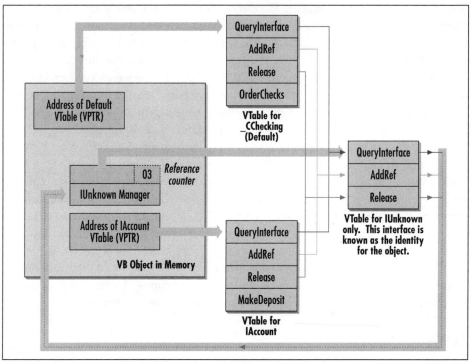

Figure 3-5. Likely representation of the memory layout of VB objects

of the CChecking class, it will allocate three vtables in memory. Each vtable definition begins with the members of IUnknown. Figure 3-5 shows you how each
vtable is constructed. VB allocates three subobjects in memory for each interface.
The first thing in memory for each little object is the vptr to the corresponding
vtable. VB also creates a separate vtable containing only the functions for the
IUnknown interface and another object (looking at the debug symbols for the VB
runtime, this might be an instance of the CUnkPriv internal class) that holds the
vptr to this vtable. However, this other object that will be responsible for implementing the methods of IUnknown also allocates memory for a private member
variable that will hold the reference counter. This IUnknown handler object is what
VB hands out when someone calls *QueryInterface* and specifically asks for the
IUnknown interface.

> When a client specifically asks for the IUnknown interface, the object
> that the server hands out to the client is known as the identity of the
> COM object.

With this new information, let's study what happens in the client code once more:

```
Dim Acct As IAccount
Set Acct = New CChecking
Dim SD As ISaveToDisk
Set SD = Acct
Dim Acct2 As IAccount
Set Acct2 = Acct
Set Acct = Nothing
Set SD = Nothing
```

The client code is slightly different. It contains an extra declaration for a variable named Acct2, and it sets Acct2 to Acct. When VB executes the `Set Acct = New CChecking` line, it calls *QueryInterface* asking for the `IAccount` interface. Internally, VB calls the *QueryInterface* function of the `IUnknown` handler object (the object that ultimately handles all the methods of `IUnknown`). This object is the master controller for all the subobjects VB creates to represent each interface. It is the object that makes all the subobjects appear as if they are one unit representing the entire CChecking class. Its job is to return the address of the little object that has the vptr for the requested vtable.

When the program executes the `Set SD = Acct` statement, the Acct variable is holding on to the memory address of the object that stores the vptr for the `IAccount` vtable. The code is going to call *QueryInterface*, but how? Well, the rule is that every vtable must contain the methods of `IUnknown` in exactly the same order. In fact, the compiler knows that *QueryInterface* is the first function of every vtable. So the compiler uses the address for the function listed in the first entry of the `IAccount` vtable to request the `ISaveToDisk` object. The object simply forwards the call to the main `IUnknown` controller, which is responsible for all the *QueryInterface* calls. This function then increases the reference count by 1. At this point, the reference count is at least 2. (It turns out that we can't say with certainty that it is 2 because other internal functions in VB are allowed to affect the count.) But for the sake of the discussion, it makes sense to say that this value is 2.

When the code executes the line `Set Acct2 = Acct`, VB does not need to do a *QueryInterface*. That is because Acct2 is of the same type as Acct. Therefore, all that VB does is call the *AddRef* function, telling the object that there is another variable using the same memory. The code calls the *AddRef* entry in the `IAccount` vtable (function number 2). The code for the server simply forwards this method call to the `IUnknown` controller object. This object then increases the count to 3. If the client used the code `Set Acct2 = SD`, then the compiler would have translated that call to another call to *QueryInterface*. The only difference is that it would make a call using the first entry of the `ISaveToDisk` vtable. But again, the VB server code simply forwards the call to the same instance of the `IUnknown` controller object. Thus, the `IUnknown` controller object keeps a reference count for the object as a whole.

When the program executes the line `Set Acct = Nothing`, the code calls the *Release* function through the `IAccount` vtable. This call also is forwarded to the internal `IUnknown` controller object and it decreases the count by 1—the count is now 3. The next line, `Set SD = Nothing`, calls the *Release* function through the `ISaveToDisk` vtable, which forwards the call again to the `IUnknown` controller object and decreases the count by 1—the count is now 1.

The code does not have a statement `Set Acct2 = Nothing`, so how does the count ever get to 0? It does because VB has a fail-safe method in case the developer forgets to set the variable to `Nothing`. If the variable goes out of scope, VB automatically calls the *Release* function. At that point, the count goes to 0, and the `IUnknown` controller object, which has knowledge of all the subobjects responsible for their vtables, destroys all of them and releases itself from memory. Thus, all the memory is cleaned up.

VB does all this behind the scenes so that you never have to see `IUnknown` or a reference counter. Creating a COM object in C++ would be a different story. You could code the object from scratch and write code for the methods of `IUnknown` and include a variable for reference counting. Or you could use one of the two COM libraries that Microsoft provides that offer a default implementation of the `IUnknown` methods. These two libraries are the ActiveX Template Library (ATL) and the Microsoft Foundation Class (MFC) library.

If by chance the client requests an interface that is not implemented, *QueryInterface* is able to return an error to the client. Thus, *QueryInterface* works for handing out references to objects in memory or for simply finding out if an interface is supported.

Now that you know how VB finds out if an object supports an interface with *QueryInterface*, can you guess what happens when you use the `TypeOf/Is` operator in VB? If you guessed that it calls *QueryInterface*, you are correct. Since it does not need to get a reference to the object, it calls *Release* immediately afterward if the call was successful.

IDispatch

Until now we have been talking about how the Visual Basic compiler generates code to talk to a COM object via an interface. Essentially, the compiler had to know several things at design time. It had to know the interface that we wanted to use when communicating with the object. A developer specifies the interface through a `Dim` statement, such as `Dim Acct As IAccount`. This statement tells the compiler that we are going to use the `IAccount` interface. The compiler then

Spying on Calls to IUknown

Included in the downloadable software for this book is a COM server I created called *UnkFilter.dll*. This server has one interface definition called `IUnk-Monitor` and one object called `UnkFilter`. This object enables you to monitor when VB calls the methods of `IUnknown` for any VB object. It will not work with just any COM object. It is meant to work only with VB objects. To use it, you must implement the `IUnkMonitor` interface in the class that you would like to monitor. Then you create an instance of the `UnkFilter` object outside the class and call its *ReplaceUnk* function, passing an instance of the class you want to monitor. The way it works is that the `UnkFilter` object constructs a vtable replacement for the `IUnknown` interface's vtable. It then replaces the vtable of the `IUnknown` controller object (perhaps `CPrivUnk`) with the new vtable. The result is that when a method in `IUnknown` is called, the call really goes to functions in *UnkFilter.dll*. The *DLL* then calls the functions in `IUnkMonitor` to enable you to see when each function is called. After sending your object a notification, it forwards the call to the methods in the old vtable. Thus, the object continues to work as before, except that calls go though the *UnkFilter.dll* functions first. A description of the methods and examples of how to use the tool are available in the *readme.txt* file included with the download-able software for this book.

reads from the definition of the interface from the type library. It has to know the calling convention to use and the position of the function within the vtable. The end result of the compilation is assembly code that calculates a "jump" address based on a vptr and a vtable.

This procedure is known as *early binding*. Early binding is when the compiler fig-ures out at design time the offset of the function you wish to call. To make VB use early binding, you need to do two things: include the type library through project references and declare a variable using an interface as the type (remember that using the class name as the type simply tells VB to use the default interface, which is still early binding).

What if the information required for early binding is not available at design time? Let's take, for example, a client program like Internet Explorer (IE). IE is a client that can host COM objects. Authors of HTML pages specify the object that they want to use. It would be impossible for the designers of IE to account for every interface a developer may come up with. It would also be too time consuming for IE to locate the type library for an object and build a vtable layout on the fly for each interface that the object implements. Therefore, IE, as well as scripting cli-ents such as Windows Script Host (WSH), do not use early binding to talk to inter-faces; instead, such clients use a mechanism called *late binding*.

The solution for clients that cannot do early binding is to use early binding only to talk to one all-purpose interface called `IDispatch`. The `IDispatch` interface enables a client to make a function call using its name instead of its address in a vtable. The developer of the server component implements the `IDispatch` interface the same way that it would implement `IAccount`. The client makes a call through `IDispatch`, and the server makes the actual method call on behalf of the client. In other words, the server does the work of early binding on the client's behalf. This is called late binding, because from the perspective of the client code, the actual binding to a function (the code that makes a jump into the function) does not take place until runtime.

The `IDispatch` interface has four functions, but the important ones that make this possible are *GetIDsOfNames* and *Invoke*. When the scripting client creates an object, the first thing it does is ask for the `IDispatch` interface. Then when the scripting client encounters a line of code such as `Obj.MakeDeposit(5000)`, the program (IE for example) calls the function *GetIDsOfNames*. The *GetIDsOfNames* function enables the client to pass in the function name, in this case *MakeDeposit*. The COM object is responsible for making sure it has a function that matches that name and assigning a numeric ID to the function. This numeric ID is known as a DispID (or dispatch ID). The DispID is a programmer-assigned number. Once the client obtains the DispID, it then calls the *Invoke* function. The *Invoke* function enables the client to make a method call. The function requires a DispID for the method to invoke and an array of variants with the parameters for the method call.

In the case of the method call `Obj.MakeDeposit(5000)`, the client would call *GetIDsOfNames* first to obtain the DispID. The method would return a number (5, for example), and then the client would call the *Invoke* function, passing ID 5 and an array of variants with only one element containing the number 5000. The COM object would then receive the *Invoke* method call, unpackage the parameter containing the array of variants, and make the method call itself. The *Invoke* function has an output parameter for the return value from the function, if there is any. Thus, the server component can make the method call and package the result of the function into a variant and send that back to the client.

In the case of the client making a call like `Obj.Balance`, the scripting client would first call *GetIDsOfNames* and receive a DispID (e.g., 1000). Then the client would call *Invoke* with ID 1000 and send in an empty array. The server would then make the call to its own *Balance* function. Next, it would take the output parameter of the function, the balance, and stuff it into a variant variable, then send that back at the end of the *Invoke* call.

Although scripting clients can cache the DispIDs for each method name, IE does not do this. It simply executes the two method calls, *GetIDsOfNames* and *Invoke*, for each method call, even if the client calls *MakeDeposit* a hundred times in a row. As you can see, this makes method invocation from a scripting client slower than method calls from a client that can bind to any interface.

The good news for VB developers is that VB automatically adds support for the IDispatch interface to every COM class you create. It does this by making every interface that is created with Visual Basic derive from IDispatch. You may be thinking, "What about IUnknown? I thought every vtable had to have the functions of IUnknown as the first three members." That is absolutely right. The answer is that IDispatch itself is derived from IUnknown. So the COM rules say that every interface has to be derived from IUnknown, or from another interface that is derived from IUnknown. The outcome is always the same: the methods of IUnknown will always be first in the interface's vtable. If every interface created with VB derives from IDispatch, this means that the vtable representations shown thus far in this chapter are slightly inaccurate. Figure 3-6 shows the true representation of the vtables for the interfaces defined thus far.

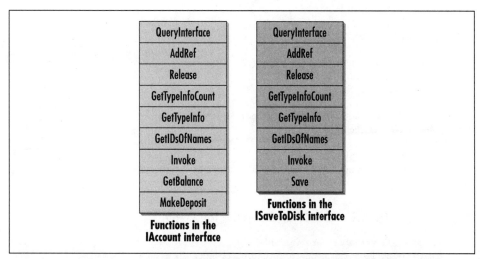

Figure 3-6. vtable representation of the interfaces implemented in the CChecking object

Any interface that a programmer defines that derives directly from IUnknown is known as a *custom interface*. An interface that derives from IDispatch is known as a *dual interface*. In VB, all the interfaces you define are dual interfaces. To define a custom interface, you must define it outside VB.

There is a big limitation with scripting clients. Since they know how to talk only to IDispatch, it is not possible to write code for a scripting client that asks for another interface. What's more, every variable in scripting clients is of type Variant, so it is impossible to define a variable of the interface type that you would like to request. For example, the following code is illegal in a scripting client:

```
' Illegal
Dim SD As ISaveToDisk
Set SD = Acct 'where Acct has a reference to which interface — IDispatch
```

The IDispatch implementation that VB provides knows how to talk only to functions that are part of the default interface. Some developers erroneously try to overcome this using a trick shown in the following code. Please realize that although the following code works under certain circumstances, it is not recommended. Many aspects of the COM remoting layer prevent it from working in all cases. It is presented here simply because it is something that many developers are tempted to do at one time or another.

```
' Class CChecking

Option Explicit

Implements IAccount

Private m_cBalance As Currency

Public Function GetAccountInterface() As IAccount
    Set GetAccountInterface = Me
End Function

Private Property Get IAccount_Balance() As Currency
    Balance = m_cBalance
End Property

Private Sub IAccount_MakeDeposit(ByVal Amount As Currency)
    m_cBalance = m_cBalance + Amount
End Sub
```

The scripting client code would look like the following:

```
Dim Acct 'All variables are variant
'CreateObject is a function for creating objects in a
'scripting language
Set Acct = CreateObject("BankServer.CChecking")
Dim AcctInterface
Set AcctInterface = Acct.GetAccountInterface()
AcctInterface.MakeDeposit(5000)
```

The client code first creates an instance of the object and asks for the IDispatch interface. If you recall, VB creates subobjects for each interface that is implemented in the CChecking class plus one for the default interface. The default interface has only whatever has been marked as public in the class. At this point, the class has one public function, *GetAccountInterface*. The client code calls this function. You may recall that the scripting client simply calls *GetIDsOfNames* and *Invoke*. The VB implementation for IDispatch is unique to each interface. If VB gets a request of

GetIDsOfNames from the _CChecking vtable, then *GetIDsOfNames* returns IDs for only the member functions in that vtable. When the code encounters the *GetAccountInterface* method, the implementation in the CChecking VB source responds as follows:

```
Public Function GetAccountInterface() As IAccount
    Set GetAccountInterface = Me
End Function
```

The preceding code actually triggers *QueryInterface* on the Me reference, which forwards the call to the IUnknown manager in memory and asks for the IAccount interface. This has the effect of returning to the client a reference to another vtable—the vtable for the IAccount interface. Because the vtable also has support for IDispatch, the client does not request the IDispatch interface again. If it did, VB would return the vtable for the default interface. Because the client does not request IDispatch again and assumes it already has it (which is legal, since it has a vtable with IDispatch), it simply uses the new vtable in subsequent calls. When the client executes the AcctInterface.MakeDeposit(5000) line, it uses the IAccount vtable to call *GetIDsOfNames* and then *Invoke*. This is a nice trick because it enables the scripting client to make calls on various interfaces by forcing the server code to call *QueryInterface* for it. However, this trick will work only if the COM server is shipped as an ActiveX DLL. It will not work with a COM object that is part of an ActiveX EXE. The reason is too complicated to explain in this chapter. You will learn the reason in Chapter 5. When using components from an ActiveX EXE, the only functions the scripting client may call are the ones for the default interface.

Summary

If your head is spinning, it is because this is difficult stuff. The good news is that VB does almost everything for you automatically.

In this chapter you learned the memory layout of interfaces. The main thing to remember is the memory layout of an interface is the same in every language: a memory address known as a vptr points to a vtable. A vtable is nothing more than an array of pointers to functions. Each vtable begins with pointers to functions of the IUnknown interface. In fact, the true definition of a COM object is an object that implements the IUnknown interface. IUnknown enables us to do two main tasks. First, it gives us a mechanism by which we can accomplish polymorphism (through *QueryInterface*). Second, it gives us two methods (AddRef and Release) by which we can do reference counting.

Some clients are not able to use just any interface directly. For these clients, Microsoft provides a special interface known as IDispatch. IDispatch enables a client to ask the server to execute a method on its behalf using its name. A client using `IDispatch` first asks for a DispID for a certain method using the *GetIDsOfNames* function. Then, it calls the *Invoke* function to execute the method. VB automatically adds support for `IDispatch` to every COM object. In fact, every interface created in VB is a dual interface. A dual interface is one that is derived from `IDispatch`, instead of directly from `IUnknown`.

In the next chapter, you will learn how VB COM objects are packaged. We are also going to fill in some of the holes of how clients communicate with servers in COM.

4

In-Process Servers

In the last chapter, you learned about the memory layout of VB COM objects. In particular, you learned how VB allocates memory for objects with multiple interfaces. You also learned how VB enables you to request different portions of this memory using the *QueryInterface* method of the IUnknown interface (henceforth referred to as *QI*). Most important was the idea that all interfaces are created equal. In other words, the memory layout of an interface in any language is basically the same—it is a virtual table pointer (vptr) pointing to a virtual table (vtable). A vtable is nothing more than an array of pointers to the addresses of functions in memory. COM rules state that the first three functions in the vtable of a COM interface must be the methods of IUnknown: *QueryInterface*, *AddRef*, and *Release*. You learned from Chapter 3 that Visual Basic built a little object to manage the IUnknown implementation for the entire object. You also learned some of the COM rules for allocating memory in the last chapter. One rule discussed in the chapter was that memory for COM objects must be allocated by the server code. You also learned that the server provides the definitions of its COM objects for the client through a file called a type library.

In this chapter, you will learn the whole story of activation for ActiveX DLLs. The term *activation* refers to the process that occurs at the API level from the time the client requests a new server object to the time it can use this object. For example, consider the following code:

```
Dim Account As IAccount
Set Account = New CChecking
Call Account.MakeDeposit(5000)
```

In this chapter, we are going to focus on what happens in the second line of code: Set Account = New CChecking. However, before we go into too much detail on the activation process, let's see how it is that COM components are packaged and used from a client application at a high level.

Client-Server Communication: A High-Level View

To many of you, this will be review. Nonetheless, let's take a minute for a high-level examination of the process of building a COM server and using it from a client program at a high level.

Building an ActiveX DLL

Using the same classes as in the last chapter, let's build a COM server and use it from the client. The first step in building the server is to decide on the packaging. The packaging comes in three flavors: ActiveX EXE, ActiveX DLL, and ActiveX OCX. This book does not discuss ActiveX OCXs, although for all practical purposes they are the same as ActiveX DLLs except that the COM components they export can be inserted into ActiveX containers (such as the VB Form object). In this chapter, we will focus on the ActiveX DLLs. You will learn about ActiveX EXEs and the COM remoting architecture in the next chapter.

If you have not already done so, start Visual Basic 6. When you see the New Project dialog box, double-click on the ActiveX DLL entry. You should now have a project called Project1 with a single class module called Class1. Change the name of the class module to **IAccount**, and add the following code:

```
Option Explicit
Public Property Get Balance() As Currency
End Property
Public Sub MakeDeposit(ByVal Amount As Currency)
End Sub
```

You may recall from Chapter 2 that this class serves as an interface definition. Because it is meant to be an interface and not a standalone class, change the Instancing property to **2 - PublicNotCreatable**. Add a second class module to your project using the Project → Add Class Module menu option. Change the name of the class to CChecking and enter the following code in the module:

```
Option Explicit
Implements IAccount

Private m_balance As Currency

Private Property Get IAccount_Balance() As Currency
    IAccount_Balance = m_balance
End Property
```

```
Private Sub IAccount_MakeDeposit(ByVal Amount As Currency)
    m_balance = m_balance + Amount
End Sub
```

If you are unsure why there is a line that reads **Implements IAccount**, refer back to Chapter 2. The preceding class definition comes straight from Chapter 2. CChecking is a class that implements the **IAccount** interface.

Change the name of the project to BankServer. Then choose File → Make Bank-Server.dll to compile your project. You have just built a full COM server with one COM class, CChecking. To use the CChecking class, you must build a client program.

Building a Client

Choose File → New Project to begin a new project and double-click on the Standard EXE icon. You should have a project with a single Form module. Change the name of the Form to frmClient. Then change the name of the project to Bank-Client. Add a CommandButton control to the form, change its name to cmdCreate, and change its caption to "&Create Account".

The first step in using the server components is to tell VB to read the definition of the CChecking class from an external file. Without reading this external file, VB knows nothing of the CChecking class. This external file is called a type library. You learned a little about type libraries in Chapter 3. Later on in this chapter, you will learn more about them. The type library contains the definitions of the classes and interfaces that a server exports. To tell VB to read a type library file, choose Project → References from the IDE. You will see the References dialog box as depicted in Figure 4-1.

Select the entry that reads BankServer and click OK. You may now enter code in the cmdCreate button to create an instance of the CChecking class and use it. Double-click on the cmdCreate button and enter the following code in the code window:

```
Private Sub cmdCreate_Click()
    Dim Acct As IAccount
    Set Acct = New CChecking
    Call Acct.MakeDeposit(5000)
    MsgBox Acct.Balance
End Sub
```

Notice that the code makes use of the **IAccount** interface. The alternative would have been to use **Dim Acct As CChecking**, but that would not work because the default interface for the class, the **_CChecking** interface, does not have any public members—all the functionality comes from the implementation of the **IAccount** interface.

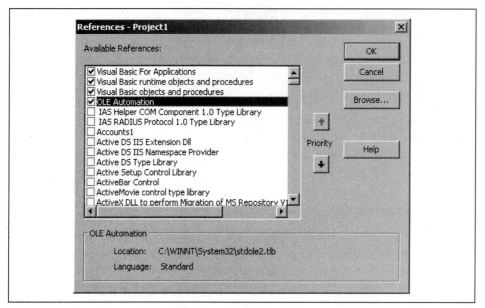

Figure 4-1. The References dialog box has a list of type library files to use in your project

After declaring the Acct variable, the code then creates an instance of CChecking and calls the MakeDeposit method. Finally, it displays the balance by reading the Balance property.

Run your application from within the IDE. Then, click the Create Account button to make sure all is well. You should see a message box with the number 5000.

As you can see, it is fairly easy to create and use COM components in Visual Basic. All you need to do is create an ActiveX DLL project and add class modules to it. Then you build the DLL. To use it, you create a Standard EXE project and add a reference to the server project using the References dialog box. After adding the reference to the server project, you can create instances of the exported classes and use them as you have done in the previous code.

It is now time to turn our attention to what is happening underneath to make the mechanism work.

Client-Server Communication: A Low-Level View

Let's begin by examining what is required for a client to be able to create a COM object that lives in a DLL. (In Chapter 5, you will see that the process is slightly different for ActiveX EXEs.) But first you must learn the true name of a COM component.

GUIDs

As we noted in the "COM Standard Interfaces: IUnknown and IDispatch" section in Chapter 3, the official name for classes and interfaces is not the string name you assign to the class or interface while developing in VB. You may recall that *QI* enables developers to ask an object for a particular interface implementation. It also enables developers to find out if an object in fact supports an interface. The first parameter in *QI* is the interface "name." It is an **input** parameter. The second parameter is an **out** parameter returned by the object with a pointer to the vptr of the requested interface.

The name **IAccount** is not unique enough for *QI* to work for every interface ever defined. Think about how many companies writing COM-based banking applications may use the name **IAccount** for their primary interface definition. *QueryInterface* would not know if you were asking for company A's **IAccount** or company B's **IAccount**. Therefore, Microsoft decided to use another mechanism for naming interfaces. Instead of using the string name, COM identifies each interface by a number—a very big number known as a globally unique identifier, or GUID.

A GUID is a 128-bit number. An example of a GUID is 36B1C83C-62D0-4199-AF2E-A7A73505EA65—the registry is full of them. In fact, most of COM's registry keys can be found in four locations: **HKEY_CLASSES_ROOT**, **HKEY_CLASSES_ROOT\ CLSID**, **HKEY_CLASSES_ROOT\TypeLib**, and **HKEY_CLASSES_ROOT\Interface**. If you look at the registry with *Regedit.exe*, you will notice that the registry hierarchy is divided into four main trees. Microsoft has suggested that the **HKEY_ CLASSES_ROOT** tree in the registry (normally abbreviated as **HKCR**) should be used for storing information about COM components. Microsoft provides an API function called *CoCreateGUID* in *OLE32.DLL* that uses a special algorithm to generate unique GUIDs. GUIDs were not conceived by Microsoft developers. GUIDs, normally called UUIDs (universally unique identifiers), were first introduced by the Open Software Foundation (OSF) as part of their Distributed Computing Environment specification. They are also the creators of the algorithm to generate unique numbers and the ones who specified the format in which they are written (xxxxxxxx-xxxx-xxxx-xxxx-xxxxxxxxxxxx).

The algorithm for generating GUIDs uses, among other things, the unique number of your network adapter (if your computer has a network adapter). Each network card has a unique identifier assigned by the manufacturer. The algorithm for generating GUIDs has been declared statistically guaranteed to generate unique numbers until the year 3000 (by then our brains will be large enough that we will not need computers anymore). The bottom line is that if you use the function *CoCreateGUID*, you do not ever have to worry about getting the same number twice.

Believe it or not, there is a small controversy among COM developers about how to pronounce the acronym GUID. Some people like
to make it rhyme with the word *druid*, as in *goo-id*, while others like
to make it rhyme with the word *squid*. I must warn you that a number of famous COM authors (including my coworkers) like to make
it rhyme with squid, and this now seems to be the standard. I, however, like to say it *goo-id*, because this is the way I first learned it
five years ago, and old habits are hard to break.

The reason you may not have ever seen a GUID in VB is that VB generates GUIDs
using *CoCreateGUID* behind the scenes and hides all evidence of them. This is a
blessing and a curse, as you will see at the end of this chapter when we discuss
versioning.

In COM, GUIDs are used to name other elements aside from interfaces, such as
classes and type libraries. When a GUID is used to name an interface, it is known
as an IID (interface ID). Likewise, when it is used to name a class or library, it is
referred to as a CLSID (class ID) or a LIBID (library ID), respectively.

In reality, COM does not refer to the `IAccount` interface by its string name
`IAccount`, but by its IID (written as `IID_IAccount` in C++). In the same fashion,
COM knows nothing of the name CChecking—it knows the class by its numeric
name, the CLSID (written as `CLSID_CChecking` in C++).

VB generates an IID for each interface you define, a CLSID for each COM class
you define, and a single LIBID for the type library of the project at compile time.
Because GUIDs are guaranteed to be unique, if you were to compile the source
code for BankServer in your machine, and I were to compile it in my machine, we
would definitely end up with different numbers for IIDs, CLSIDs, and LIBIDs. Later
in this chapter you will see how these numbers are stored and how the client
becomes aware of them.

ProgIDs

GUIDs are not very readable. You cannot read a GUID and easily identify the
component to which it belongs; for example, you have never read in a manual to
"create an instance of the 36B1C83C-62D0-4199-AF2E-A7A73505EA65 class." Using
GUIDs can make programming cumbersome for scripting languages or even for
VB developers. Therefore, even though a class name such as CChecking is not
guaranteed to be unique, COM does enable a developer to refer to a class by a
string name called a Programmatic ID (ProgID). A ProgID is a string name that
identifies an object. It is not guaranteed to be unique—two companies may come
up with the same ProgID.

The ProgID is supposed to be constructed from the company name plus the name of the server plus the class name (for example, `WidgetsUSA.BankServer.CChecking`). Although this name is not guaranteed to be unique, it can be close. ProgIDs are stored in the registry under `HKCR`; COM rules say that ProgIDs are optional, but if they are assigned, each COM class in your server must have its own ProgID. Under the ProgID key, you store the GUID for the class (the CLSID). COM provides two API functions called *CLSIDFromProgID* and *CLSIDFromProgIDEx*, which search the registry for a specific ProgID and return the CLSID. Thus, a COM developer who does not know the component's GUID may use this API to obtain it from a readable name and then use the GUID in other COM calls.

Each machine maintains only one copy of a ProgID. That means that if two companies use the same ProgID, they will override each other's setting in the registry; the ProgID will point to the CLSID of the last COM server to be registered.

Microsoft decided this was too much work for us VB developers. Every time you compile a COM project (ActiveX DLL, ActiveX EXE, or ActiveX OCX), VB automatically generates a ProgID for each of your classes and adds it to the registry. VB constructs the ProgID from the project name plus the class name. So for CChecking, the ProgID is `BankServer.CChecking`. If we had a class called CSavings, we would have two ProgIDs (`BankServer.CChecking` and `BankServer.CSavings`). Notice that this can be a problem, since it is very likely that two companies can name their projects BankServer and both include a CChecking class. Nonetheless, there is nothing that can be done about this. VB does not let us choose our own ProgIDs. If you are concerned about your classes, you can always name your project *CompanyNameBankServer* and at least have a fair shot at uniqueness. If you are really concerned, you can always take matters into your own hands and come up with ProgIDs that you feel are unique, then manually add them to the registry through your installation program.

CoCreateInstance and CoCreateInstanceEx

Whether you are working with VB, Java, or Visual C++, each language eventually uses one of two API functions to create a COM object: *CoCreateInstance* or *CoCreateInstanceEx*. *CoCreateInstance* is an earlier version of the API—internally *CoCreateInstance* simply calls *CoCreateInstanceEx*, passing some default parameters. However, each works slightly differently. Both of these APIs are in *OLE32.DLL*.

CoCreateInstance has five parameters. The first parameter is the CLSID of the class you wish to create (the real name of the class). The second parameter is for a feature called aggregation, which is outside the scope of this book. (*Aggregation* enables you to make a client think that another already-compiled COM object is actually part of your object. In other words, it enables two COM objects to act as a single object. VB objects cannot be aggregated.) The third parameter is the creation flag. The creation flag enables you to specify whether the API should search for the object inside a DLL, inside an EXE in the same machine, inside an EXE in another machine, or in any possible way starting with a DLL. The fourth parameter is the IID of the interface you wish to start with. When you create the object, you can tell the COM API to do a *QI* for you so that you can execute both creation and *QI* at the same time. The fifth parameter is an output parameter that receives the memory address of the vptr of the vtable you asked for in the fourth parameter.

CoCreateInstanceEx is slightly more advanced. For one thing, it enables you to specify a remote server where the object lives. Another advantage of *CoCreateInstanceEx* is that instead of asking for a single interface, you can ask for an array of interfaces at once. This is particularly useful when creating an object remotely, since it minimizes the number of times you have to access the remote server to do a *QI*. Whenever you need to create a COM object from a remote machine, and you wish to specify the remote machine's name, you must use the *CoCreateInstanceEx* function.

However, you never see these API functions in VB because VB makes the call for you. Yet, it is good to know which one VB uses in each circumstance, because it turns out that this information is crucial when versioning your components (see Chapter 6).

Type Libraries (Revisited)

VB translates the **New** operator into a call to *CoCreateInstanceEx*. *CoCreateInstanceEx* takes as its first parameter the CLSID of the class you wish to create. This means that VB must know the CLSID of the class at compile time. Where does it get the CLSID when using the **New** command? Consider the following code:

```
Dim Acct As IAccount
Set Acct = New CChecking
Call Acct.MakeDeposit(5000)
```

You learned from Chapter 3 that the line **Set Acct = New CChecking** does two things: first, it tells the server to allocate memory for the CChecking class; second, it uses *QI* to get a pointer to the **IAccount** interface.

QI requires that you specify the interface you wish to obtain using the interface's IID. This means that VB must know both the CLSID of CChecking and the IID of **IAccount** to execute the preceding code. Not only that, but if you read the last chapter carefully, you should know that the call **Acct.MakeDeposit** is translated to a vtable call. This means VB has to know that MakeDeposit is function number 8 in the vtable for **IAccount**.

Why number 8? First, there are the three methods for IUnknown in the vtable, then the four methods for IDispatch, and then MakeDeposit.

In other words, at compile time VB needs to translate the line Acct. MakeDeposit(5000) to use the vtable, find the entry to the MakeDeposit function (i.e., read the address of function number 8 from the array of function pointers), then make the call. For this to work at compile time, VB must know the layout of the interface. Thus, there are at least three pieces of information that it needs to create that object: one CLSID, one IID, and the layout of the IAccount interface. Where does all this information come from?

All the information the client needs to create a COM object comes from the type library. The type library is a binary file that VB generates at compile time. The format for the type library file is undocumented; however, Microsoft provides tools for generating type libraries as well as an array of API functions for parsing a type library file. Type libraries are generated by VB when the server is compiled, and they provide clients with the information necessary for the client to use early binding (see Chapter 3 for details). A C++ developer defines the interfaces and COM classes first using the Interface Definition Language (IDL). Microsoft provides an IDL compiler called MIDL. This compiler can generate (along with other files) a type library file with the extension *.TLB*. The idea is that you should be able to create a COM server in Visual C++ and generate a *.TLB* file, then use the *.TLB* file in a VB client in order to give VB the information it needs to create instances of the classes in the C++ server. This is a two-way street. VC can also use the type library from a VB server to get all the information it needs to create classes in that server.

The COM specification says that a server may distribute a type library in one of two ways: as a standalone file or as part of the server file (i.e., embedded into the DLL or the EXE as a resource). VB chooses to embed the type library file into the DLL or EXE at compile time, although you can request to also have the type library as a standalone file. To have VB generate a standalone file as well as embed the file into the compiled image, choose Project → BankServer Properties. In the Project Properties dialog box, click on the Component tab, and choose the Remote Server Files option.

It is possible to see a server's raw type library information using a tool Microsoft provides with Visual Studio called OLE/COM Object Viewer. To use the OLE/COM Object Viewer, choose Start → Programs → Microsoft Visual Studio 6.0 → Microsoft Visual Studio 6.0 Tools → OLE View (see Figure 4-2).

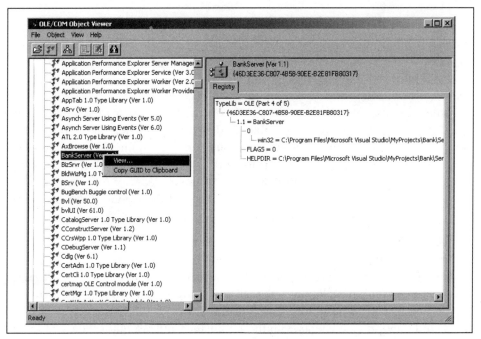

Figure 4-2. OLE/COM Object Viewer

If you compiled the BankServer code from the beginning of the chapter, you may examine the type library information embedded in the *BankServer.DLL* file. To do so, expand the Type Libraries branch and find the entry that reads BankServer. Right-click on BankServer and choose View.... Example 4-1 shows portions of the raw type library information in *BankServer.DLL*.

Example 4-1. Portions of the raw type library information in BankServer.DLL

```
// Generated .IDL file (by the OLE/COM Object Viewer)
//
// typelib filename: BankServer.dll

[
  uuid(46D3EE36-C807-4B58-90EE-B2E81FB80317),
  version(1.0),
  custom(50867B00-BB69-11D0-A8FF-00A0C9110059, 8495)

]
library BankServer
{
    [
      uuid(14172653-F73E-4BB0-8392-2E1D61528542),
      dual,
      hidden,
    ]
    interface _CChecking : IDispatch {
```

Example 4-1. Portions of the raw type library information in BankServer.DLL (continued)

```
   };

   [
      uuid(4B9095B4-809C-4669-B54B-DD9610E054A4),
   ]
   coclass CChecking {
       [default] interface _CChecking;
       interface _IAccount;
   };

   [
      uuid(36B1C83C-62D0-4199-AF2E-A7A73505EA65),
      dual,
      hidden,
   ]
   interface _IAccount : IDispatch {
       [id(0x68030000), propget]
       HRESULT Balance([out, retval] CURRENCY* );
       [id(0x60030001)]
       HRESULT MakeDeposit([in] CURRENCY Amount);
   };

   [
      uuid(E6ECF4C7-69D9-43FB-8A80-BA24AF5A4E14),
      noncreatable
   ]
   coclass IAccount {
       [default] interface _IAccount;
   };

};
```

I have condensed the code in Example 4-1 for the sake of clarity. Notice that the type library has three important pieces of information: the library block, the interface definitions, and the class definitions. What may seem strange from the code is that there are two interface definitions and two class definitions. Example 4-1 shows an interface called **_CChecking** and a class called CChecking. The following fragment from Example 4-1 includes the interface definition:

```
   [
      uuid(14172653-F73E-4BB0-8392-2E1D61528542),
      dual,
      hidden,
   ]
   interface _CChecking : IDispatch {
   };
```

Before the interface definition are attributes for the interface enclosed in brackets. One of these attributes is the **uuid** (or GUID) or, more specifically, the interface's IID. The interface is also marked as hidden. This attribute works only for VB clients—it means that a VB client is not able to see this interface in Intellisense (the drop-downs you see when you are coding) unless you select View → Object Browser, right-click anywhere in the window, and select Show Hidden Members from the drop-down menu.

If you read Chapter 2, you learned that _CChecking is the default interface for the CChecking class. The default interface contains the public members (properties and functions) of a class. The CChecking class does not have any public members of its own; it gets its functionality from implementing the IAccount interface. This is why there are no functions declared in the interface definition for _CChecking. Remember that what VB does when it allocates an instance of the CChecking class is to create two little objects in memory, one to handle calls to the default interface and one to handle calls to the implemented interface.

If you are unfamiliar with C++ syntax, you may not realize that the statement interface _CChecking : IDispatch means that _CChecking is derived from IDispatch. In fact, every interface in Example 4-1 is derived from IDispatch. In Chapter 3, you learned that all VB-generated interfaces are dual interfaces to support scripting clients.

Following the definition for the interface in Example 4-1 is the definition for the CChecking coclass (COM class):

```
[
   uuid(4B9095B4-809C-4669-B54B-DD9610E054A4),
]
coclass CChecking {
     [default] interface _CChecking;
interface _IAccount;
  };
```

CoThis and CoThat

You may have noticed already that nearly every COM API is named with the letters *Co* as a prefix. This is a standard that the COM team used for naming their APIs. It simply stands for COM. So *CreateInstance* becomes *CoCreate-Instance*, and a COM class is called a coclass. ·

Again, notice that the class has a uuid attribute, which is the CLSID for the class. Interesting, however, is that two interfaces are listed for the class. The coclass definition is an advertisement to the client of what the class supports. The interfaces listed in the coclass definition have no effect on the compiler, only on Intellisense at design time; the important thing for the compiler is the CLSID for CChecking. Note that the list of interfaces contains interface _CChecking marked with a [default] attribute. The default attribute is used only by VB clients; a C++ programmer couldn't care less if an interface is marked as the default. To obtain any interface from an object, C++ or VB has to use *QI*. So a C++ client simply creates an instance of the class and asks for _CChecking or for _IAccount. VB uses the default attribute so that at design time a programmer may write code like the following:

```
Dim Account As CChecking
Set Account = New CChecking
```

In the preceding code, Account is defined as being of type CChecking. The compiler knows that what the developer means is:

```
Dim Account As _CChecking
Set Account = New CChecking
```

In other words, VB will do a *QI* in the assignment for the default interface, which is _CChecking. In this way, VB hides the fact that interfaces even exist when using VB classes.

Example 4-1 also has a definition for the IAccount interface—except that IAccount is not the interface name. As in the example of _CChecking, VB creates a default interface for the IAccount class. The default interface is _IAccount:

```
[
    uuid(36B1C83C-62D0-4199-AF2E-A7A73505EA65),
    dual,
    hidden,
]
interface _IAccount : IDispatch {
    [id(0x68030000), propget]
    HRESULT Balance([out, retval] CURRENCY* );
    [id(0x60030001)]
    HRESULT MakeDeposit([in] CURRENCY Amount);
};
```

An interesting fact is that VB also defines a class with the name IAccount. In fact, for every class whose Instancing property is not marked as Private, VB adds two things to the type library: a default interface and a class definition. VB does not know that the intent of the IAccount class was to serve as an interface definition. It treats it as any other class at compile time. Take a look at this IAccount coclass:

```
[
    uuid(E6ECF4C7-69D9-43FB-8A80-BA24AF5A4E14),
    noncreatable
]
coclass IAccount {
    [default] interface _IAccount;
};
```

The only attribute that is different is **noncreatable**. This attribute is enforced by the VB IDE when a developer is coding a client at design time, and it is also enforced at runtime if a program attempts to create an instance of the component. A component marked as **noncreatable** lacks the code necessary for the client to create an instance of the class. Because we marked the class' Instancing property as 2 - `PublicNotCreatable`, VB added this attribute to the type library.

Not obvious from looking at the type library source is that there is no mention of the DLL file or path to the DLL file that contains this type library (except for the comment at the top that has no effect on the client). How does the client code know what DLL to use to create the objects at runtime? Or does it need to know the DLL name and path at runtime? The answer is, "No." The VB client needs to know only three things: the CLSID of the class you wish to create, the IID of the interface within the class you wish to use, and the interface layout (function position within vtables). Therefore, think of the type library as separate from the DLL—the fact that it is compiled into the DLL is only for convenience.

VB COM Creation Functions

You have already seen from the previous chapter that you are able to create COM objects in VB using the `New` operator. The VB compiler replaces the call to `New` with a call into the VB runtime *MSVBVM60.DLL*. The VB runtime executes a function called *vbaNew*. This function calls *CoCreateInstanceEx*. If you recall, *CoCreateInstanceEx* requires the compiler to know at compile time the CLSID of the class you wish to create. VB gets this information from the type library. This, in turn, requires that you tell VB what type libraries to use. You do this through the References dialog box in VB. The References dialog box lists all the type libraries available in the system. It builds a list of these type libraries from reading the registry `HKEY_CLASSES_ROOT\TypeLib` subkeys.

The advantage of VB's using *CoCreateInstanceEx* over *CoCreateInstance* is that *CoCreateInstanceEx* enables you to ask for an array of interfaces at once instead of a single interface, and VB certainly makes use of this. VB is particularly interested in four interfaces upon creation:

`IUnknown`
> By obtaining a pointer to `IUnknown`, VB can do reference counting more easily.

The object's default interface
> VB guesses when asking for the second interface. The VB team made an assumption that is accurate for many developers. However, it is not accurate for us COM-savvy VB developers. The VB team assumed that you would most likely be using the object's default interface. Therefore, the second interface asked for is the default interface. VB knows which is the default interface at compile time from reading the `default` attribute in the type library. If there is no `default` attribute, VB automatically asks for the first interface listed in the coclass definition in the type library.

IPersistStreamInit

> This third interface is a Microsoft-defined interface whose purpose is to talk to objects that are persistable. VB 6 added a property to the class module called Persistable (**True** or **False**). When you mark a class as Persistable, VB adds support for the **IPersistStreamInit** interface. This is as if you had written **Implements IPersistStreamInit** in your class. Adding support for **IPersistStreamInit** doesn't mean that a client program will definitely make use of the interface. However, VB, being the kind of environment it is, asks to see if the object has this interface and starts using it.

IPersistPropertyBag

> This fourth interface is an alternative to **IPersistStreamInit**. Both have similar methods—the idea is that if the class does not support **IPersistStreamInit**, it will try to use **IPersistPropertyBag**.

The important thing to know is that VB client programs are written to ask for these four interfaces internally: **IUnknown**, **I_DefaultInterface**, **IPersistStreamInit**, and **IPersistPropertyBag**.

VB executes the statement **Set Account = New CChecking** in two stages. The first stage is creation (the right side of the equals sign), and the second stage is assignment (the left side of the equals sign). In creation, VB calls *CoCreateInstanceEx* to create the object, and while in creation it asks the object for those four interfaces. If VB cannot find **IUnknown**, then it is not a COM object, and VB generates an error. If VB cannot find the default interface, it also generates an error. (This is unfortunate, since the default interface may not be the interface the client needs, and this is what gives us 90% of the problems with versioning). The **IPersistStreamInit** and **IPersistPropertyBag** interfaces are optional, and VB does not generate an error if it cannot find them.

In the assignment stage, VB calls *QueryInterface* and asks for the interface specified by the type of the variable. Thus, since Account is of type **IAccount**, VB will ask for what interface? Notice that **IAccount** was the name we gave to the class, and in the type library source you can see that the coclass is named **IAccount**. VB does a *QI* for the default interface of **IAccount**, which is **_IAccount**. In VB there is a one-to-one mapping of the default interface to the class name.

It is also possible to create a class from its ProgID. To do that, you must use the *CreateObject* function. This function has two parameters, although the second is optional and will be discussed in Chapter 5. The first parameter is required—it is the ProgID of the object you wish to create. VB will automatically call *CLSIDFromProgIDEx* for you to obtain the class' GUID and use that whenever it needs to make a COM call for you.

The following code shows how to use the ProgID to create an instance of the
CChecking class from the client:

```
Private Sub cmdCreate_Click()
    Dim Acct As IAccount
    Set Acct = CreateObject("BankServer.CChecking")
    Call Acct.MakeDeposit(5000)
    MsgBox Acct.Balance
End Sub
```

The code is the same as before, except that the *CreateObject* function is used
instead of the **New** keyword. What VB does internally with *CreateObject*, however,
is very different from what it does with **New**—it turns out that **New** is faster than
CreateObject in many instances. In informal tests, I found that **New** is much faster
than *CreateObject* when using components from an ActiveX DLL but that the difference is not as dramatic when the components are in an ActiveX EXE in the
same machine. If the ActiveX EXE is on another machine and you specify a remote
machine in the second parameter of the *CreateObject* function, then *CreateObject*
and **New** do almost the same thing, so the difference in speed is very small. Before
you switch all your code to use **New**, however, you should know that **New** has limitations when used with COM+-configured components (see Chapter 7 for details).

CreateObject was introduced in VB 3, which may explain why it works the way it
does. *CreateObject* does not call *CoCreateInstanceEx*; instead, it calls
CoCreateInstance. Remember that with *CoCreateInstance*, VB can ask for only one
interface upon creation. VB takes the safe route and asks for **IUnknown**. The
problem is that because VB still needs **IPersistStreamInit**, it immediately calls
QueryInterface for this interface. If it fails to find it, it asks for **IPersist-
PropertyBag**. Then comes the interesting part. Because *CreateObject* was written
for scripting clients, VB assumes that you wish to get hold of the object's
IDispatch interface (scripting clients talk only to **IDispatch**). Therefore, VB
immediately *QI*s for **IDispatch**. The *CreateObject* function fails only if it cannot
translate the object's ProgID into a CLSID or if the object does not support the
IUnknown interface. The **IDispatch** interface is optional. Remember that **New** asks
for the default interface, whereas *CreateObject* asks for **IDispatch**; this is an
important distinction, particularly when versioning your components.

Using *CreateObject* requires four round-trips before it can execute the last *QI* for
the interface you are looking for. Compare this to the **New** operator, which takes
only one round-trip to complete.

In VB 3, the only way to create a COM object was through the *CreateObject* function. The *CreateObject* function was intended to be used with the Object datatype.
In VB you can declare a variable to be of type Object as follows:

```
Private Sub cmdCreate_Click()
    Dim Acct As Object
```

```
      Set Acct = CreateObject("BankServer.CChecking")
   End Sub
```

The preceding code segment uses the Object datatype instead of the IAccount interface. The Object datatype stands for the IDispatch interface. Whenever you set a variable of type Object equal to a variable pointing to a COM object, VB does one of two things. If the variable points to a dual interface, an interface derived from IDispatch, VB simply increases the reference count for the COM object. If the variable points to a custom interface (derived from IUnknown), VB calls *QueryInterface* and asks for IDispatch. The Object type is discouraged, because each method call goes through *GetIdsOfNames* and *Invoke* (as you learned in the previous chapter) instead of using direct table binding.

There is one advantage in using the Object datatype in conjunction with *CreateObject*. The previous code sample does not require you to have a type library. Type libraries are required for early binding. The previous code uses late binding (IDispatch). What's more, the code uses a ProgID to create the object. Thus, the executable code finds out the CLSID of the object at runtime; New requires that you know the CLSID at design time (hence the need for the type library).

To summarize our discussion so far, at the server's compile time, VB assigns GUIDs to each interface and to each COM class. VB puts the information for each interface and class into a type library file and embeds the type library into the DLL. VB client programs read the type library file to read the object's definition. Upon compilation of the client, VB translates a New call into *CoCreateInstanceEx*, and it translates *CreateObject* into *CLSIDFromProgIDEx* → *CoCreateInstance* → 3 *QIs*.

There are, however, a few unresolved issues. One is that, since *CoCreate-InstanceEx* and *CoCreateInstance* require only the CLSID of a class to create it, how do they know which EXE or DLL contains that class? Second, once the server is located, how is it told to create the class? Read on!

Registry Keys

To find information about the DLL that contains the requested class, *CoCreateInstanceEx* in *OLE32.DLL* searches the registry for a key containing the CLSID requested by the client. (The CLSID information comes from the type library file that you have to import into the client project using Project References.) The piece of code in *OLE32.DLL* that is involved in searching the registry and finding the associated DLL is called the Service Control Manager (SCM). Real COM+ developers refer to the SCM as the *scum*. The code for the SCM is scattered throughout *OLE32.DLL* and *RPCSS.DLL* (a service loaded by *svchost.exe*). This makes the SCM a logical entity rather than a physical entity that you can pinpoint to a single piece of code. For that reason, activation of a COM+ component is always blamed on the SCM.

Under COM+, it is possible to make a class available at two different levels: machinewide or user specific. If the class is to be available for all users, information for the class is added to the HKEY_CLASSES_ROOT\CLSID branch. If a class is meant to be used only by a certain user, information is added to the HKEY_CURRENT_USER\Software\Classes\CLSID branch. Each COM class needs to be added to the registry. It is done in the following fashion. Suppose that the CLSID for CChecking is {7C0B41FF-4935-499D-A1BD-465E98655C89}. The registry may contain HKCR\CLSID\{7C0B41FF-4935-499D-A1BD-465E98655C89} or HKCU\Software\Classes\CLSID\{7C0B41FF-4935-499D-A1BD-465E98655C89}   or both. It is possible to add information to both branches and have slightly different information for a certain user and general information for all users. This cannot be done with VB, however; VB writes information only to HKCR. In fact, most COM developers ignore HKCU; it is an enhancement that never caught on. If you want to use HKCU, you have to write the registry key manually with code or use your setup program of choice. COM+ always searches the HKCU branch first, then the HKCR key (even if it finds information under HKCU).

If the SCM finds the CLSID in one of the two branches, it searches for other subkeys. The first subkey that it searches for is TreatAs. The TreatAs key enables a developer to redirect the key information to another key. In other words, it is possible to tell *OLE32.DLL* that whenever it encounters key A, it should really look in key B for information. After searching for the TreatAs subkey, *OLE32.DLL* searches for the InProcServer32 key. The InProcServer32 key provides the location of the COM server DLL in 32-bit Windows. In 64-bit Windows, *OLE32.DLL* searches for the InProcServer64 key. Assuming you are using 32-bit Windows, the CChecking may have the following information in the registry:

```
HKCU
    CLSID
        {7C0B41FF-4935-499D-A1BD-465E98655C89}
            InProcServer32    (Default) C:\Bank\BankServer.DLL
```

What if it cannot find the InProcServer32 key? It then searches for a LocalServer32 key. You are going to learn more about this key in the next chapter when we discuss EXE servers. However, for now, realize that the SCM prefers for classes to be in DLLs, so it searches for the InProcServer32 key first. This key is meant to store only a path to a DLL. If you build a server as an EXE, the path to that file must be stored in the LocalServer32 key. The term local server is used in the COM spec to denote an ActiveX EXE server that lives on the same machine as the client program.

When the SCM locates the registry information for the CLSID, it adds the information to an internal cache. This means that if you request the information a second time, the SCM does not search the registry again; it simply gets the information from its internal cache.

If there is an `InprocServer32` key, the SCM reads the path to the DLL file. It then calls the WIN32 API function *LoadLibrary*. This function causes the kernel to load the DLL file into the same memory space allocated for your executable. In Windows, each process is given a virtual memory space. In Windows 2000, an application has an address space of 4 GB. Into this memory space Windows maps the system DLLs as well as any COM Server DLLs that *OLE32.DLL* loads (as well as *OLE32.DLL* itself). The end result is that it appears as though your application is running by itself in the machine and it can reach any of the functions in its memory. This is required by the Windows architecture: for an executable to make a direct function call into a DLL, the functions need to be in the same address space as the process.

Once the SCM loads the DLL with the *LoadLibrary* function, it calls the Win32 API function *GetProcAddress*. This function enables the SCM to find the location in memory of a certain function in the DLL. The SCM uses this function to find the function *DllGetClassObject*. *DllGetClassObject* is one of the required functions for every COM Server DLL. The COM+ specification says that every COM+ DLL must have four functions that can be called externally. (This does not mean that your component must have four functions; rather, the DLL itself must.)

The reason you may never have known that every COM DLL has four exported functions is that VB automatically adds them to the DLL image at compile time.

DLL Exports

To the operating system, an ActiveX DLL is like any other DLL. DLLs export functions. DLLs do not have the necessary code to be standalone programs. They must be run from within a process.

When you run an executable in Windows 2000, the OS allocates 4 GB of virtual memory (in 32-bit Windows) for your executable; each executable has its own address space. The details of how virtual memory translates into physical memory are beyond the scope of this book. Nonetheless, these 4 GB of virtual memory are known as your application's address space. Each executable has a region of this memory available for storing variables and allocating objects. The variables that are allocated in each executable are visible only to the executable (or to DLLs loaded by the executable). In other words, two executables cannot see each other's memory contents. This means that an executable that makes a mistake with its memory and crashes will not affect the memory contents of another executable.

Also within this memory is the code for the executable. When an executable loads a DLL, the DLL code is mapped into this portion of the executable's address space. Also, any variables that are global to the DLL will be allocated into the address space of the executable. In fact, when an executable loads a DLL, the DLL in a sense becomes part of the executable. The DLL code is able to reach the memory of the executable, and the executable is able to make calls into functions of the DLL as if they were functions in the executable. In theory, a faulty application should not bring down the OS. A faulty DLL, on the other hand, can cause a process to crash, because once it is loaded, it is part of the executable's address space. It is the same as the executable itself crashing.

The DLL functions that are available to the client are known as *exported functions*. VB does not enable developers to have functions that are exported directly. Instead, functions are exported through COM objects. Yet, for the ActiveX DLL to function, it must export functions that the executable can call. The COM specification says that for a DLL to be considered an ActiveX DLL (or simply a COM DLL), it must export four functions: *DllRegisterServer*, *DllUnregisterServer*, *DllGetClassObject*, and *DllCanUnloadNow*.

For the SCM to find the COM server DLL, it must find the CLSID key in the registry. Who puts this registry information there? The registry information comes from the COM server DLL itself through its *DllRegisterServer* function. In Visual C++, for example, developers have to write code to add their COM classes as well as their type library information to the registry. (This is very tedious code to write. Luckily, C++ offers premade code through ATL or MFC to make this easier.) Because a DLL cannot run on its own, another program must run it to enable it to add itself to the registry. Microsoft provides the program: *RegSvr32.EXE* (an eight-character filename—the habit is hard to break). When you run this program, you must specify the location of the DLL you wish to register. *RegSvr32* takes this path and loads the DLL into its address space with *LoadLibrary*. Then it finds the *DllRegisterServer* function with the aid of the *GetProcAddress* WIN32 API and executes it. It is the responsibility of the developer of the COM server to write code in this function to add a CLSID key in the registry and an `InprocServer32` key. After adding itself to the registry, the function ends and *RegSvr32* exits.

VB automatically calls the *DllRegisterServer* function immediately after it compiles the COM DLL. This means that as soon as you compile your COM DLL, you can start using it. InstallShield and Wise Installation System have an option to autoregister DLLs. These programs also simply find the *DllRegisterServer* function.

The *DllUnregisterServer* function's job is to remove the registry keys for the server. Again, this is done by the DLL itself. The developer authoring the server is responsible for writing code to remove the registry keys when a program calls this function. You can use *RegSvr32.EXE* to unregister the DLL as well. To do so, simply run *RegSvr32.EXE* with the /U switch followed by the path to the DLL. In this case, *RegSvr32.EXE* simply calls the *DllUnregisterServer* function. Notice that this helps programs like InstallShield and Wise to clean up registry keys, since they do not have to remember what the DLL added to the registry—they simply call this function, and the DLL itself takes care of removing the keys.

The function *DllCanUnloadNow* tells a process if it is OK to unload the DLL. If you were writing a COM server in C++ from scratch, you would have to keep track of outstanding references to any of your objects. In other words, every time someone calls *AddRef* in any of your objects (to notify you that they are using your object), you must increase a global counter for all the objects in the DLL. In the same fashion, you must decrease the counter every time someone calls *Release* in any of the objects. This is a different counter from the reference counter through Iunknown—that is a per-class counter that lets you know when to remove an instance of the class from memory. This counter knows when to unload the entire server from memory. The developer of the COM DLL simply checks the counter and returns 0 (the C++ constant is S_OK) if the counter reaches 0. If the counter is greater than 0, then the developer returns 1 (the C++ S_FALSE constant).

To create an instance of the class the client requested, the SCM calls the *DllGetClassObject* function.

Class Factory

When a client requests an instance of a class through *CoCreateInstanceEx*, the function first retrieves a COM class object. The COM specification says that creation happens in two steps. When you define a class module in VB, say CChecking, it serves as a template for creating instances of the CChecking object in memory. When you compile your project, however, if your class' Instancing property is set to a value that makes your component creatable, VB creates another class, which we refer to as the *class factory*. (Values that result in a creatable component are 5 - MultiUse and 6 – GlobalMultiUse for ActiveX DLL classes and 3 – SingleUse, 4 - GlobalSingleUse, 5 - MultiUse, and 6 – GlobalMultiUse for ActiveX EXE classes.) It is called the class factory because VB adds the implementation to this class for the IClassFactory interface. The SCM loads the DLL that contains the requested class and calls *DllGetClassObject*. The purpose of this function is to return an instance of the class factory class, not the class you defined. The IClassFactory interface has a method called *CreateInstance*. The *CreateInstance* function has an incoming parameter of the IID for the interface the client wishes to use. *CreateInstance* returns a pointer to the object that implements this interface. Therefore, each creatable class you create in VB has a class factory class that VB creates. The SCM requests the class factory object and calls *CreateInstance* to create instances of your class. Once it creates one instance of your class, it releases the class factory object.

Observations About Activation

So why do you need to know about the process of activation? It is possible to live a healthy and fruitful life without knowing how COM in-process activation works, and in fact many VB developers build complex applications with COM objects without knowing anything at all about the process. Although you may want to learn COM simply for the sake of knowing what's happening underneath, I feel it necessary to outline some of the benefits of knowing this information. Consider the following situation.

A developer offers you an ActiveX DLL for which you write a client. Before you can use the DLL, you must make sure it is registered. Why do you need to register the DLL? Because, as you may recall, *CoCreateInstanceEx* finds the ActiveX DLL by reading the `InprocServer32` key from the registry. You can register the DLL with *RegSvr32.EXE*. Registration also adds a type library entry to `HKCR\TypeLib`. This is important for two reasons. One has to do with COM's remoting layer; you will learn about it in the next chapter. The other is that it will cause VB to include the type library in the References dialog box. Why do you need to add the type library as a reference? You need it for early binding. For early binding the compiler needs to know three things from the type library: CLSIDs, IIDs, and interface layouts. VB reads the CLSIDs and IIDs from the type library in order to translate the New statement into *CoCreateInstanceEx*. VB also uses IIDs when it needs to make a call to *QueryInterface*.

Another need for understanding the activation story is to know what to do when versioning your DLLs (covered in Chapter 6).

Summary

It is now time to put together all the pieces that constitute in-process activation. The following list offers a step-by-step summation of the process:

1. Developer compiles ActiveX DLL.

2. VB creates a type library file and embeds it into the DLL image. It also compiles in the image a class factory class for each class you defined and adds entry points for the four COM DLL required functions: *DllRegisterServer*, *DllUnregisterServer*, *DllCanUnloadNow*, and *DllGetClassObject*.

3. VB automatically calls *DllRegisterServer* on the DLL.

4. Server code for *DllRegisterServer* adds a registry key for each `HKCR\CLSID`. It also adds a registry key for the type library under `HKCR\TypeLib`.

5. VB automatically runs the registration code for your server when you compile it. If you move the DLL to another machine, then you can use *RegSvr32.exe* to execute the registration code in *DllRegisterServer*.

When There Is No Type Library

What if you don't have a type library? You can use the *CreateObject* function along with the Object datatype. Although it is better to use direct table binding than IDispatch methods, it is useful to use the Object datatype with *CreateObject* when the type library is not available. Think of the reasons you need the type library. One reason is that VB needs to know the CLSID of the object you wish to create when you use the New operator. However, *CreateObject* internally calls *CLSIDFromProgIDEx*, which simply gets the CLSID from the registry using a ProgID. That eliminates the need for having to know the CLSID at compile time. A second reason for the type library is to know the IIDs for any interfaces requested through a Set statement. However, if you use the Object datatype, the Set asks for IDispatch. VB knows the IID of IDispatch without having to read a type library. Thus, by using the Object datatype, you eliminate the need to know any IIDs. The third reason for using the type library is to know the layout of the vtable in the desired interface. This is done so that when you make a method call such as obj. MakeDeposit(5000), the call is translated into a call into the vtable. However, using the Object datatype (IDispatch), you do not have to know the entries of the vtable. IDispatch calls are basically translated into *GetIdsOfNames* and *Invoke*. Therefore, you also eliminate the third reason for the type library by using the Object datatype. There is a fourth need for the type library that has to do with COM's remoting layer, and you will learn about it in the next chapter. However, if the only interface you need is IDispatch (i.e., you are only going to use the Object datatype), it turns out that COM's remoting layer knows everything there is to know about remoting the IDispatch interface, so you do not need a type library in this case either. In conclusion, you can eliminate the need for the type library if the server is a VB ActiveX DLL and the client uses the Object datatype with the *CreateObject* function.

6. The developer authoring the client code uses the References dialog box to locate the type library.

7. At compile time for the client, VB reads the CLSIDs and IIDs for each class you specified in New. It then translates each New call into *CoCreateInstanceEx*.

8. At runtime, the client code executes New, which is translated into the *vbaNew* function in the VB runtime, which is translated into *CoCreateIntanceEx* asking for four interfaces: IUnknown, IDefaultInterface, IPersistStreamInit, and IPersistPropertyBag. If you used *CreateObject* instead of New, then the call is translated into *CLSIDFromProgIDEx* followed by *CoCreateInstance* asking for IUnknown, then three *QI*s: IDispatch, IPersistStreamInit, and IPersistPropertyBag.

9. *CoCreateInstanceEx* is a function in *OLE32.DLL*. It searches the registry for the CLSID you specified. It searches under HKCR\CLSID. When it finds the key, it searches for the InprocServer32 subkey to find the path to the DLL.

10. It loads the DLL with the *LoadLibrary* function. Then it calls the *DllGetClassObject* function in the DLL.

11. It retrieves from the DLL an instance of the class factory object for your class and stores it in an internal cache.

12. It then calls *CreateInstance* on the class factory to create an in-memory instance of the class you defined.

13. It returns a pointer to a vptr to a vtable for the interface you specified.

14. The client makes method calls using the vtable. It knows which method in the vtable to call from having read the type library definition for the interface at compile time.

In the next chapter you are going to learn about COM's remoting architecture and how the process activation works. In Chapter 5, we will also modify the activation story for both in-process and out-of-process servers slightly to account for the remoting architecture.

5

Out-of-Process Servers and COM's Remoting Architecture

In the last chapter, you learned about in-process activation. You learned what information is stored in the type library and what the client has to do to use vtable binding. We have also been talking about what constitutes an interface. An interface stored in a VB variable is simply the address of a vptr to a vtable. In the last chapter, you also learned about the process by which COM loads DLLs into memory. We discussed that when you call New, VB translates the New command into a call to *CoCreateInstanceEx*, the function responsible for creating instances of a class.

In this chapter, you will learn about COM's remoting layer. You will also learn about apartments. Apartment architecture enables components that are thread safe to talk to components that are not thread safe.

ActiveX EXEs

EXEs load in their own address space. While there are tricks for sharing memory between two executables, for the most part, every executable loads in its own protected memory space. The memory space is 4 GB. This doesn't mean that by installing Windows your machine receives 4 GB of RAM. Most of us mortals have far less physical memory than that. However, the operating system simulates that each process runs in a memory space of 4 GB. In reality, the OS uses a swap file to map virtual memory to physical memory. The details of how the memory mapper works are beyond the scope of this book. However, it is sufficient for us to know that the memory of one process is protected from another process. This means that if you launch an executable twice so that there are two running instances of it, they do not share memory. In other words, if your code uses global variables, each executable has its own copy of those global variables.

It is possible to have a COM server live in an executable. You do this in VB by creating an ActiveX EXE project. An ActiveX EXE is a COM server like an ActiveX DLL, but because it is an executable instead of a DLL, there are a few differences in the way they work:

- By putting components in an ActiveX EXE, you are declaring that the client program and the server process will live in different address spaces. The fact that the server and the client do not share an address space means that potential defects in the ActiveX EXE (i.e., bugs) will not make the client crash. More importantly, if the client program crashes, it will not make the ActiveX EXE crash, unless it manages to bring down the OS, which is very difficult to do in VB.

- In the case of a DLL, variables in the DLL cannot be shared among different client programs. Why? The answer is that, as we mentioned earlier, a DLL does not run in its own address space. Each instance of the client program will load its own copy of the variables in the DLL. In the case of an executable, each client will use components that live in the same executable. Therefore, each instance of a COM object can share state through global variables (with certain exceptions to be discussed later).

- In COM, some security settings are controlled at the process level; you will learn more about this in Chapter 9. It is enough right now to know that because certain security settings are handled at the process level, by the time a DLL loads, the client program has already determined these security settings for the DLL. In the case of an ActiveX executable, the executable can set these security settings before creating COM objects.

- Perhaps the biggest difference between an ActiveX DLL and an ActiveX EXE has to do with performance. An ActiveX DLL performs a lot better than an ActiveX EXE. You will understand why this is the case at the end of this chapter.

In the last chapter, you learned that DLLs have four entry points (or exported functions): *DllRegisterServer*, *DllUnregisterServer*, *DllGetClassObject*, and *DllCanUnloadNow*. However, executables do not have entry points like DLLs. So what performs the tasks of these four functions in the case of ActiveX EXEs? Let's start with registration and unregistration.

Registering and Unregistering an ActiveX EXE

Executables do not have entry points like DLLs, but they do have command-line parameters. For example, you may enter the path to a text file when you run Notepad, as in:

```
notepad.exe c:\windows\mytest.txt
```

The second portion of this command is a command-line parameter. Like an ActiveX DLL, an ActiveX EXE is supposed to add its COM class information to the registry. The COM specification defines how to tell an EXE to add itself to the registry: it defines the command-line switch /RegServer. If you run an ActiveX EXE with this switch, the executable will know to add itself to the registry and then to automatically exit.

You do not have to worry about implementing this code. VB automatically adds this code to the executable image. The only thing you have to know is how to cause the EXE to self-register when you move it to another machine—you run it with the /RegServer switch, as in:

```
BankServer /RegServer
```

Unregistering an ActiveX EXE is done the same way, except with the /UnregServer switch. For example:

```
BankServer /UnregServer
```

There is a difference, however, in the keys that the server writes to the registry. You may recall that COM DLLs add an InprocServer32 key under the CLSID for each class to specify the path to the DLL server that implements the class. If you think about the fact that the key is named InprocServer32, you may guess that this key is only for DLLs. Thus, an EXE uses a different key called LocalServer32. Therefore, an EXE server registers its class and its location as follows:

```
HKEY_CLASSES_ROOT
    CLSID
        LocalServer32   C:\BankServer\BankServer.exe
```

The name LocalServer comes from the different names for EXE servers. EXE servers fall into two categories. When an ActiveX EXE is run on the same machine as the client EXE, we say that it is a *local server*. If it is run from a different machine, it is called a *remote server*. You may wonder at this point if there is in fact a RemoteServer32 key under CLSID. The answer is: not quite.

COM defines a *COM application* as a group of COM classes. What makes these classes appear to be an application is not that they are together in the same EXE. It is simply that they are assigned the same AppID. An AppID is a GUID. There is no rule for how to come up with an AppID—it is just a GUID that may be generated with *GuidGen.exe* (see Chapter 4 for details), or it may just be the CLSID from one of the classes in the group. The point is that each class that wants to be part of the COM application receives the same AppID. To assign them an AppID, you must enter a subkey under CLSID called AppID and assign to this subkey the value of the GUID. Thus, the registry keys for the classes belonging to the COM application will appear as follows:

```
CLSID_1
    AppId {GUID 1}
CLSID_2 {GUID}
    AppId {GUID 1}
```

Then you add the AppID GUID under the `HKEY_CLASSES_ROOT\AppId` branch. The following is an example of an AppID GUID:

```
HKCR
    AppId
        {GUID} ServerDescription
            RemoteServerName = www.servername.com
```

As you can see, it is customary to add a description or readable name to the AppID. Then, under the AppID GUID, you may add a `RemoteServerName` subkey. In this subkey, you may specify the name of the server that has that EXE. The remote machine's name may be an IP address, a NetBios name such as \\ *Goofy*, or a DNS name such as *www.develop.com*.

VB 6 does not automatically create an AppID and group the classes together with their ActiveX EXE. If you want this to happen, you must generate a key yourself with GuidGen and add code to your setup program to add the key. If you are concerned about this, do not be. COM+ provides an easier way to add an AppID, and we will discuss it in Chapter 7.

In theory, it is possible for all three keys—an `InprocServer32` key, a `Local-Server32` key, and a `RemoteServerName` key—to appear in the registry. In C++, you can specify to the SCM which of these keys to look for first. However, when you use a VB client, VB tells *CoCreateInstanceEx* to use the `CLSCTX_ALL` flag when performing a search. The `CLSCTX_ALL` flag tells *CoCreateInstanceEx* to look first for an `InprocServer32` key, then for a `LocalServer32` key, and only then for an `AppID` key and for its `RemoteServerName` key.

What if you would like the SCM to just activate the class on a remote machine and not worry about the registry keys? There is a way to do this in VB. In the last chapter you learned about the VB *CreateObject* function. The *CreateObject* function has two parameters. The first parameter you already learned about from the last chapter—it is the ProgID. Remember that VB translates *CreateObject* first into a call to *CLSIDFromProgIDEx*. Then it calls *CoCreateInstance*. However, as of VB 6, *CreateObject* has been enhanced to accept a second optional parameter: the name of a remote server. This tells the SCM not to search for the server in the registry but to go directly to a different machine. You use the second parameter as follows:

```
Set Obj = CreateObject("ProgId","RemoteMachine")
```

If you use the current machine for the name of the remote machine parameter, you do not receive an error; VB simply treats the call as if you had not entered the second parameter. However, if you set the second parameter to a remote machine name, VB will call *CoCreateInstanceEx*. This form of the creation API enables VB to do two things:

- Specify a remote machine.

- Ask for several interfaces at once. This is important because, as you will learn later, asking for interfaces from a remote machine is a costly operation. Each request for an interface with *QI* may cause COM to do a round-trip across the network. Therefore, VB asks for four interfaces—`IUnknown`, `_DefaultInterface`, `IPersistStreamInit`, and `IpersistPropertyBag`—from the server at once.

This means that *CreateObject* with a remote server parameter works identically to the `New` operator, except that it searches for the server remotely. By the way, if you happen to have a `RemoteServerName` key under `AppID` specified in the registry and you use the *CreateObject* function with its second parameter, the SCM will use the second parameter and not bother looking at the registry for the remote server name. It will also tell the SCM not to search for an `InprocServer32` key or a `LocalServer32` key. In fact, it tells the SCM not to look for a CLSID subkey on the local machine. All that we need in the registry on the client side when we use remote activation are the ProgID key, the interface IDs, the type library ID, and the path to the file. The reason we need to have information about the interfaces will become clear shortly.

That takes care of self-registration and self-unregistration. What about the other tasks? Specifically, how does the SCM access the class object that implements the `IClassFactory` interface?

Getting the Class Objects

When the SCM wants to create an instance of a class out-of-process, it searches for `LocalServer32`. If there is a `LocalServer32` key, the SCM searches in the system's class table for the class object that implements class factory. The OS maintains a systemwide class object table that enables an executable to register its class factory objects. The table has instances of the class factory objects for each executable mapped by the CLSID of the class that the class factory object is meant to build. The SCM searches for an entry using the CLSID. If the SCM cannot find the class object in the class table, it then looks at the `LocalServer32` key to get the path of the executable that implements the class object. The SCM then launches the executable with the `-Embedding` command-line switch and waits.

It is the executable's job to add its class objects to the class table. It does this by calling a function in *OLE32.DLL* called *CoRegisterClassObject*. This is particularly interesting to VB developers because there are two ways of registering a class in the class table. The executable can mark the class as being good either for a single use or for multiple use. If the class is marked for single use, when the SCM gets hold of the class object, it removes the class object from the class table. This means that the next time a client requests an instance of the class, the SCM will not find it in the class table. This in turn means that the SCM will need to launch another copy of the ActiveX EXE in order for the EXE to add the class object to the table. In other words, by marking a class object as being good only once (SingleUse), we are telling the SCM to launch another copy of the ActiveX EXE each time the user requests a new instance of the class. If a class object is marked as being good for many uses (MultiUse), the SCM will not remove the class object from the class table. Then each time a client requests an instance of the object, the SCM will use the same class object, which means that all the instances of the class will be hosted by the same executable.

You can control whether the class object for each class (remember, the class object is not the class you write but the class factory class) should be marked as SingleUse or MultiUse using the class' Instancing property.

You may have seen the word *singleton* used in Visual C++ documentation. Some programmers erroneously assume that it refers to marking a class as SingleUse. A singleton and a SingleUse class have absolutely nothing to do with each other. A singleton is a class for which there is only one instance in memory. It does not have to do with the class factory being marked as SingleUse. To have a singleton means that each time a client requests a new instance of a class, the class factory class does not allocate new memory for the class. It keeps a reference to the object before it is handed out and always hands out the same object. This means that if the singleton object lives in a DLL, each process has its own unique copy of the class that is marked as singleton, but every instance of that class created within the process points to the same object. If the singleton is in an ActiveX EXE, it means that every client shares the same instance of the class. There is no instancing property in VB that produces that behavior.

Server Lifetime

Lifetime management for an ActiveX EXE is a little different from an ActiveX DLL. In the case of ActiveX DLLs, the executable loading the DLL unloads it by calling *CoFreeUnusedLibraries*, a function in *OLE32.DLL* that calls the *DllCanUnloadNow* function. *DllCanUnloadNow* is a function that VB automatically adds to every ActiveX DLL. We did not cover this function in great detail, but it is sufficient to know that to implement it correctly, VB must increment a counter each time someone calls AddRef on an object or a class factory object.

ActiveX executables have to terminate their process on their own; COM does not terminate them automatically. The logical thing for an ActiveX EXE to do is to terminate when nobody is using references to its objects, but this is a little difficult to assess. For one thing, an ActiveX EXE registers its class factories with the COM system's class table—doing so causes COM to call AddRef on the class factory object. In the case of an ActiveX DLL, this increases an internal global counter and in turn causes *DllCanUnloadNow* to report `False` when asked if it is OK to unload. If an ActiveX EXE server increased a counter in each AddRef to the class factory object, just like a DLL, the count would always be at least 1, and the EXE would never know to shut down. For this reason, ActiveX EXEs do not keep track of each AddRef to the class factory objects. Instead, the SCM calls the `IClass-Factory::LockServer(True)` function when it uses the class object to create an instance of an object. It then calls `IClassFactory::LockServer(False)` when it is done using the class factory. The executable terminates itself when the Lock-Server count is set to 0 and all the object references are gone.

Threads

Every process in the operating system begins executing code with a single thread. The OS does not really see processes when it is time to run code—it sees threads. When the operating system starts a process (an executable), the code for that executable begins with a thread. The first thread (the one that every process gets when it is launched) is called the main thread. A process continues to live as long as the main thread lives. The OS assigns each thread a unique thread ID. Any process can reach a thread (if it has the right permissions) by using its ThreadId. In the same fashion, the OS also assigns each process a process ID, or PID.

Every thread defines an execution sequence. The OS demands that each thread be attached to a procedure called the thread procedure, or ThreadProc. The main subroutines's thread procedure is *main* in console applications or *winmain* in Windows applications. In Visual Basic, the code for the *winmain* procedure executes the VB procedure `Sub Main`, if there is one. In fact, as you will see later, `Sub Main` is a procedure that Visual Basic runs for every thread that it launches.

Threads are kernel objects, which means that the code in *kernel.dll* is responsible for creating, destroying, and managing threads for the system.

The OS does not wait for each thread to be done with its task. The OS has a scheduler that gives each thread a certain amount of time to run based on the thread priority. Each thread receives a portion of time, known as a *quanta*, to execute code. When its time has expired, the system then suspends the thread and gives another thread a chance to run. In fact, the OS code itself runs in a thread, so the OS sets up a hardware interrupt that occurs regularly and allows the OS to take over. Because each thread must share physical memory and CPU registers, the OS has to save a thread's state information, then load the registers and memory with information for another thread. This switch of information is called a thread switch.

Herein lies the problem with creating multithreaded software: it is virtually impossible for a thread to know when it is going to be suspended to permit another thread to execute. Why is this a problem? It is a problem when two threads need the same resource (memory, files, or a COM object, for example). When two threads try to perform an operation on a shared resource, there is no guarantee that one thread will complete its entire task before another thread is given the chance to use the resource. Imagine what would happen if two threads were using the same array of employee records. Let's say that Thread 1 tries to move one of the employee records in the array to the end of the array. Thread 1 first tries to remove the record from its current position and then insert it at the end of the array. However, after Thread 1 removes the employee record and before it inserts it back into the array, Thread 2 gets to execute code. The code in Thread 2 analyzes the array to find out if an employee is part of the company. If the code in Thread 2 tries to find the employee record that Thread 1 was in the process of moving, it may incorrectly assume that the employee does not exist.

Every process begins with one thread, the main thread, but it doesn't have to stay that way. A process may ask the OS to create another thread. This is done to perform different tasks simultaneously. To tell the kernel to create a new thread, we use the *CreateThread* function. *CreateThread* takes the address to a function as a parameter. Consider for example an application like Word. As I am typing this information, Word is running spelling and grammar checkers, apparently in the background. Although the details of how Word works specifically are unknown to this author, one way to make this feature work is to execute the spelling- and grammar-checking code in a different thread from the thread used to edit the document. If the two pieces of code were to execute in the same thread, you would see both tasks competing for time, and it would greatly affect performance. However, there is also some coordination between the threads. As I type in Word, the spellchecker waits until I finish a word to tell me if the word is correct or not. So while I type, signaling needs to take place between the code that handles the output to the screen and the spellchecking code. The text in this case is a shared resource. It does not make sense for the spellchecker to do anything while I am in the middle of typing a word.

For this coordination to take place, the kernel provides *synchronization objects*. Synchronization objects come in the following forms:

Mutexes

A mutex grants a thread exclusive access to a shared resource. The developer of the application writes code in each thread to request the mutex before executing its code and to release the mutex after completing the task. If a thread requests a mutex that another thread is using, the OS will block the requestor thread until the first thread releases it. If every thread follows the rule that it must obtain the mutex before using the resource, then only one thread will use the resource at a time.

Semaphores

A semaphore allows a fixed number of threads to gain access to the shared resource. A semaphore has an initial count (2, for example). Each thread that wants to use the shared resource requests the semaphore. If a thread obtains the semaphore, the count for the semaphore goes down. When a thread has completed its work, it releases the semaphore, and the count goes up. If a thread requests a semaphore and the count is 0, then the thread is blocked until one of the other threads releases the semaphore.

Events

An event enables threads to wait in a blocked state until another thread is done performing a task. One thread performs the task, then signals the event. All the threads waiting for the event then become unblocked, and they can do their tasks.

Critical sections

A critical section prevents more than one thread from executing the same piece of code at the same time in a program. However, critical sections are not kernel objects.

In the example of Word and its spellchecker, synchronization is necessary to give the user a good experience, but one could argue that without synchronization the worse that could happen is that the word processor would check for correct spelling more often than it needed to. However, there are times when not synchronizing access to a shared resource could produce incorrect results and even cause the application to crash.

To better illustrate the problems with creating multithreaded applications, let's write a simple program in VB that uses multiple threads. It is not impossible to write multithreaded applications in VB if you understand how VB treats threads. I am going to show you a technique that is not documented (though any undocumented technique is not guaranteed to work with the next service pack) but that works only partially with VB 6 SP 3. Later in this chapter, you will learn a much safer and simpler way to write multithreaded ActiveX EXEs.

You are going to write a multithreaded drawing program in VB. Not quite! The idea is that there will be a form with a listbox. The listbox will store coordinates for rectangles to draw. There will be two threads drawing rectangles at the same time. Each will loop 2000 times calling a *Draw* function that resides in a form. The *Draw* function has access to four form-level variables: *ptLeft*, *ptTop*, *ptWidth*, and *ptHeight*. The drawing function writes the coordinates to a listbox and increases each of the coordinates by 1. For the project to be successful, the listbox should end up with 4000 unique entries: 0,0,0,0   1,1,1,1   2,2,2,2... 3999,3999,3999,3999.

Start a new Standard EXE Project in Visual Basic. Change the name of the project to SuperDraw. Change the name of the form to frmDraw. You may also change the form's caption to Draw. Add a listbox to your form, and change its name to lstRectangles. Add to the project a new Module (chose Project → Add Module). Change the name of the module to Threads and add the following declarations:

```
Public Declare Function CreateThread Lib "kernel32" ( _
ByVal lpThreadAttributes As Long, ByVal dwStackSize As Long, _
ByVal lpStartAddress As Long, ByVal lpParameter As Long, ByVal _
dwCreationFlags As Long, lpThreadId As Long) As Long

Public Declare Function TlsGetValue Lib "kernel32" ( _
ByVal dwTlsIndex As Long) As Long

Public Declare Function TlsSetValue Lib "kernel32" ( _
ByVal dwTlsIndex As Long, lpTlsValue As Any) As Long

Public Declare Function CoInitialize Lib "ole32.dll" _
(ByVal lReserved As Long) As Long
```

The first function is *CreateThread*. The name makes really obvious the purpose for the function. The purpose of the two other functions is not as obvious; they are for reading and writing to the thread's local storage block. Every thread in the system gets a memory block that is to be used by only that thread—it is protected from other threads. It is called thread local storage (TLS). Memory that is allocated outside of TLS can be shared among all the threads in the process (remember that memory is protected for each process). Every thread needs to call the fourth function, *CoInitialize (or CoInitializeEx)*, before it can access a COM object. Normally, you do not have to do this in VB, because VB calls the function for you. However, you are now creating threads on your own, so you must call this function. *CoInitialize* has only one parameter, which must be 0.

VB uses thread local storage extensively. In fact, when VB creates threads, each thread acts as if it were an application of its own. As you will see later when we talk about VB's thread-pooling mechanism for EXEs, each thread gets its own copy of global variables, the Err object and the App object. The information for the location of those objects in memory is stored in each thread's TLS.

This makes it very difficult to create multithreaded applications in VB. VB will have no knowledge of the threads we are going to create; we are in a sense hacking the system. The main problem is that normally after you make a call in VB, VB internally checks for errors and populates the Err object (even if there were no errors after the call). Because VB did not create our thread, it does not have the necessary information for locating the Err object in TLS. To make things worse, the designers of VB did not think we would be creating other threads; Visual Basic reads the location in TLS and tries to use the value stored in that location as a memory address without checking if, in fact, our thread has a valid value stored in TLS. The result is that VB tries to write to nonexistent memory addresses (0) and it crashes.

The fix is for us to make VB think that our thread is legitimate. To do that, we are going to read the required address from the TLS of a true VB thread, then we are going to write this memory address into our TLS. It sounds more difficult than it actually is, as you will see shortly.

As the **Declare** statement presented earlier shows, the *CreateThread* function has a number of parameters. We are going to ignore all of them but two: *lpStartAddress* and *lpParameter*. *lpStartAddress* is the address of the function you wish to run in a separate thread. *lpParameter* is a parameter you wish to send to the thread procedure. Add the following thread procedure to the Threads module:

```
Function ThreadProc1(lParam As Long) As Long
    Dim counter As Long
    Call TlsSetValue(4, lParam)
    Call CoInitialize(0)

    For counter = 0 To 1999
        Call frmDraw.Draw
    Next

End Function

Function ThreadProc2(lParam As Long) As Long
    Dim counter As Long
    Call TlsSetValue(4, lParam)
    Call CoInitialize(0)

    For counter = 0 To 1999
        Call frmDraw.Draw
    Next

End Function
```

The Win32 SDK defines the signature of the *ThreadProc* functions: it accepts one Long parameter and returns one Long value. Our thread procedure first fixes the TLS problem described earlier, then enters a loop where it calls the *Draw* function in the form 2000 times. Now add the following routine to the same module:

```
Sub Main()
    'this code will get the value of index 4 from tls so
    'that the other thread can use it
    Dim ThreadInfo As Long
    ThreadInfo = TlsGetValue(4)

    frmDraw.Show
    Call CreateThread(0, 0, AddressOf ThreadProc1, ThreadInfo, 0, 0)
    Call CreateThread(0, 0, AddressOf ThreadProc2, ThreadInfo, 0, 0)
End Sub
```

The Sub *Main* procedure is running in a VB-created thread (the main thread). Therefore, it has the correct information in TLS. It reads the information from TLS and sends it as a parameter to the *CreateThread* function. Notice that Sub *Main* shows the form and then creates two threads to use the form.

Now let's add the code to the form. Enter the following code in the frmDraw object:

```
Private m_ptleft As Long
Private m_pttop As Long
Private m_ptwidth As Long
Private m_ptheight As Long

Public Sub Draw()
    lstRectangles.AddItem m_ptleft & "," & m_pttop & "," & m_ptwidth & _
                      "," & m_ptheight
    m_ptleft = m_ptleft + 1
    m_pttop = m_pttop + 1
    m_ptwidth = m_ptwidth + 1
    m_ptheight = m_ptheight + 1
End Sub
```

That's all there is to it. Switch the Startup Object in the Project Properties dialog box to Sub Main (Project → Properties), then compile the program. Do not run the program inside the VB debugger; it was not meant to debug multithreaded applications, and you will have problems. Run the program outside the debugger.

If you examine the output in the listbox, you will notice several problems. Some entries are duplicated, and some entries are wrong. You may see, for example, 600,255,255,255 as one of the entries. It is difficult to browse through all the entries in the listbox; however, in the sample code included with this book, I have included a button called Examine that checks the integrity of the entries in the listbox.

What went wrong? Why are there duplicate entries, and why are some entries wrong? There are three threads involved: two are requesting drawing, and the third is drawing and moving the rectangle coordinates. It seems that because only one thread is changing the member variables, it should have worked correctly. The problem is that the scheduler makes no guarantees of when a thread is going to be blocked. It just gives each thread an opportunity to process. This means that while the method is in the process of handling a *Draw* call from one thread but before it is finished changing the coordinates of the rectangle, the thread is paused and another thread gets to call the Draw method. Thus, when the second thread executes, the information in the variables may or may not be accurate, since the function was in the middle of changing them before it was interrupted by the system in order to handle another call. Because there is no guarantee of when a thread will be blocked or allowed to continue, the resource is not protected from corruption even if the code that changes the resource is correct and centralized.

To solve the problem, we can use a mutex. With a mutex, a thread blocks other threads from using the shared resource until it is done doing its work. The other threads are suspended until the first thread releases the mutex, then another locks the mutex while it is doing its work. The code in Example 5-1 uses a mutex to synchronize the two threads.

Example 5-1. Using a mutex to synchronize two threads

```
Public Declare Function CreateThread Lib "kernel32" ( _
ByVal lpThreadAttributes As Long, ByVal dwStackSize As Long, _
ByVal lpStartAddress As Long, ByVal lpParameter As Long, ByVal _
dwCreationFlags As Long, lpThreadId As Long) As Long

Public Declare Function TlsGetValue Lib "kernel32" ( _
ByVal dwTlsIndex As Long) As Long

Public Declare Function TlsSetValue Lib "kernel32" ( _
ByVal dwTlsIndex As Long, lpTlsValue As Any) As Long

Public Declare Function CoInitialize Lib "ole32.dll" (ByVal lReserved As Long) As Long

Public Declare Function CreateMutex Lib "kernel32" Alias "CreateMutexA" _
(ByVal lpMutexAttributes As Long, ByVal bInitialOwner As Long, _
ByVal lpName As String) As Long

Public Declare Function ReleaseMutex Lib "kernel32" ( _
ByVal hMutex As Long) As Long

Public Declare Function WaitForSingleObject Lib "kernel32" ( _
ByVal hHandle As Long, ByVal dwMilliseconds As Long) As Long

Private hMutex As Long              'Handle to mutex
```

Example 5-1. Using a mutex to synchronize two threads (continued)

```
Public Const INFINITE = &HFFFF        'Infinite timeout

Function ThreadProc1(lParam As Long) As Long
    Dim counter As Long
    Call TlsSetValue(4, lParam)
    Call CoInitialize(0)

    For counter = 0 To 1999
        Call WaitForSingleObject(hMutex, INFINITE)
        Call frmDraw.Draw
        Call ReleaseMutex(hMutex)
    Next

End Function

Function ThreadProc2(lParam As Long) As Long
    Dim counter As Long
    Call TlsSetValue(4, lParam)
    Call CoInitialize(0)

    For counter = 0 To 1999
        Call WaitForSingleObject(hMutex, INFINITE)
        Call frmDraw.Draw
        Call ReleaseMutex(hMutex)
    Next

End Function

Sub Main()
    'this code will get the value of index 4 from tls so
    'that the other thread can use it.
    Dim ThreadInfo As Long
    ThreadInfo = TlsGetValue(4)

    frmDraw.Show
    hMutex = CreateMutex(0, 0, "")

    Call CreateThread(0, 0, AddressOf ThreadProc1, ThreadInfo, 0, 0)
    Call CreateThread(0, 0, AddressOf ThreadProc2, ThreadInfo, 0, 0)
End Sub
```

The Sub *Main* procedure creates the mutex. Each thread calls *WaitForSingleObject* first before calling the *Draw* function. The *WaitForSingleObject* function blocks the thread if another thread is using the mutex. If not, it locks (or signals) the mutex and continues. When the function is done, it releases the mutex, enabling another thread to access it. If you run the code again, you will notice that all entries are now correct. The example that is included with the book asks first if you would like to run using the mutex or not.

Apartments

The COM architecture addresses two aspects of multithreaded programming. The first is called *thread affinity*, which determines what threads can make calls into the object. The second is *concurrency*, which determines how many threads can access the object at the same time.

If you have never heard of apartments in reference to COM, you may be inclined to think the word has something to do with a living space. That is not far off. An *apartment* is a place for objects that have the same thread affinity to live in.

Thread affinity is a big term that gets tossed around a lot. It simply means that certain objects have specific requirements for what threads can call its methods. ActiveX controls, for example, are placed inside a form. The form runs on a certain thread. The form registers its window event procedure (the internal function that receives messages from the operating system) to be executed on a certain thread. Keep in mind that a form is not a thread. It is possible and likely that a number of forms run on the same thread. However, objects that require all their code to run in a certain thread need to let COM know that they have this requirement. When an object has a requirement for all of its calls to come from a single thread (like UI components), we say that that object has *high thread affinity*. Other objects can receive calls from a certain group of threads, and only from that group of threads. We say that these objects have *low thread affinity*. Then there are objects that can receive calls from any thread. We say that these objects have *no thread affinity*. Except for the latter group, objects in general always have a degree of thread affinity. *Apartments* group objects that have the same thread affinity.

Let's look at an example of thread affinity. In the last section, I mentioned that Visual Basic writes information to TLS. When a thread creates a VB COM object, the VB runtime adds information to the thread's TLS. Whenever the VB COM object receives a call, the VB runtime assumes that the thread making the call has the necessary information in its TLS. (A VB object must always get calls from the same thread—the thread that created it.) If a VB object receives a call from a thread that does not have this information in its TLS, the VB runtime code crashes. This is why in the multithreading example earlier in this chapter you needed to write information to the TLS of the newly created object before calling a function in the form object; without this information the program would crash. This is an example of an object that has high thread affinity. Nearly all COM objects have some degree of affinity.

To better understand concurrency issues, consider the problems we had before using the mutex in the previous example. Suppose for the sake of argument that the code in a form was code in a COM object and that the client created a multi-threaded program that used the object from inside the thread to maximize its work. It is easy to do the right synchronization when the same set of program-mers write both the client code and the server code. But COM was designed to accommodate the sharing of objects that different developers create. The question is, who is responsible for synchronization? Is it the client or the server, and if it is the server, do you want to bother protecting every method in an object with mutexes simply because a client may use multithreading? The designers of COM decided this was a detail they wanted to worry about for you.

To control which threads have access to a COM object (thread affinity issues), COM introduced the concept of apartments. Apartments mainly answer the first concern, but one of the apartments also addresses the second. To address all the situations with concurrency, MTS and COM+ introduced Activities. You will learn about Activities in Chapter 7.

COM provides three types of apartments: single-threaded apartments (STAs), multi-threaded apartments (MTAs), and thread-neutral apartments (TNAs). The STA also provides some protection against concurrency.

Apartments are specific to a process. In other words, two processes will not share the same apartment. Objects that live in the STAs receive calls from only one thread, and always from the same thread for the lifetime of the object. Objects that have high thread affinity must live in the STA. Because VB objects have high thread affinity, they always live in the STA. MTAs enable multiple threads to exist within them. Only threads that have requested to enter the process' MTA can make direct calls on objects in the MTA. Objects that have low thread affinity (for example, they do not require information from the thread's TLS) can live in the MTA. TNAs do not allow any threads to exist within them. A thread using an object that lives in the TNA enters the TNA while it is making a call to the object, then exits the TNA. Objects in the TNA cannot have any thread affinity; they can receive calls from any thread.

While the STA offers protection against concurrency, objects in the MTA or TNA must assume that multiple threads may call their methods concurrently.

In this chapter we will concentrate on the STA because at the moment that is the only apartment for VB servers and clients.

Every thread must declare its threading intentions before it uses COM. It does this by calling *CoInitializeEx*. Any thread that tries to use COM without calling *CoInititalizeEx* (or *CoInitialize* or *OleInitialize*) receives an error. In our multi-threaded VB example, each custom thread was careful to call *CoInitialize* before doing its work. When you call *CoInitializeEx* (or one of its derivatives), the COM runtime adds information to the thread's TLS. If you attempt to make a call to any COM function without this information in TLS, the call will fail. The VB syntax for *CoInitializeEx* is:

```
Public Function CoInitializeEx(ByVal ApartmentType As Long, _
                        ByVal Reserved As Long) As Long
```

CoInitializeEx is a function in *OLE32.DLL*. It enables you to specify whether your thread should run inside an STA or an MTA (no threads can enter the TNA). The first parameter in the function is the apartment type.

Both clients and servers specify their threading requirements at startup. It is easier to understand why the server needs to specify its requirements but a little less obvious why the client needs to specify its requirements. The reason the client needs to specify its threading requirements is that it also needs protection. It is possible for a client to provide the server object with a COM object for the purpose of callbacks. In the earlier multithreading example, the client helped the server code by synchronizing its threads with a mutex. The server code might have done a similar thing using a critical section.

When you write an ActiveX EXE, the EXE code begins with one thread. VB automatically calls *OleInitialize* (a variation of *CoInitializeEx* that also enables various OLE services, such as OLE drag and drop). The main thread in a VB ActiveX EXE specifies that it wishes to enter an STA. It then creates its class factory objects, and COM places them in the STA as well. The important thing to understand in this discussion is that your components live in an STA apartment.

When a thread enters an STA, *OLE32.DLL* creates a hidden window. The class name for this window is `OleMainThreadWndName`. There is a hidden window for each STA. For each method call that a client makes, *OLE32.DLL* posts a message to this hidden window that in turn causes the thread in the apartment to execute the method call. If two threads make method calls on objects that are in the same STA, both requests will be posted to the hidden window, but only one of the requests from the message queue will be handled at a time. The other client will be blocked until the first call is completed. There is one exception to this that we will explore later, but the outcome is that calls to the STA are serialized so that the objects living in it do not experience concurrency.

There is another aspect of the STA that is particularly important to VB. There is always only one thread in the STA, and it is always the same thread for the lifetime of the object. That means that code on the STA will always be executed in the same thread. What this means is that VB is able to put information into the thread's TLS. VB definitely uses this extensively. In fact, each time VB creates a new STA in an application, it is as if you were starting a brand new application. This may seem strange at first, but the reality is that every time VB begins a new thread, it makes a copy of all the global variables, the Err object, and the App object, and internally it goes as far as running the same code as if you were starting a new instance of the EXE. Therefore, global variables are not really global variables. They are in fact global only within a thread. If your VB ActiveX server ends up placing two instances of the same class in separate threads, the two objects will not be able to share global variables, even within the same process. Each will have its own copy of the global variables.

At first glance, this does not seem like a good idea, but the designers of VB did not want you to have to worry about synchronizing memory between two threads. The best way to ensure this was to first use the COM STA model and then use TLS to guarantee that your variables are visible to only one thread at a time.

Let's put this information into a concrete example by going back to our banking application. Let's say that you are writing a BankServer COM server. Suppose that each new account you create receives a unique number. Suppose that this unique number is generated from a number stored in a global variable in the project. (Granted, there are better techniques, but let's assume this is the way it is stored for the sake of argument.) A client creates a new account by first creating a component called CBankManager and using the **IAccountManager** interface. The following is the definition of **IAccountManager**:

```
'Interface IAccountManager
Public Function CreateAccount() As IAccount
End Sub
```

The following code uses the **IAccountManager** interface in the client program:

```
Dim NewAcct As IAccount
Dim AcctMgr As IAccountManager
Set AcctMgr = New CBankManger
Set NewAccount = AcctMgr.CreateAccount()
NewAccount.ClientName = "Jose Mojica"
```

Whenever the client calls the *CreateAccount* function, the server code reads the value of the *AccountID* global variable, creates a new Account object, then populates a property called AccountNumber with the value in *AccountID*. It then adds 1 to *AccountID* and exits. The following code represents what the server object may do:

```
Implements IAccountManager
Private IAccountManager_CreateAccount() As IAccount
    Dim Acct As IAccount
    Set Acct = New CCheckingAccount
    Acct.AccountNumber = g_AccountID
    g_AccountID = g_AccountID + 1
    Set IAccountManager_CreateAccount = Acct
End Function
```

Suppose each of two clients creates an instance of the CBankManager object from an ActiveX EXE. The two clients are running in different threads. Both instances of CBankManager use the same global variable. If the two clients make calls at the same time, it is possible that both would execute the code before either is able to increment the global variable. Thus, both clients would end up with bank accounts that have the same AccountNumber.

To prevent this, VB places all objects in an STA apartment. In this way, one of two things may happen:

- Both objects are created in the same STA. Because the STA provides synchronization, only one of the clients would get to execute the code, and the global variable is incremented correctly.

- Each object may end up in different STAs. In this case, both clients may make calls concurrently. The fact that VB writes global variables to TLS means that each of these objects will have its own copy of the global variables. Therefore, in the previous code example, each object would have its own copy of *g_AccountID*, and therefore a call from one client will not affect the state of another client.

Later in this chapter, you will learn how to tell VB what mechanism to use (all of the objects in the same STA, each object in a different STA, or a mixture of the two). Also, you may be wondering what to do to share data between STAs. For example, what if you do want to have the same counter for both threads but with synchronization? COM+ provides a mechanism for sharing state between two apartments using the Shared Property Manager. Using the Shared Property Manager is not covered in this book, but is not a difficult component to use, and there is a lot of documentation on it in MSDN.

Life in an MTA apartment is quite different. Objects in the MTA do not receive any protection against concurrency from the apartment architecture. Any thread that has requested to enter the MTA in its call to *CoInitializeEx* may call upon methods simultaneously.

What advantage does the MTA offer over the STA or vice versa? The STA helps with synchronization, but at a price. The STA does not differentiate between two calls made from different threads from the same client or two separate clients. Therefore, the STA limits concurrency and makes your system less scalable. In other words, the more clients using objects from the same STA, the worse the system will perform. Clients will be blocked while a single client executes a method. In the MTA, many clients can execute at the same time, but resources have to be protected with code.

Why do clients also need to be in an apartment? Because of callbacks. It is possible for the client to create a COM object and pass a reference to the server through a method call. Then the server may make a call that will be received by the client. That means that if the client has resources that need to be protected from concurrency, it may wish to be in an STA. If it does not have resources that require protection or it wants to handle protection by other means, it may choose to be in an MTA.

The Message Filter

You learned that the way COM implements an STA is by creating a hidden window. Method calls are posted as window messages. It is possible for a client program to override the message-handling procedure and install its own. A thread that is going to display forms may want to do this in order to control what messages get handled. The thread is able to handle not only COM requests but also any type of messages, including paint messages and user input messages. Visual Basic installs its own message filter and overrides the default STA message filter. By doing this, VB is able to monitor user input to a form waiting for the result of a COM call. When VB is busy processing COM calls and detects user input, it displays the message box seen in Figure 5-1.

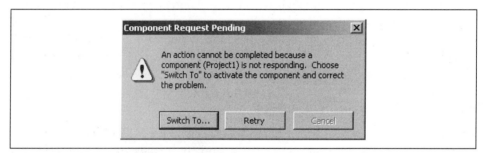

Figure 5-1. The server busy dialog box

Threading Options for DLLs

An ActiveX DLL cannot call *CoInitializeEx* (or *OleInitialize*) on its own. The client using the DLL must call *CoInitializeEx* before it can create a class in the ActiveX DLL. What happens if the programmer of the DLL component meant for the component to live in the STA, but the client enters an MTA? ActiveX DLLs can declare to COM what type of apartment they want to live in. You can specify the apartment type where your object is to live in the registry. You do this in the `InprocServer32` subkey by adding a value pair called `ThreadingModel`, as shown:

```
HKCR
    CLSID
        InprocServer32
            (default)          PathToDLL
            ThreadingModel     Apartment
```

Thus, you can specify an apartment type for each class. However, VB's registration code uses the same apartment type for all the classes in the server. The choices are **Single**, **Apartment**, **Free**, **Both**, and **Neutral**. If you specify that your component can live in only a certain apartment that is different from the apartment the client is in, then COM will create an apartment for your object that meets your requirements.

If **ThreadingModel** is **Single**, or if there is no value specified, you are indicating that your object must live in an STA. Furthermore, you are indicating that all of your objects must live in the main STA. The main STA is the first thread to request an STA apartment. This option is available only for legacy reasons. In the first revisions of COM, there was no apartment model. Therefore, COM does not presume that it can put an object in just any STA. Before VB 5 SP 2, the VB runtime assumed that there would be only one copy of global variables and that all instances of a component would share the same copy without need for synchronization. It would have been wrong for COM to assume that all objects could live in any STA, because then, conceivably, two objects would end up in different threads and both have access to the same global variables, requiring the developer to protect global variables against concurrency. The safest thing is for COM to place all legacy components in the same apartment. Today there is no reason to choose this option.

A **ThreadingModel** of **Apartment** tells COM that your object must live in an STA, but it is not limited to the main STA. Let's assume that a client creates two threads and creates two instances of your class, one in each thread. When the threads enter the STA apartment, if the component's threading model were marked as **Single**, then both objects would live in the first thread. The second thread would need to communicate with its object through cross-apartment mechanisms that you will learn about later. If the **ThreadingModel** is **Apartment**, when each thread creates an instance of an object, COM places the object in the creator's apartment. This is a more scalable option, since it enables both threads to make calls concurrently.

The other options are not available to VB. Setting **ThreadingModel** to **Free** means that the object must live in an MTA. Setting **ThreadingModel** to **Both** means that it can live in the STA, the MTA, or the Neutral apartment. A **ThreadingModel** of **Neutral** means that it can live only in the TNA. We will talk more about the other models throughout the book as I show you the COM+ services.

If a thread that entered the MTA creates an instance of a component marked as apartment-threaded, then COM creates a special STA apartment known as the *host STA*. The host STA contains any of the objects that must live in the STA but that are created from an MTA thread. The host STA is different from the main STA. If the host STA is the first STA thread in the process, then it is also the main STA, but it is possible for the host STA and the main STA to be different apartments.

On the other hand, if an STA thread creates a component marked as wanting to live in the MTA, COM creates an MTA apartment for the process. A process may have multiple STA apartments, but it always has at most one MTA and at most one TNA. The only way for an object to live in the TNA is to be in an ActiveX DLL and to have the `ThreadingModel` set to `Neutral`.

To specify the threading model for a DLL, use Project → Properties, and change the Threading Model option, as shown in Figure 5-2. The choices are `Apartment` or `Single`, and the default is `Apartment`. You should leave this option as `Apartment`. The only time you may need to use `Single` is if you are creating an ActiveX control that will contain a legacy control marked as `Single`. In this case, your control must also be marked as `Single`; the two controls cannot live in separate apartments. You are not expected to check each control for this setting; VB will let you know if you are using a control that is marked as `Single`. If it does not warn you of this, then leave this setting as `Apartment`.

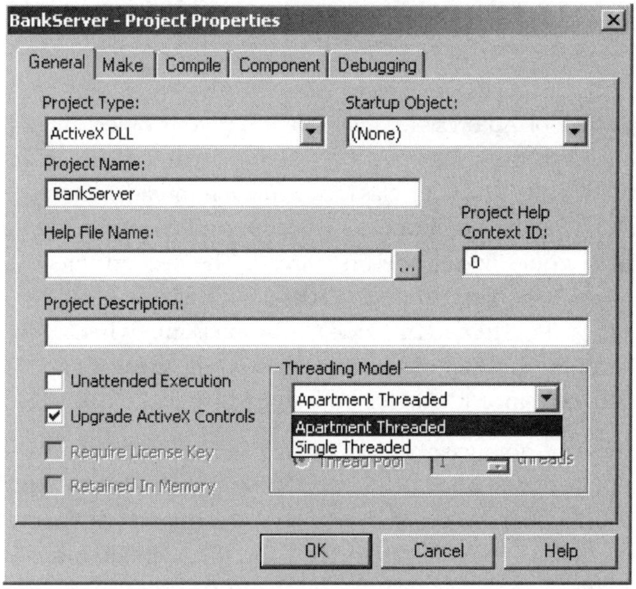

Figure 5-2. The ThreadingModel options in Project Properties

Cross-Apartment Communication

What happens when a client speaks to a server object and the client is in a different apartment? This could happen in one of several ways. In the case of VB, the most frequent way for this to happen is that the client is talking to an object in an ActiveX EXE. The client and the server in this case will always be in different apartments (because apartments are specific to a process). But it may happen in other ways. It is possible that the client and the object are in the same process, but one is in an STA and one is in an MTA. This may happen if your client creates an object that was written in C++ that is meant to work in an MTA.

Whenever a client wants to use an object that is in a separate apartment, the call does not happen directly; it happens through an interceptor. Most of the time, when a client is in a different apartment than the object, the client is also in a different thread than the object. This could happen, for example, if a client is in another process, as is the case when a client program creates an object in an ActiveX EXE. In Chapter 3, you learned what your code does to make a method call. Remember that a call to a function is a jump to a certain location in memory. The call stacks for each thread are different. Thus, an interceptor is needed for COM to step in and simulate a synchronous call. If a client in one thread makes a call to an object that lives in a different thread, COM needs to pause the caller until the object completes the call. If the threads are in different processes, then a memory location in one process is meaningless in another process. The interceptor needs to intercept the call in the calling process and replay the call in the process where the object lives. In fact, part of the COM architecture's job is to perform this function, enabling the client and the object to live on different machines.

The interceptor also guarantees the safety of objects that have high thread affinity. With objects that have high thread affinity, COM does not let just any thread make a call into the object. It intercepts the call and ensures that the actual call is made from the correct thread. To intercept calls, COM uses *proxies* and *stubs*.

Proxies are objects that have the same interface as the real object. However, they do not implement the actual code; they do nothing but forward the call through the COM mechanism to the real object. The proxy is a COM object that looks to the client as the real object and lives in the apartment of the client. When a client requests to use an object in another apartment (for example, a client EXE calls the New function to create a component in an ActiveX EXE), the object's interface reference needs to be exported from the apartment the object lives in and imported into the apartment of the client. The process of exporting an object from one apartment and importing it into another is called marshaling the interface. *Marshaling an interface* means constructing a byte stream (a message in a sense) that has information about where that object lives, the process that is hosting it, and the apartment as well as the interface ID (IID). To build this information is to marshal the interface.

When COM marshals the interface, it builds a COM object called the stub that has a reference to the true object. The stub object is an object that represents the client and lives in the apartment of the object. The marshaled information in a byte stream is taken to the client by the COM transport (which is discussed later). On the client side, the information is used to construct the object's interface on the apartment of the client. To build an interface from the information is to unmarshal the interface. COM then sets up communication between the proxy and the stub objects.

The outcome is that the proxy acts as the object on the client side, and the stub acts as the client on the server side. Both the client and the server are not aware that these impostors are in between themselves.

Therefore, every time you create an object that lives in an ActiveX EXE, you receive a proxy instead of the actual object. This makes sense if you think about it in terms of the client and the process being in different memory spaces. If the server code uses memory that lives in the server process, the client cannot be jumping to certain memory addresses directly on the client side. If we were to reproduce the memory on the client side, we would also have to reproduce all the memory that object needs, including the memory on the server side. Instead, COM gives you an interface reference that looks like the real thing but forwards each call only to the actual object, waits for the object to do its work, and gives back to you the response from the server. COM builds a separate proxy and a stub for each interface.

So if a client creates an object in another apartment, it receives a proxy for the interface it requested. If the client creates an object that can live in its own apartment, then it receives a raw pointer to the object's interface (no interceptor).

Here is the tough question: what if the client then passes to the remote object a reference to an interface in its local object? If the client passes an interface reference through a method call, COM automatically marshals the reference and creates a stub, then unmarshals on the receiving side and gives the remote object a proxy to the client object's interface. What if the remote object hands the interface reference back to the client through yet another method? To summarize, the client created the object in its apartment, passed it through a method call to a remote object, then the remote object passed it back to the client. It would be silly for the client to now be holding to a proxy to its local object. The COM architecture is smart enough to know the origin of the object and does not give the client a proxy when it does not need one. The architecture is smart enough to create only one proxy. The situation in which a proxy talks to another proxy never arises. If, for example, a client receives a proxy to an object's interface and passes this proxy reference to another client program, COM rewires the proxy so that the second client holds a proxy that talks directly to the object.

ByVal and ByRef with Interface Parameters

Now that you know about proxies and stubs, it is important to understand that the meaning of `ByVal` and `ByRef` changes when you use interface parameters such as `ByVal Acct As IAccount`.

Suppose we have an ActiveX DLL with a class named CPoint defined as follows:

```
'class CPoint
Public x As Long
Public y As Long
```

Suppose also that we have an ActiveX EXE with a class named CDraw defined as follows:

```
'class CDraw
Public Sub MovePointA(ByVal pt As CPoint)
    pt.x = pt.x+5
    pt.y = pt.y+5
End Sub
Public Sub MovePointB(ByRef pt As CPoint)
    pt.x = pt.x+5
    pt.y = pt.y+5
End Sub
```

A client program enters the STA. (If it is a VB or a scripting client, this happens automatically.) If it is a C++ client, the client calls *CoInitializeEx* with the `COINIT_APARTMENT` flag as the first parameter. Suppose that CPoint is marked as an STA component. Since we are assuming this is a VB class, then the component is always an STA component. The client's main thread creates an instance of CPoint. CPoint lives in a DLL and therefore the objects produced from the class will live in the same process as the client. Because the client thread and the object have requested the STA model, they both share the same apartment, and therefore the client has a direct pointer to the object.

The client program then creates an instance of CDraw. CDraw lives in another executable. Therefore, by definition, objects produced from the CDraw class are in different apartments (apartments are specific to a process). The client program, therefore, receives a proxy to the object's default interface. Let's say the client calls the MovePointA method in the CDraw component and passes an instance of the CPoint class it created. First, when the object code in MovePointA uses the *pt* variable, is the *pt* variable pointing to a raw object or to a proxy? The *pt* variable in MovePointA receives a proxy to the object that actually lives in the client's apartment. The *pt* parameter is marked as `ByVal`. Normally, this means that changes to the variable's value inside the code do not change the client's actual value, but `ByVal` does not have the same meaning when dealing with interfaces. The code in MovePointA makes modifications to the data in the CPoint object by setting properties in the object's default interface. Setting the properties is just making a method call through the proxy. The actual change occurs on the client side. The fact that the parameter is a `ByVal` parameter does not mean that the code cannot make method calls through the proxy. The code in MovePointB also receives a proxy and can also make method calls through the proxy. Thus, at first glance, these two options appear identical. The following piece of code will show the difference:

```
'class CDraw
Public Sub MovePointA(ByVal pt As CPoint)
    Set pt = New CPoint
End Sub
Public Sub MovePointB(ByRef pt As CPoint)
    Set pt = New CPoint
End Sub
```

Calling the two routines indicates that `ByVal` and `ByRef` produce different behavior. In MovePointA, the parameter is passed `ByVal`. The code sets the point to a new instance of the CPoint class. This time, the instance is being created on the server side. Upon execution, the function receives a reference to a proxy. The object lives on the client side. Then the server code replaces this with an object created on the server side. However, because the parameter is `ByVal` when the call returns, the server-side object is discarded and the client still retains its original object. In MovePointB, the behavior is different. Because the parameter is passed `ByRef`, when the server code replaces the proxy reference with a reference to a server-side object when the call returns, COM releases the client object, and the client receives a proxy to the object that lives in the server. In other words, the client had a reference to a local object before the call without a proxy, and after the call the client holds a reference to a proxy for an object that lives on the server.

In short, `ByVal` and `ByRef` have to do with the way that COM has to marshal the interfaces. In `ByVal`, marshaling occurs only from the client side to the server side. In the case of `ByRef`, marshaling occurs in both directions. You should use `ByVal` whenever possible; the less marshaling the system has to do, the better your performance will be.

Communication through a proxy is slower than direct communication by an order of magnitude. You do not want a proxy if you can help it. If the object lives in a different process (i.e., is an ActiveX EXE), the client EXE will always receive a proxy; but it can also happen within the same process. If your objects come from an ActiveX DLL and the `ThreadingModel` is `Single`, then if two threads create instances of the component, one of them will get a direct pointer to the object; the other will get a proxy. If you create an object in an MTA for a VB client, the VB client will get a proxy to the object. A more common occurrence is what happens when you use ActiveX EXE's thread-pooling mechanism, discussed shortly.

Marshalers and the Type Library Marshaler

Cross-apartment communication involves the creation of interface proxies and interface stubs. The job of the proxy is to take the parameters of a call and package them into a byte stream to be sent to a stub, where the byte stream is unpackaged.

When COM decides that it needs to export an interface from one apartment, it asks the object if it is going to handle the packaging of parameters itself. It does this by asking the object if it supports the `IMarshal` interface. If an object supports the `IMarshal` interface, it is said to support custom marshaling. *Custom marshaling* enables an object to put whatever it wants into the byte stream.

If an object does not want to do its own marshaling, COM needs a helper to tell it the parameter types involved in the call in order to package the parameters into a byte stream. It also needs a helper on the server side to unpackage the parameters from the byte stream. The helper object can come in two flavors. When you use MIDL (the IDL compiler), not only does it generate a type library file, but it also can generate code to build what is called a proxy/stub DLL. A proxy/stub DLL has information on how to package and unpackage parameters for each call. You do not have to do this for Visual Basic COM servers.

There is a second helper object that is known as the universal marshaler, or type library marshaler. The type library marshaler is in *oleaut32.dll*; it packages and unpackages parameters into a byte stream. In order to use the type library marshaler, you must tell COM that the interface is using the type library marshaler.

I said earlier that the parameters of a method call can be marshaled in three ways. One is to use custom marshaling. Custom marshaling occurs when the object answers yes to the request for the `IMarshal` interface. If the answer is no, COM searches the registry under the `HKCR\Interface` key for the IID of the interface that needs marshaling. Under the `Interface\IID` subkey, you must specify the GUID of the object that will do the marshaling. If the object is an object generated with source from MIDL, the object will live in a proxy/stub DLL. If the interface wishes to use the type library marshaler, then it must use CLSID {00020424-0000-0000-C000-000000000046}, the CLSID for the type library marshaler. The type library marshaler understands how to package and unpackage parameters from the type library.

The type library marshaler builds proxies and stubs on the fly at runtime by reading the definition of your interface from the type library. Because the type library marshaler needs access to your type library, your interface needs another subkey to tell COM the LIBID of the type library (`HKCR\Interface\IID\TypeLib = LIBID`). COM uses the LIBID to do a search in the registry. The LIBID must be in the registry under `HKCR\TypeLib\LIBID`. This key must have an `HKCR\TypeLib\LIBID\1.0\0\win32` subkey that contains the path to the type library file. Notice that after `LIBID`, the registry key has a 1.0 subkey. This is the library's version number. You can specify different versions of the type library. Thus, you may have 1.0 and 2.0 subkeys. In fact, you may wish to do this if you have objects in a COM server that are no longer part of the latest version of the server but are needed for backward compatibility. The interfaces for these objects will not be in the latest version of the type library, but they will be in the old version. Thus, you must register both type libraries if the object is to be used across apartments.

In conclusion, for cross-platform communication, marshaling takes place. Any time marshaling takes place, COM requires information about how to marshal the parameters. This means that each interface must appear in the registry on both the client machine and the server machine. It also means that you must register the type library on both the server and the client.

Does that mean that you must copy the server DLL or server EXE to the client machine and register it? Not necessarily. You must register the type library. As a default, VB embeds the type library as a resource in the image of the DLL or EXE. However, you can ask VB to also generate a standalone type library file (.TLB). To do so, choose Project → Properties; select the Component tab, and check the Remote Server Files option. This will result in several extra files when you build the server. One of those is the type library file. You can take the type library file to the remote station and use a program called *Regtlib.exe* to register it. (*Regtlib.exe* is included with Visual C++.) Registering the type library adds information to the registry about the interfaces and the type library file itself, not about the classes.

Thread Pools in ActiveX EXEs

When you compile an ActiveX EXE, you have the option of using a thread pool to handle activation requests. VB can create a thread pool in one of three ways: it can create a thread per object, use a single thread, or use a fixed number of threads. The thread-pooling options are in the Project → Properties dialog box (see Figure 5-3 for details).

A thread per object means that every time a client creates an instance of an object, VB will create a new thread using the *CreateThread* function. This new thread will enter a new STA with *OleInitialize*. Then, it will create a new instance of your object and place it in the newly created STA. The outcome is that every object will

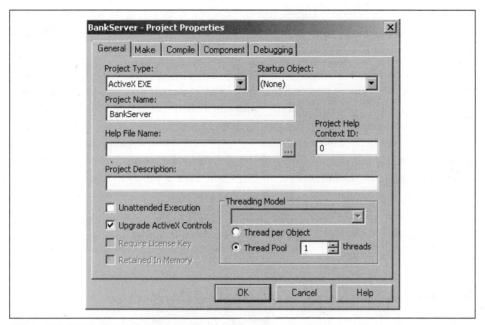

Figure 5-3. Thread-pooling options for ActiveX EXEs

live in its own STA. The advantage of this approach is that if we assume that each object is requested by a separate client, then by placing them in separate STAs, the clients are able to make concurrent calls. This is not the case if both objects live in the same STA.

There are two problems with this approach. One is memory consumption. Each thread consumes memory. The other problem is global variables. Any variables that are public in a module cannot be shared between the two different threads. Each thread keeps its own copy of global variables, the Err object, and the App object in thread local storage.

Another option when compiling is to have a thread pool of one thread. A thread pool of one thread means that VB will place each new instance in the same thread and therefore in the same STA. This approach takes less memory, but at the same time it does not enable two clients to make calls at the same time.

The last option is to limit the thread pool to a certain number of threads above one. Having more threads means greater concurrency. However, the more threads you have, the more resources your program is going to consume. Also, the question of sharing global variables becomes unpredictable. If, for example, you have a thread pool of five threads, after the client creates five instances of an object, VB will begin to reuse threads for future activations. That means that certain objects will share state through global variables (the objects that share an apartment).

Along the same lines, some clients will be blocked depending on where the object lives. If two objects end up in the same thread, one call may prevent another call from occurring even if they are meant for two different objects.

In the previous section, I mentioned that it might be possible to end up with a proxy instead of a direct reference to the object even within the same executable. This can happen in an ActiveX EXE. Suppose that the ActiveX EXE is marked as having a thread per object. If a client creates object A and then creates object B, both objects will be in different threads. Now, suppose the client passes object A to object B. Although object A and object B live in the same process, they live in different apartments, and therefore object B will have a proxy to object A.

Another interesting side effect is that forms are duplicated per apartment. If one object in one apartment issues the method Form1.Show and another object in a second apartment calls the same method, then each apartment will show a different copy of the form—there will be two forms displayed.

Remoting and Location Transparency

Before COM there was RPC, a protocol defined by the Open Software Foundation and known as Remote Procedure Calls (RPC) for a Distributed Computing Environment (DCE). Microsoft implemented this protocol in Windows NT as MS RPC. RPC is a binary protocol meant to run on top of any other network protocol, such as IP or UDP.

MS RPC uses the concept of interfaces. A developer defines an interface using the Interface Definition Language (IDL). The developer also generates code for two stubs (in RPC terminology, both the sender and the receiver are known as stubs). The stub on the client side basically looks like the interface. In other words, it has methods with the same signatures and names as the methods and signatures on the server side. However, the methods in the client stub do not do the real work. They take the parameters of a call and build a byte stream according to the format dictated by RPC. Network Data Representation (NDR) is used to convert the parameters into a representation that can be understood by a number of operating systems. Information is also added about the destination of the byte stream. On the receiving side, an RPC service listens for RPC data on a well-known port. The port number depends on the protocol the server can accept. The service listens for requests, then interprets the byte stream to figure out to which server stub information should be forwarded. The RPC listening service dispatches a thread to communicate with the stub on the server side. The server-side stub receives the information and unpackages it using NDR once again. The server-side stub builds a parameter list and calls the function specified in the byte stream. The client thread is blocked for the duration of the call. When the server stub executes the call and the call finishes, it sends the client a response message. The response message will contain the return parameters from the call. The client stub is then unblocked. The result is that the client believes it is making a call locally when it is in fact making a call with a remote server.

So why do we not use MS RPC? We do, but it has been enhanced. MS RPC had several limitations:

- The RPC specification did not address how to send an object reference through a method call. In other words, it was not possible to send an interface through a parameter.

- RPC required the server to be running and listening for requests. MS RPC did not address activation.

- MS RPC did not use an efficient system for garbage collection.

- Perhaps the most prominent, you had to write different code for communicating with objects in a DLL than for communicating with objects in an RPC server.

COM is built on the concept of *location transparency*—you write your code the same way whether you are talking to an object in a DLL, an object in a separate EXE in the same machine, or an object in an EXE in a separate machine.

Microsoft defined its own variation of RPC called Object RPC, or ORPC. ORPC is the protocol that DCOM uses. ORPC is not placed on top of RPC; rather, it uses the RPC message structure to include its own information. ORPC calls are legal RPC calls. In essence, a DCOM server is an enhanced RPC server.

The SCM serves as an RPC server, listening for remote requests. When you ask the local SCM to create a remote object with *CreateObject*, the local SCM contacts the remote SCM through an ORPC call. The remote SCM instantiates the object using its normal activation mechanism. Then it gives the local SCM the information necessary to set up ORPC communication between the proxy object in the local machine and the stub object in the remote machine.

Pinging Mechanism

Another function of the SCM is to handle the pinging mechanism. It is easy for a client to know when a server is no longer available due to a crash. If a client tries to make a call to a server object that is no longer available through an interface proxy, the COM interceptor will generate an error. It is not so easy for the server to know if the client has crashed. The local SCM sends the remote SCM a ping every two minutes. The ping contains information about active clients. Each ping does not list all the clients in the machine, but rather the change in the number of clients from one ping to the next. If the server realizes that the client is no longer connected, it releases the outstanding references for that client. If the server misses three pings from the client, as in the case when the client's machine has been disconnected from the network, the server will automatically release all the references from any clients from the missing machine. In other words, if a client crashes, six minutes later the server finds out and releases the client's references to its objects. There is no way to change the ping interval or the number of pings that must be sent before the resources are reclaimed.

Summary

In this chapter, you learned about out-of-process servers. The first thing you learned was that like DLLs, EXEs have to perform four main tasks: registration, unregistration, proper termination, and object creation (exposing their class objects using class factories). Registration and unregistration are done with command-line parameters: `/RegServer` and `/UnregServer`. To expose its class objects, the SCM uses the command-line switch `-Embedding`. The `-Embedding` switch tells the ActiveX EXE to register its class objects with the system's class table. The SCM then searches the class table for the class objects. If the class table does not have a class object that meets the client's request, the SCM launches the executable.

COM objects live in apartments. VB COM objects live in single-threaded apartments (STAs). Whenever communication occurs between apartments, it happens through a proxy and a stub. Communication through proxies and stubs is much slower than direct communication. To use an object from another apartment, we must export the object's interface from one apartment and import it into the client's apartment. To export the object's interface means to marshal it. Marshaling the interface creates a stub. To create the stub, the universal marshaler needs to have access to the server's type library. This is also the case when the object needs to be imported into the client's apartment. In this case, the universal marshaler needs to build a proxy from the type library. This means that both the client's machine and the server machine must have the type library registered. In the case of a VB client program using *CreateObject* with a remote parameter, you must also register the ProgID. Remember that the ProgID is the string name of the class (project name + "." + class name).

Communication between a client and an object that lives in a different machine is done through ORPC. The ORPC protocol is built on top of RPC. When you specify to create an object remotely, the SCM does not search the registry for an `InprocServer32` key or a `LocalServer32` key. Instead, it contacts the SCM in the remote machine through an ORPC call and asks it to instantiate the server. The remote SCM then gives the local SCM information to set up the RPC communication between the client and the object. The result of the call is that the client ends up with a proxy that represents the object, and the server object ends up with a stub that represents the client.

In the next chapter, you are going to learn how to version your components in a way that will not break existing clients. You will also learn how to write type libraries using the Interface Definition Language (IDL).

6

Versioning

If you know the phrase *binary compatibility*, you and I share the same pain. If you have never heard these words, then this chapter will spare you from the pain. This chapter is about versioning your COM components. Whenever I teach a course at a company, there is always a student who wants to know COM's versioning scheme. People often have the idea that COM has a great versioning story. The truth is that COM's versioning mechanism is very simple—once you have published an interface, you are not allowed to change it ever again. That's it! If you never change interfaces that you have published, then you do not have a problem with versioning.

The reality, however, is that often we cannot live with an interface after it has been released without modifications. At the very least, we would like to extend the interface to add new functions. The truth is that COM interfaces cannot be changed, period, not even to add functionality. To understand why, let's first discuss the goal of COM's rigid versioning rule. Then we'll discuss the different kinds of client programs and what each of them requires in terms of versioning. After that, we'll talk about why it is difficult to version things in Visual Basic. Once we have discussed the problems, I will show you the mechanism that Visual Basic offers for versioning. Although I am a big fan of Visual Basic in general, I am not fond of VB's versioning scheme. Therefore, at the end of the chapter, I will show you a better way to version your interfaces using the Interface Definition Language (IDL).

The Goal of COM Versioning

Many of the rules of COM have to do with solving the problems faced by the designers of COM. One problem was locating COM servers (DLLs and EXEs). In the days of VB Version 1 through Version 3, Visual Basic developers used a specialized form of DLLs known as VBXs. VBXs were renamed DLLs that had, aside from *DllMain,* specialized entry point and termination functions. VBX controls were essentially window controls. The main problem with VBXs was that their window message loop functions required five parameters instead of the four parameters that all standard window message loops had. The extra parameter was a VB-assigned handle to the control. Therefore, every message that was sent to one of these specialized windows had not only the window handle (that every window object must have) but also the VB handle that the developer needed to use for the control to interact with the environment. It was a fairly good system if the VBX was going to be used only with VB, but it had almost zero extensibility because it required other programming environments to change the way they interacted with window objects. A major problem with VBXs (and with DLLs in general) was difficulty assuring that the correct versions of all components were shipped with an application.

If you were ever involved in the distribution of Visual Basic applications in Visual Basic 3, you know that half of your technical support problems were related to what people refer to as DLL Hell. DLL Hell is concerned with these two issues: do we have all the DLLs the application needs, and do we have the right versions?

The problem with finding the DLLs stemmed from the absence of clear guidelines for where to put DLLs and VBXs. Microsoft had theirs in the *Windows\System* directory. Some vendors preferred putting things in the Windows directory, and some vendors had components in their installation directory. Sometimes an application needed to ship a later version of a component that was shared by multiple applications from different vendors. Often this caused a major problem, because indubitably one of the older applications from a different vendor would stop working. An even bigger problem was that a single machine could contain multiple copies of a DLL or VBX. Vendor A would release an application and install VBX Z in the *Windows\System* directory, then Vendor B would install another version of VBX Z in its application directory, but because of Windows search criteria, both applications would end up using the version of Z that was in the *Windows\ System* directory. This would normally result in a technical support call in which the technical support engineer would begin by instructing the client to search for all copies of VBX Z and compare the dates and versions.

Supposing we can guarantee that the client's machine has only one copy of the VBX, how do we make sure that the copy he has works with our application? Suppose that our application uses a database component, and suppose that other applications rely on the same component. Then suppose that the developer of the component decides to modify one of the function signatures in the component. What if one of the companies compiles its application against this new version and replaces the component on the client's machine (upon installation) with the latest version of the component? Our application would no longer work. What if a client then decides to leave the new version of the other application installed but replaces the database component with the older version so that our application will work well once again. Now the new application crashes, so the client decides to reformat the drive and reinstall Windows.

Granted, in many cases, it may be unrealistic to expect a client program to work with a different version of the component than the one it was compiled against. However, the end result should never be that the program just crashes. There may be no way for the client application to work without the functionality in the new version of the component, but the program should not leave the client without a clue of what happened. It should notify the client that component Z is older than what the program expected and that the application is unable to work. There may even be situations in which the new functions in the component are not crucial to the application, and it would be nice to degrade to old functionality gracefully.

The main problems the COM team was addressing were:

- How do we guarantee that the client's machine uses only one copy of the COM server?

- How do we make sure that new versions of the COM server continue being backward compatible?

- How do we guarantee that our application can handle the situation gracefully if it encounters the wrong version of the server?

The solutions to these problems focus on two principles. The first is that GUIDs are used to name component classes and interfaces. The advantage of using a CLSID to name a class is that the registry tells COM the location of the only DLL that matters. The registry key HKCR\CLSID\{*Class_CLSID*}\Inprocserver32 or Localserver32 points to the COM DLL or EXE, respectively, that contains the CLSID the client program needs. It does not matter how many copies of the COM server are present in the machine; the one that matters is the one that appears in the registry. If activation fails, we can always look at the registry to find out what DLL or EXE is responsible for the problem (or if there is even one registered).

The second principle is that interfaces are immutable. That means that once they are published, they can never be changed. Each interface has an IID, and clients refer to the interface by this IID. This means that once the interface is published, when the client requests an IID, it expects the interface to always look the same. The client does not know what version of the DLL or what version of the EXE it is talking to, it only knows that it needs an interface and that it expects the interface to look a certain way.

Let's talk about the problems you may encounter as a developer if versioning is not done correctly. To analyze the problems, it is best to first talk about the kinds of clients that you are designing. This is important because clients normally fall into two categories: vtable-bound clients and scripting clients.

Client Requirements

Vtable-bound clients are clients that can talk to an interface directly. They include Visual Basic client programs in which you `Dim` a variable as an interface type (or as a class—VB interprets this as a request to use the default interface), Visual C++ clients, Delphi clients, and VBA clients (such as Word and Excel scripts). Scripting clients are clients that do not use interfaces directly. They include ASP scripts, client-side VBScript or JScript, Windows Script Host scripts, and so on. The requirements for these two types of clients are different. The former group has more stringent requirements than the latter.

Scripting Clients

Let's begin with the easy group—the scripting clients. Scripting client code looks like the following:

```
Dim Checking
Set Checking = Server.CreateObject("BankServer.Checking")
Call Checking.MakeDeposit(500)
```

But it may also look like the following:

```
<object id="Acct" classid=clsid:C5D33E92-591E-4D3B-B796-1918DA093531></object>
<SCRIPT Language=VBScript>
Call Acct.MakeDeposit(500)
</SCRIPT>
```

If you examine the first example, you will notice some things that need to stay the same in the next version of the component for the code to continue to work unchanged. One thing that must stay the same is the ProgID, **BankServer. Checking**. Remember that the ProgID comes from the project name plus the class name. The second dependency is the name of the function *MakeDeposit*. How about the parameter types? The only datatype that scripting clients let you use is the Variant. The Variant type is similar to a UDT, with data members to store the different types that the Variant supports and one data member that tells the code what type is currently being stored in the Variant. The following VB UDT represents roughly (and in part) what the Variant type looks like:

```
Enum VariantTypeConstants
    VT_I2=2,
    VT_I4=3,
    VT_I8=20,
    VT_BSTR=8,
    VT_BOOL=11,
    VT_UNKNOWN=13,
```

```
        VT_DISPATCH=9
        'There are many other type constants supported in the VARIANT type
    End Enum

    Type VARIANT
        vt As VariantTypeConstants
        lVal As Long
        bVal As Byte
        iVal As Integer
        fltVal As Single
        dblVal As Double
        boolVal As Boolean
        bstrVal As String
        punkVal As IUnknown
        pdispVal As Object
        'There are many other types supported in the VARIANT UDT.
    End Type
```

As you can see, the Variant type is the equivalent of a UDT that has storage member variables for the different datatypes that the Variant supports, and one data member (*vt*) that tells the code which of the "value" data members is currently set. For example, if the Variant contains a Boolean, then the scripting engine uses the *boolVal* data member and sets the *vt* data member to VT_BOOL. When you make a function call in the scripting client, the scripting engine can take any literal values (like in `DrawPoint 5.5,10`) and package them as Variants.

If you are writing interfaces for scripting clients, your **ByVal** parameters can be of any type compatible with the Variant datatype. These include the native types like Integers, Singles, Doubles, and so forth, as well as interface parameters and the Object datatype (which translates to `IDispatch`). When the scripting client sees a call to a method, it just packages the values in Variants, forms a Variant array, and sends it as one of the parameters in its call to the Invoke method in the `IDispatch` interface of the object (read Chapter 3 for details).

However, **ByRef** parameters are different. When you make a method call to a function that has a **ByRef** parameter, you must allocate the memory for the variable in code before making the call, and what you are sending is not a value that the variable stores, but rather the address of the variable that is going to receive the value. Because the only type that you can allocate in scripts is a Variant, the scripting client only supports sending addresses to Variants for **ByRef** parameters. This means that **ByRef** parameters in your VB interfaces must be Variant parameters.

The return value of a function is a special type because VB itself is responsible for allocating the memory for the output Variant, so you can have a strongly typed return value in that case.

In summary, any **ByVal** parameters can be typed parameters, as can the output parameter in the case of a function, but **ByRef** parameters must be Variants.

Scripting languages do not use specific interfaces per se; they use the IDispatch interface. As you may recall from Chapter 3, the basic procedure in using the IDispatch interface is for the client code (in this case the scripting execution engine) to use the GetIDsOfNames method in IDispatch and then to call the Invoke method. In the call to Invoke, the client code sends the ID number for the method it wishes to call as well as the parameters for the call packaged in an array of Variants. Because the scripting client code sends in the parameters as Variants, VB takes care of unpackaging the parameters before issuing the actual call, and in doing so, it can perform certain conversions. For example, if the parameter is of type long and the client sent in a short, VB simply converts the short to a long and executes the call. This makes it possible for you to modify the parameter types, within reason, without breaking the client code. For example, the first version of MakeDeposit may have a Long parameter for the amount to deposit, but later you realize it should be a Double. You can easily make this change without breaking compatibility. You may even turn the parameter into a String parameter—this would work as well. If all else fails, you may turn the parameter into a Variant.

One other thing you can do with scripting clients is to extend the number of parameters as long as the new parameters are marked as optional in the class method. For example, the first version of MakeDeposit may look like the following:

```
Public Sub MakeDeposit(ByVal Amount As Double)
```

The second version may look like the following:

```
Public Sub MakeDeposit(ByVal Amount As Double, Optional ByVal Available As Double)
```

If you do not make existing parameters optional, then you have to change the scripting code, because VB will make sure that the number of parameters the client sends are equal to the number of parameters in the call.

The second scripting code example at the beginning of this section requires a little more attention; it uses the <OBJECT> tag to create an instance of the COM component. The object tag uses the CLSID of the class you wish to create. This means that we must ensure that the CLSID for the class remains the same in the next release, and that it appears in the registry. When you use a ProgID, the CLSID can change from one release to the next because the code looks up the CLSID at runtime based on the ProgID. You will learn later in this chapter how to ensure that the CLSID remains the same.

Vtable-Bound Clients

Vtable-bound clients use interfaces. Remember that client programs do not refer to an interface by its readable name; they refer to the interface by its IID. Thus, the IID must remain the same from one release to the next. If the IID changes, the client program will ask the object through *QueryInterface* for the IID, and the object will answer with, "I don't know what you are talking about." This is characterized with error code 429, "Interface not found."

If the call to *QueryInterface* succeeds because the object still supports the IID, then it is important for the layout of the vtable to always remain the same. This means you cannot change the parameters of the function in any way and that you may not delete or insert methods to the interface. Even changing an integer parameter to a long parameter causes the client code to stop working. It may seem as if such a change should work; after all, a Long holds a larger number than an Integer, and both parameter types are numeric. In reality, however, the two parameters are very different. With the Integer parameter, the client code pushes a 16-bit number onto the stack. If you were to change the parameter to a Long parameter, the server code would read 32 bits from the stack. This means the server code would read memory from the stack that did not belong to the parameter. If a client program asks for an interface, then the interface has to be the same interface as the one it was compiled against.

Inserting functions in the middle of the vtable will change the order of the functions, and, as you know, client programs do not remember the function names— they only know about the function offsets. Thus, this is also not a good thing to do with a published interface. But what about adding functions to the end of the vtable? This is all right 90 percent of the time. It works if an old application obtains the new vtable, because it simply doesn't care about new functions at the end of the vtable (the program was not written to use them). It also works for the new client program, of course, since it was written specifically to use that version. This approach does not work only when a new client program encounters an old version of the vtable. In other words, the new program is trying to use the old version of the interface. Of course, you may think that a new client program should not work with an old version of the interface, but, in all cases, we do not want the client program to just crash. We would like it to notify the user of the situation, and in some cases the new program may be able to use old functionality.

So we depend on the IIDs remaining the same and on the interface layout remaining the same. What about the CLSIDs? Well, this varies according to how you write your code. You may recall from Chapter 4 that if you use the New keyword, the binary code writes the actual CLSID of the class into the compiled image. This means that if you use New, you must keep the CLSIDs the same. If you use *CreateObject* instead, VB looks up the CLSID at runtime; thus, you do not have to ensure that the CLSID remains the same.

COM's Versioning Story

COM's versioning solution for vtable-bound clients is that every interface receives an IID and that interfaces are immutable once they are published. Once you publish the interface, you must keep it the same—no changes whatsoever. If you change an interface, then according to the COM rules you must assign it a different IID. If you assign a new IID to the interface, then you must decide what happens when a client requests an old IID. You have a choice in this case. You may decide that old clients must continue to run, in which case you do not touch the old interface. You simply create a new interface with the old methods plus your changes, and you implement both the old interface and the new interface in the component. For example, let's say that the first version of the **IAccount** interface is defined as follows:

```
'interface IAccount version 1
Public Sub MakeDeposit(ByVal Amount As Long)
End Sub
```

Then the code for version 1 of the **CChecking** class may be the following:

```
'class CChecking
Implements IAccount

Private m_Balance As Long

Private Sub IAccount_MakeDeposit(ByVal Amount As Long)
    m_Balance = m_Balance + Amount
End Sub
```

Let's say that later you must change *Amount* to be a Double instead of a Long. Then you would define a new interface:

```
'Interface IAccount2 (IAccount version 2)
Public Sub MakeDeposit(ByVal Amount As Double)
End Sub
```

Now that there is a new interface, the new version of CChecking would support both interfaces, as follows:

```
'class CChecking version 2
Implements IAccount
Implements IAccount2

Private m_Balance As Double

Private Sub IAccount_MakeDeposit(ByVal Amount As Long)
    Call IAccount2_MakeDeposit(Amount)
End Sub

Private Sub IAccount2_MakeDeposit(ByVal Amount As Double)
    m_Balance = m_Balance + Amount
End Sub
```

Notice that the implementation of the old interface simply forwards the calls to the new implementation.

What if it does not make sense to support the `IAccount` interface any longer? Then you have two options. You can continue to implement the old interface but return an error with a nice description informing the user that she must obtain a new version of the interface. The second option—dropping support for the old interface altogether—is very risky. However, you must have foresight. Before you write the first version of the client program, you must be aware that the interface you are using may be dropped in later releases. That means that you must code the client program with special logic from the start. For example, all VB interfaces have something in common—they are dual interfaces. That means that they have support for `IDispatch`. One thing you can do is declare your first variable as type Object and then find out from the interface you obtain if it supports the interface you need for vtable binding. The following example shows how to do this:

```
Dim AcctTemp As Object
Set AcctTemp = CreateObject("BankServer.CChecking")

If TypeOf AcctTemp Is IAccount Then
    Dim Acct As IAccount
    Set Acct = AcctTemp
Else
    MsgBox "The client program you are using is too old. " & _
           "You must obtain a new version."
End If
```

The preceding code shows how to write the first version of your client program to account for the possibility that you may eventually drop support for the old interface.

How Visual Basic Versions Your COM Objects

The good thing about VB is that it does almost everything for you; the bad thing about VB is that it does almost everything for you. What I mean is that sometimes it would be easier if the developers of VB let you take control of certain features. There are many times that I wish the toolbar had a button called Manual Mode that would let me take out the autopilot. Versioning is one of those categories in which VB's help actually makes it harder for you.

The problem is that you never deal with GUIDs directly in VB. They are generated for you automatically when you compile your program or when you run your program in the debugger. Because of the nature of GUIDs (the fact that they are guaranteed to be unique), you must tell VB when it is appropriate to generate a new GUID or when it must keep the GUIDs the same. If VB were to change some crucial GUIDs, such as the IID of an interface, any client programs that depend on the GUID would stop working.

Visual Basic has three options that enable you to control how it generates GUIDs. (Remember that GUID generation occurs when you compile your server or when you run your server code in the debugger.) These three options produce four different configurations. You will find the three settings in the Project → Properties dialog box, under the Component tab, as shown in Figure 6-1.

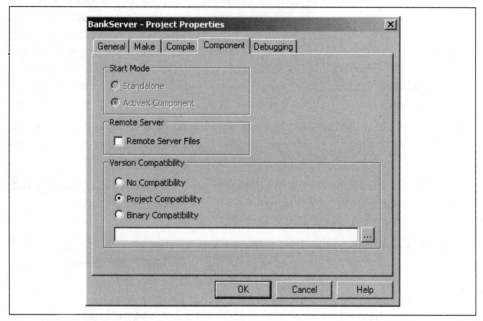

Figure 6-1. Version configurations

The three settings are Binary Compatibility, Project Compatibility, or No Compatibility. However, when you choose Binary Compatibility, you may end up with two different configurations: Binary Identical or Binary Compatible.

Binary Compatibility

If your clients use vtable binding, then they expect all interface IIDs to remain the same. Binary Compatibility tells VB to keep all the GUIDs the same. This includes LIBIDs, CLSIDs, and IIDs. Notice that this is *not* the default. The default is Project Compatibility. You will learn about Project Compatibility shortly, but for now keep in mind that the only option that ensures that you have the same GUIDs is Binary Compatibility.

When you choose Binary Compatibility, you must tell VB what ActiveX DLL or ActiveX EXE to use as a reference when generating the GUIDs. VB will read the type library of the old server you specified in the input field (see Figure 6-1) so that it can use the old GUIDs for the new version of the type library.

The procedure for using Binary Compatibility is usually the following:

1. The very first time you build your server, you must use Project Compatibility (which is the default setting).

2. Take the resulting DLL or EXE and move it to a separate directory. I always create a subdirectory under the target directory for the server called *Rel1* (or *Rel2*, *Rel3*, etc). For example, if the project name is BankServer, I normally have a directory called *Projects\BankServer* where I build the ActiveX DLL (or ActiveX EXE). Then I have a subdirectory *Projects\BankServer\Rel1*. As soon as I build the DLL or EXE, I move a copy of the image file to this directory. This is the DLL or EXE that VB will use as a reference.

3. Set the option to Binary Compatibility and set the field under the Binary Compatibility option to point to that copy of the DLL or EXE. In this case, the complete path may be *Projects\BankServer\Rel1\BankServer.dll*.

Each time you run the project in the debugger or compile your program, VB will use the type library in the *Rel1* copy of the DLL as a reference and try to match all the GUIDs to the GUIDs in that type library.

By default, VB will try to point the reference DLL or EXE path to the target directory, but this causes problems. I recommend that you choose two different directories, as I have described earlier. The reason is that there seems to be a glitch in the building process in VB; it sometimes tries to build the new version of the DLL or EXE at the same time it tries to read the old type library, and the building step fails with a message that the file is locked. The only way to build your project then is to exit VB altogether and try again. This gets old rather quickly. The solution is to have two different files, one for reading the type library and one for the compiled DLL or EXE. The easy way to do this it to place a copy of the built DLL or EXE in a different directory and use that file for reading the type library.

By building with binary compatibility, you are instructing VB to keep all the GUIDs identical. Of course, VB cannot violate the rules of COM. It can keep the GUIDs the same only if you abide by the rules of COM. That means that you must keep all the public functions in every class identical.

Let's talk about all the possible changes you may want to make. Let's suppose that we have a Bank COM server called BankServer. The BankServer project is a DLL (an EXE would have exactly the same issues). The project has four classes. The first class is `IAccount` and, as in the previous chapters, `IAccount` has a Make-Deposit method and a GetBalance function, as shown in the following code:

```
'class IAccount
Public Sub MakeDeposit(ByVal Amount As Double)
End Sub

Public Function GetBalance() As Double
End Function
```

The `IAccount` class Instancing property is marked as 2 – `PublicNotCreatable`. The project has two implementation classes, CChecking and CSavings. Both of these classes have their Instancing property set to 1 – `MultiUse`. The following code shows the implementation of the `IAccount` interface in the CChecking class. The code for `CSavings` is identical at this point and has been omitted for convenience.

```
'class CChecking (same code for CSavings)
Implements IAccount
Private m_Balance As Double

Private Sub IAccount_MakeDeposit(ByVal Amount As Double)
    m_Balance = m_Balance + Amount
End Sub

Private Function IAccount_GetBalance() As Double
    IAccount_GetBalance = m_Balance
End Function
```

The fourth class in the project is called BankConstants, and it contains public enumerated constants for the error codes. The following code shows the Bank-Constants class:

```
'class BankConstants
Public Enum BankErrorConstants
    beNotEnoughFunds = vbObjectError + 1000
    beInvalidAccount = vbObjectError + 1001
End Enum
```

This project represents a typical COM server. It contains an interface class, several implementation classes, and one class to store constants that will be published in the type library. The only thing that VB takes into consideration when performing binary compatibility are public members that have GUIDs assigned to them. For some reason, however, the VB team decided to assign GUIDs to every element that appears in the type library—not just to classes and interfaces but to enums as well. Thus, if we were to take an X ray of the BankServer project so that we could see all the GUIDs that matter for binary compatibility, we would have the following:

```
'class IAccount
{IID-_IAccount} contains MakeDeposit and GetBalance
```

```
{CLSID-IAccount}

'class CChecking
{IID-_CChecking} no methods
{IID-_IAccount}  contains MakeDeposit and GetBalance
{CLSID-CChecking}

'class CSavings
{IID-_CSavings} no methods
{IID-_IAccount} contains MakeDeposit and GetBalance
{CLSID-CSavings}

'class BankConstants
{IID-_BankConstants} no methods
{GUID-BankConstantsEnum} contains error constants
{CLSID-BankConstants}
```

Remember that every class has a default interface. Thus, the CChecking and CSavings classes each has two interfaces—the default interface and the IAccount interface. The BankConstants class also has a default interface—it is a COM class just like the others.

The simplest change to make is to extend an interface. For example, you may want to add a new method to IAccount (like MakeWithdrawal). Or you may want to add public members to the CChecking or CSavings class. Adding public members to these two classes extends the default interface of each class. Although enums are not interfaces, they follow similar rules when it comes to versioning. Extending the enum (i.e., adding a new constant) also falls in the same category of change. Under the rules of COM, this constitutes a new interface altogether. You are not allowed to extend an interface without renaming the interface.

Suppose we added the MakeWithdrawal method to the IAccount interface as follows:

```
'class IAccount
Public Sub MakeDeposit(ByVal Amount As Double)
End Sub

Public Function GetBalance() As Double
End Function

Public Sub MakeWithdrawal(ByVal Amount As Double)
End Sub
```

According to the COM rules, this change requires a new IID for the IAccount interface. VB does not break the COM rules. Instead, it assigns a new IID to the interface IAccount, but it also keeps support for the old IID. This behavior occurs only if you have versioning set to Binary Compatibility and only if you extend an interface.

If you add a constant to an enum, VB also assigns the enum a new GUID. However, supporting the old GUID is somewhat irrelevant, because when a client uses an enum, it does not address the enum by its GUID. The compiled image of the client program does not have any references to enum GUIDs nor to the constant names, only to the constant values themselves. The COM specification does not say that enums should have GUIDs—this was a decision of the VB team. There is one side effect to extending the enum, however. Not only does the enum get a new GUID, but the default interface of the class where the enum was defined also receives a new IID. Thus, after extending the interface for **IAccount** and adding a constant to the BankConstants class, the class GUIDs VB creates would look like the following:

```
'class IAccount
{IID-_IAccount-Version2} contains MakeDeposit, GetBalance and MakeWithdrawal
{IID-_IAccount-Old} forward any requests for this interface to the new version.
{CLSID-IAccount}

'class CChecking
{IID-_CChecking} no methods
{IID-_IAccount-Version2}  contains MakeDeposit and GetBalance and MakeWithdrawal
{IID-_IAccount-Old} forward any requests for this interface to the new version.
{CLSID-CChecking}

'class CSavings
{IID-_CSavings} no methods
{IID-_IAccount-Version2} contains MakeDeposit and GetBalance and MakeWithdrawal
{IID-_Account-Old} forward any requests for this interface to the new version.
{CLSID-CSavings}

'class BankConstants
{IID-_BankConstants} no methods
{GUID-BankConstantsEnum} contains error constants
{CLSID-BankConstants}
```

As you can see, VB assigns a new IID to the **IAccount** interface and adds support for the old interface.

Let's see how such a change affects client code. Assume that the first version of the client program has the following code:

```
Dim Acct As IAccount
Set Acct = New CChecking
```

The important line of code is the creation line. Remember to evaluate first the right side of the equals sign and then look at the left. If you recall from Chapter 4, **New** calls *CoCreateInstanceEx* and asks for four interfaces: *IID-IUnknown*, *IID-_CChecking* (the default interface), *IID-IPersistStreamInit*, and *IID-PropertyBag*. The *CoCreateInstance* function also requires the CLSID of the class you wish to create, *CLSID_CChecking*. If you examine the GUID X ray after extending the **IAccount** interface, you can see that none of the GUIDs involved in the right side of the equation are affected by the change. The only IID changed was IAccount. Now, look at the left side of the equation. The left side calls *QueryInterface* on the CChecking object and asks for *IID-IAccount-Old*. VB adds code to the CChecking class to handle requests for the old IID. The code simply returns the new vtable.

Why is it OK for VB to return the new vtable? Because it has support for all the old methods as well as the new. The old client programs do not care about the new methods. Client code that was compiled against the new interface definition would call *QueryInterface* requesting the new IID. This means that both old and new client programs would work fine with a new version of the COM server. We say that this new version is *binary compatible* as opposed to *binary identical*.

One more situation that VB needs to account for is the type library. VB does not add a definition for the old interface to the type library. If you were to examine the type library resulting from extending the interface, you would see the following (in pseudocode IDL):

```
library BankServer
{
    [IID-_IAccount-Version2]
    interface _IAccount
    {
        HRESULT MakeDeposit([in] double Amount);
        HRESULT GetBalance([out,retval] double *Amount);
        HRESULT MakeWithdrawal([in] double Amount);
    }

    [CLSID_CChecking]
    coclass CChecking
    {
        [default] interface _CChecking;
        interface _IAccount;
    }
}
```

The client code doesn't use the type library after it has been compiled. However, if the interface is going to be used across apartments, as you learned in Chapter 5, there must be a proxy and stub generated. The type library marshaler builds the interface proxy and stub from the interface definition in the type library. However, the type library does not have a definition for the old interface. It has a definition for the new interface, which is compatible with the old, but the name for the interface is different. VB also adds code to the registration function to add a special key to the registry. In Chapter 5 you learned that when the type library marshaler gets a request to build a proxy or a stub, it looks in the registry for the interface under HKCR\Interface\{*IID_Interface*}. Under this key, the type library marshaler finds a **TypeLib** subkey that tells it the LIBID of the type library that contains the interface definition. VB adds a **Forward** key under the interface key as follows: HKCR\Interface\{*IID_Interface*}\Forward. The value for this Forward key is the IID for the new version of the interface. This key tells the type library marshaler to treat the old interface as the new interface.

You may be wondering what happens if you extend the interface a second time—will you have two Forward keys? You may, depending on which version of the type library you use for binary compatibility. If you extend the interface once and rebuild your project using version 1 of the type library as a reference, then extend the interface again and again still using version 1 as the reference, VB will treat the new interface as if you had added two functions to the original. Therefore, it will need to add only one Forward key for the old IID. If you extend the interface once, then replace the reference DLL or EXE with the last DLL or EXE you built, then extend the interface again and rebuild, VB will notice that there were two changes to the interface. In other words, you started with *IID_Version1*, then you added a function that resulted in *IID_Version2*, then you added a third function that resulted in *IID_Version3*. VB will add support to the DLL or EXE for all three IIDs and forward *IID_Version1* to *IID_Version2*, then forward *IID_Version2* to *IID_Version3*.

Breaking Compatibility

You sometimes need to change or remove an existing function in the interface, just as you sometimes need to remove or change an enum from a constant. If you make a change to one of the existing functions, VB does not have any tricks that can help you. You are forced to break compatibility, and VB will let you know with the dialog box in Figure 6-2.

You will get this dialog box if you have version compatibility set to Binary Compatibility and you remove a function, you change the parameters in a function, you add a parameter (even if it is optional) to a function, you change the result parameter of the function, or you attempt to rename the function. It could also happen, however, if you remove or change the value of one of the constants in an enum. The dialog box gives you two options. The first option is to break compatibility. The second option—Preserve (Advanced)—is available only if you do not remove an existing function or constant. Let's talk about the second option first.

If you choose to preserve compatibility, which certainly seems like a useful option, client programs that use the interface definition will crash. That's right, they will crash. This option tells VB to keep the IID for the interface the same. It should have been named Force Compatibility—it is telling VB to forget the rules of COM and just treat the new interface as the same interface. You should choose this version only while you are developing and testing. Yes, you will have to rebuild clients using the interface, but you will not have to rebuild every client as you would with the first option.

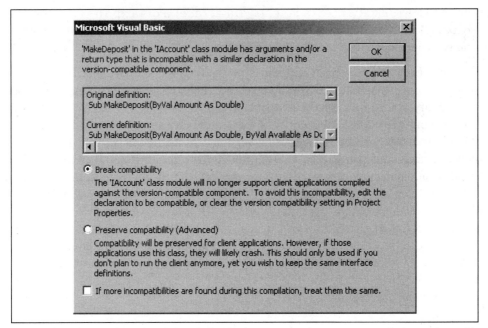

Figure 6-2. The Break compatibility dialog box

If you choose to break compatibility, VB will build your project as if you had chosen Project Compatibility.

Project Compatibility

Project Compatibility also uses an existing type library as a reference when building your new project. However, it tells VB that the interfaces are currently in flux and that you do not want it to attempt to make them compatible. This mode causes VB to generate new IIDs for every class in the project but to keep all CLSIDs and LIBIDs the same. This option also tells VB to generate new GUIDs for enums and structures if they are in the type library.

When you have your project set to Binary Compatibility and you make a change by which binary compatibility cannot be maintained, if you choose the Break Compatibility option in the dialog box in Figure 6-2, all the IIDs for every class will change, and the classes will not have support for the old IIDs. An X ray of the classes in the project would reveal the following IIDs:

```
'class IAccount
{IID-_IAccount-New} contains MakeDeposit and GetBalance
{CLSID-IAccount-Old}

'class CChecking
{IID-_CChecking-New} no methods
```

```
{IID-_IAccount-New}  contains MakeDeposit and GetBalance
{CLSID-CChecking-Old}

'class CSavings
{IID-_CSavings-New} no methods
{IID-_IAccount-New} contains MakeDeposit and GetBalance
{CLSID-CSavings-Old}

'class BankConstants
{IID-_BankConstants-New} no methods
{GUID-BankConstantsEnum-New} contains error constants
{CLSID-BankConstants-Old}
```

If you consider the following client code once again, you will see that the client will no longer work:

```
Dim Acct As IAccount
Set Acct = New CChecking
```

The right side of the equation asks for *CLSID-CChecking-Old*, *IID_IUnknown*, *IID-_CChecking-Old*, *IID_IPersistStreamInit*, and *IID_IPersist-PropertyBag*. The code will find *CLSID-CChecking-Old* but not *IID-_CChecking-Old*, and it will fail with error 429. Even if the right side were to succeed, the left side of the equation would ask for *IID-IAccount-Old* and would fail.

Notice that Project Compatibility is the default, which is why—if you compile a COM server, then build a client, then recompile the COM server (without making any modifications)—compiled client programs will stop working. You must immediately switch compatibility to Binary Compatibility.

You may think that this is not a serious problem, since it makes sense that if an interface changes, you must rebuild the client program. True, but consider the case in which you have three interfaces: IAccount, ISaveToDisk, and IAdmin. Then suppose that you have three client programs: one that uses IAccount exclusively, another that uses ISaveToDisk exclusively, and a third that uses IAdmin exclusively. You may change IAccount in a way that requires VB to break compatibility. If you change a parameter in one of the functions in IAccount, VB will give you the option to break compatibility or to preserve compatibility (as in Figure 6-2). If you choose to preserve, then only the client program using IAccount would stop working—all other IIDs would be preserved. However, if you choose to break compatibility (and remember, this is your only option if you remove a function or rename it, since that is the same as removing a function and adding a new one), VB will change all IIDs. Therefore, every single client program, and not just the one using IAccount, will need to be recompiled. What is even worse is that, in our example, removing a constant from the BankErrors enumerated type would also result in a change that would require all client programs to be rebuilt.

What is the advantage of project compatibility? As far as versioning, project compatibility does keep all CLSIDs and LIBIDs constant. The advantage of keeping CLSIDs constant is for scripting clients that use the <OBJECT> tag with a CLSID. If you write scripting clients using the <OBJECT> tag, then you depend on CLSIDs remaining the same; therefore, this option is ideal. There is another reason why this setting is useful, and it has to do with the LIBID.

When you build a client program in VB and add a type library through project references, VB stores the LIBID of the type library you imported in the project file. If you open a saved project, VB will locate the type library from the LIBID. If the LIBID were to change, when you opened your project, VB would not find the type library and would tell you that one of your references is missing, as shown in Figure 6-3.

Figure 6-3. Missing reference

Therefore, one nice aspect of having project compatibility is that it keeps you from having to add project references every time you change the code.

No Compatibility

The last option in the versioning settings is No Compatibility. It just tells VB to change every GUID every time you recompile and every time you run the program in the debugger. Every CLSID, IID, enum GUID, and struct GUID will change. You choose this option when you want a clean start. Sometimes this is useful if you have been developing your DLL or EXE using one of the other compatibility settings, then the time comes to finally ship your server and you want to make sure that the type library is clean and that there is no code in the registry functions to add Forward keys and so on.

Versioning Wrap-up

If you decide that you can live with the versioning rules in VB, you may find the following guidelines useful. Normally, when you begin the process of developing your components, you make a lot of changes to the interface. In this case, it is best to leave your version compatibility setting to the default value—Project Compatibility. This will enable you to recompile the client application without having to reimport the type library for the DLL.

At some point in your development, it makes sense to freeze the interface changes. This is usually done well before release so that the interfaces may be properly tested and documented. At the point you wish to freeze the interface, switch the version setting to No Compatibility. This will give you a fresh set of GUIDs. This also means that you must reimport the type libraries and rebuild the clients, but you will end up with a fresh set of GUIDs.

Once you generate the fresh copy of the DLL, make sure to set it aside in a separate directory. From then on, always compile with the version property set to Binary Compatibility. If there is a problem before the version is released to the project, then you may make changes to the interfaces. When VB warns you that your interface is no longer binary compatible, you must decide on the risk factor. If you choose Break Compatibility, then every client must be recompiled.

Once you recompile the COM server, use this new version for binary compatibility. If the change did not involve removing a method, you may want to choose Preserve Compatibility. This will minimize the number of clients you will need to recompile. Do this with the understanding that if the clients are not recompiled, they will crash in testing.

When the components are released to the public, you are committed to supporting those interfaces. From that point on, make sure to set the version option to Binary Compatibility, and if you need to make a change to an interface, add a new interface to your project and implement both the new and the old interfaces in your object. Remember that VB enables you to add members to the interfaces without breaking binary compatibility.

Using IDL

If you believe, as I do, that VB's versioning scheme is more trouble than it is worth, a better way to gain complete control over GUIDs is to define your interfaces with the Interface Definition Language (IDL). Defining your interfaces in IDL has several advantages:

- You eliminate the overhead of having a class for each interface in a VB project.

- You have complete control over when GUIDs change and why.

- If you use IDL and use *CreateObject* in your client code (for reasons that will be obvious shortly), then you can set the versioning setting in VB to anything you wish and it will not affect whether the clients work or not.

The only disadvantage in using IDL is that you have to learn how to use it, and for some reason VB developers shy away from it.

You learned about IDL in Chapter 4. IDL is not a full language in the sense that it does not allow you to write loops or have if...then...else statements and so on. IDL is a syntax language for defining interfaces. IDL enables you to build stand-alone type library files. Once you define your interface in IDL, you can compile it with MIDL, the Microsoft IDL compiler. MIDL can produce a variety of files, including header files for C++ clients, proxy-stub code for standard marshalers, and, most importantly for us, a standalone type library file. It would be impossible for me to show you every aspect of IDL in this section of the chapter, so I am going to show you the essentials for building a type library in IDL.

Reverse-Engineering Type Libraries

In Chapter 4, you learned that you can reverse-engineer a type library and obtain the source for the type library in IDL using OLE/COM Object Viewer. In addition to showing you the source for a type library, COM Viewer lets you save the source to a text file.

By far the easiest way to generate IDL is to start with a prototype project in Visual Basic. The prototype project can contain the definition of all the interfaces in your project. You can then compile the project and use COM Viewer to extract the IDL. When you are satisfied, you can then forget about the prototype and manage the interfaces through the IDL source code. The best part about it is that everything that you can define in Visual Basic can be represented in IDL; the VB compiler would stop you from compiling something that would be illegal in IDL syntax.

If you are going to use the reverse-engineering approach, you must know about a few caveats. One is that OLE/COM Object Viewer may shift the order of interface definitions at any time. The end result is that if you attempt to compile IDL source as is, sometimes you will get compile errors. In IDL, order matters. For example, if you reference an interface as a parameter in another interface, then the other interface must be declared first. If you have a situation in which interface A and interface B need to know about each other—for example, IA serves as a parameter type in IB and IB serves as a parameter type in IA—then you can use a technique called *forwarding*, which simply means that you add a declaration line first without describing the interface. The following code shows an example of forwarding:

```
interface IA;

interface IB
{
    HRESULT DoSomethingWithA([in] IA *param);
};

interface IA
```

```
{
    HRESULT DoSomethingWithB([in] IB *param);
};
```

The first line in the code simply states that IA is an interface that will be defined later in the script. Without this one line, the compiler would get to the method DoSomethingWithA in IB and complain that IA was not defined.

The only other caveat with using IDL source from a reverse-engineered type library is that VB adds a number of things to the type library that are not really needed (for example, keywords such as `odl`, `hidden`, `nonextensible`, and `ids` can be omitted). In the remainder of this chapter, you will learn the necessary elements that produce a type library.

Defining Elements in IDL

Let's look at all the most common elements in a VB type library. In doing so, the chapter is going to build a type library for the BankServer project discussed before.

To build a type library from IDL, you need two tools: a text editor (Notepad is fine) and MIDL (the IDL compiler). To get the latest version of MIDL, you can install the Platform SDK. You also get MIDL if you install Visual C++. One thing to remember if you install Visual C++ is to register environment variables. The installation program asks you in a dialog box at the end of installation if you would like to register environment variables. Saying yes will enable you to run MIDL from any directory. (Otherwise, you can run *VCVARS32.bat* from the command line.)

Library section

The first element in every type library is a `library` block. The following code shows the definition of the BankServer type library:

```
[   uuid(3AD84662-D0FC-4792-9AB0-593013939269),
    helpstring("BankServer Interface Definitions Version 1.0")
]
library BankServerLib
{
    importlib("stdole2.tlb");
};
```

All other elements will be defined inside the `library` block. The first thing to notice from the code is that there is a set of attributes before the library declaration. Each element in IDL may contain attributes. Attributes are defined within square brackets. The attributes in this case are `uuid` and `helpstring`. The `uuid` attribute is required and contains the LIBID for the type library. To generate this number, use the tool *GUIDGEN.EXE* that Microsoft provides when you install Visual C++, the Platform SDK, or the Enterprise Edition of Visual Basic. Figure 6-4 shows you GUIDGEN.

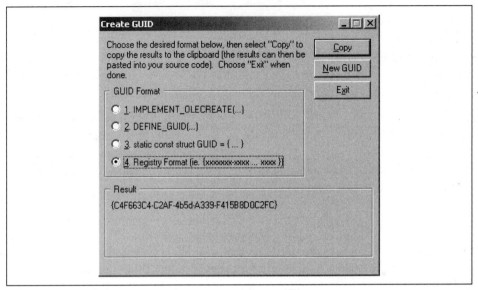

Figure 6-4. GUIDGEN

When you use GUIDGEN, choose option number 4, Registry Format. This format
is what IDL expects, except that it adds curly brackets before and after the GUID.
You will need to remove the curly brackets.

The `helpstring` attribute is optional. If you use a `helpstring`, VB will display the
help string in the Project References dialog box. Otherwise, VB will display the
name of the type library, BankServerLib in this case. IDL uses C++ syntax so, as you
can see, every element definition uses curly brackets and has semicolons at the end.

Inside the `library` block, there is a directive to import another type library. The
type library, *stdole2.tlb*, has a few definitions such as `IUnknown`, `IDispatch`, different font and picture structures, and so forth. You should always include this
type library.

Interfaces

Let's add an interface definition (which is shown in boldface) to the IDL script:

```
[   uuid(3AD84662-D0FC-4792-9AB0-593013939269),
    helpstring("BankServer Interface Definitions Version 1.0")
]
library BankServerLib
{
    importlib("stdole2.tlb");

    [
        uuid(812A55AE-5013-463d-B2DD-D630230CDB68),
        object,
```

```
    oleautomation
]
interface IAccount : IUnknown
{
    HRESULT MakeDeposit([in] double Amount);
    HRESULT GetBalance([out,retval] double *Amount);
};

};
```

The preceding code shows the definition for the IAccount interface. The first thing to notice about this definition is that, like the library definition, it has an attribute block. The attribute block contains three important attributes. The first is uuid, the IID for the interface. As before, you can generate the IID using *GUIDGEN.EXE*. The second attribute is object, which tells the MIDL compiler that this is a COM interface. If you omit this keyword, MIDL would think that the interface is an MSRPC interface, and MSRPC interfaces have different restrictions. The third attribute is oleautomation, which tells MIDL to do two things. One is to add information in the type library for registering the keys for the interfaces that are outside the library block. Remember that it is possible to declare interfaces outside of the library block, and if you do, then by default when you register the type library the interface keys would not be added. These keys are needed for marshaling. Second, this attribute tells the compiler that all declarations within the interface should be automation compatible. The compiler issues warnings if you add definitions that are not automation compatible. It turns out that VB uses automation types for all of its interface declarations as well. In essence, you are instructing the compiler to let you know if one of your definitions will not be VB compatible.

Another interesting thing to notice from the declaration is that IAccount derives from IUnknown. Visual Basic interfaces must derive either from IUnknown or from IDispatch. You are not allowed to implement an interface in a VB class that does not derive from one of these two interfaces. It makes sense to choose IUnknown rather than IDispatch. Implementing an interface that derives from IDispatch means that VB will need to add extra code to add support for the IDispatch interface. This is unnecessary because, as you learned in earlier chapters, IDispatch support is necessary only for scripting clients. Scripting clients, however, will not be able to use the interfaces you define in IDL. When a scripting client requests the IDispatch interface from a Visual Basic component, the component returns only the default interface. Any interface you implement using a custom type library will not be the default interface.

If you examine each method, you should notice that the return value of each method is an HRESULT. HRESULTs are 32-bit error (or success) codes. In the Visual Basic definition of IAccount, MakeDeposit was a subroutine and GetBalance was a function that returned a Double. IDL lets you simulate this behavior by adding attributes to each parameter. The attributes that work with Visual Basic are [in], which translates to ByVal; [in,out], which translates to ByRef; and [out,retval], which translates to the return value of a function. If Visual Basic sees the [out,retval] attribute, it turns the method into a function. Visual Basic also hides all evidence of the HRESULT. If VB gets an HRESULT that translates to an error, VB raises a trappable error instead. If VB gets a success HRESULT, it simply discards it. Also, if you are not familiar with C++ syntax, whenever you want to declare a ByRef parameter, you must make it a pointer parameter. This is why we have double *Amount as the parameter type. The asterisk in front of the Amount field denotes a pointer parameter.

Instead of having a GetBalance function, we may want to have a property that enables us to both read the Balance and set the Balance. You can simulate this behavior in VB as well in the following fashion:

```
interface IAccount : IUnknown
{
  HRESULT MakeDeposit([in] double Amount);
  [propget] HRESULT Balance([out,retval] double *Amount);
  [proput]  HRESULT Balance([in] double Amount);
};
```

In the preceding code example, Balance has two declarations in the interface definition. IDL lets you do this only when defining properties. You tell IDL that you are defining a property by specifying an attribute in front of the declaration. One attribute is [propget] for the property get function, and the other is [propput] for the property let. What if you want to mimic a property set? Then you would use the [propputref] attribute and make sure that the parameter type is a certain interface. Which leads us to the topic of using interface parameters in a declaration.

You can have interfaces as parameters in a declaration. To do so, make sure to declare the interface to be used as the parameter before the declaration of the method that uses it, or write a forward declaration. Then write the method as shown in the following example:

```
[
    uuid(BDF699F1-0C71-47f2-A1C3-E15981063142),
    object,
    oleautomation
]
interface IAccountFactory : IUnknown
{
    HRESULT CreateNewAccount([out,retval] IAccount **NewAccount);
    HRESULT CopyAccount([in] IAccount *Old, [out,retval] IAccount **Copy);
    HRESULT FetchAccountInfo([in] IAccount *AnyAccount);
};
```

The preceding code shows three methods in a different interface that use the IAccount interface as a parameter type. The first method returns a pointer to the IAccount interface. Notice that this method uses a double pointer for the parameter type. The reason: in COM, interfaces are abstract (noncreatable) entities. Therefore, interface parameters are pointers to an interface to begin with. This is evident in the second declaration. The first parameter in the CopyAccount function is of type IAccount *. So interface parameters use one pointer level for ByVal parameters and a double pointer for ByRef parameters and for return values.

You may also add enums and user-defined types (UDTs) to type libraries. In fact, even if you decide that IDL is too much trouble, you may want to consider IDL just for defining enums. This will enable you to adjust constants without having to break compatibility in your project. The following code shows you how to define an enumerated type in two ways:

```
#define vbObjectError 0x80040000
enum BankErrors
{
    beNotEnoughFunds = vbObjectError + 1000,
    beInvalidAccount
};
typedef enum AccountType
{
    atChecking,
    atSavings
} AccountTypeConstants;
```

The preceding code should be placed inside the **library** block. You declare enumerated types using the **enum** keyword. Enumerated values begin at 0 unless you explicitly set a starting value. In the first example, I defined a compiler constant to stand for the **vbObjectError** constant. Separate constants with commas. If you do not set a value for the constant, the compiler will automatically add 1 to the previous value in the enumeration. In the second example, I used the **typedef** directive. This is useful if you need to refer to the enumeration later in the script. For example, we can use the enumeration as a parameter type, as in the following definition:

```
HRESULT CreateNewAccount([in] AccountTypeConstants *AcctType,
                [out,retval] IAccount **NewAccount);
```

Using **typedef** tells the compiler to assign a name to the combination "enum AccountType"; otherwise, you would have to use "enum AccountType" whenever you referred to the enumeration. If you use an enum for a parameter type, then when a developer uses the method he will see a list of constants. Notice that I did not assign a GUID to the enumeration—you do not have to assign one.

To define a UDT, you use the **struct** keyword, as follows:

```
typedef struct AccountInfo
{
    BSTR AccountNum;
    DATE DateCreated;
    VARIANT_BOOL Active;
} AccountInfo;
```

The preceding code shows the definition of a structure. As in the enum declaration, you can use the **typedef** directive to assign an alias to the "struct AccountInfo" phrase; otherwise, you would have to use the entire phrase "struct AccountInfo" each time you wanted to refer to the structure. The structure has three members. The first member, *AccountNum*, is of type string. Visual Basic strings are of type **BSTR** (or basic strings). **BSTRs** are variable-length Unicode strings with a prefix that contains the length of the string. The second member, *DateCreated*, is of type Date. The third member, *Active*, is a Boolean. Boolean values must be declared with the type **VARIANT_BOOL**. The **BOOL** type in C++ translates to a Long value in Visual Basic.

You can use UDTs as parameter types in methods, as shown in the following code:

```
HRESULT FetchAccountInfo([in] BSTR AcctNum,
                         [out,retval] AccountInfo *Info);
```

In Visual Basic, UDTs can be used as parameters only if they are **ByRef** parameters or the return type of a function. Therefore, you must use the attribute **[in,out]** or **[out,retval]** **attributes**, and the parameter must always be a pointer.

This is by no means a complete guide to IDL; there is a lot more you can do with it, like declare optional parameters, parameter arrays, and so forth. The best way to learn all the combinations is to declare the interface in VB, compile the project, and then look at the IDL with OLEViewer.

Creating the Type Library

Collecting all the pieces of code scattered throughout the chapter results in the following IDL source:

```
[ uuid(3AD84662-D0FC-4792-9AB0-593013939269),
    helpstring("BankServer Interface Definitions Version 1.0")
]
library BankServerLib
{
    importlib("stdole2.tlb");

    #define vbObjectError 0x80040000
```

```
typedef struct AccountInfo
{
    BSTR AccountNum;
    DATE DateCreated;
    VARIANT_BOOL Active;
} AccountInfo;

enum BankErrors
{
    beNotEnoughFunds = vbObjectError + 1000,
    beInvalidAccount
};

typedef enum AccountType
{
    atChecking,
    atSavings
} AccountTypeConstants;

[
  uuid(812A55AE-5013-463d-B2DD-D630230CDB68),
  object,
  oleautomation
]
interface IAccount : IUnknown
{
  HRESULT MakeDeposit([in] double Amount);
  HRESULT GetBalance([out,retval] double *Amount);
};

[
  uuid(BDF699F1-0C71-47f2-A1C3-E15981063142),
  object,
  oleautomation
]
interface IAccountFactory : IUnknown
{
  HRESULT CreateNewAccount([in] AccountTypeConstants *AcctType,
                           [out,retval] IAccount **NewAccount);
  HRESULT CopyAccount([in] IAccount *Old,
                      [out,retval] IAccount **Copy);
  HRESULT FetchAccountInfo([in] BSTR AcctNum,
                           [out,retval] AccountInfo *Info);
};

};
```

You may save the source in a text file, *BankInterfaces.IDL* for example. Once you have the IDL source in a text file, you run the MIDL compiler to produce a type library. If you registered the C++ environment variables, you may run MIDL using a command prompt from the directory where you saved the source, as shown:

```
MIDL BankInterfaces.idl
```

After running the MIDL compiler, you should see a new file called *BankInterfaces. tlb* in the directory. Before you can use the type library, you must register it. There are two ways of registering the resulting type library. One is to use a tool that ships with the Platform SDK called *regtlib.exe*. You can run *regtlib.exe* from the directory that contains the type library as follows:

```
regtlib BankInterfaces.tlb
```

The second way is to use the Browse button in the Project References dialog box. The type library does not appear in the list of references until you register it. However, the project references dialog box has a Browse button that lets you locate the .TLB file, and it will register it for you.

Using the Custom Type Library

Once you register the type library, you can include it in your BankServer project through the Project References dialog box. If you are using the previous source code, you should see an entry in the dialog box that reads BankServer Interface Definitions Version 1.0. With the interface definitions in a separate type library, there is no need to have the **IAccount** class. We also can take out the Bank-Constants class because it is now defined in the external type library. All you need to do is implement the **IAccount** interface in the CChecking class and in the CSavings class as you have before. The following code shows the implementation of the **IAccount** interface in the CChecking class:

```
'class CChecking (same code for CSavings)
Implements IAccount
Private m_Balance As Double

Private Sub IAccount_MakeDeposit(ByVal Amount As Double)
    m_Balance = m_Balance + Amount
End Sub

Private Function IAccount_GetBalance() As Double
    IAccount_GetBalance = m_Balance
End Function
```

Let's take an X ray of the project to reveal the GUIDs:

```
'class CChecking
{IID-_CChecking} no methods
{IID-IAccount-}  defined in external type library
{CLSID-CChecking}

'class CSavings
{IID-_CSavings} no methods
{IID-IAccount-}  defined in external type library
{CLSID-CSavings}
```

What would happen if we were to make a change to the IAccount interface? How would it affect the GUIDs in the BankServer project? The only things that VB considers when making decisions about binary compatibility are the public methods in the Visual Basic classes. When you define an interface in an external type library and implement it, the methods are private in the implementation class; they do not affect the versioning for any of the classes in the project. Let's shift back to the client program. Consider the following client code once again:

```
Dim Acct As IAccount
Set Acct = New CChecking
```

The definition for IAccount is now in the custom type library. The way the code is written, however, imposes a requirement on the VB BankServer type library as well. This is because, as you learned in Chapter 4, the New operator assumes that you want the default interface for CChecking (defined in the BankServer project) and requires the CLSID for CChecking (also in the BankServer project) to be known at compile time. If you use the New operator, then, you must set the versioning setting in the BankServer project to Binary Compatibility. This is because New asks for the default interface, and, in order for the client program to continue working, *IID-CChecking* must remain the same.

A much better approach is to change the client code to use *CreateObject* instead, as follows:

```
Dim Acct As IAccount
Set Acct = CreateObject("BankServer.CChecking")
```

The way the client code is written now, you need to include only the custom type library as a reference—the type library in the BankServer project is no longer needed. *CreateObject* does not ask for the default interface; it asks for the IUnknown interface, then calls *QueryInterface* for IDispatch, IPersistStream, and IPersistPropertyBag. It also does not depend on the CLSID; it searches for the CLSID dynamically at runtime. If you use the preceding code, you also do not have to worry about versioning settings in VB. You can leave the versioning setting on Project Compatibility or even No Compatibility. Even if VB were to generate a new GUID for every element, your client programs would continue to work correctly.

Summary

In this chapter, you learned how to version your COM servers. The degree of versioning has to do, to a certain extent, with the type of client you are developing. It is easier to develop for scripting clients because they do not use interfaces directly. That means that you can change your interfaces without breaking existing client code. You can, for example, add optional parameters to methods. You also do not have to worry about versioning settings in your VB project, unless your scripting code uses the <OBJECT> tag with the CLSID property. Then you must ensure that all CLSIDs remain the same.

When vtable-bound clients use your components, you have to be careful that interface definitions do not change. The COM specification says that once an interface has been published, it must not be changed. A change to the interface means that you must change the IID for the interface—in other words, you must rename it.

Visual Basic automatically generates GUIDs for you each time you compile and each time you run your project in the debugger. For this reason, you must tell VB when you wish to keep GUIDs the same and which GUIDs to keep the same. Your options are Binary Compatibility, Project Compatibility, or No Compatibility. If you choose Binary Compatibility, you are telling VB to preserve all GUIDs. Project Compatibility tells VB to preserve only the LIBID and all CLSIDs. No Compatibility tells VB to generate brand new GUIDs for everything.

You learned in this chapter that it is very easy to break Binary Compatibility and that, when you break Binary Compatibility, all IIDs (not just the one for the class that broke compatibility) change. A change to all IIDs means that all your vtable clients must be rebuilt.

To take full control of versioning, it is better to use IDL to define your interfaces. IDL enables you to define an external type library. If you use an external type library plus the *CreateObject* function, the setting you use for versioning in your VB project does not matter.

7

COM+ Applications

Chapter 1 through 6 focused on what is typically known as the core COM architecture. It gave you an inside view of what interfaces look like in memory as well as how in-process servers are activated and deployed and how out-of-process servers differ. Chapter 7 through 10 are all about the COM+ architecture and services. In this chapter we move beyond the core COM architecture and begin exploring what COM+ is.

The COM+ principle is based on the following idea: let Microsoft do it for you. If you think about the success of Visual Basic, a lot of it can be attributed to the vast number of third-party controls. Third-party controls offer a lot of features and enhancements that can be instantly added to your application to create rich user interfaces. With controls, another group of developers creates and maintains the functionality. Imagine how long it would take you to create an application if you had to create your own grid control or your own 3-D charting tool.

Along the same lines, a number of features that would be too difficult to implement by hand are necessary in distributed business applications. These features include group-based (or role-based) security, distributed transactioning, component load balancing, automatic data replication, the creation of client setup programs, synchronization, thread pooling, sharing of resources, and so on. All of these features or services are too time consuming to add by hand, yet they are a critical component of most distributed business applications. It would be nice if all you had to do was focus on the business logic for your middle tier and then add these features later when the client requested them. That is the core idea behind COM+. Microsoft would like for you to focus on the development of your components, then for you to entrust your components to them. They offer an environment in which you can add your components and, without having to recompile your application (at least that's the hope), automatically add the features mentioned earlier with the flick of a switch. In other words, you create your banking components, and later if you wish to add something like role-based security, all you have to do is create security groups and check a checkbox that turns on security checks.

What's the catch? There are several:

- The functionality is designed with the concept that "one size fits all." A lot of the services do not enable you to control the details of how they work.

- Not all the services are available to VB components.

- You cannot create components that work well outside of the COM+ environment as well as inside. You must make a decision about where your components are going to live. The reason is that, in order for your components to use some of the services, you will need to interact with the environment. Your code will therefore expect that environment to exist.

- Adding services to your application consumes resources.

Shortcomings aside, however, Microsoft does provide a lot of features to your application that, if you were to add them by hand, could easily add another year or more to your delivery date. And the best part is that they are all given for free as part of the operating system.

I know as a developer you are most likely dying to write some COM+ code; however, before you can write COM+ code, you must learn about the environment: how to create a COM+ application and how to add your components to it. This chapter is about how to create and administer COM+ applications and what services you gain by using COM+.

Creating a COM+ Application

Let's create a COM+ application to get a feel for the "big picture." COM+ applications are created with a tool that ships with Windows 2000 (in all of its flavors) called Component Services. Component Services is an add-in for the Microsoft Management Console system (MMC). All this means is that it has a very recognizable frontend and works similarly to other MMC add-ins. To run this tool, choose Start → Programs → Administration Tools → Component Services. Figure 7-1 shows the Component Services administration tool.

As the tree-view pane in Figure 7-1 shows, there are three main branches: Component Services, Event Viewer, and Services. The only branch of interest for our discussion is Component Services. If you expand it, you will find a Computers folder and, if you expand that folder, you will find the My Computer entry.

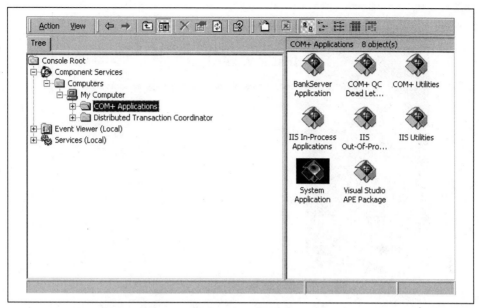

Figure 7-1. The Component Services Administration tool

It is possible to manage multiple Windows 2000 computers from one console. You do this by right-clicking on the Computers folder and choosing New Computer from the pop-up menu, then entering the name of the computer you wish to manage. Chances are that you will not have security privileges to make changes to the other machine's settings. (I will show you how to restrict access to other machines in Chapter 10 when we discuss security.)

 If you right-click on a branch and do not see the menu options I am describing in the pop-up menu, it may be because of a quirk with Component Services. Menu options are based on the item that has the focus. Therefore, you may need to click on the branch first to give it focus, then right-click to see the appropriate pop-up menu.

If you expand the My Computer branch, you will find two folders: COM+ Applications and Distributed Transaction Coordinator. The Distributed Transaction Coordinator (DTC) is a piece of software that enables multiple resource managers (databases, for example) to participate in a single transaction as one unit. You will learn all about the DTC in Chapter 9. If you expand the COM+ Applications branch, you will see a number of COM+ applications. To create a new application, right-click on the COM+ Applications folder and select New → Application. This will invoke the COM Application Install Wizard (see Figure 7-2).

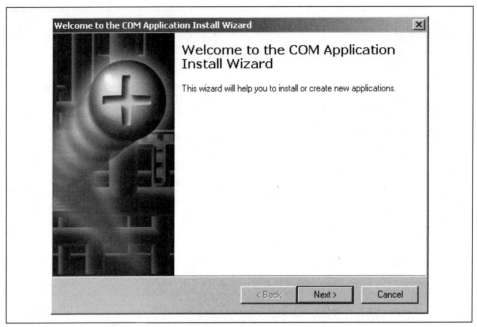

Figure 7-2. The COM Application Install Wizard

If you choose Next, the Wizard will prompt you with two choices: Install Prebuilt Applications or Create an Empty Application (see Figure 7-3).

You use the "Install pre-built application(s)" option to export an already-made application from one server and import it to another. For example, if you have created a COM+ application on your development machine and now want to move it to a production machine, you can export the application from the development machine and import it to the production machine using this option. The export process will create a Microsoft System Installer (MSI) file. The "Install pre-built application(s)" option will let you locate the file and use it to recreate the application on the other machine.

To create a new application, choose "Create an empty application." The wizard will then ask you for a name for the package as well as the activation type, as depicted in Figure 7-4.

The name of the application in Figure 7-4 is not the true name for the application; it is only the readable name. When you create an application, COM+ assigns it a GUID. This GUID is the true name. In fact, if you would like to recreate the application on another machine, you must ensure that the other machine has the same GUID for the application. The only way to do this is to export the application from one machine and import it into the other machine. You may add spaces to the readable application name, as in Bank Server, for example.

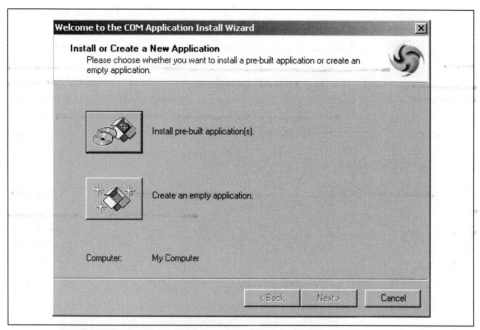

Figure 7-3. Install or Create a new application step in the wizard

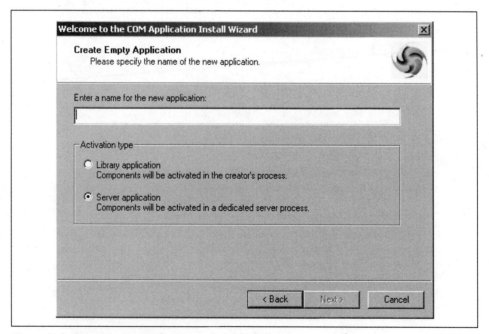

Figure 7-4. Create Empty Application step in the wizard

There are two choices for activation type: Library or Server. This question translates to: do you wish your application to run in-process to its client or out-of-process? If your application is going to be used remotely, you would choose Server. In fact, most of the time you will want to run your application as a server application. The reason is that server applications offer more services than library applications. This is because server applications run within a Microsoft-provided surrogate process, thus Microsoft has more control over the process itself. Library applications run within the process of the client; therefore, they do not get all the services that the Microsoft surrogate process provides (unless the hosting application is a COM+ server application).

One of the limitations of library packages over server packages has to do with security. There are two main types of security checks: application-level and component-level. Application-level security, which is the security that is normally associated with DCOM, cannot be managed in a library application. The client hosting the application would have to set its own security setting either through code or through registry keys.

If you choose to create a library application, this is the last step in the wizard. If you choose a server application and select Next, you will be prompted with the dialog box in Figure 7-5.

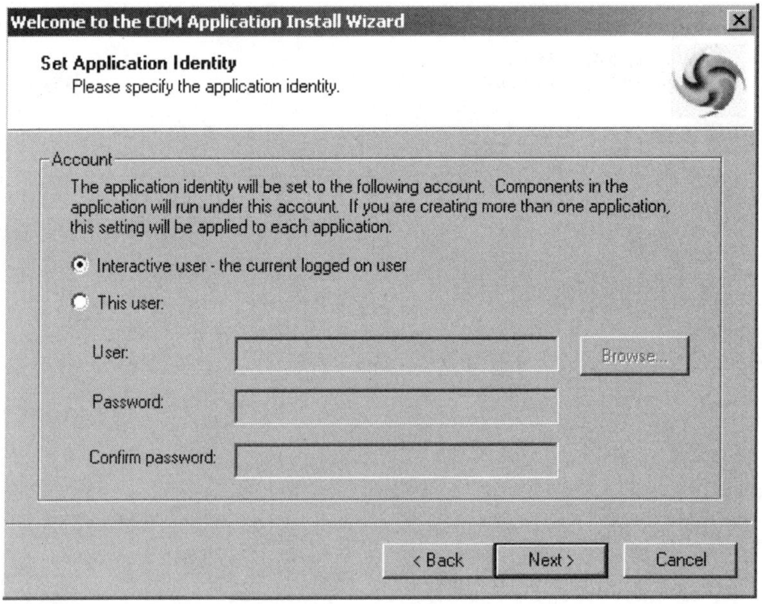

Figure 7-5. Set Application Identity step in the wizard

You will learn more about this option in Chapter 10. However, for now it is sufficient to know that this option asks you for the credentials you would like to use when your process runs. If your application needs to access resources on other machines (or even your own machine), it will use the credentials you specify in this dialog box. Your choices are to run as the interactive user or as a distinguished user (the option labeled "This user"). These options will not mean much until Chapter 10, but for now the choice comes down to whether you are deploying the COM+ application on a production machine or on a development machine. If you are currently developing your application, you will want to choose the default "Interactive user." If you are deploying the application on a production machine, you will want to choose the "This user" option.

Choosing "Interactive user" means that COM+ will use the credentials of whomever is logged in. This means that someone must be logged into the machine. This is why this option is not a good option in a production environment—because someone would have to be logged in for the server components to run. Furthermore, it is hard to predict what resources the application will have access to, since it is based on the access privileges of whomever is logged in at the time. In a production environment you will want to control this by creating an account for the server and using the account as the application identity.

Choosing a distinguished user has its shortcomings when developing. When an application runs under a certain set of credentials (even if the credentials are the same as the user logged in), the application runs in what is called a separate WinStation. Chapter 10 will explain WinStations further. For now, think of a WinStation as a separate virtual machine. Each WinStation gets its own desktop. Only one desktop is visible at a time, and the desktop for the other WinStation is not going to be the desktop you are currently working with. This means that if you display a message box in your program (or show a form), the message box will be displayed in an invisible desktop. Thus, you will hear a beep telling you the message box has appeared, but you will not be able to close it (or see it) because it is in another desktop. Therefore, while developing, make sure to set the identity to the interactive user.

After you choose Next, the wizard will let you know that you are done with the process; click the Finish button to continue. If you look at the list of applications in the Component Services listview pane, you now have a new application folder. If you expand the folder for your application, there are two folders: Components and Roles. The Roles folder has to do with role-based security; this topic is deferred until Chapter 10. The Components folder will contain a list of the components you add to your application.

The downloadable software for this book has a COM server called *TestComponents. DLL.* You will find this server and its source under *Chapter07\TestComponents.*

This server has three COM components called CompA, CompB, and CompC. These components are useful when researching "what if" scenarios. The software also includes a server application. To set up a testing environment, you can recreate the application I used for testing purposes by importing it. You will find the application in the *\Chapter07\TestApplication* folder. This directory contains two files: *TestComponents.MSI* and *TestComponents.CAB*. You can recreate the application in one of two ways:

- You may simply execute the *TestComponents.MSI* file. This will run a simple install program that will recreate the application in your machine. (I did not write the MSI file myself. All I did to give you this file was to export my application—a feature we will explore further later in this chapter.)

- Simply right-click in the COM+ Applications branch and choose New → Application. Instead of creating an empty application, choose "Install pre-built application(s)." The wizard will prompt you with a File Browse dialog box (see Figure 7-6). Choose the MSI file that you've downloaded.

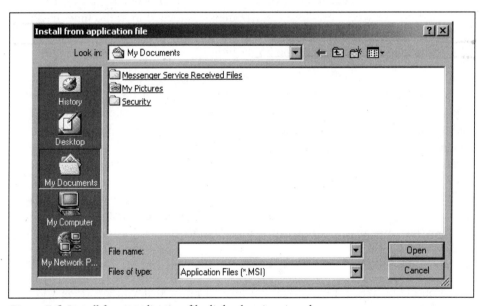

Figure 7-6. Install from application file dialog box in wizard

If you look at the "Files of type" drop-down box, you can see that the dialog box has support for MSI files or PAK files. PAK files are application files that were exported from Microsoft Transaction Server (MTS). If you do not have experience with MTS, think of MTS as the earlier version of COM+ that was available in Windows NT 4.0. COM+ is essentially the next version of MTS. PAK files were text-based scripts with information about the application (in MTS, applications were called packages, and thus the extension PAK). This means that you are able to export a package from MTS and import it into a COM+ server. You cannot do the opposite: take a COM+ application and use it within MTS.

Whether you choose to import it or simply run the MSI file directly, the outcome should be the same—you should have a new COM+ application named Test Components. The Test Components application has three components listed in the Components branch.

Adding Components

COM+ applications host middle-tier COM objects. Your components must be inside an ActiveX DLL (throw away your ActiveX EXEs—they cannot be used inside a COM+ application). The other requirement is that they are compiled as Apartment-threaded. Other languages can use Free-threaded, Apartment-threaded, and Neutral-apartment components. Any language, however, should avoid using the Single-threaded option. As mentioned in the last chapter, this option is available for legacy purposes and is not to be used in COM+ applications. You will learn more about the side effects of using this option when we discuss thread pools in Chapter 8.

You can add your own components to an existing application in one of several ways. The easiest way is to select the Components branch so that the left pane shows the Components branch highlighted, and the right pane shows the contents of the Components branch (which may be nothing). Then you can drag and drop the DLL file that contains the components from Windows Explorer onto the right-hand pane. This will automatically add all the components in the DLL to the package. As soon as you add the component file to the application, COM+ will register your components. If you remove it from the application, COM+ will unregister your components.

You can also add components by right-clicking in the Components tab and choosing New Component. Selecting this option will start the Component Install Wizard (see Figure 7-7).

If you select Next, you will be prompted with three options, as shown in Figure 7-8. The three options are to install a new component, import components already registered, or install new event classes. The third option, event classes, has to do with a new service in COM+ to send event notifications to multiple subscribers. This feature will not be discussed in this book, because the event notification service in COM+ is arguably very limited for building distributed applications. The first and second options seem identical, except for the fact that one is for importing components already registered and the other is for adding components not already registered. However, they are very different options.

Figure 7-7. The Component Install Wizard

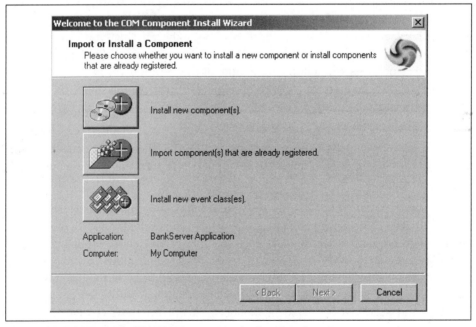

Figure 7-8. Import or Install a Component step in the wizard

"Install new component(s)" enables you to select a DLL and a type library (TLB) file. You cannot add a TLB file without adding a DLL file as well. Adding a TLB file to your application will be beneficial when exporting the application. Selecting this option will add all the components of the DLL to the application. You can later delete from the application the components you do not wish to include. You do this by simply highlighting the component you do not want to include in the application and pressing the Delete key or by right-clicking on the component and choosing the Delete option. You do not have to have all the components in a DLL in the same application. You can, for example, split the components within several applications or simply not add them to any application.

If you wish to take a component from one application and move it to another application, you must use the Move option. Right-click on the component you wish to move and select Move. This option will display the dialog box shown in Figure 7-9.

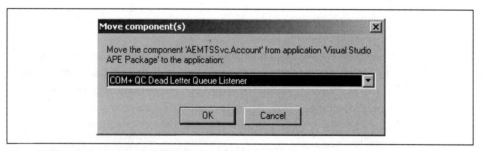

Figure 7-9. Move component(s) dialog box

A component that lives inside a COM+ application is said to be a *configured component*. Adding a component to an application does two things. One, it registers the component with *regsvr32.exe*. In Chapter 4 you learned the registry keys associated with in-process components. These same registry keys must be present for your configured component to work properly. Second, it saves the COM+ configuration information, such as whether the component is transactional. This other information is kept in the COM+ catalog. The COM+ catalog is stored in a series of files with the extension .CLB under *WINNT\Registration*. Microsoft does not publish the format to the catalog files. You can manipulate the catalog through code with the aid of COM+ Administration components. The COM+ Administration components are three COM components that enable you to create and manage applications, the same way that you would through the COM+ Services Administration program. Later in this chapter you will learn how to use these components.

If you remove a component from the application, COM+ will unregister the application.

The next question is: can the information in the registry and the catalog information tion ever get out of sync? For example, is it possible to unregister a component using *regsvr32.exe* while it is part of a COM+ application, and how will it behave then? The answer is, "Yes"; you can unregister the component manually using *regsvr32.exe* with the /u option. The components will remain in the COM+ application, but they will not function properly. When a test client attempts to create an instance of the object, it will receive runtime error 429, "ActiveX Component Can't Create Object." If this is an error you receive while running the client program, you may reregister the components using *regsvr32.exe* without having to read the components to the COM+ application. Also, if you right-click on your application's Components folder and select the Refresh option from the pop-up menu, COM+ will warn you that several components are not registered. If you get this option, you may register the components again using *regsvr32.exe*. If you add the components again using the "Install new component(s)" option, you will lose the existing configuration information.

The "Import component(s) that are already registered" option enables you to add components that are already registered to a COM+ application. This option has, however, a few limitations. There appears to be a bug with it, and, in fact, the documentation in MSDN hints that you should avoid it. If you add a component to an application with the "Import component(s) that are already registered" option, you will not be able to configure some of the attributes in your component. Normally, when you add components using the "Install new component(s)" option or when you drag and drop a DLL onto the application, the COM+ Component Services Administration program lists the interfaces for the component and lists each method in each interface. Interfaces and methods have attributes that you can configure through the Administration program. However, when you add components with the "Import component(s) that are already registered" option, COM+ does not display the interfaces or methods for the component, and you will not be able to configure them. Also, when you export the application, as you will learn later, you will not be able to use the components remotely. Why does this option exist? Good question—it is of no advantage over simply installing the components using the "Install New Component(s)" option.

 Do not use the "Import component(s) that are already registered" option. To add components to your application, use "Install New Component(s)." You may also add components to an application by dragging and dropping the DLL on the application in the Administration program.

A component may be part of only one application. If you want two applications to use a configured component and to have in-process access to it, you must put the component in a library application. The other reason for using a library application has to do with security. Access rights are checked at the application boundary; when you place components in a library application, you define another security checkpoint. Read Chapter 10 for more information.

Deploying COM+ Applications

Once you have created a COM+ application and added components to it, you will want to deploy it. There are two possibilities for deploying your application. You may want to deploy it with the idea of using it on another server. For example, you may be working on a development machine and want to deploy the application on a production machine. Or you may want to deploy the application on a client machine. Whether you seek to deploy your application for server use or for client use, you will want to export it. To export the application, right-click on the application you wish to export and choose Export from the menu. After the wizard's welcome screen, you will see the options depicted in Figure 7-10.

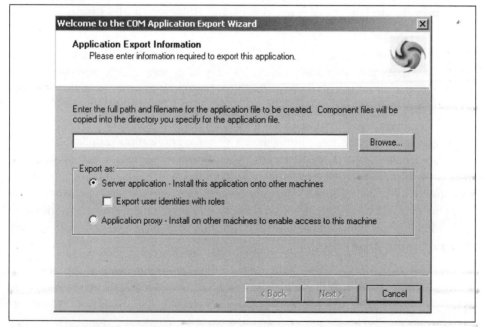

Figure 7-10. Application Export Wizard

Server deployment

When deploying your application for server use, as when you're moving the application from a development environment to a production environment, you'll want to choose the "Server application" option in the wizard. Enter the name and the path for the exported files. The export command will produce two files: a Microsoft System Installer (.MSI) file and a CAB file. The MSI file will have all the components in the package, along with any type library (.TLB) files you may have added. The CAB file contains the MSI file—it is for use in web sites.

You can, for example, create an HTML page that uses the components in client-side scripts. In this case, the components must be installed in the client machine. (Note that ASP pages are server-side scripts, and clients do not require that the components be installed in their machine). As part of the scripts, you can use the CODEBASE tag to tell IE where to find the CAB file that contains the components in case they are not installed in the client's machine and IE needs to install them. The following code shows how to use the CODEBASE tag:

```
<OBJECT ID="checking"
    CLASSID="CLSID:F2D83912-8B32-4820-8E55-A565622EC309"
    CODEBASE="http://www.banksoft.com/download/bankapp.cab
    #Version=1,0,0,0">
</OBJECT>
```

In addition to adding a CODEBASE tag, you must do a few other things in your component to declare it safe for download. However, a discussion of those requirements is beyond the scope of this book.

When you choose to export as a server application, the wizard also gives you the option to export user identities with roles. If you do not check this option, the wizard will export information about the roles but not about the users in the roles. Roles have to do with role-based security, which you will learn about in Chapter 10; however, for now it is sufficient to know that roles are groups of users—you grant access to different levels of your application (application, component, interface, or method) to various roles. Roles may contain individual users or security user groups. When you include identities with roles, and you install the resulting MSI file in the server machine, only system groups such as Administrators, Guests, or Backup Operators will be added to the target roles. Any information pertaining to individual users or to groups you have defined will not be replicated in the target server.

Once you have exported the application and the wizard generates the MSI and CAB files, you copy the MSI file to a temporary directory in the target machine and execute the MSI file from Windows Explorer. You may also use the COM+ Component Services Explorer to import the application. To do so, right-click on the application's folder and choose New → Application. Then choose "Install pre-built application(s)" from the wizard. When you choose the MSI file, you will be asked for the target directory for the components in the CAB file, as seen in Figure 7-11.

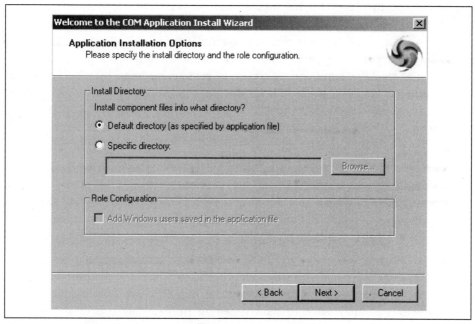

Figure 7-11. Destination directory for components in MSI file

You may choose a specific target directory or use the default directory. The default directory for installing a COM+ application is *Program Files\ComPlus Applications\{Application GUID}*, where *{Application GUID}* is the GUID that COM+ assigned the application when it created it. (If instead of adding the application through COM+ Component Services Explorer, you run the MSI file directly from Windows Explorer, the MSI file will install the application without prompting you for a target directory for your components; in this case, the components will be installed to the default directory.) Regardless of what option you choose, the installer script will copy the components as well as any type library files and register the DLLs in the application.

You can import the application definition only once. If you wish to reimport it, you must first delete the application, then go through the installation process once more.

Client deployment

COM+ is built on top of DCOM. The requirements for a client to run a COM+ application are the same as for a client running a DCOM application. When the client runs its program and tries to create an instance of a COM object that is on another machine, the client may create the component in one of two ways:

- If the client is a scripting client such as VBScript, the client will use the *CreateObject* function. The VBScript version of *CreateObject* has only one parameter, the ProgID. This means that the VBScript client (unlike a VBA client calling the *CreateObject* function) cannot enter the name of the server from which it wishes to run the components. Instead, the VBScript client relies on the registry. In the previous chapter, you learned that it is possible to tell the SCM that the components are on a remote machine by associating the component with an application ID. In the registry you may add an application ID GUID under `HKCR\AppId\{AppId GUID}`. Under the AppID GUID, you may add a `RemoteServerName` subkey. In this subkey, you can specify the name of the remote machine.

When the scripting client calls *CreateObject*, the SCM will first search for an `InprocServer32` subkey (for in-process activation), then for a `LocalServer32` subkey (for out-of-process local activation). If these two keys are missing, it will use the `RemoteServerName` subkey under the AppID GUID key.

- In the case of a VB client, you may use the registry mechanism if you do not specify a second parameter (the computer name) in the `CreateObject` function, or you may use the `New` operator. This may be a good writing style, since otherwise you may have to read a setting from a database or the registry telling you what name to use for the remote machine's name, or you may have to prompt the user. As you will learn shortly, Windows 2000 clients can change the `RemoteServerName` registry key using the COM+ Component Services Explorer.

Regardless of what creation method you use, if you use the *CreateObject* function, you may recall from Chapter 4 that this function calls the function *CLSIDFromProgIdEx* in *OLE32.DLL*. *CLSIDFromProgIdEx* requires that the registry contain a ProgID key with a subkey for the CLSID. What the SCM really needs is the CLSID. If you specify a remote name in *CreateObject*, all that the SCM needs is the CLSID GUID itself. It will not search the local registry for the CLSID, since it knows that the class the client requested is on another machine. However, it will need the ProgID to find out what this CLSID is. If you use `New`, then unfortunately `New` does not let you specify a remote machine, so the SCM will need to find the CLSID in the registry. Once the SCM creates a component remotely, the client code will most likely ask for a certain interface. You may recall from the previous chapter that *CreateObject* asks for `IUnknown`, `IDispatch`, `IPersistStreamInit`, and `IPersistStream-PropertyBag`. All these interfaces are system interfaces. Therefore, you do not need to do anything in the local machine to use these interfaces remotely. However, normally you assign the results of *CreateObject* to a variable, as in the following lines of code:

```
Dim Acct As IAccount
Set Acct = CreateObject("Bankserver.CChecking","RemoteServer1")
```

If you remember from Chapter 3, the left side of the equals sign in the second line of code results in a *QueryInterface* for the **IAccount** interface. When you ask for the **IAccount** interface and the object lives in a different apartment, the interface pointer needs to be exported (or marshaled). The marshaling process invokes the services of the type library marshaler to create a server-side stub for the interface. The SCM on the client machine then needs to import the interface into the apartment of the client program. This process is called unmarshaling the interface. Unmarshaling the interface also requires the services of the type library marshaler to create a proxy in the client's apartment to represent the object. To create this proxy, the type library marshaler requires the interface definition in the type library. In Chapter 6 you learned how to write a custom type library. In the preceding code snippet, you can see that the interface the client needs is the **IAccount** interface, which in Chapter 6 was declared in the *BankServerInterfaces.TLB* file. Thus, the client machine must also have this file present and registered for the client to be able to access and use the remote components.

In conclusion, if you use custom interfaces and the *CreateObject* function, the client machine needs to have the ProgID of the class and the type library file with the interface definitions registered. If you do not code using custom interfaces and instead use the default interface, you would then have to register the type library that VB generates for you as part of the DLL.

What is important for you to realize is that you do not have to have the actual DLLs with the components on the client's machine. In fact, your goal should be for you to have a client setup that does not require the clients to have the actual component DLL files. For this, you want to make sure to add the type library files the client requires as standalone files to the COM+ application. You may recall from the previous section that when you add a component to an application, you may also add a type library file. If you add a type library file, then when you export the application for client setups, the MSI file will not contain the actual components; it will have only the type library files. If you do not include the type library files as part of your application and you rely on the type library that is embedded into the DLL image, the MSI file will contain the components, since that is the only way for the client to have the type library registered on her machine. Therefore, even if you do not use custom interfaces and wish to use only the default interface, you will want to generate a standalone type library file and add this file separately to the application.

You can generate a standalone TLB file using the Remote Server Files option. You will find this option in the Project Properties dialog box under the Component tab. Checking this option makes Visual Basic generate a TLB file in addition to the one embedded into the image.

To generate a client-side setup, you ask COM+ to export the application, but this time instead of choosing a Server Application, you choose an Application Proxy. The Application Proxy is an MSI file that installs the necessary files and enters the necessary registry keys in the client's machine so that you may use the components in the application remotely. The export process, as in the Server export, results in two files: an MSI file and a CAB file. The MSI file contains the TLB files that your application requires. The MSI script installs the files to the *Program Files\ ComPlus Applications*\{`Application GUID`} directory. The installer also adds support for uninstall.

When you install an application proxy on a client machine, the MSI script will enter the registry keys necessary to run the application remotely. Among these keys are the ProgID of the components, the CLSIDs, the interfaces, and the type library registration keys. Interestingly, the MSI script does not bother putting either an `InprocServer32` key or a `LocalServer32` key under CLSID. The script also creates an AppID registry key (the AppID is the application GUID) and assigns each CLSID the AppID GUID. The script adds to the AppID GUID a `RemoteServerName` subkey and points this subkey to the machine from which the application was exported. If the client machine is a Windows 2000 machine, you will find the client application listed as a COM+ application in the COM+ Component Services Explorer. A cool feature in Component Services Explorer is that if you delete the application folder, Component Services Explorer will instantly run the uninstall program for the application.

The difference between an application you create and an application proxy you install, from the user's point of view in the explorer, is that the application proxy has all its settings at the application, interface, and method levels disabled except for one setting in the Activation tab of the application's Properties dialog box: Remote Server Name. This setting originally has the name of the server from which the application was exported. You can change this setting to the name of another server from which you want to run the components. Changing this setting has two effects: it updates the catalog (COM+ persists the information in this field in the catalog), and it changes the value of the `RemoteServerName` subkey under `AppId` to match the value in the catalog. An interesting feature in COM+ is that *CoCreateInstanceEx* has been changed to look for the Remote Server Name in the catalog rather than in the `RemoteServerName` subkey under `AppId`. Therefore, when you are using COM+ proxies, the `RemoteServerName` subkey is ignored for remote activation and instead the value of the Remote Server Name field is used.

If you know that the client will want to create components on a different machine than the one you are using to export the application, you can also change the default Remote Server Name before you export the application. To do so, right-click on the My Computer branch in COM+ Component Services Explorer and click on the Options tab (see Figure 7-12).

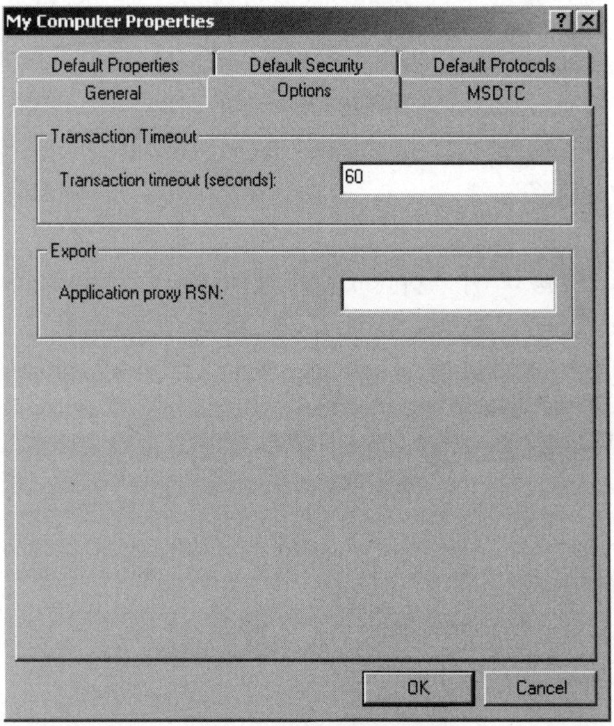

Figure 7-12. The Options tab in the My Computer Properties dialog box

Enter the name of the computer that clients are to use as a default in the Application Proxy RSN field. The application proxy will then have this name for the `Remote Server Name` field. Even though the value of this field under COM+ takes precedence over the `RemoteServerName subkey`, you can always override it by using *CreateObject* and specifying a remote machine name in the second parameter.

The two previous paragraphs describe the way things should work. However, at the time this book was written, there was a problem with this mechanism: if you export an application that has both the type library embedded in the DLL and the standalone type library file, the export procedure generates the following error:

```
Error occurred writing to the application file. Either the path
cannot be accessed or an existing file cannot be overwritten.
Make sure you entered the full path for the application
definition file. The application was not exported.
```

One solution to this problem is to not include the standalone TLB file, but this will result in a client setup MSI file that includes the DLL file. Another solution is to basically force Component Services Explorer to generate the application proxy correctly. To do this, you must have only the standalone TLB file; therefore, you must get rid of the embedded TLB file. You can do this by using the Visual C++ IDE. Do not do this before adding the components to the package, however; do it only when you are in the process of creating the client application proxy.

To remove the embedded TLB from the Visual Basic DLL using the Visual C++ IDE, do the following:

1. Choose File → Open.

2. Change the "Files of type" option in the dialog box to Executable Files.

3. Change the Open As option in the dialog box to Resources.

4. Select the DLL file and click the Open button. You should see the resources for the DLL, as shown in Figure 7-13.

5. Notice that in the resources there is an entry for the type library file. You can delete this entry from the resources, then choose File → Save.

You now have a DLL server without a TLB file. Do not worry about losing the TLB file completely; when you recompile, VB will regenerate it. What this allows you to do, however, is to create the client-side setup without running into problems. Once you generate the application proxy, you will want to recompile the VB DLL to restore it to its normal condition.

Services Overview

Now that you know how to create a COM+ application, add your components to it, and deploy it, you may be wondering about the advantage of having a COM+ application in the first place. The advantage is that adding components to your application enables you to use a number of COM+ services. If you examine the properties of a component in the COM+ Services Administration program (right-click on the component and choose Properties), you will notice that there are a number of services, which are available at different levels: the application, component, interface, and method levels of a COM+ object. The following list briefly

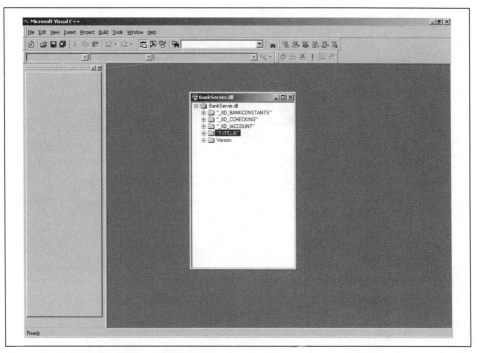

Figure 7-13. Resources for a COM VB DLL

describes each service and indicates whether it is available to library applications—if the item does not read "server applications only," the service is available
for both library applications and server applications:

Process-level security (server applications only)

Helps you set up DCOM security. DCOM security affects how a client gains
access to the application. Without COM+, you would have to configure DCOM
security manually using *dcomcnfg.exe*. You will learn more about this feature
in Chapter 10. (See the dialog box on the left in Figure 7-14.)

Component-level security

Enables you to restrict or grant access to a component's method by assigning
access rights either at the component, interface, or method level based on
roles. Roles are a collection of user accounts or groups. Only users in the role
have access to the element to which you assign the role. You will learn more
about this feature in Chapter 10. (See the dialog on the right in Figure 7-14.)

Activation

Determines whether your application will run out-of-process or in-process. For
out-of-process activation, set the activation setting to Server. For in-process
activation, set it to Library. You will learn about this feature in this chapter and
in the chapters that follow. (See Figure 7-15.)

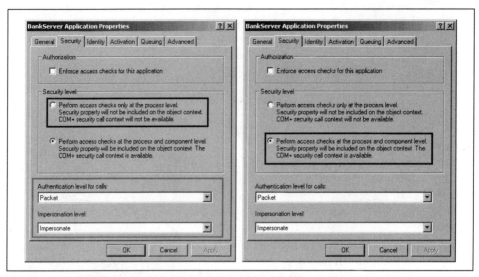

Figure 7-14. Application Security Properties

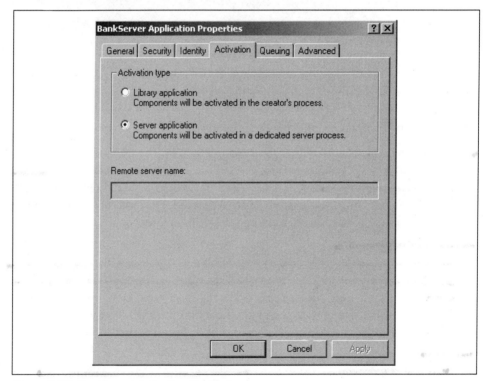

Figure 7-15. Component Activation Properties

Queuing (server applications only)

Enables a client to communicate with the application asynchronously through messaging. This option offers limited Microsoft Message Queue (MSMQ) functionality. MSMQ and queued components are not discussed in this book. (See Figure 7-16.)

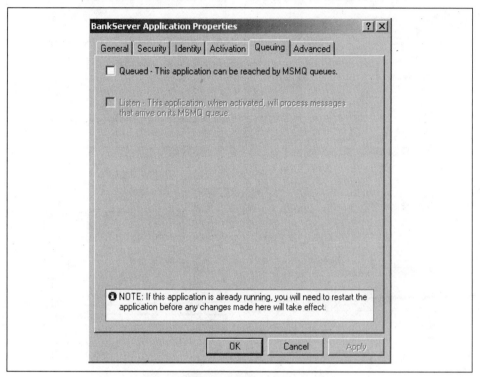

Figure 7-16. Application Queueing Properties

Server Process Shutdown (server applications only)

Controls how long the application runs after all the references to the COM+ objects are released. Starting an out-of-process application takes time. You may decide to continue running the server application for a certain amount of time after all the clients have released references to the objects. This means that if another client creates a component, the application will already be running, thus activation can be faster. You will learn about this feature later in this chapter. (See the dialog on the upper left of Figure 7-17.)

Permission

Controls whether the application settings can be modified and whether the application can be deleted. You will learn about this feature later in this chapter. (See the dialog on the upper right of Figure 7-17.)

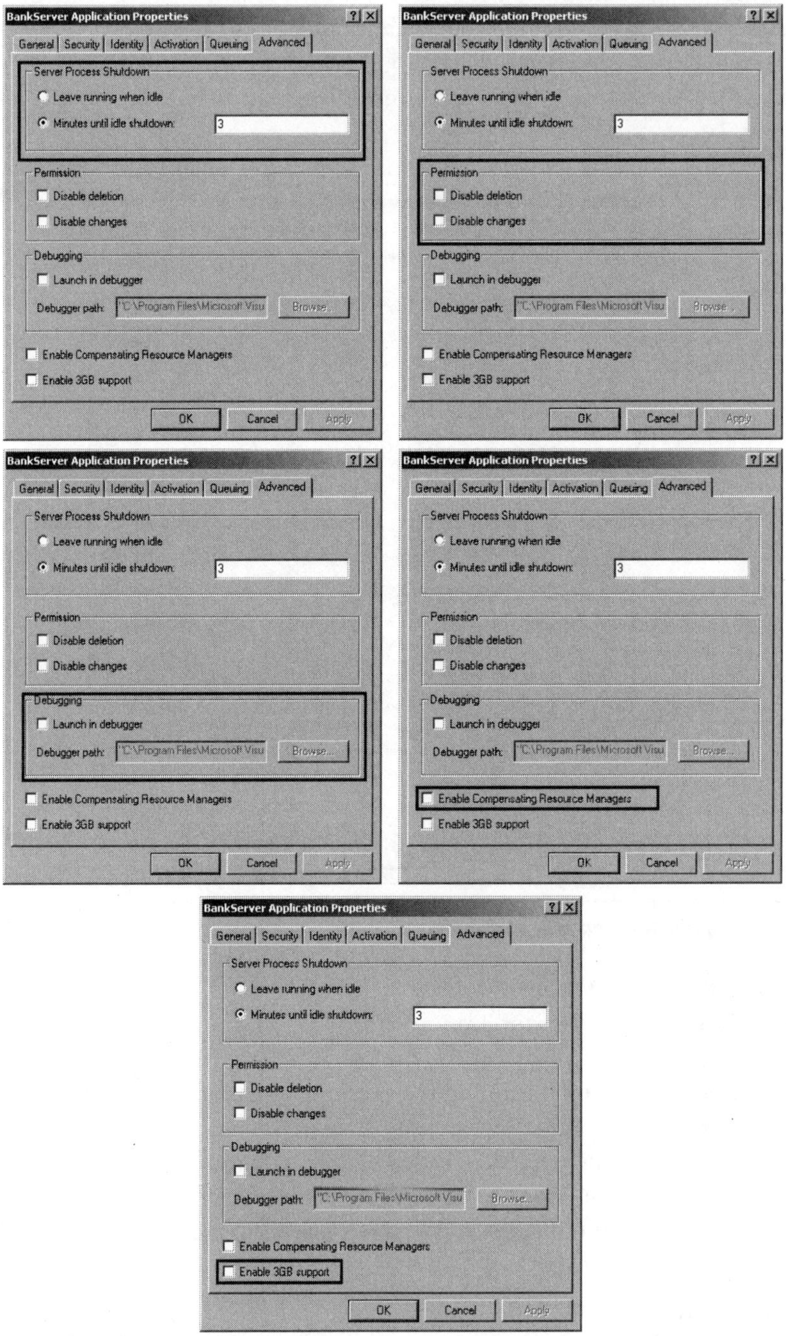

Figure 7-17. Application Advanced Properties

Debugging (server applications only)

Determines whether COM+ automatically launches the Visual C++ debugger (or a debugger of your choice) when the client program requests the creation of one of the components in the application. You will learn about this feature in Chapter 8. (See the dialog in the middle left in Figure 7-17.)

Enable Compensating Resource Managers (server applications only)

Compensating resource managers enable you to involve a custom resource (things like a registry key or a text file) in a distributed transaction. You will learn about this feature in Chapter 9. (See the middle right-hand dialog in Figure 7-17.)

Enable 3GB support (server applications only)

Windows 2000 applications run within a virtual memory space of 4 GB. Of these 4 GB, applications have 2 GB they can use to allocate to applications. It is possible to tell Windows to provide you with 3 GB of application memory, but this means that there is less memory for the operating system. This feature is not covered in this book. (See the bottom dialog in Figure 7-17.)

Start/Stop application (server applications only)

Enables you to start and stop the application from within the administration program. You will learn more about this feature later in this chapter. (See the top dialog in Figure 7-18.)

Export (limited support for library applications—importing in another server option only)

Enables you to recreate the application in another machine or to set up client machines to use the server application remotely. You will learn about this feature later in this chapter. (See the bottom dialog in Figure 7-18.)

Thread pooling

Runs components in different threads. You will learn about this feature later in this chapter.

Distributed transactioning

Uses the services of the Distributed Transaction Coordinator (DTC) to coordinate transactions from multiple database systems. You will learn about this feature in Chapter 9. (See Figure 7-19.)

Object pooling

Enables you to create a pool of objects. COM+ will automatically create a number of instances of a class when the application starts and maintain the pool. You can set the minimum number of instances and a maximum number of instances. You will not learn about this feature in great detail, since it is not available to VB components. (See the upper left-hand dialog in Figure 7-20.)

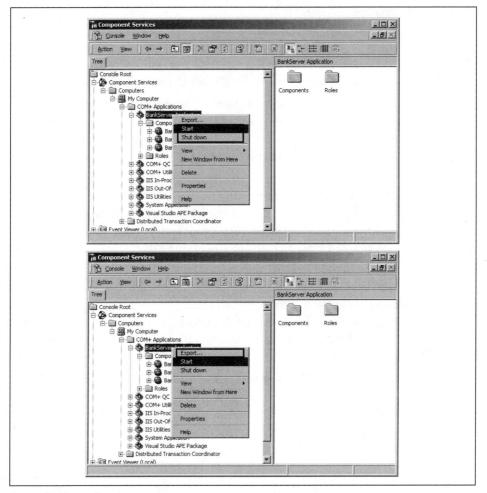

Figure 7-18. Application pop-up menu

Construction string

A string that COM+ passes to a component whenever COM+ creates an instance of the object. You use this string to send the component configuration information. You will learn about this feature in Chapter 8. (See the dialog in the upper right of Figure 7-20.)

Just-in-time activation (JITA)

Delays activation of an object until the first method call into the object. It also adds the ability for an object to be deactivated and destroyed after each method call. This functionality is required when using distributed transactioning. You will learn about this feature in Chapter 9. (See the lower left-hand dialog in Figure 7-20.)

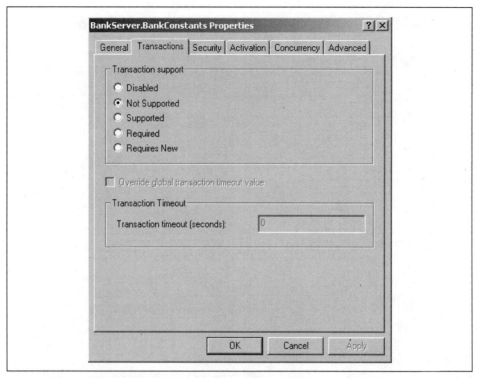

Figure 7-19. Component Transaction Properties

Events and statistics (limited support for library applications—events only)

Notifies you of various events, such as when an object is created, when a thread is added to the pool, and so on. The Administration program can also display statistics, such as how many objects have been created, how long a call has lasted, and so forth. You will learn about this feature in Chapter 8. (See the lower left-hand dialog in Figure 7-20.)

Synchronization

Offers two services in one. It correlates instances of objects that were created from a single call from a certain client. These objects act as one entity. Synchronization also blocks other clients and other threads from making calls into objects that are grouped together. You will learn about this feature later in this chapter. (See Figure 7-21.)

COM+ Administration Components

It is possible to administer a COM+ application through code. The code can be in a C++ client, a VB client, or even a VBScript or JavaScript client. To administer COM+ applications through code, you use the COM+ Administration Components.

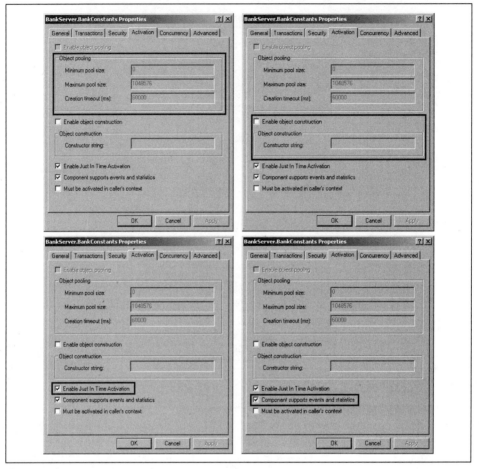

Figure 7-20. Component Activation Properties

The first step in using these components in a VB client program is to reference the type library: choose Project → References and then select COM+ 1.0 Admin Type Library from the dialog box.

The type library contains definitions of three coclasses: COMAdminCatalog, COMAdminCatalogCollection, and COMAdminCatalogObject. Each of these coclasses has a default interface: ICOMAdminCatalog, ICatalogCollection, and ICatalogObject, respectively. COMAdminCatalog is the main component—this is the component you use to accomplish most of the administrative tasks. From COMAdminCatalog, you can request certain collections. When you ask for a collection through the GetCollection method in ICOMAdminCatalog, it returns a reference to an ICatalogCollection interface (the default interface of COMAdminCatalogCollection). You can then use the ICatalogCollection interface to navigate through the collection. To use a certain item in the collection, you

Figure 7-21. Component Synchronization Properties

call the Item method in the `ICatalogCollection` interface; that method returns a reference to the `ICatalogObject` interface. You can then use the `ICatalog-Object` interface to set properties for an individual item in the collection.

Creating a COM+ Application

The following code fragment first deletes a COM+ application named BankServer if it already exists, then creates the application:

```
Dim cat As ICOMAdminCatalog
Set cat = New COMAdminCatalog

'connect to the catalog
Dim AppColl As Object 'ICatalogCollection
Set AppColl = cat.GetCollection("Applications")

'define an array of variants to use in the PopulateByKey function
Dim Keys(0 To 0) As Variant
Keys(0) = "{2EA3007E-7B96-450a-B37A-FFD7C621C6CA}"
Call AppColl.PopulateByKey(Keys)

Dim BankServerApp As ICatalogObject

'if the application already exists
If AppColl.Count > 0 Then
    '...change deleteable property so that we can delete it
    Set BankServerApp = AppColl.Item(0)
    BankServerApp.Value("Deleteable") = True
```

```
      Call AppColl.SaveChanges
      '...delete it
      Call AppColl.Remove(0)
      Call AppColl.SaveChanges
End If

'add a new application
Set BankServerApp = AppColl.Add

'set the application properties
BankServerApp.Value("ID") = "{2EA3007E-7B96-450a-B37A-FFD7C621C6CA}"
BankServerApp.Value("Name") = "BankServer"
BankServerApp.Value("Description") = "Bank Server Application"
BankServerApp.Value("Activation") = COMAdminActivationLocal
BankServerApp.Value("Changeable") = False
BankServerApp.Value("Deleteable") = False
AppColl.SaveChanges
```

This code has several points of interest. It first uses the **New** keyword to create a catalog object. Then it asks the catalog object for the Applications collection. (You can get a complete list of all the collections you can ask for by searching MSDN for the article titled "Administration Collections.") The GetCollection method returns the **IDispatch** interface. Normally you would just *QI* for **ICatalogCollection** (**Dim AppColl As ICatalogCollection**). However, I have declared my variable as Object. The reason for this is that I want to use the PopulateByKey method in the collection object. However, this method was defined incorrectly. The parameter was declared as an **[in]** SafeArray parameter, and SafeArrays have to be declared as **[in,out] SafeArray** * in order to use them from a VB client with vtable binding. The workaround is to use the **IDispatch** interface instead.

Once the code obtains the catalog collection object, it uses the PopulateByKey method to trim the items in the collection to only the item we are interested in. The MSDN documentation also shows you that each collection has a key associated with it. The PopulateByKey method takes as a parameter an array of Variant values containing the keys to filter by. It works like the ADO Recordset object's Filter method, in the sense that it does not return a value; it simply applies a filter to the result set so that as you navigate through it, you see only items that meet the criteria. The documentation for the Applications collection indicates that the unique key for an application is the Application ID (or Application GUID), so we filter the collection by the Application GUID. After calling this method, the collection will have either no items (if the application has never been added) or a single item (if the application has already been added). You can check whether the application already exists by examining the Count property of the AppColl object.

If the application is already in the collection, the script deletes it. To delete it, however, you have to change the Deletable setting to **True** first in the event that its Deletable setting has been set to **False** (as the portion of this code that creates and saves the application does). The code does this in the following lines:

```
BankServerApp.Value("Deleteable") = True
Call AppColl.SaveChanges
```

Notice that changes to a property in an item or in a collection do not take effect immediately. You have to call the collection object's SaveChanges method before the change takes place. Thus, deleting the application in this case is a two-step process: first you change the Deletable property to **True** and call SaveChanges; then you delete the application with the following lines of code:

```
Call AppColl.Remove(0)
Call AppColl.SaveChanges
```

After deleting the application if it already exists, the code adds a new application. Notice from the code that when you add an application using the COM+ Admin objects, you can assign the application an Application GUID instead of letting COM+ generate one automatically. This is useful because the true name of the application is its GUID. Remember that if the application is deployed on two machines, the system knows it is the same application by the Application GUID. Therefore, it is to your advantage to keep this GUID the same. You can do this through code, as shown in the following portion of the previous code fragment:

```
Set BankServerApp = AppColl.Add
BankServerApp.Value("ID") = "{2EA3007E-7B96-450a-B37A-FFD7C621C6CA}"
BankServerApp.Value("Name") = "BankServer"
BankServerApp.Value("Description") = "Bank Server Application"
BankServerApp.Value("Activation") = COMAdminActivationLocal
BankServerApp.Value("Changeable") = False
BankServerApp.Value("Deleteable") = False
AppColl.SaveChanges
```

The code first creates a new item in the collection using the Add method. This mechanism is a little different than the Add method in a native VB collection. The Add method does not accept any parameters; it simply returns a brand new COMAdminCatalogObject object. To set properties for this object, use the Value property. The Value property has one parameter—the property you want to set. Then you set the property equal to the value you wish to set. For example, the code sets the ID (or Application GUID) to a specific GUID, {2EA3007E-7B96-450a-B37A-FFD7C621C6CA}. (For your own application, you can generate this GUID using GUIDGEN, as you learned in Chapter 6.) As before, you must call SaveChanges for the changes to take effect.

Adding Components and Setting Their Properties

The following code builds on the previous code sample. It first installs new components to an application. Not all the components in the DLL will be added to the application, so the code deletes the components that should not be there. The code then shows how to configure the components.

```
'Change changeable property so that we can install new components
BankServerApp.Value("Changeable") = True
AppColl.SaveChanges

'Install the components in a DLL to the application
Call cat.InstallComponent("{2EA3007E-7B96-450a-B37A-FFD7C621C6CA}", _
                          "C:\TestComponents\TestComponents.dll", _
                          "", _
                          "")

'Remove any components that should not be there
Dim BankComponents As Object 'ICatalogCollection
'...first get the Components collection
Set BankComponents = AppColl.GetCollection("Components", _
                          "{2EA3007E-7B96-450a-B37A-FFD7C621C6CA}")
Call BankComponents.PopulateByKey(Array( _
                          "{9EE44A1F-F4A6-46A9-858B-BB2AA8967BC2}"))
'...then remove the item and save changes
Call BankComponents.Remove(0)
Call BankComponents.SaveChanges

Call BankComponents.Populate
Dim Component As ICatalogObject
'Navigate through all components and change properties
For Each Component In BankComponents
    Component.Value("Synchronization") = COMAdminSynchronizationRequired
    Component.Value("Transaction") = COMAdminTransactionRequired
Next

'Save changes does not have to be called each time a change
'is made. In this case we are calling it after we have made
'all the changes.
Call BankComponents.SaveChanges

'Set the changeable property back to False
BankServerApp.Value("Changeable") = False
AppColl.SaveChanges
```

The code first changes the Changeable property to **True** so that we can make modifications to the application. As before, you have to call the SaveChanges method in the collection in order for the changes to take effect. Next, the code calls the InstallComponent method in the catalog object. This method is equivalent to the Install New Component option in the Add New Components wizard. Its first parameter can be the application name or the application GUID. The application GUID is the only way to guarantee uniqueness, since it is possible to have two applications with the same readable name but with different GUIDs. The second parameter is the name of the DLL. The third parameter is the name of the standalone TLB file. If you are using only the TLB file embedded in the DLL, you can set this parameter to an empty string. The fourth parameter is for use with C++ components—it is the path to a proxy/stub DLL. Your VB components will use the type library marshaler, só you can send it an empty string for this parameter as well.

After adding the components, the code removes any unwanted components. In our example, we have one component that should not be configured. To remove the component, you first need to get the Components collection for the application. This is not very straightforward—instead of getting the collection from the catalog object, you must get the collection from the Applications collection object. If you read the MSDN collection documentation, you find out that the Components collection is available only through the Applications collection. Therefore, you must call GetCollection from the AppColl object. The GetCollection method in the `ICatalogCollection` interface has two parameters. The first is the name of the collection, which in this case is Components. The second is the ID or name of the application whose components you wish to obtain. Once the code obtains the components in the collection, it uses the PopulateByKey method to retrieve a reference to the component we need to remove. The code uses the CLSID of the component as the parameter in PopulateByKey. Notice from the code that the parameter type is an array of Variants, so the code uses the *Array* function (the function produces a variant array from several elements) to save time. After finding the item, the code simply calls Remove followed by SaveChanges.

The final task in the code is to go through each item and set a few properties. In this case, we are changing the Synchronization property and the Transaction property. Before you are able to loop though the remaining components in the application, you must remove the filter that resulted from the call to PopulateByKey; you do this by calling the Populate method in the collection object.

One more thing to realize is that you do not have to call SaveChanges each time you change a property. The collection remembers all the changes you make. Then when you call SaveChanges, the collection saves all the changes. The COM+ Administration objects use transactions to ensure that either all the changes are committed or none of them is. If a problem occurs while SaveChanges is taking place, none of the changes will be saved.

Exporting and Importing an Application

So far you have learned how to create an application, how to add components to it, and how to configure the components in the application. The last major task is to export the application, connect to a remote server, and install the application.

You can use the following code, for example, to export an application from your development machine to a production machine:

```
Call cat.ExportApplication("{2EA3007E-7B96-450a-B37A-FFD7C621C6CA}", _
                            "C:\BankServer.MSI", _
                            COMAdminExportForceOverwriteOfFiles)

Call FileCopy("C:\BankServer.MSI", "\\MOJICA\CDRIVE\BankServer.MSI")

Call cat.Connect("\\MOJICA")
Set AppColl = cat.GetCollection("Applications")

Keys(0) = "{2EA3007E-7B96-450a-B37A-FFD7C621C6CA}"
Call AppColl.PopulateByKey(Keys)

If AppColl.Count > 0 Then
    Set BankServerApp = AppColl.Item(0)
    BankServerApp.Value("Deleteable") = True
    Call AppColl.SaveChanges
    Call AppColl.Remove(0)
    Call AppColl.SaveChanges
End If

Call cat.InstallApplication("C:\BankServer.MSI", _
                            bstrUserId:="buck", _
                            bstrPassword:="chloe")
```

The first step is to produce the MSI file. You do so by calling the Export-Application method in the catalog object. The first parameter in the Export-Application method is the application name or application GUID. The second parameter is the name of the exported file and path. The third parameter tells the ExportApplication method whether you want to export a server application or a proxy application (for a complete list of options, see the MSDN documentation).

After you produce the MSI file, you must copy the MSI file to the machine on which you wish to install it. This is because the InstallApplication method, which you are going to use later to import the application on the other server, interprets the path to the application as a local directory. The code uses the VB *FileCopy* function to copy the file to the other server. You can then connect to the catalog in the remote machine using the Connect method of the COMAdminCatalog object, passing the DNS, IP Address, or NetBios name of the server. Once you connect to another catalog, all the methods you call will do their job on the remote catalog instead of the local catalog. The code, like before, checks that the application does not exist; if it does, it deletes it. The last step is to import the application. To do so, you must use the InstallApplication method in the COMAdminCatalog object. The Install method takes as a parameter the path to the MSI file. You can optionally send in a set of credentials to use to install the application in case the System package does not allow everyone to make changes (more on this in Chapter 9).

Summary

In this chapter, you learned how to create COM+ applications using both COM+ Services and COM+ Administration Components. COM+ applications are packages that hold configuration settings for a group of components. These settings are known as services; a component that lives in a COM+ application is called a configured component. The goal of configured components is to provide functionality to your application without your having to add code. The dream is that you will be able to turn functionality on and off by simply changing a few settings in the COM+ Component Services Explorer. This may be true at some level, but the reality of the environment is that, to take advantage of some of the services, you have to code your components in certain ways. In fact, in the next chapter, you will learn how to interact with the environment. The bottom line is that for this code to work, your components expect to be running in the COM+ environment.

COM+ applications fall into two main categories: server applications and library applications. Server applications run out-of-process to the client. Library applications run in the same address space as the client. You use library applications when you want to share a component among two or more applications and you want the components to run in-process to the applications.

This chapter also focused on deploying the application for both server and client use. One of the main points in this chapter is that, in addition to your components, you can add standalone TLB files to a COM+ application. The reason you may want to do this is because it enables you to create client-side application proxies that do not require the DLL containing your components to be present and registered in the client machine. However, there appears to be a problem with the export process in COM+ that does not let this feature work if you add a standalone TLB file and the DLL contains an embedded TLB file as a resource. A workaround is to temporarily delete the TLB embedded in the DLL when creating the application proxy. You can do this using the VC++ IDE, viewing the DLL's resources, deleting the TLB, and saving the changes to the DLL. After creating the application proxy, you can restore the DLL to normal by recompiling it.

In the next chapter, you'll learn about how to write code that can interact with the COM+ architecture. You are also going to learn about the COM+ architecture itself.

8

Writing and Debugging COM+ Code

In the last chapter you learned how to create a COM+ application and how to administer it. You also learned about some of the services COM+ offers. Now, let's turn our attention to writing code for use in COM+ components to use those services. As I alluded to earlier, it is not really possible to develop components that work well inside COM+ and outside COM+. In order to take advantage of some of the COM+ services, you will want to code your components differently. Coding your components differently means that your component will expect the COM+ environment to exist.

To write COM+ components that interact with the COM+ environment, you must reference the COM+ Services Type Library in your project (Project → References and then select the COM+ Services Type Library from the listbox). There are a number of interfaces, classes, user-defined types, and enumerated types in the type library. In this section you will learn about only a few of the objects. You will get a better taste for the rest of the objects and interfaces in the type library as we discuss each service throughout the book.

Before you can write COM+ code, however, you must learn about the COM+ architecture.

COM+ Architecture

So far, you have learned how to manage applications at a high level through the Component Services Administration program or through code using the COM+ Administration Components. In this section, you will learn about how COM+ applications work internally.

Server applications run within a surrogate process. You may recall from Chapter 5 that a surrogate process is a process that enables you to run in-process components in an out-of-process fashion. The name of the surrogate process is *DllHost.exe*. Library applications run differently. They do not need *DllHost.exe* because they run in the process of the client.

A client creating a COM+ component has no idea whether the component is in-process, out-of-process on the same machine, out-of-process on a remote machine, configured, or nonconfigured. The client always creates the component using *CreateObject* or New. The call is translated into *CoCreateInstance* or *CoCreateInstanceEx*, as you learned in Chapter 4. *CoCreateInstance* and *CoCreateInstanceEx* are API calls in *OLE32.DLL*.

The activation process is the same as without COM+ from the client's point of view. From the server standpoint, the story is a little different. *OLE32.DLL* must ensure that the services you have requested are started automatically when the object is created. What's more, some services require that COM+ monitor methods before execution, after execution, or both before and after.

For services to work, COM+ defines several boundaries. In Chapter 5, you learned about one of these boundaries: the apartment. The apartment is a boundary that separates objects that do not have the same threading requirements. Objects with the same threading requirements can be in the same apartment; objects with different threading requirements must live in different apartments. Other services require objects to live in different boundaries. Objects that have the same service requirements can live within the same boundary; objects that have different requirements must live outside the boundary.

Context

Every COM object (whether it is configured or not) lives in a *context* under Windows 2000. Contexts are the lowest-level living space or boundary for a component. COM+ uses the context to monitor method calls before and after they are executed. When you turn on a service for a configured component that requires COM+ to monitor method calls from the client either before the call takes place, after the call takes place, or both, COM+ places that configured component in its own context. If an object does not have requirements for method-level monitoring, then the component will live in the same context as its creator. Calls from one context to another are slightly more expensive in performance than calls made to a component directly; they also consume more memory.

When COM+ places an object into its own context, calls to the object have to go through a lightweight proxy—COM+ gives the client a lightweight proxy instead of a direct reference to the object. The purpose of the proxy is to enable COM+ to monitor the calls to the object and start or enforce the service the author of the component specified. (I refer to this proxy as a lightweight proxy because it does not consume as much memory as a proxy between threads.) The services that require this type of monitoring are the following:

- At the application level (in the Security tab), choosing to check access rights at both the application and the component levels. This service requires COM+ to place every instance of every object in the application in its own context regardless of any other settings.

- At the interface level (in the Transactions tab), turning on distributed transactioning support. An object that has this option set to anything other than Disabled requires the use of another service called Just-in-time activation (or JITA). As you will see in the next bullet, JITA requires the object to have its own context.

- At the interface level (in the Activation tab), using JITA. Just-in-time activation means that COM will let you know when your object receives its first method call. It also enables your object to be destroyed and deactivated after a method call. This means that COM+ must monitor the method calls; thus, COM+ must place the object in its own context. You will learn a lot about JITA in the next chapter.

- At the interface level (in the Activation tab), choosing "Component supports events and statistics." This service requires that the object live in its own context and is useful for monitoring what is happening in your application.

- At the interface level (in the Concurrency tab), choosing a synchronization option other than Disabled that is not compatible with the creator's synchronization state. Suppose that object A creates object B; if object A is set to Required or Requires New, object B will be in the same context only if B is set to Required or Supported. If object A is set to Not Supported, object B will be in the same context as A only if object B is set to Not Supported or Supported. If object A is set to Supported, object B will share a context with object A if it is set to Supported, Not Supported, or Required. To guarantee that the two end up in the same context, set object B to Disabled.

You can ensure that an object will be in the same context as its creator by turning off the preceding services. This means that you have to set the application's security level to "Perform access checks only at the application level," and disable the distributed transactioning property, JITA support, events and statistics reporting, and synchronization support. If you do, COM+ places the object in the context space of its creator. The advantage of doing this is that access to the component is direct; it is, therefore, faster and requires less memory.

In fact, COM+ provides a checkbox under the component's Activation tab called "Must be activated in caller's context." This setting ensures that your object can be created only in the creator's context space. Turning on this option does not automatically cause COM+ to place the object in its creator's context. It generates a runtime error only if COM+ was unable to place the object in the context of its creator. The runtime error is -2147467228 (&H8000424), "The specified activation could not occur in the client's context as specified." You cannot set this option on the first component that the client will create, only on components that follow. In fact, if you do not need any of the previous features, this is a way to guarantee that the object is not created directly by the client program. An object that is created directly by the client is called the root object. Objects that are created from the root object are known as secondary objects. COM+ always places nonconfigured components in the context space of their creator as long as they have compatible threading models.

What does it mean for two objects to share the same context other than that communication between the objects happens without a proxy in the middle? It means that you have to be very careful. For example, if you have multiple objects inside the same context, you should never give the client access to more than one of the objects—the results are hard to predict.

When a client creates an object, that object lives in a context. If the client creates a second instance of the object, COM+ puts the object in another context even if the objects are in a library application and even if the objects end up in the same thread as the client's thread. Because the client thread itself is not inside a context, each activation request results in the object living in its own context. For two objects to end up in the same context, one object must create the other. Therefore, for the client to have access to more than one object, one of the objects inside the context must give the client a reference to another object in the context.

Here is an example of what can happen when a client obtains a reference to more than one object in the same context. Let's say that CompA and CompB both have the same interface, `ITestComponent`. Let's say also that CompA is set to use JITA. The details of JITA will be explained in Chapter 9; for now it is sufficient to know that, with JITA, you can enable another feature at the method level called "Automatically deactivate this object when the method returns." Suppose we turn on this feature on the Method1 method in the `ITestComponent` interface. This means that after the client makes a call into Method1 through CompA, COM+ will automatically destroy the object. Then, suppose the client creates CompA. CompA creates CompB and gives the client a reference to CompB so that the client has a reference to both CompA and CompB. Now the client makes a call to Method1 through CompB. The result is that COM+ destroys the instance of CompA. This is because the proxy the client receives is a proxy to a context. The rules of the context are to destroy CompA when there is a call to Method1 through the `ITestComponent` interface. A call through the proxy for Method1 satisfies the deactivation rule regardless of what object the client is talking through. However, to the client, this is not the expected behavior. The client expects the object to be destroyed only when the call is being made through CompA, as would be the case if CompB had its own context. The bottom line is that the client should not have references to multiple components within a context.

Apartments (Revisited)

A group of contexts may share a single apartment. The first decision that COM+ makes is whether the object requires its own context. The second decision is whether the object requires a different apartment. You learned about apartments in Chapter 5. Apartments are used to separate objects with different threading requirements. An object is always part of some context. Two objects may share a context, but there can never be an object without a context boundary. Along the same lines, a context may never be part of two different apartments. If two objects are in different apartments, then by definition they are in different contexts.

You may have realized from the previous discussion that it is possible to have interception through a proxy in COM+ even when the objects are in the same apartment, if the objects end up in different contexts. But what if the objects need to be in different apartments and at the same time require their own context because of the services mentioned earlier? COM+ will never give you a proxy to a proxy. This means that if the component has a requirement for its own context because it is using one of the services described before and the object is also being used from a different apartment, such as when the object runs out-of-process from the client, COM+ creates a single proxy that handles both services. This is a heavyweight proxy because it consumes more memory and more resources than a cross-context–only proxy.

In Chapter 5, you learned that one reason for apartments was to offer protection from concurrency to non–thread-safe components. This is accomplished by posting method calls as windows messages to a hidden window. (You can break this mechanism by doing something that will process messages while executing a method, like calling *DoEvents*, displaying a message box, or displaying a form.) On the other hand, in the case of VB objects, global variables are only global per apartment. This means that you cannot share state using global variables across apartments. It is beneficial to group all the objects that belong to a single call from a client in the same thread and other objects that belong to other clients in a different thread. In that way, all clients can make concurrent calls, and all the objects working on behalf of a client can share state. COM+ accomplishes this with the use of an STA pool. You will learn about the STA pool after you learn about a new concurrency model called the activity.

Activities

An *activity* is a logical boundary that has two purposes. (When I say a logical boundary, I mean that the activity is a piece of data, a GUID in fact, that is propagated across calls, as opposed to a more physical boundary like a thread or a process.) The first purpose for the activity is to tell COM+ what objects belong to a single call from a single client. By placing instances of objects in an activity, COM+ knows what objects are acting on behalf of a client. For example, in Chapter 9 when we talk about transactions, you will learn that for objects to vote on the outcome of the same transaction, they must be in the same activity. The second purpose for the activity is protection from concurrency.

In Chapter 5, you learned that one of the purposes for the STA was to prevent concurrent calls. An activity has the same goal. If you recall, MTA objects written in C++ did not have protection from concurrency in plain COM. The activity in COM+ was designed to add protection from concurrent access to MTA objects. It was also designed to add protection from concurrency to objects of multiple apartment types. This means that the activity can group together MTA objects, STA objects, and even TNA objects that are working on behalf of a client and protect the group from multiple threads using the objects at the same time.

When a client creates an object that is marked as requiring synchronization (protection from concurrent access from multiple threads), COM+ creates an activity and assigns the object to the activity. COM+ refers to each activity by a GUID. Each creation request results in a different activity, which means that if a client creates two instances of the same object, each object instance will be in a different activity. The only way for other objects to be part of the same activity is for an object already inside the activity to create the object. The object that the client creates is known as the root object. Any object the root object creates is known as a secondary object. If the secondary object has the same synchronization requirements as the root object, the secondary object will be part of the same activity. Figure 8-1 shows the different synchronization settings for an object.

COM+ begins an activity when there is a request for the creation of an object with its synchronization property set to Required or Requires New. For a secondary object to be in the same activity, the object's synchronization property must be set to Supported or Required. If the synchronization property for the secondary object is marked to Requires New, then COM+ will begin a new activity. When an object is marked as synchronization Supported, then it will be part of an activity only when an object already in the activity creates it. If an object outside the activity creates the secondary object, then it will not be part of the activity.

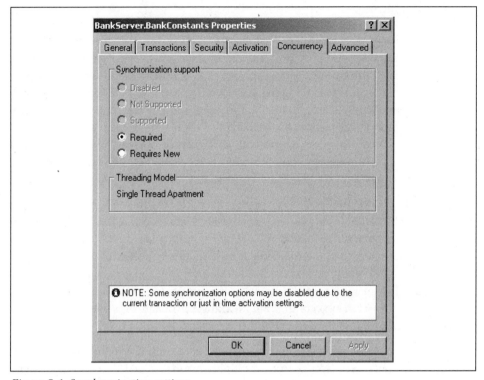

Figure 8-1. Synchronization settings

There is a subtle difference between the Not Supported option and the Disabled option. Not Supported means that the object will never be part of the activity. Disabled tells COM to ignore this setting altogether. If an object already in the activity creates an object with synchronization Disabled and COM+ can place the object in the same context as its creator, then the object will be part of the activity—remember they must be in the same context, which means all those settings discussed earlier must be turned off. The Disabled property has been added so that the object may share a context with its creator if possible. If the object is marked as synchronization Not Supported, COM+ will always place the object in its own context outside of the activity regardless of the setting of its creator.

Activities group contexts; a context belongs to only one activity (or to no activity). There is no direct relationship between an activity and an apartment unless the activity involves STA objects. In the case of STA objects, activities are mapped to apartments. However, an activity may encompass more than one apartment; an activity may include an apartment from one server application and an apartment from another server application. In fact, the activity may span multiple machines. Think of an activity as a piece of data—a GUID that gets propagated through a single call chain made on behalf of a single client.

Figure 8-2 illustrates the different boundaries and how they relate to one another. In Chapter 9 you will also learn about another boundary known as transaction streams.

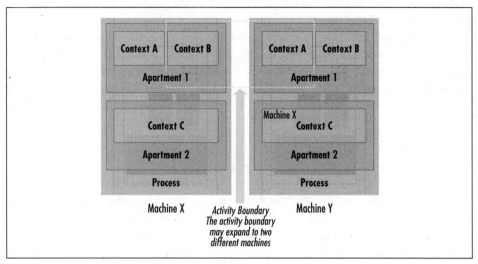

Figure 8-2. Contexts, apartments, and activities

Activity lock mechanism

An activity prevents multiple threads from accessing objects in the activity concurrently. It does this by implementing an activity lock. The activity lock code controls access to the activity by using a semaphore. The semaphore is created when the activity is created; the semaphore is created with an initial count of 1 and a limit of 1. COM+ assigns each thread that calls *CoInitialize[Ex]* a causality ID. (You may recall from previous chapters that *CoInitialize[Ex]* is a function in *OLE32.DLL* that every thread must call before creating or using COM objects.) When the thread makes a call, COM+ propagates the causality ID through the call chain. If a method call results in another method call, the causality ID is propagated through that call as well. You can find the causality ID by using the function *CoGetCurrentLogicalThreadId* within a function. The following code has the declaration for the *CoGetCurrentLogicalThreadId* function. The function returns the causality ID GUID. Since the function returns a GUID, and a GUID is not a VB native type, you must also declare the GUID type as shown:

```
Private Type VBGUID
    Data1 As Long
    Data2 As Integer
    Data3 As Integer
    Data4(0 To 7) As Byte
End Type

Private Declare Function CoGetCurrentLogicalThreadId Lib "ole32.dll" ( _
        ByRef guid As VBGUID) As Long
```

COM+ places a lock on the activity so that only one causality may enter the activity at a time. When a call enters the activity, the activity lock code examines the causality ID. If there are no causalities yet in the activity, then the semaphore count goes down by 1. When another causality (from a second thread, for example) enters the activity, the activity lock code calls *CoWaitForMultipleHandles* and tells the function to wait for the semaphore. The second client will be blocked at that point until the first call releases the semaphore. When the first call completes, the activity lock code releases the semaphore. The second causality is then allowed to enter.

CoWaitForMultipleHandles is a new COM+ synchronization function that can recognize if the call is being made from within an MTA or an STA. In the case of an MTA, *CoWaitForMultipleHandles* simply blocks the thread until the semaphore is available. In the case of an STA, *CoWaitForMultipleHandles* enters a window message loop, which enables the STA thread to continue processing messages. Whether the activity involves MTA objects, STA objects, TNA objects, or a mixture of all three, the code was written to account for reentrancy from the same causality. In other words, if a client calls object A, object A makes a call to object B and object B makes a call back to object A, then the activity lock must allow the second call to execute; otherwise, we would have a deadlock. The deadlock would be the result of B not being able to call into A because of the client's call, but the client call would never end because it would be waiting for B to finish. The activity handles this scenario with the causality ID. If a client calls object A, object A makes a call to object B, and object B makes a call back to object A, the causality ID of the client is propagated throughout the call chain so that when object B calls back into A, the activity lock code knows that it is part of the same chain and thus lets the call through.

For an STA object to allow reentrancy, it must process window messages. Remember that the STA handles method calls through messaging. RPC threads post requests from clients as window messages to a hidden window. When an STA thread object makes a call outside its apartment, it does not block the thread; instead, it continues to process messages to enable reentrancy. Reentrancy prevents deadlocks, as explained earlier. However, there is a problem with the way STA threads work in conjunction with the activity lock.

Activities and deadlocks

There are situations in which you can cause COM+ calls within activities to deadlock. When working with STA objects (i.e., all VB objects), two client threads should never have access to objects within the same activity. This can happen if a client creates an object inside the activity, then passes the object to another thread, perhaps to an ActiveX EXE object, or if one of the objects in the activity hands the client itself or another object in the activity.

The problems stem from the way the activity lock was coded. One can say that the activity lock code is inside the STA boundary. Suppose that two clients try to make calls into the same object in the STA. The STA mechanism serializes the calls. The serializing mechanism fails if the STA processes messages. This can happen if the client makes an out-of-process call, calls *DoEvents*, displays a message box, and so on. The problem is that when an object in an STA makes an out-of-process call, COM+ places the thread in a message loop by calling *MsgWaitForMultipleHandles*. It will continue looping and processing messages until one of two things happens: an incoming message for another COM call is posted to the message queue, or a completion event occurs—this event is a kernel object event that COM uses to synchronize the return of a call. You may recall from the previous chapter that COM turns the server into an RPC server. A thread is created in the process to listen for RPC requests. The RPC thread waits for the out-of-process call to complete. When the call completes, the RPC thread gets an RPC message and signals the event. The STA thread can then continue with the next call.

If the RPC thread receives an incoming call, it posts a message to the hidden window. This means that the STA message loop is interrupted and the new COM call is dispatched. The new call is then confronted with the activity lock code. If the call comes from a second causality (from a different thread), the call will be blocked in yet another message loop waiting for the activity lock to be released. The problem is that this other loop doesn't know about the completion event from the RPC thread; it only knows about the semaphore for the activity lock. Therefore, when the out-of-process call completes and the RPC thread raises the event, the STA thread does not receive it. The activity lock will never be released because the call that first locked the activity in essence never finishes. This results in a deadlock.

To prevent this deadlock situation, if you are planning on making out-of-process calls, never have two threads make a call concurrently into the activity. This restriction includes ADO calls talking to SQL Server or Oracle.

It seems funny to say that the activity lock works as long as you do not make concurrent calls, since that is what the activity lock is supposed to protect you against, but this is the reality when working with STA threads. In fact, when working with STA threads, the COM+ model should be that each client must have a single instance of an object in the application—the root object. The root object then creates other objects. Because the activity will not give you any more concurrency benefits than the STA thread, you may be tempted to disable synchronization support. However, synchronization support also influences how objects are mapped to threads in the STA pool.

STA Thread Pool

COM+ maintains a pool of STA threads to enable concurrency from multiple clients. The idea is that objects that are created on behalf of a client are mapped to one thread in the pool, while objects belonging to a different client are mapped to a different thread in the pool. This mechanism enables multiple clients to make calls concurrently and allows objects that belong to the same client to share state.

Each application (this is done per application boundary) has a thread pool with the minimum number of threads equal to 7 plus the number of processors in the machine and a maximum number of threads equal to 10 times the number of processors. The number of threads can be expressed by the following set of relationships:

```
7 + Number Of Processors <= Threads in pool <= 10 * Number Of Processors
```

Each server application maintains its own thread pool. A library application maintains a thread pool only if it is not loaded in the process of a COM+ server application. If the library application is loaded in the process of a COM+ server application, there will be only one thread pool—the one for the COM+ server application. If a non-COM+ server application client loads the library application, then COM+ will create the STA thread pool. If a COM+ server application uses components in another COM+ server application, there will be two STA thread pools. The bottom line is there will always be one thread pool per process.

When a client creates an STA object that is marked as synchronization Required or synchronization Requires New, COM+ immediately creates the minimum number of threads using the formula shown earlier. Then it assigns the object to one of the threads in the pool and binds the activity to the thread.

For the sake of the discussion that follows, let's assume that the machine we are dealing with has a single processor. In this case, COM+ will create eight threads when the first client creates the first STA component requiring synchronization. From then on, any objects the root object creates will be placed in the same thread as long as they do not require their own thread. Secondary objects will require a different thread only if they are marked as synchronization Requires New. In other words, activities are mapped onto STA threads; any time COM+ starts a new activity it will try to place that activity on a new thread. Keep in mind that COM+ will use a second thread from the pool only if the first client still holds references to objects in the first activity. When a client releases all of its references to objects in the activity, the thread returns to the pool.

After all the threads are used from the pool, COM+ will not allocate new threads immediately. Call number 9 in our example will result in another activity, but COM+ will map the activity to one of the existing threads. Thus, one of the threads will have two activities mapped to it. Call number 10 results in two threads from the pool having two activities mapped; call number 11 results in three of the threads having two activities mapped; and so on. Objects in the second activity will not execute their code until the objects from the first activity are done or until the objects in the first activity make a call that results in the processing of window messages. For example, if an object calls *DoEvents*, displays a message box, and calls another object in a server application or in an ActiveX EXE or even if the object makes an ADO call to SQL Server or Oracle, the result is that the STA will process messages and allow the second activity to come through.

COM+ will continue to map activities onto the same apartments until every apartment in the pool has five activities mapped to it. This means that only after 40 calls (in the case of a single processor) will COM+ allocate thread number 9. COM+ will then map the next five requests (41, 42, 43, 44, and 45) to the new thread in the pool. After the ninth thread has five activities mapped to it, COM+ will create thread number 10. In the case of a single processor, this is the maximum number of threads. This means that after thread 10 has five activities mapped onto it, COM+ will go back to one of the threads in the pool and assign a sixth activity onto it.

Two things influence whether two objects end up in the same thread. You already know that to even have a thread pool, each root object must have synchronization support turned on. After the root object is placed in a thread from the pool, the only other requirement for secondary objects is that they have synchronization set to something other than Requires New. This means that if a root object with synchronization marked as Required creates a secondary object with synchronization marked as Not Supported, the two objects will still end up on the same thread from the pool.

ObjectContext and CallContext

As you learned previously, every COM+ object lives inside a context. The context offers two things:

Object context information
  Information that is specific to that context.

Call context information
  Information that is propagated throughout the call chain. In this release of COM+, there is only one type of call context information besides the causality ID: security information. You will learn about security in Chapter 9.

Because there are two types of information that you may want to interact with, the starting point of COM+ code is the call to one of two functions: *GetObjectContext* or *GetSecurityCallContext*. *GetObjectContext* enables you to reach into the context and affect the context specific to your object. Remember that several objects may be sharing the same context—in this case, the changes you make will influence all the objects sharing a context. *GetSecurityCallContext* enables you to examine call context information, in particular security call context information.

GetObjectContext

The *GetObjectContext* function returns an instance of the `ObjectContext` interface, a VB-friendly version of the `IObjectContext` interface. For now, it is sufficient to know that `ObjectContext` is the starting point for a number of COM+ services. With `ObjectContext`, you can request other interfaces or execute methods specific to the `ObjectContext` interface.

The following code shows you how to reach into context with the `Get-ObjectContext` function:

```
Dim ctx As ObjectContext
Set ctx = GetObjectContext()

If Not ctx Is Nothing Then
'...do something useful here
End If
```

Make sure to test if you indeed have a valid pointer after the call, since the call may return `Nothing`. *GetObjectContext* has one optional parameter: the name of an ASP intrinsic object. The story is that, in Internet Information Server Release 4, the runtimes for MTS and IIS were merged. The outcome is that if an ASP script creates a COM+ component, IIS places a reference to the ASP intrinsic objects in context, and you can retrieve these objects by using the function, passing the name of the intrinsic object you would like to get, as in:

```
GetObjectContext("Response")
```

This syntax is actually shorthand for a call to the `ObjectContext` interface's Item function, as in:

```
GetObjectContext.Item("Response")
```

Once you have the `ObjectContext` interface, you can execute one of the methods in the interface. The methods in `ObjectContext` fall into two categories: transaction methods and security methods. There are two methods, however, that do not fall in one of these categories: CreateInstance and ContextInfo.

CreateInstance is in the `ObjectContext` interface for backward compatibility with MTS. In MTS, whenever you created another object, COM had no concept of the MTS architecture. Whenever a client created an MTS component, MTS would place the object in an activity—there was no way to avoid activities. However, once the client created the root object, if the root object wanted to create secondary objects in the same activity, the root object would call a special MTS creation method called CreateInstance. CreateInstance would tell MTS that the new object should be part of the same activity as its creator. Without this function call, MTS would think another client was creating the object and would place the object in its own activity. This function is no longer necessary because the native COM functions such as *CoCreateInstance[Ex]* know all about the MTS model (i.e., COM+). In fact, as you learned in Chapter 1, COM+ is really the integration of the MTS model with the core COM APIs plus a few new services. However, having the method available means that your MTS code will continue to run fine. CreateInstance now simply does the equivalent of *CreateObject*.

There is a problem, however, if you create secondary objects using the **New** operator in COM+. The **New** operator has different behaviors depending on where you use it. If you use it to create a component that is in the same DLL as its creator, VB skips COM+ activation altogether. This means that the object will live in the context of its creator—the object will not have a context of its own, and the COM+ settings for the component will not take effect. If you issue **New** to create a component outside of your DLL, then **New** will use COM+ activation and will work correctly. The *CreateObject* function always uses COM+ activation and is the preferred function when writing COM+ code. Notice also that because **New** may not do the correct activation, depending on where the components are, you should also avoid using `Dim Obj As New CObj`, since this syntax will use **New** as the creation operator.

Another interesting method in the `ObjectContext` interface is ContextInfo. The ContextInfo property returns the `ContextInfo` interface, which reports various characteristics about the context you live in. You can get the following information: activity GUID (GetActivityId), context ID (GetContextId), OLE transaction object (GetTransaction), transaction Stream ID (GetTransactionId), and whether or not your component is currently involved in a transaction (IsInTransaction).

The following code shows you how to reach into context and get the activity ID:

```
Dim ctx As ObjectContext
Set ctx = GetObjectContext
Dim ctxinfo As ContextInfo
Set ctxinfo = ctx.ContextInfo
Debug.Print ContextInfo.ActivityId
```

This code can also be compacted into one line, as follows:

```
Debug.Print GetObjectContext.ContextInfo.ActivityId
```

Constructor String

In addition to objects that enable you to interact with the environment, COM+ also offers a number of interfaces you can implement to get notifications of certain events. We will discuss a number of these interfaces in the course of the book. For

the sake of illustrating how to implement a COM+ interface and the kind of notifications you may receive, let's look at one of the interfaces, `IObjectConstruct`.

You can get notifications whenever someone creates an instance of your class by
implementing the `IObjectConstruct` interface. `IObjectConstruct` has a single
method, Construct, which COM+ invokes when a new instance of the component
is created; Construct, in other words, corresponds to a Visual Basic event. The following code illustrates how you may implement the interface:

```
Implements IObjectConstruct

Private Sub IObjectConstruct_Construct(ByVal pCtorObj As Object)
    Dim sComp As String
    sComp = pCtorObj.ConstructString

    If sComp <> "" Then
        Set Account2 = CreateObject(sComp)
    End If

End Sub
```

COM+ passes the Construct method a creation object in the variable *pCtorObj*. All
that you can do with *pCtorObj* is get a construction string, which is the string you
assign to the object through the Activation tab of the component's Properties
dialog box, as shown in Figure 8-3.

To enable the ability to receive notification when your class is created, first check
the Enable Object Construction option shown in Figure 8-3, then enter a string in
the "Constructor string" text box. If you enable this feature, then you must implement the interface, or clients will not be able to instantiate the object. In fact, you
can prevent a client from creating an instance of your object by raising an error
within the Construct method implementation. The *pCtorObj* object supports the
`IDispatch` interface, as seen in the preceding code example, but it also supports
the `IObjectConstructString` interface. Thus, another way of retrieving the construction string is to cast the interface as follows:

```
Dim objstr As IObjectContructString
Set objstr = pCtorObj
Dim sComp As String
sComp = objstr.ConstructString
```

The Construct method/event takes place after Class_Initialize. The previous example
uses the constructor string to create an instance of another component. The constructor string is meant as a mechanism for setting configuration information for
your class without having to use the registry or change code and recompile.

Now that you have a taste for the context of COM+ programming, you need to
understand one more topic—how to debug COM+ applications—before
embarking into in-depth COM+ programming in the following chapters.

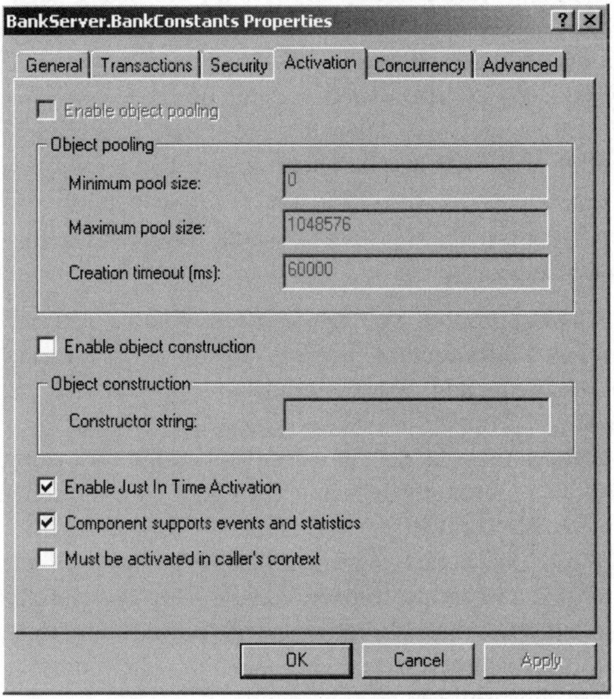

Figure 8-3. Constructor String text box in Activation tab

Debugging COM+ Applications

Because the Visual Basic 6 debugger is very limited, debugging COM+ applications is not a trivial task. The biggest limitation is that the debugger cannot attach itself to a running process; it only knows how to debug code that is being interpreted and running under the VB 6 process. This means that you cannot debug COM+ server applications in Visual Basic, since these applications run inside *DllHost.exe*. A second limitation is that it can debug only single-threaded processes, which means that you cannot debug things like the STA thread pool. Note that you can debug all these things using the Visual C++ debugger. Therefore, one option for debugging VB COM+ code is to use the Visual C++ debugger, which is discussed as the second of the following debugging options; another option is to use trace messages by calling the Win32 *OutputDebugString* API.

Option 1: Use the VB Debugger

VB offers you limited debugging support for COM+ applications by simulating a COM+ library application environment. In order to offer you debugging support, VB does the job of *DllHost.exe* and acts as a surrogate process. Because VB treats your application as if it were a library application, debugging support is limited to features for library applications—you cannot debug server-only application features (see Chapter 7 for a complete list of server-only services). You also cannot debug the way your objects are created in different threads. This means that if you mark a component as synchronization Requires New, you cannot detect that the component has been created in a different thread. Furthermore, you also cannot test whether components are created in the STA thread pool correctly, since the VB environment does not support multithreading. However, it does enable you to test a number of features, such as role-based security and transactions.

To enable debugging support, you need to tell VB that it should simulate the COM+ environment. Unfortunately, there is no option that explicitly tells VB to turn on COM+ debugging. The roundabout method is to change the MTSTransactionMode property in each of your class modules to something other than 0 – `NotAnMTSObject`, its default value. You could, for example, set it to 1 – `NoTransactions`. This property is mainly for controlling the transactional setting for the component, as you will see in Chapter 9, but it also tells VB to run your component in the COM+ debugging environment. The only other requirement is to compile your DLL and set the version compatibility option to Binary Compatibility—this is the only way that VB knows to match the source to a particular component instance. You can then place breakpoints in your source code and choose Run → Start to run your program from within the IDE.

When your program runs, VB invokes some private functions in *comsvcs.dll*, the DLL that manages the COM+ services. These functions enable VB to create a hidden application if you have not already created one. The best way to debug your application is to compile your components and add them to an existing COM+ application. This will give you control over the settings for your components. If you add your components to a server application, VB will temporarily change the activation property of the application to Library while you are debugging, then back to Server when you are done.

One problem that developers often run into while debugging COM+ applications is that after the client program finishes, they attempt to make a change to the DLL source and rebuild the DLL only to get a "Permission Denied" error from the VB IDE. This can happen because of a feature in COM+ that keeps your server application running. In the Advanced tab of the application Properties dialog box, there is a "Minutes until idle shutdown" setting that defaults to 3 minutes. The first time COM+ launches the application, it takes a noticeable amount of time for the first object to be created. When all the clients release their references to your objects, you have the option to leave the application running so that if another client immediately creates an instance of an object in the application, the creation can happen instantly without having to relaunch the application. However, while you are developing, you will most likely want to turn off this feature. Otherwise, the COM+ application will have loaded instances of your DLL and you will not be able to recompile it. To turn off this feature, set the minutes to 0. You can also shut down the application explicitly by right-clicking on the application and choosing "Shut down."

There are times when you want to shut down an application, but the application will not respond. You may kill the application through the Task Manager, but if there are other server applications running, there will be multiple entries of *DllHost. exe* in the task list. COM+ has a cool feature that lets you know the process ID (or PID) for each running COM+ application. You can use this PID in the Task Manager to shut down a particular *DllHost.exe* instance. You can view the list of process IDs by clicking on the COM+ Applications folder in the explorer. Then choose the View → Status menu option. Figure 8-4 shows a list of running processes.

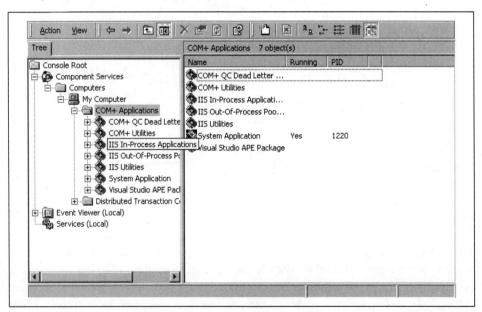

Figure 8-4. List of running COM+ applications; Status View shows the PID for each process

Since VB debugs COM+ applications as library applications, the VB debugger is useless if you specifically need to debug a feature that's specific to server applications. In that case, you'll have to use one of the debugging options discussed in the next two sections.

Option 2: Use the VC Debugger

You can step through VB code in the Visual C++ debugger if you compile your DLL with symbolic debugging information. You can do this by checking the Create

Symbolic Debug Info option and selecting the No Optimization option in the Compile tab of your project's Properties dialog box, as seen in Figure 8-5.

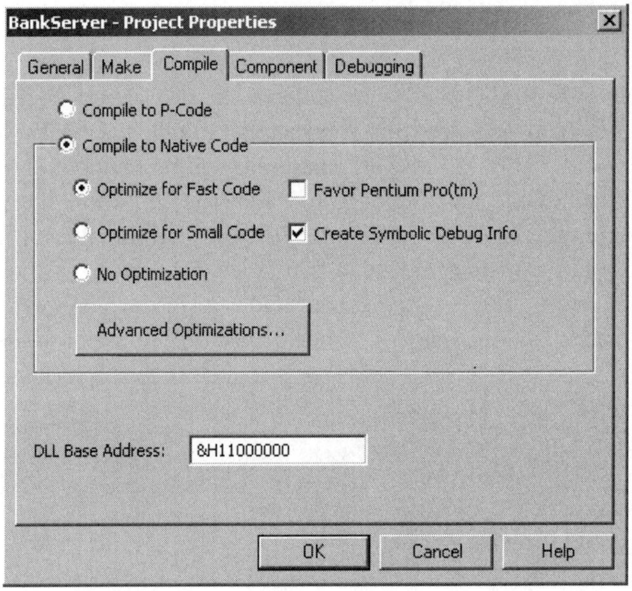

Figure 8-5. Compiling with symbolic debug information

Once you have compiled with symbolic debug information, you can ask COM+ to automatically launch the VC debugger when a client creates an instance of a component in your application. You do this by enabling the "Launch in debugger" option in the Advanced tab of the application Properties dialog box. When COM+ launches the debugger, you will see that the VC toolbar (which is shown in Figure 8-6) includes two buttons for starting the application, one with a code icon with a down arrow, the other with a red exclamation mark. The latter runs the program without going through the debugger, while the former runs the program through the debugger. You have 30 seconds to click either of these two run buttons. This is because if COM+ cannot obtain a reference to the object within 30 seconds, it assumes that there is a problem and returns an error to the client.

Figure 8-6. Visual C++ Build toolbar

To stop at a portion of code in the VB program, you have to first make sure the VB DLL is loaded into memory. You can do this by choosing Project → Settings, then clicking in the Debug tab of the dialog box (see Figure 8-7).

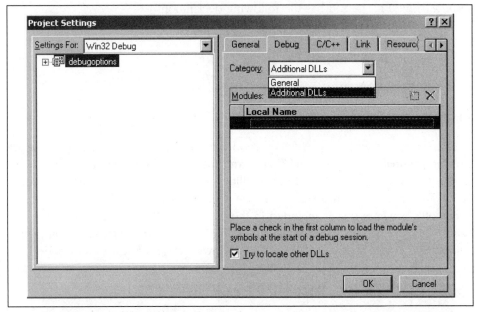

Figure 8-7. The Project Settings dialog box

In the Debug properties, choose Additional DLLs from the category drop-down box. In the Modules listbox, click the first entry. The dialog box will enable you to type the path to your DLL, or you can browse using the "..." button. Once you add the path to your DLL, you can close the dialog box, then choose File → Save Workspace from the IDE to save your changes. Saving your changes means that the next time COM+ launches the VC debugger, it will automatically load your DLL into memory as well.

Choose File → Open to open a VB class library source file (.CLS). The extension CLS is not one that the VC team included in its list of file type choices, so you must enter ***.cls** in the Filename field, and the dialog box will open the CLS source file. You can then set a breakpoint on a VB line of code by placing the cursor on the line and pressing the F9 key or by right-clicking on the line and choosing Insert Breakpoint from the menu. When the VC debugger hits the binary code corresponding to the line where you placed the breakpoint, the debugger will stop. You can then single-step through by pressing the F11 key.

You can use the VC debugger in this fashion only to step through code and examine the application flow and to test variable values, but you will not be able to use it to modify variable values or to change code and continue executing.

Going through the VC debugger is the only way to debug server-related services and multithreading features.

You can output messages to the VC output debug window using the *Output-DebugString* API. The API has the following declaration:

```
Private Declare Sub OutputDebugString Lib "kernel32" _
        Alias "OutputDebugStringA" ( _
        ByVal lpOutputString As String)

Call OutputDebugString("Object A Initialized" & vbNewLine)
```

Option 3: Use Trace Messages

In fact, using *OutputDebugString* is a good way to generate trace output. There are several standalone programs that can display strings coming from the *OutputDebugString* API. One of these utilities is dbmon. dbmon is a console application that displays strings output by the *OutputDebugString* function. dbmon is Microsoft's program that is included in the Platform SDK. A nicer option is dbgnt, from SysInternals (see Figure 8-8). You can download this program from *www. sysinternals.com*. This program offers a Windows GUI and a few other options.

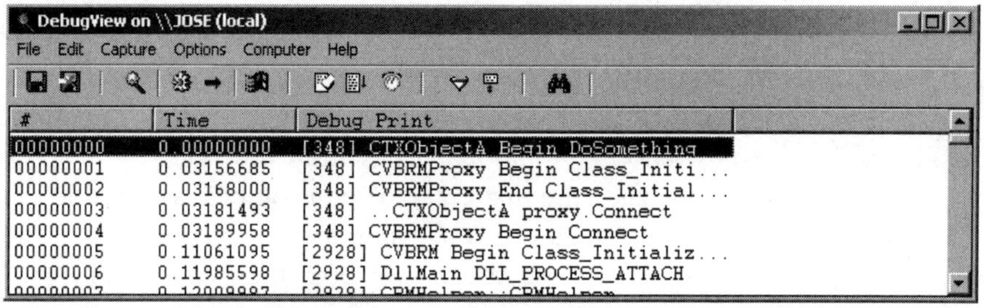

Figure 8-8. dbgnt from SysInternals

In addition to your own trace messages, one of the COM+ services, event reporting, can give you inside information about when objects are created, how activities are started, how many threads there are in the STA pool, and so on. You can turn on event reporting by selecting the "Component supports events and statistics" option in the Activation tab of the class Properties dialog box. To get notifications, you must also implement several notification interfaces. The only problem is that not all these interfaces can be implemented in VB classes. I have included a C++ COM object with the downloadable code for this book that implements all these interfaces and reports the events through *OutputDebugString*. To see a list of all the events you can get notifications for, see the article entitled "COM+ Instrumentation Interfaces" in MSDN.

To get notifications, you must create what is called a transient subscription. You create a transient subscription with the COM+ Administration Objects. You cannot create a transient subscription from within an object running in a COM+ application. This means that to get reporting, you will want to create an instance of the component I have provided in a separate EXE. All you need to do is instantiate the object, and the object automatically registers itself for reporting. To create an instance of the object, use the *COMPlusTrace.DLL* file in the *Chapter07\ COMPlusTrace* directory of the downloadable software for this book. Add the reference to the "VBCOM Book: COM Plus Event Tracing" type library, then create an instance of the component as follows:

```
Dim er As EventReporter
Private Sub Form_Load()
    Set er = New EventReporter
End Sub
```

The reporting tool will receive events from any application as long as the program that contains the previous code is running. The component will use *OutputDebugString* to output the trace messages.

Internally, the C++ component has to implement the event interfaces, then register for receiving events. The following is part of the C++ code translated to VB (the interface method implementations are not exactly accurate, since the methods have parameter types that VB does not support):

```
Implements ICOMMethodEvents

Private Sub EvMethods_OnMethodCall(ByVal guidCid As String, _
                                   ByVal guidRid As String, _
                                   ByVal iMeth As Long)
End Sub

Private Sub EvMethods_OnMethodException(ByVal guidCid As String, _
                                        ByVal guidRid As String, _
                                        ByVal iMeth As Long)
End Sub

Private Sub EvMethods_OnMethodReturn(ByVal guidCid As String, _
                                     ByVal guidRid As String, _
                                     ByVal iMeth As Long, _
                                     ByVal hResult As Long)
End Sub

Private Sub Form_Load()
    'First create an instance of the catalog object
    Dim cat As COMAdminCatalog
    Set cat = New COMAdminCatalog

    'Get the TransientSubscriptions collection
    Dim eventcoll As COMAdminCatalogCollection
```

```
      Set eventcoll = cat.GetCollection("TransientSubscriptions")

      'Add a new item to TransientSubscriptions
      Dim eventobj As COMAdminCatalogObject
      Set eventobj = eventcoll.Add

      'Set the subscription properties
      eventobj.Value("Name") = "EV:IComMethodEvents"
      eventobj.Value("EventCLSID") = _
              "{ECABB0C3-7F19-11D2-978E-0000F8757E2A}"
      eventobj.Value("InterfaceID") = _
              "{683130A9-2E50-11d2-98A5-00C04F8EE1C4}"
      eventobj.Value("SubscriberInterface") = Me
      eventcoll.SaveChanges
End Sub
```

The code implements the **ICOMMethodEvents** interface. Remember that this is only pseudocode, since the methods in **ICOMMethodEvents** have parameters that VB can't handle. The code then creates a COMAdminCatalog object and requests the TransientSubscriptions collection. The code then subscribes to receive event notifications. The subscription procedure involves adding a new item to the collection, setting its properties, and saving the changes. As soon as the changes are committed, the object will begin to receive notifications. The properties for the subscription element are:

Name
> A developer-provided name for the item

EventCLSID
> The CLSID of the object that reports the COM+ event; this GUID is always the same for all the event notifications interfaces

InterfaceID
> Tells COM+ what event interface you are implementing (i.e., what type of event notifications you are requesting)

SubscriberInterface
> Gives COM+ an instance of the class that will receive notifications

Figure 8-9 shows the output of some of the events that COM+ reports.

One caveat is that asking COM+ for event reporting forces the object into its own context, so you cannot get this type of information for objects that share a context with other objects.

Not a Debug Option: MsgBox

Whatever you do, do not display message boxes. Message boxes have the side effect that they cause messages posted to the STA hidden window to be processed. What this means is that while you are displaying the message box, another

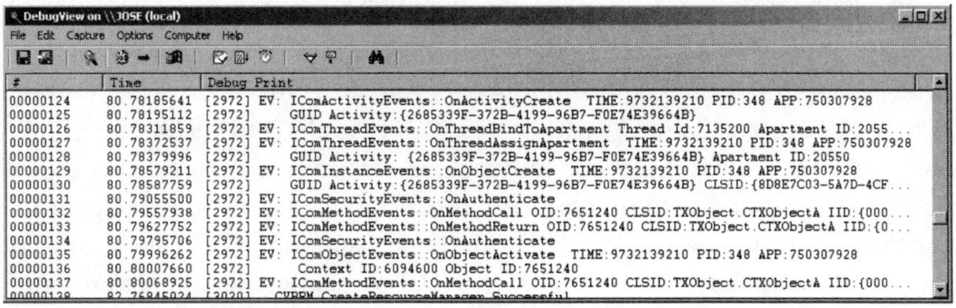

Figure 8-9. Events that COM+ reports for analyzing your application

call may come into your thread. This can cause you to get different results while you are debugging than when you are in production.

Summary

Some of the COM+ services require COM+ to monitor the calls made into your object both before the method call and after the method call. Every time that COM+ needs to monitor your component at the method level, it places your component in a living space called a context. Communication between separate contexts requires an interceptor or a proxy. The job of the interceptor is to ensure that your component runs within an environment that has support for the features you have specified. Having each component in its own context consumes more memory and degrades performance. If you do not need the services that demand their own context, you may want to turn the services off, as long as you never give a client access to multiple objects within the same context.

COM+ adds a new boundary called the activity that tells COM+ what objects are doing work on behalf of a single client. Each time a client creates an object that has its synchronization property set to Required or Requires New, COM+ creates a new activity. The first object the client creates is called the root of the activity. The root of the activity then creates secondary objects to be part of the same activity. COM+ maps STA objects in activities to a thread from the STA thread pool. Each time a client creates an instance of an object that requires a new activity, COM+ places that object in a new thread from the STA thread pool. The number of threads in the pool is determined in part by the number of processors in the machine.

You can get into trouble while using activities if you give a reference to objects in the same activity to multiple clients, then make out-of-process calls. There is a problem with the way the activity lock was implemented that makes this situation result in a deadlock. To prevent these situations, make sure to never have more than one client holding references to the same object or to other objects that are in the same activity and in the same thread.

To write COM+ code in your components, you program against the COM+ services type library. The starting task in most COM+ code is to reach into context to interact with the context environment for your component. You do this by calling the *GetObjectContext* function. You have three options for debugging your COM+ application. You can use the VB IDE with limited support. VB treats your application as a library application. If you want to debug server-specific features such as synchronization and multithreading, you may want to use the VC debugger or simply trace messages. I have provided a component that can report internal COM+ events so that you can get rich trace output messages.

In the next chapter you will learn about transactions, both local transactions and distributed transactions. You will also learn about resource managers, in particular SQL Server and Oracle, and how they implement their locking mechanism while they are in a transaction.

9

Transaction Services

Perhaps the most important feature in COM+ services is transactions. If you think about it, the predecessor to COM+ is Microsoft Transaction Server (MTS); the name implies that the main purpose of the product is to manage transactions.

In this chapter, you will learn about transaction services. A lot of COM+ programming has to do with concurrent data access. In large systems, a number of clients may be using the same COM+ application, and each client may be calling the same methods and accessing and modifying the same data. To guarantee that each client can change data safely, we use transactions.

What Is a Transaction?

A transaction in a database environment is usually defined as the movement of one or two pieces of data from one location to another in a way that guarantees their integrity. The definition of a transaction, however, is not limited to data in a database. It is also possible to involve other resources in the transaction. For example, COM+ transactions may involve MSMQ messages. (A full discussion of MSMQ—a product from Microsoft for sending and receiving messages—is beyond the scope of this book.) In order to ensure the integrity of data involved in them, transactions must meet the ACID rules. The acronym ACID stands for Atomic, Consistent, Isolated, and Durable. These terms have the following meaning:

Atomic
> The operation must succeed completely or be rolled back completely. In other words, it is an all or nothing operation. Atomicity is not usually the job of a client program; it is normally the job of the database system or the transaction coordinator.

Consistent

Even though the data may not meet the rules of integrity for the database while a portion of the transaction is executing, by the time the transaction ends, the data must follow the rules of integrity. In other words, if the database rules state that a program may not delete a record from the database but may move it from one table to another, it is possible that at any given point the data in the database may not reflect the rule. For example, the program may add the record to the destination table and then delete it from the source table. In the first step, there may be two records that are identical, one in each of the tables. However, when the transaction succeeds, the data must meet the rules. Consistency is usually the job of the middle-tier component code. Only the middle tier can be certain of how many changes must be made to keep the database in a consistent state.

Isolated

Transactions run as if they were the only transaction executing in the system. A high level of isolation prevents one transaction from seeing intermediate changes from another transaction. A number of systems control the isolation level by placing locks on the data.

Durable

If the transaction succeeds and the system crashes during or immediately afterward, the changes must be preserved when the system is restored. Durability is the responsibility of two entities: the database system and the transaction coordinator.

Players in a Transaction

There are at least four major players in a typical COM+ transaction:

The client

We will refer to the client as the piece of code that originates the transaction, whether the client is a Visual Basic program or simply a DHTML page inside a browser.

The middle-tier component

In truth, when we study the process of declarative transactions in COM+, you will see that the middle-tier component can be further subdivided into two categories: the root object and secondary objects.

The transaction coordinator

The transaction coordinator begins and ends the physical transaction. It follows the commands of either the client directly or the middle-tier components or, in the case of declarative transactions, the commands from COM+ itself.

The resource manager

The resource manager is the piece of software that manages durable state. The resource manager is normally a database system like SQL Server or Oracle, but it could also be something like MSMQ. Database resource managers enable a number of transactions to run simultaneously. In order to manage concurrency, resource managers place locks on the data. When writing distributed applications, it is very important to know what locks are placed on the data by each transaction, how the locks block other transactions, and how long the locks are held.

In "local" transactions (in database terms, these are transactions that involve a single resource manager and that are usually driven through ADO directly), the transaction manager is part of the resource manager.

Types of Locks

We will discuss the three basic types of locks in this chapter: shared locks (or read locks), exclusive locks (or write locks), and update locks.

Depending on the isolation level, whenever you read data within a transaction, SQL Server will place shared locks on the data. Whether the locks are placed on a single record, a page of records, an index range, or the entire table is not important for our discussion. However, shared locks do not prevent other transactions from placing shared locks on the same data. Two transactions may read the same data and in so doing place shared locks on the data.

Shared locks, however, do prevent exclusive locks from being placed on the data. In other words, if Transaction A (TXA henceforward) has shared locks on record A, then Transaction B (TXB) will not be able to modify the record. Modifying the record (either through UPDATE or DELETE) would require SQL Server to place an exclusive lock (or write lock) on the record, and the shared lock would prevent it. This means that TXB would be blocked until TXA releases its read locks on the piece of data that TXB needs. As you may already see, it is also important to know how long locks are held. The isolation levels mostly affect how shared locks are honored.

Write locks or exclusive locks prevent any other locks from being placed on the data. This means that if TXA is updating a record and thus the record has an exclusive lock on it, if TXB tries to read the record, TXB will be blocked until the lock is released. In transactions that meet the ACID rules, write locks are always held for the duration of the transaction. The amount of time shared locks are held is affected by the isolation mode.

Isolation

Isolation modes determine the locking scheme that the database engine will use while executing your transaction. The higher the isolation mode, the more protected your data will be; the lower the isolation mode, the less protected your data will be. Concurrency, however, is affected inversely by the isolation level. The lower the isolation level, the more operations that can run concurrently, and the higher the isolation level, the fewer operations that can run concurrently. The trick is to figure out what isolation level you can live with. The problem is that, depending on the isolation level, you may encounter problems such as dirty reads, unrepeatable reads, or phantom records.

The isolation levels that SQL Server supports are read uncommitted, read committed, repeatable read, and serializable. Serializable offers the highest protection at the cost of the least concurrency. With any other isolation mode, you risk one of the problems mentioned earlier. Let's take a look at each isolation mode.

Read uncommitted

The read uncommitted mode tells SQL Server not to honor shared locks or exclusive locks and, moreover, not to place shared locks on read data. This isolation mode suffers from all the access problems listed before.

Let's see exactly how this isolation mode works by using the Query Analyzer tool that ships with SQL Server. The easiest way to test isolation modes is to run Query Analyzer (Start → Programs → Microsoft SQL Server 2000 → Query Analyzer) and to open two query windows, as seen in Figure 9-1.

Each query window has its own connection. Before opening the second query window, make sure to switch the database you are going to use to the Pubs database by selecting Pubs from the drop-down box on the right side of the window's toolbar. Create a second window by selecting Query → New Query. Once you have two query windows, you may enter the following code in one of the windows:

```
BEGIN TRAN
UPDATE AUTHORS SET au_lname='Black' where au_lname='White'
ROLLBACK TRAN
SELECT * FROM AUTHORS
```

In the second window, enter the following:

```
SET TRANSACTION ISOLATION LEVEL READ UNCOMMITTED
SELECT * FROM AUTHORS
```

Do not run any of the code in the windows yet. Return to the first query window and highlight the first two statements. A feature of Query Analyzer allows you to run only the highlighted lines. Execute the first two lines by pressing F5 or by selecting Query → Execute. Then go to the second window and execute the entire query.

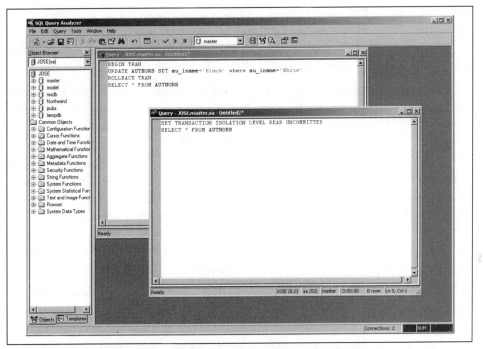

Figure 9-1. The SQL Server Query Analyzer tool with two Query windows

The first line in the second query script sets the isolation mode to read uncommitted. It is true that the script does not have a `Begin Tran` and `Commit Tran`. I left those statements out on purpose to illustrate changing the isolation level for the connection and that individual SQL statements are basically run within a transaction that lasts only for the duration of the statement. If you study the results of the query, the first record in the result set has the name Johnson Black. The original name for the author was Johnson White, but the first transaction changed the author's last name to Black. However, the first transaction has not ended. Return to the first transaction and execute the second two statements. If you look at the results of the `SELECT` statement in the first window, you will notice that the record has been restored to Johnson White. This means that the second query was able to look at data from changes that had not been finalized. This is known as a dirty read. You must decide whether your queries can live with dirty reads.

To understand the danger of dirty reads, imagine two transactions in a bank operation. The first transaction moves $1,000 from a customer's savings account to her checking account; the second transaction evaluates a loan application for the client based on the funds in the checking account. You can see that if the second transaction is able to see the $1,000, the loan decision may be evaluated incorrectly. It is possible for the transfer to fail, for example, if the program discovers that the client does not in fact have $1,000 in her savings account. In that case the transaction would be aborted; the checking account never really had $1000. A dirty read would occur, though, if the checking account balance was increased and the balance was read before the transaction was aborted.

Given the danger of dirty reads, why would you want to run a transaction with read uncommitted? To see the benefits of running certain queries with read uncommitted, let's examine the next isolation level, read committed.

Read committed

The read committed isolation level, the default for both SQL Server and Oracle, exists to protect against dirty reads. It, however, suffers from two other problems: unrepeatable reads and phantom records. In the read committed isolation level, the database honors shared locks. It also places shared locks on data, but only for the duration of the read. In other words, the shared locks are not held for the duration of the transaction.

Let's use Query Analyzer once again to test this scenario. Use two query windows as before. In the first query window, enter the following:

```
BEGIN TRAN
UPDATE AUTHORS SET au_lname='Black' where au_lname='White'
ROLLBACK TRAN
SELECT * FROM AUTHORS
```

In the second window, enter the following script:

```
SET TRANSACTION ISOLATION LEVEL READ COMMITTED
SELECT * FROM AUTHORS
```

Again, instead of executing the entire script in the first window, highlight only the first two lines in the script and execute the query. Execute the entire script in the second window. You will notice that the **SELECT** query in the second window will not show results. The query is blocked because one of the records needed to finish the query has an exclusive lock on it. The query attempts to place a shared lock on the record while it is executing the statement and is prevented from doing so. Now return to the first window and execute the remaining two statements. You will notice that the query in the second window immediately completes after the transaction in the first window finishes.

Let's try another scenario to understand more about this mode. Leave the same query script in the first window, but change the query script in the second window to the following:

```
SET TRANSACTION ISOLATION LEVEL READ COMMITTED
SELECT * FROM AUTHORS WHERE au_lname='Bennet'
```

If you run only the first two statements in the first query script and then the entire second script, you will notice that now the query in the second script executes without being blocked. In this case, the query in the second script does not attempt to access records that have exclusive locks on them.

The read committed isolation level prevents you from doing dirty reads. However, it does not prevent two other common problems—unrepeatable reads and phantom records. With unrepeatable reads, it is possible to run the same query twice within a transaction and obtain different results.

To illustrate an unrepeatable read, change the script in the first window to the following:

```
BEGIN TRAN
UPDATE AUTHORS SET au_lname='Black' where au_lname='White'
COMMIT TRAN
UPDATE AUTHORS SET au_lname='White' where au_lname='Black'
SELECT * FROM AUTHORS
```

The second **UPDATE** statement in the preceding query is there only to restore the records to their original state; it is not really necessary to illustrate the problem. Change the query in the second window to the following:

```
SET TRANSACTION ISOLATION LEVEL READ COMMITTED
BEGIN TRAN
SELECT * FROM AUTHORS WHERE au_lname='White'
SELECT * FROM AUTHORS WHERE au_lname='White'
COMMIT TRAN
```

Instead of executing code in the first query window first, this time select the first three statements from the script in the second window and execute them first. The output for the script will show the record that contains the author Johnson White. Then select the first three statements in the script for the first window and execute them. Return to the second window and select the remaining two statements and execute them. The results for the second window will display no records with the last name White. You may execute the remaining statements in the first script to restore the record.

The second transaction ran the same query twice within the same transaction and both times had different results. After the second script read the record the first time, another transaction—the one in the first window—changed the record. Script 2 then read the record a second time and noticed that the record was gone. Transaction 2 is placing shared locks on the records it reads. The shared locks should prevent a record from being updated by another transaction because a change requires an exclusive lock, and exclusive locks cannot be obtained on a record that has a shared lock. The problem is that the shared lock in this isolation mode is held only for the duration of the statement and not for the duration of the transaction.

Repeatable read

The repeatable read isolation mode prevents unrepeatable reads but does nothing to prevent phantom records. First, let's see what happens if we run the previous example using the repeatable read isolation mode instead. Using the two-query-window mechanism as before, enter the following script in the first query window:

```
BEGIN TRAN
UPDATE AUTHORS SET au_lname='Black' where au_lname='White'
COMMIT TRAN
UPDATE AUTHORS SET au_lname='White' where au_lname='Black'
SELECT * FROM AUTHORS
```

Then enter the following script in the second window:

```
SET TRANSACTION ISOLATION LEVEL REPEATABLE READ
BEGIN TRAN
SELECT * FROM AUTHORS WHERE au_lname='White'
SELECT * FROM AUTHORS WHERE au_lname='White'
COMMIT TRAN
```

Notice that the only difference in this second script is the isolation mode. Highlight the first three statements in the second script and execute them. Then highlight the first three statements in the first script and execute them. This time, the first script is blocked from changing the record. This is because the shared locks from the second script are held for the duration of the transaction. If you return to the second window, you may execute the remainder of the statements. This will make it possible for the transaction in the first window to continue. Execute the remaining statements from the first script as well.

Repeatable read prevents unrepeatable reads by placing shared locks on the records and holding the locks for the duration of the transaction. This mode must be used with caution, however. Imagine what would happen if you were to execute the following script in the second window instead:

```
SET TRANSACTION ISOLATION LEVEL REPEATABLE READ
BEGIN TRAN
SELECT * FROM AUTHORS
COMMIT TRAN
```

Now every record in the table has a shared lock on it. This means that you cannot update any of the records from another transaction because it would be impossible for the other transaction to obtain an exclusive lock. To complicate things further with this mode, examine what would happen if you were to have the following script on both windows:

```
SET TRANSACTION ISOLATION LEVEL REPEATABLE READ
BEGIN TRAN
SELECT * FROM AUTHORS
UPDATE AUTHORS SET au_lname='Black' where au_lname='White'
COMMIT TRAN
```

```
UPDATE AUTHORS SET au_lname='White' where au_lname='Black'
SELECT * FROM AUTHORS
```

If you were to execute the first three lines in the script on both windows, then attempt to execute the first **UPDATE** statement in each of the windows, both of the transactions would be blocked. In fact, the situation is called a deadlock: the first transaction cannot place an exclusive lock, because the second transaction has a shared lock on the data; at the same time, the second transaction cannot place an exclusive lock because the first transaction has a shared lock on the data. The problem with shared locks is that any transaction may place shared locks on the data—they are shared.

SQL Server has a deadlock detection mechanism, the details of which are beyond the scope of this book; however, the outcome is that SQL Server decides on a loser for the transaction and automatically aborts one of the two transactions. Oracle does not suffer from the same deadlock issues because it does not use read locks (unless you explicitly ask it to hold read locks with a **For Update** clause in a SQL statement), and it never escalates a lock; it always uses row-level locks.

Repeatable read mode guarantees that if you run a **SELECT** query, another transaction will not be able to change or delete a record in the query, but it does nothing about inserts. Repeatable reads do not prevent the problem of phantom records; for that, you need the serializable isolation mode.

Serializable

In the serializable isolation mode, phantom records—records that may appear the second time you run a query—are prevented. In the repeatable read isolation mode, it is possible to run a query such as **SELECT * FROM AUTHORS** and get one result set, and then for another transaction to insert a record in the AUTHORS table. This means that running the same query twice would give different results.

To illustrate the problem of phantom records, let's use two Query Analyzer windows as before. In the first query window, enter the following script:

```
SET TRANSACTION ISOLATION LEVEL REPEATABLE READ
BEGIN TRAN
SELECT * FROM AUTHORS WHERE au_lname='Ringer'
SELECT * FROM AUTHORS WHERE au_lname='Ringer'
COMMIT TRAN
```

In the second query window, enter the following script:

```
SET TRANSACTION ISOLATION LEVEL REPEATABLE READ
BEGIN TRAN
INSERT INTO AUTHORS (au_id,au_lname,au_fname,contract) VALUES('111-22-
3333','Ringer','Jose',0)
COMMIT TRAN
DELETE FROM AUTHORS WHERE au_id = '111-22-3333'
```

As before, do not run the entire script for the first window; highlight the first three lines in the first query window and execute them. Then, in the second query window, select the first four lines—everything except the DELETE instruction (this line is here only to restore the data to its original state)—and execute them. The output for the first query window should list two entries from the table. The output for the second query window should indicate that one new record was added. Return to the first query window and execute the last two lines. You will notice that the output now contains three rows. What has happened is that another transaction has added a record that meets the selection criteria of the query. This means that in repeatable read mode, it is possible to get phantom records. The second query would have been blocked if there had been an attempt to delete a record or update a record that would have been part of the result set of the SELECT query, but in this case the second query inserted a record. To fix the problem of this type of insertion (or phantom record) you can repeat the test, but this time change the first script to the following:

```
SET TRANSACTION ISOLATION LEVEL SERIALIZABLE
BEGIN TRAN
SELECT * FROM AUTHORS WHERE au_lname='Ringer'
SELECT * FROM AUTHORS WHERE au_lname='Ringer'
COMMIT TRAN
```

You may leave the second script the same. Again execute the first three lines in the first query window. Then execute the first four lines in the second query window. This time, the second transaction is blocked from inserting a record that would fall in the range of the SELECT query in the first transaction.

In order for SQL Server to accomplish this, it has to lock a range of records based on an index. Sometimes this range may include a page or even the entire table, depending on what would take the least amount of memory and on whether the table has a primary key. With the serializable isolation mode, the transaction runs as if it were the only transaction running in the system—changes from other transactions do not affect it. As a result, this mode offers the least concurrency because it has great potential to block other transactions. Imagine if you ran a query such as SELECT * FROM AUTHORS in serializable isolation. In order to prevent phantom records, SQL Server has to do the equivalent of locking the entire table. This means that no other transaction is able to modify, delete, or insert any records.

The read committed mode suffers from the other problems discussed earlier: unrepeatable reads and phantom records. You can get unrepeatable reads, because if you were to read data that was presently being changed, the data would come from the rollback log, but if you read it again after the change had been completed, you would read the latest data. The same explanation applies to phantom records.

Locking Mechanism in Oracle Databases

Oracle is the only major database on the market that does not use shared locks. Not using shared locks makes it possible for Oracle to offer greater concurrency. However, the cost of greater concurrency is that the potential for failure increases (I will explain how shortly). Instead of using shared locks, Oracle maintains two logs: a rollback log (or undo log) and a redo log. When a client requests to modify data within a transaction, several things happen.

First, the change is assigned a system change number, or SCN. The SCN is used to correlate changes to a certain transaction. Then the prechanged data (the state of the data before the data is changed) is saved to the Rollback log. While the data is being changed, the row that contains the data is locked exclusively. Oracle will never scale up a lock to include a page, table, index, and so on; it locks only the records that are being modified. An exclusive lock tells a reading operation from another transaction to do one of two things: either read the information from the rollback log or simply fail the operation and return an error to the user. Once the change has occurred, the lock is released.

Oracle does not typically update the actual record. Instead, it commits the change to the redo log in memory. The change information in the redo log is not a snapshot of the data changes but rather a snapshot of the operation that caused the change. It is in a sense a recording of the steps necessary to reproduce the data as it is. Once you commit a transaction, Oracle still does not touch the physical data in the disk; instead, it commits the redo log information in memory to disk. Then when Oracle detects that there is enough information in the redo log to warrant a change to the actual data on disk, it will start synchronizing the redo information with the log information.

If there is a failure in the system before it has a chance to update the actual data on the disk, as soon as the server comes back up, it will detect that it was not shut down properly the last time and will begin to replay the instructions in the redo log. If by some chance the server goes down in the middle of a transaction, Oracle assumes that the transaction was aborted.

Oracle supports two isolation modes: read committed and serializable. You may recall from the previous section that read committed guards you from the dirty read problem. How does Oracle do this? Before a change takes place to a record, the state of the record is saved in the rollback log. If a transaction running in the read committed state attempts to read data that is being changed, Oracle reads the data from the rollback log instead.

—Continued—

You may be wondering why this is a good thing, since the data will most likely be changed after it has been read. Think about the true purpose of a transaction: to provide consistent data—not the "latest" data. The rollback data gives you an accurate picture of what the data looked like at one point in time. The fact that it is being changed at the moment is irrelevant. Even in a system like SQL Server (such as DB2 and Sybase), in which the transaction would be blocked from reading the data until the change has been committed, the system does not guarantee that you have the latest data.

Consider the time that it takes to populate an HTML page for the client with the data the other transaction has read. It is very likely that by the time you are done reading the information, another transaction may have come in and changed the data. Or again, consider the process of purchasing a book through Amazon.com. When you do a search for the book, the HTML page reports how soon the book is expected to arrive at your door. This estimate is based on a quantity of books. However, by the time you actually purchase the book, it is possible that other clients may have bought all the copies of the book. The data was accurate at the time it was read, but it was only a snapshot in time. Therefore, it makes no difference whether you are getting the latest data or the data just before the most recent changes were begun; what matters is that the data you read is consistent.

Distributed Versus Local Transactions

We use the term *local transaction* to describe a transaction that involves a single resource manager (RM). The term does not have to do with the proximity of the RM; it simply has to do with where the transaction coordinator resides. In a local transaction the transaction is managed by the RM's internal transaction manager.

A *distributed transaction* is one that involves more than one resource manager. We will discuss shortly exactly what this means. For now, think about the difficulties of coordinating a transaction between two different databases like a SQL Server database and an Oracle database. COM+ components are designed to work with this type of environment. In the case of transactions in which two or more resource managers are involved, a transaction coordinator must run the two-phase commit (2PC) protocol. In phase 1 of the 2PC protocol, the transaction coordinator asks each RM involved in the transaction if it is ready to commit. If every RM involved answers yes, then the DTC notifies all of them to commit in phase 2. If one RM answers negatively in phase 1, then every RM is told to abort. This is a simplified view of the two-phase commit and, in fact, you will learn quite a bit more about it in this chapter.

COM+ transactions use the services of the Microsoft Distributed Transaction Coordinator (DTC) to execute the 2PC protocol. The DTC is a program, *msdtc.exe*, that runs as a service in Windows NT and Windows 2000. When you use the transactioning services of COM+, you automatically use the DTC to run a distributed transaction even if your transaction involves a single RM. The DTC employs an optimization if, in fact, it is dealing with only a single RM. The RM is notified in phase 1 of the 2PC protocol that it is the only RM. The RM can then tell the DTC that it does not need phase 2. SQL Server uses this optimization, but Oracle does not. This means that Oracle distributed transactions that involve only one Oracle database still go through both phases of the 2PC protocol.

A number of developers assume that, because the COM+ mechanism for transactioning uses the DTC, you cannot use local transactions in your components. The truth is that it is often faster to use local transactions.

Local transactions

A client starts a local transaction in ADO through the `ADODB.Connection` component (that is, the ADO Connection object). The following piece of code sets the isolation level of the transaction and begins a transaction:

```
Dim conn As Connection
Set conn = New Connection
conn.IsolationLevel = adXactReadCommitted
conn.BeginTrans
```

Once you have done the database work within the transaction, you have the option of committing or aborting the transaction. To commit the transaction, you can use the CommitTrans method of the Connection object. To abort the transaction, you can use the Connection object's RollbackTrans method.

In addition to starting and completing a transaction in code, you may also write stored procedures that begin and end a transaction. The following piece of code represents a stored procedure that changes the author's name from the AUTHORS table in the Pubs database when given the author's ID:

```
DECLARE PROCEDURE ChangeAuthorsName @AuthorId nchar(5), @NewName nchar(30)
    SET TRANASACTION ISOLATION LEVEL SERIALIZABLE
    BEGIN TRAN
    UPDATE Authors SET au_name=@NewName where au_id = @AuthorId
    COMMIT TRAN
END PROCEDURE
```

A question that may come to mind is, "What happens if you begin a transaction with code and, within the transaction code, you call a stored procedure that also begins a transaction?" Are the two transactions related somehow, or do they behave like two different transactions?

When your transactional code calls on a stored procedure that itself calls BEGIN TRAN, SQL Server maintains a transaction counter; each call to BEGIN TRAN, whether in a stored procedure or in SQL code, increases the counter by 1. The transaction can be committed only when you call COMMIT TRAN as many times as BEGIN TRAN was called. A word of caution, however: if you call ROLLBACK TRAN from either your code or the stored procedure, the transaction is rolled back and terminated regardless of how many times you called BEGIN TRAN.

Distributed transactions

Distributed transactions are transactions that involve the DTC and often more than one resource manager. Having more than one resource manager involved means that distributed transactions are harder to manage. For example, a distributed transaction may involve an Oracle database and a SQL Server database. A program task may be to move data from the Oracle database to the SQL Server database. These operations must be done atomically. If you try to do this manually with local transactions, you may tell one database to commit the transaction only to find that the second database is not able to commit its transaction. At this point, it would be too late to tell the first database to abort the transaction. To fix this, an external transaction manager runs the distributed transaction.

The external transaction manager in Windows is the Distributed Transaction Manager, better known as the DTC. The DTC is a piece of software that runs in Windows NT or Windows 2000 as the service *MSDTC.EXE*. This software is known as a Transaction Processing Monitor, or TP monitor. A TP monitor is a piece of software that controls distributed transactions by running an algorithm known as the *two-phase commit protocol* (2PC). The two-phase commit is an industry-standard algorithm that works as follows: In phase 1, known as the *prepare phase*, each resource manager (Oracle and SQL Server, for example) is asked if it is able to commit the transaction. If one of the resource managers says no, then every other resource manager is told to abort the transaction in phase2. If all the resource managers say that they can commit the transaction, then all of the resource managers are told to commit the transaction in phase.

You do not have to use COM+ to use the DTC; you can use the DTC directly, although some of the interfaces are not Visual Basic friendly. In the downloadable software for this book, I have included an ATL COM component called DTCProxyVB to facilitate communication with the DTC.

However, it is important to know how the DTC works, because COM+ internally calls on the DTC. There are three entities involved in communication with the DTC: the client program, the resource manager proxy, and the resource manager. All three entities communicate with the DTC in one way or another. The DTC manages transactions and returns pointers to the ITransaction interface that represents each transaction. The client program is the entity that begins a transaction with the DTC. The process of talking to the DTC is roughly as follows:

First the client program contacts the DTC. The machine the client is on does not have to have the MSDTC service running (the MSDTC service runs only on Windows NT 4 and Windows 2000). This is possible because contacting the DTC is done through the DTC proxy core, a set of COM components that enable a client to communicate with the DTC.

The client contacts the DTC through the *DtcGetTransactionManager* function in the MSDTC Proxy Core Object in *xolehlp.dll*. The function has a number of parameters, but most of them are reserved and must be null. The Visual Basic version of this function has the following syntax:

```
Public Function VBDtcGetTransactionManager(ByVal HostName As String, _
    ByVal iidInterface As String) As IUnknown
```

The first parameter, *HostName*, is the name of the computer with the DTC that will serve as the coordinating machine. You can leave this parameter blank to use the local DTC if the client is running on a Windows NT or Windows 2000 machine with the *MSDTC.EXE* service running. The second parameter, *iidInterface*, is the interface ID with which you would like to start. Client programs ask for the **ITransactionDispenser** interface. The function returns an **IUnknown** pointer to the interface you requested.

To contact the DTC directly through the *VBDtcGetTransactionManager* wrapper function, do the following in code:

```
Dim pTxDisp As IUnknown
Set pTxDisp = VBDtcGetTransactionManager("Computer1", "ITransactionDispenser")
```

The function returns a pointer to an **ITransactionDispenser** interface. With this interface, you can ask the DTC to begin a new distributed transaction by calling the **ITransactionDispenser** interface's BeginTransaction method. However, this and the other methods in the interface are not VB friendly. Therefore, I have added a function called *BeginTransaction*. The *BeginTransaction* function has the following syntax:

```
Public Function BeginTransaction(ByVal pTxDisp As IUnknown, _
    ByVal IsoLevel As VBISOLEVEL, ByVal TimeoutMilliseconds As Long, _
    ByVal Description As String) As IUnknown
```

The first parameter, *pTxDisp*, is the pointer to the **ITransactionDispenser** interface you obtained from the earlier call to *DtcGetTransactionManager*. The next parameter, *IsoLevel*, is the isolation level for the transaction. The DTC does not really care what you choose; it simply passes this value onto the resource manager later. The isolation level constants represent the isolation levels you learned about earlier. The choices for isolation level are **ISOLATIONLEVEL_READCOMMITTED**,

ISOLATIONLEVEL_REPEATABLEREAD, and ISOLATIONLEVEL_ISOLATED (or
ISOLATIONLEVEL_CURSORSTABILITY or ISOLATIONLEVEL_SERIALIZABLE).
Notice that cursor stability and serializable are synonyms for isolated. The third
parameter, *TimeoutMilliseconds*, enables you to set a timeout period for the
transaction. If you exceed the transaction period, the DTC will abort the transaction. You can enter 0 for this value if you wish the transaction to last indefinitely.
The fourth parameter, *Description*, is a programmer-assigned description for the
transaction. The function returns a pointer to an ITransaction interface.

The following code example shows you how to begin a transaction:

```
Dim Tx As IUnknown
Set Tx = VBBeginTransaction(pTxDisp, VBISOLATIONLEVEL_SERIALIZABLE,6000, _
                "My distributed transaction")
```

The values I chose for the isolation level and the timeout period are not random;
these are the values that COM+ chooses when you are using distributed transactions.

A distributed transaction, though, involves more than the client and its local DTC.
A distributed transaction attempts to ensure the integrity of data in multiple
resource managers, each of which may be running on a different machine. The
DTC that the client used to begin the transaction is known as the *coordinating
DTC.* For a resource manager to be involved in a distributed transaction, the DTC
service must also be running on the same machine that the resource manager is
on. Thus, it is likely that more than one DTC service is involved in the same transaction—one on the machine where the code to begin the transaction resides and
one for each machine with a resource manager. Each resource manager talks to
the DTC service on the same machine, and each DTC service communicates with
the coordinating DTC.

As we've mentioned, you begin a transaction by calling the *BeginTransaction*
function, which returns a pointer to an ITransaction interface. So what good is
a pointer to an ITransaction interface? Well, by itself, this pointer serves as just
a handle. What we must do is get every resource manager involved in the transaction to do all their database work using this transaction handle. Resource managers also talk to the DTC through the DTC proxy core. Instead of asking for
ITransactionDispenser, they ask for IResourceManagerFactory. The details
of how they enlist and participate in the transaction are beyond the scope of this
chapter. However, I have included an example of a VB resource manager (this is
an ActiveX EXE that simulates the work of SQL Server in a distributed transaction). With this sample code, you can learn how resource managers say that they
want to participate in a transaction.

A resource manager enlists itself with the DTC without knowing anything about
the transaction a client has begun. A third entity connects the client to the resource

manager; this entity is known as the *RM proxy*. ADO through the OLEDB provider serves as the RM proxy. The job of ADO is to grab the `ITransaction` pointer handle and carry its information to the resource manager so that the DTC for the resource manager can communicate with the coordinating DTC and vice versa. For ADO to take this `ITransaction` handle, you must enlist the ADO connection in the distributed transaction.

The problem is that if you look through the methods and properties of the ADO Connection object, you will not find a way to do this. The BeginTrans method is for local transactions, not for DTC transactions. There is a trick to do this from Visual Basic, but it involves using another function in the DTCProxyVB DLL I have included for download. The trick is that all ADO Connection objects are wrappers for the OLEDB Session cotype (normally referred to as the Session object). OLEDB providers that support distributed transactions implement the `ITransactionJoin` interface. Once you have the Session object, you can *QueryInterface* (*QI*) this interface for `ITransactionJoin` and call its JoinTransaction method.

We have to get at the Session object that the ADO Connection object is wrapping but that is not exposed to Visual Basic developers. Fortunately, there is a way to do this, but it requires a little help from the DTCProxyVB component I included with the book. The trick is to access the `ADOConnectionConstruction` interface. This interface serves as a bridge between the ADO Connection object and its underlying Session object. You can *QI* an ADO Connection object for this interface to obtain a pointer to the Session object, then you can use the get_Session method to retrieve the Session object pointer. With this in mind, I added a function called *VBJoinDistributedTransaction* to the DTCProxyVB DLL. This has the following syntax:

```
Public Sub VBJoinDistributedTransaction(ByVal ADOConnection As IUnknown, _
            ByVal Tx As IUnknown, ByVal IsoLevel As VBISOLEVEL)
```

The first parameter, `ADOConnection`, is a pointer to the ADO Connection object. The second parameter, `Tx`, is the pointer to the `ITransaction` interface you obtained earlier from the DTC. The last parameter, `IsoLevel`, is the isolation level. You may be thinking, "But wait, why do we need the isolation level in this call when we specified it earlier?" According to the documentation, it is not necessary to specify the isolation level; however, some resource managers, like SQL Server, let you switch the isolation level of the transaction in the middle of the transaction. So if you are using a resource manager with this capability, this method will override the existing isolation level. It turns out that even though the documentation says you can omit this value, you must specify a value for isolation level, or the call will fail.

The following code shows how to enlist an ADO connection in a distributed transaction:

```
Dim Conn As Connection
Set Conn = New Connection
Conn.Open "Provider=SQLOLEDB;User Id=sa;Password=;Initial Catalog=Pubs"
Call VBJoinDistributedTransaction(Conn,Tx, _
                     VBISOLATIONLEVEL_SERIALIZABLE)
```

One resource manager hardly makes a distributed transaction worthwhile, so if you want to take advantage of this function, you may want to create a second connection and enlist both connections in the same transaction. All you have to do is create a second connection to another database, even if it is on a different machine and even if it uses different provider, then call *JoinDistributedTransaction* again, but this time passing the second connection object as the first parameter.

Once you have a Connection object enrolled in the transaction, any work you do with the ADO connection will occur within the confines of the transaction. Naturally, at some point, you will want to commit or abort the transaction. You can do so through the `ITransaction` interface. There are two ways of committing and aborting a transaction: it can be done synchronously or asynchronously. When you do it asynchronously, you must also implement the `ITransactionOutcomeEvents` interface. This interface lets you know if the transaction was committed, aborted, or placed in doubt (which will be explained shortly). This chapter will discuss how to do this only synchronously.

Let's examine committing and aborting a transaction synchronously. To commit a transaction, you must cast your transaction object to an `ITransaction` pointer, then call the `ITransaction`'s Commit method. However, even though the `ITransaction` interface is defined in the COM+ Services Type Library, two of the parameters in the Commit method are not VB compatible. Therefore, I have defined a VBCommit method that can be used as follows:

```
Call VBCommit(Tx, 0, VBXACTTC_SYNC_PHASEONE,0)
```

The first parameter is the transaction object you obtained from the VBBegin-Transaction method you used earlier. The second parameter tells the DTC whether to begin a new transaction immediately after committing this one. The value 0 means not to begin another transaction; 1 means to begin a new transaction. Currently the DTC does not support a value of 1. The second parameter controls whether the call is synchronous or asynchronous and when you expect the DTC to notify you of the outcome. The choices are XACTTC_ASYNC_PHASEONE, XACTTC_SYNC_PHASEONE, or XACTTC_SYNC_PHASETWO, XACTTC_SYNC. The XACCT_SYNC constant is the same as XACTTC_SYNC_PHASETWO. The other three constants determine if the DTC is to return notification after phase 1 or after phase 2 and whether it is a synchronous or an asynchronous commit. Phase 1 and phase 2 refer to the phases in the two-phase commit protocol. They determine whether you are notified after the conclusion of phase 1 or after the conclusion of phase 2. Remember that, in phase 1, each resource manager is asked if it can commit the transaction. If all resource managers say yes, the transaction will succeed. If at least one of the transaction managers says no, the transaction will fail. So after phase 1, it is a sure bet that you will know the outcome of the transaction. Currently, the XACTTC_SYNC_PHASETWO value is not supported. The third parameter must be 0.

To abort the transaction, you call the Abort method in the ITransaction interface. As I mentioned earlier, the definition of this interface is included in the COM+ Services Type Library. If you include this type library through the Project References dialog box, then you can use it, and the good news is that the Abort method is supported in VB. Let's look at some code that aborts the transaction and then discuss the parameters in the call:

```
Dim pTrans As ITransaction
Set pTrans = Tx
Dim reason As Boid
Call pTrans.Abort(reason,0,0)
```

The Abort method has three parameters as well. The first parameter is a pointer to a BOID structure that describes the reason the transaction was aborted. This is not a required piece of information, so you can set this parameter to a variable of type BOID. The BOID structure is used to set a reason for the failure that makes sense to your application. It is meant to be a value you provide through the BOID's array of bytes, but there is currently no documentation explaining how this value is used by the DTC, and it is certainly not needed. The second parameter tells the DTC whether it should start another transaction immediately. As in the Commit method, 0 means not to begin another transaction, and 1 means to begin a new transaction immediately. Again, the value 1 is not currently supported; you must pass 0. The last parameter is a Boolean that tells the DTC whether you want asynchronous notifications; 0 means synchronous, and 1 means asynchronous. Notice that unlike the Commit method, you do not have two phases to worry about. That's because your code is run before the two-phase commit protocol. Thus, an Abort method call before the two-phase commit protocol begins tells the DTC to just tell each resource manager to abort the transaction.

Declarative Transactions

As you know, a number of COM+ features can be set through declarative attributes. One is setting transactions at the component level, known as *declarative transactions*. You can set the transactioning attribute of each component by using the component's Transactions tab in the Component Services administration program. The options are Disabled, Not Supported, Supported, Required, and Requires New. Through this declarative property, components decide whether they wish to participate in the outcome of the transaction. Every object that wants to participate in a transaction has one vote. All operations that the object performs occur during a transaction. At the end of the operation, all the votes are collected. Then the system either aborts the transaction or commits the transaction. You have to know when the transaction begins, when the transaction ends, what objects participate in the transaction, and how the components vote on the outcome of the transaction.

Declarative transactions differ from local transactions in several ways. First, when you use declarative transactions, you do not call BeginTrans, CommitTrans, or RollbackTrans. Your code never manages the physical transaction directly. You specify the transactional requirements of your component through declarative properties. COM+ will begin the physical transaction when needed. Your code will simply vote on the outcome of the transaction. At the end, COM+ will collect all the votes and call CommitTrans or RollbackTrans on your behalf. Second, declarative transactions use distributed transactions instead of local transactions—they involve the DTC.

To understand how components vote on the outcome of the transaction and how the COM+ plumbing manages the DTC transaction, you must first understand how transaction streams work.

Transaction Streams

COM+ includes the concept of a *transaction stream*. Components in the same transaction stream participate in the outcome of the transaction. To become part of a transaction stream, a component specifies its transaction requirements through the Transactions tab of a component's Properties dialog box in the Component Services administration program. If you examine Figure 9-2, you will see the declarative attributes of a component.

As you can see, the transaction options are Requires, Requires New, Supported, Not Supported, and Disabled. As with other services in COM+, COM+ attributes greater importance to the first object that the client creates in the application. The first object to be created with transactioning turned on becomes the root of the transaction. As you will see shortly, the root of the transaction controls the lifetime of the DTC transaction. When you create a component that is marked as Transaction Requires or Transaction Requires New, COM+ begins a transaction stream. COM+ assigns to each transaction stream a unique identifier known as the transaction ID.

Once the client creates a transactioning component, COM+ begins the transaction stream but does not begin a physical connection with the DTC immediately—it tries to delay this until it is needed. In fact, it delays talking to the DTC until COM+ makes the first interesting call, which is the first call that needs access to an

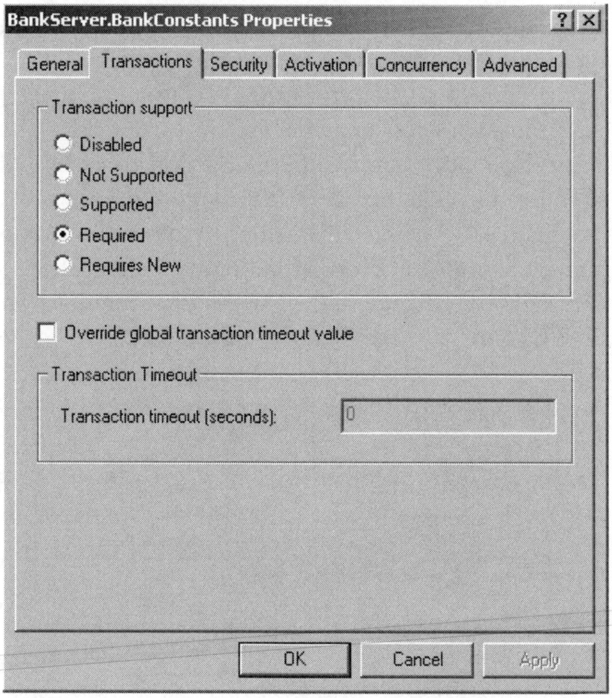

Figure 9-2. Transaction settings for a component

TransactionId

You can tell if two objects are part of the same transaction stream by examining the properties of the context the objects live in as follows:

```
Dim ctx As ObjectContext
Set ctx = GetObjectContext()
Dim ctxinfo As ObjectContextInfo
Set ctxinfo = ctx.ContextInfo
Call TRACE("Transaction Stream Id=" & ctxinfo.TransactionId)
```

This code reports the GUID assigned to the transaction stream.

`ITransaction` pointer. (Remember that the `ITransaction` pointer is the resource dispensed by the DTC.) The first interesting call occurs when you make an ADO connection or when you try to access the `ITransaction` pointer yourself in code. Once the first interesting call occurs, the COM+ plumbing contacts the DTC and tells it to begin a distributed transaction (the details of this operation were described earlier, in the "Distributed Versus Local Transactions" section). Thus, COM+ delays contacting the DTC as long as possible, then contacts the DTC after the first interesting call and tells it to begin a new transaction. As part of the call to begin a transaction, the client tells the DTC two important pieces of information: the first is the expiration time for the transaction, and the second is the isolation level. The expiration time for the transaction is set by default to 60 seconds. However, you can change this default through scripting code or through the administration program. To change this setting through the Component Services administration program, right-click on My Computer, then choose Properties. In the Properties dialog box, change the value in the "Transaction timeout (seconds)" field on the Options tab. See Figure 9-3 for details.

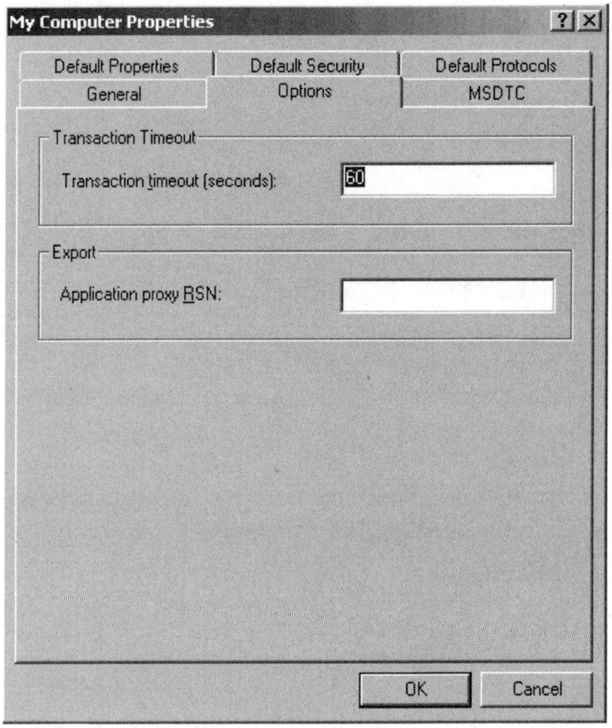

Figure 9-3. Machine Transaction timeout default

You can also change the default timeout per root component. If the creation of the component begins a transaction stream, then the setting for that particular component can override the system's default. You can set the component's timeout by right-clicking on the component, choosing Properties, and then choosing the Transactions tab. The lower half of the screen lets you override the default timeout for transactions (see Figure 9-4).

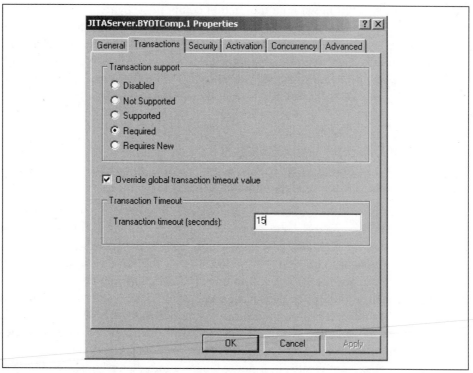

Figure 9-4. Transaction Timeout for components

Unfortunately, you cannot change the default isolation mode. But that does not mean that the isolation mode is fixed. Remember that resource managers like SQL Server enable you to change the isolation level in the middle of a transaction. Therefore, if you wish to change the isolation level from serializable to something else, you can do it in two ways. One way is to run a stored procedure that sets the isolation level with a line like the following:

```
SET TRANSACTION ISOLATION LEVEL READ UNCOMMITTED
```

The other way is to use query hints. SQL Server 7.0 and above enable you to specify in a query the isolation level for the query. The following query uses a query hint to change the isolation level temporarily to read uncommitted:

```
select * from author (readuncommitted)
```

Once the COM+ plumbing begins a physical transaction, it stores the **ITransaction** pointer reference in context. You can retrieve this **ITransaction** pointer from context using the **ContextInfo** interface, as shown:

```
Dim Tx As ITransaction
Set Tx = GetObjectContext.ContextInfo.Transaction
```

When you use ADO from within a transaction component, by default, OLEDB Services checks the context space for a transaction handle (in essence, it runs the preceding code). If there is one, then it automatically joins the transaction using the procedure we talked about in the distributed transaction section. You can turn off this behavior by specifying OLE DB Services = 0 in the connection string, as follows:

```
Dim Conn
Set Conn = New Connection
Conn.Open "connection string here, OLE DB Services=0"
```

You can use the preceding code whenever you need to run a query that does not need to hold locks for the existing transaction.

So far we have been talking about a single object being part of the transaction. To include other objects in the same transaction, objects already in the transaction must create them. In addition, you must choose the appropriate transaction setting in the component's attributes. To be included in the same transaction stream, the secondary component must be marked as Transaction Required or Transaction Supported. The difference between Required and Supported is that Required begins a new transaction if a nontransactional component or the client creates the component, but it joins the existing transaction if a transactional component creates it. A component marked as Transaction Supported joins a transaction only if a transactional component creates it; it never begins a transaction stream on its own. If you mark a secondary component as Requires New, the secondary component will begin a new transaction stream. This is not a nested transaction, but rather a new transaction, independent from the existing one. The Not Supported setting forces the object outside of the transaction (it simply does not participate in or vote on the transaction). The Disabled setting is available for raw configured components—it tells the SCM not to look at this property when deciding whether the component needs its own context. Thus, a component with the transaction setting set to Disabled will be part of a transaction stream only if the SCM can place it in its creator's context.

An interesting thing about transaction streams is that they are not bound to one application; they can in fact extend to multiple applications, and they can even span across machines. Objects involved in the transaction stream will most likely interact with a resource manager and then vote on the outcome of the transaction.

JITA

To understand how the voting mechanism works, you first need to understand how JITA works. JITA stands for Just-in-time activation. It is a service that can normally be turned on or off through the component properties. Figure 9-5 shows the JITA checkbox in the component Properties dialog box.

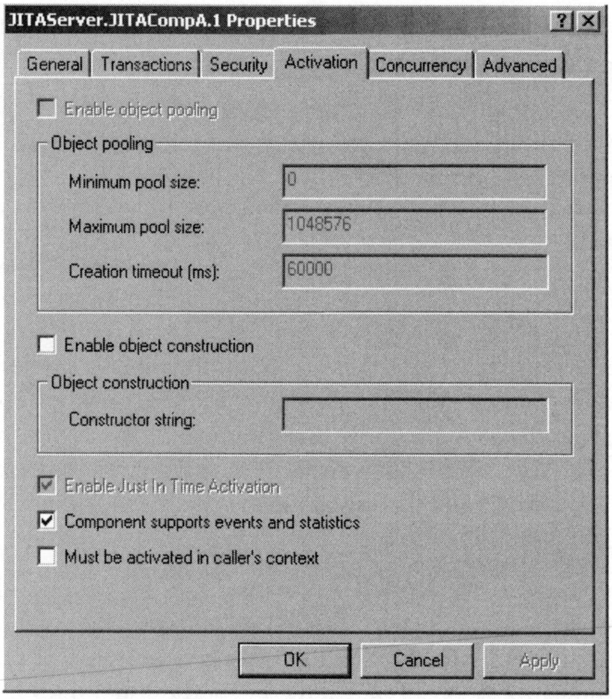

Figure 9-5. Just-in-time activation setting

When you turn on transactioning for a component, the component will always use JITA—you cannot turn it off. JITA means that the COM+ architecture will create instances or destroy instances of your component on demand. The fact that the JITA service will destroy your object on demand means that using JITA also implies Just-in-time deactivation (but JITD doesn't sound cool).

With JITA, your component's life cycle follows a four-step process:

Creation

   Occurs when the client creates an instance of the component. In COM+, there is little distinction between creation and the next phase, known as activation.

Activation

   Occurs when the client makes the first method call into the component. In MTS (the predecessor to COM+), context information was not available until the activation phase. In VB components for Windows 2000, there is always full context information at creation time. Thus, activation can just be seen as the time when the client makes its first method call.

Deactivation

Occurs when the client releases the object. In the case of VB components, deactivation is always followed by termination.

Destruction

Occurs when all references to the object are released. For VB components, it happens right after deactivation.

You may have noticed that I have been careful to not use words like *always* in the previous list without the phrase *in the case of VB components*. The reason is that activation and deactivation can potentially work differently if you use another service called object pooling. *Object pooling* enables you to return an object to a pool of objects after it is deactivated. If that happens, then it is possible to have deactivation without destruction. VB objects cannot use the pooling service because it requires the objects to have very low thread affinity, and, as you have learned in previous chapters, VB objects have very high thread affinity. Therefore, in the case of VB components, deactivation is always immediately followed by destruction.

It is possible, however, for a component to be deactivated before the client releases the reference to it. Every object running with JITA support runs in its own context. Part of the context space for a JITA component is a flag known as the done bit. The done bit controls when an object is deactivated. If you set the done bit to **True** during a method call, when the method call returns, COM+ will deactivate the object and (in the case of a VB object) destroy it. You can set the done bit to **True** programmatically or through the administration program. The following piece of code shows you how to set the done bit programmatically:

```
Dim ctxState As IContextState
Set ctxState = GetObjectContext()
Call ctxState.SetDeactivateOnReturn(True)
```

To control the done bit, you use the SetDeactivateOnReturn method in the `IContextState` interface. The first step is to cast the `ObjectContext` interface obtained from *GetObjectContext* into `IContextState`. Then call the SetDeactivateOnReturn method, passing the value of **True** to turn on the done bit or **False** to turn it off. The function has no effect until the call returns and passes through the proxy for the context. You may also do this through the Component Services administration program. Just choose the method whose done bit you want to set and view its properties. Figure 9-6 shows you the method Properties dialog box. If you check the "Automatically deactivate this object when this method returns" box, then the done bit will be set for that method, and, when the method completes, the object will be deactivated and destroyed.

If you set the done bit to **True** for the context and the call returns, then the object is deactivated and destroyed, but the client may not have released the object. So from the client's point of view, the client is still holding on to the object. In reality,

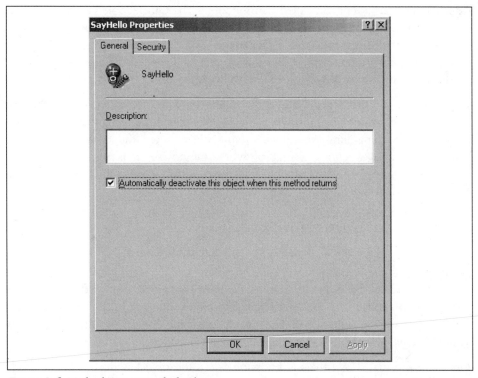

Figure 9-6. Method Properties dialog box

the client holds the proxy. If the client tries to make another method call, the COM+ plumbing creates another instance of the component and executes the call. Thus, your component goes through the construction and the activation phase again.

You can detect when your component goes through the four phases of JITA. Creation and destruction are detectable through the normal Initialize and Terminate events in all VB classes. To detect activation and deactivation, you must implement the `ObjectControl` interface. The `ObjectControl` interface has the methods shown in the following code fragment:

```
Implements ObjectControl

Private Sub ObjectControl_Activate()
End Sub

Private Sub ObjectControl_Deactivate()
End Sub

Private Function ObjectControl_CanBePooled() As Boolean
End Function
```

If you notice, the interface has Activate and Deactivate methods that report the activation and deactivation phases of the JITA service. You may also notice that this interface also has a function called CanBePooled. The CanBePooled method is unrelated to the JITA service; it really is part of the object pooling service, which also makes use of the `ObjectControl` interface. The CanBePooled method asks the object if it wants to return to the pool of objects or if it wants to be destroyed. This method will not fire for VB objects, since they cannot use the object pooling service.

One could argue that JITA is useful for telling us when the client makes the first method call into the object and when the plumbing is done using the object. However, a more compelling reason is for an object to tell the COM+ architecture when it is done executing a unit of work. Otherwise, it is impossible for the plumbing to know when your object is done with a certain task. This leads us back to transactions.

Voting on a Transaction

JITA tells the COM+ architecture when the objects involved in a transaction are done with all the necessary steps to complete the transaction. COM+ ends the transaction when the object that is the root of the transaction is deactivated. In fact, the JITA service is used for all the components involved in the transaction. An object votes on the outcome of the transaction using some functions I will show you later. The vote is final when the object is deactivated.

One problem that JITA solves is knowing when the object is done with its work. This problem could have been solved by assuming that the object is done when it is destroyed. However, that would mean one of two things: either the client would have to destroy the object, or the COM+ architecture would have to destroy it. Having the client destroy the object is not a good idea, because it places the client in control of the transaction. Placing the client in control of the transaction means that the client code must contain the logic to execute all the steps in the transaction. This means that each step will be executed potentially across the Internet, greatly decreasing the performance of the application. If the duration of the transaction depends on several round-trips across the Internet, locks obtained for the transaction will be held longer than if the round-trips occurred from middle-tier components on the server machine. The longer the locks are held, the less concurrent your application will be. This is because locks from one transaction will block other transactions from doing their work. Also, when working with the DTC, there is the potential problem that a transaction will time out after a certain period of time. Remember that when you begin a transaction with the DTC, you must specify a timeout period—COM+ sets this timeout to 60 seconds by default. You may think that this can be easily fixed by increasing the timeout period, but it would not be a good idea to increase it significantly. The timeout period is a safeguard for cases in which a deadlock situation may arise that the resource manager cannot resolve. By automatically ending a transaction after a certain period of time, you guarantee that a deadlock will not halt your server forever.

It is important to optimize your application's performance and concurrency by moving all the transaction code to middle-tier components where round-trips to the database are much faster. If you move all the transaction logic to a middle-tier component, there must be a mechanism by which the object can tell COM+ that it is done with a certain transaction. The object could tell COM+ that it is done by invoking a special method. However, there is a second problem. Objects do not really know the true outcome of a transaction. To an object that votes to commit a transaction, it appears as if the transaction has succeeded. The truth is that even after all the objects vote to commit the transaction, it is possible for the transaction to fail during the 2PC—one of the resource managers may have gone offline, for example. It would be bad for an object to assume that a transaction has succeeded and for the object to hold data that was calculated during the transaction. For example, after removing an item from inventory, an object may decide to cache the total count of inventory items. However, if the transaction is rolled back, the object may be holding incorrect data.

To be safe, COM+ destroys the objects that were involved in a transaction before beginning the 2PC. In that way, the next transaction occurs with a fresh set of components. This leads us to the second scenario—the object has, in a sense, destroyed itself by telling COM+ that it was done executing a transaction. But what if the client code is not done using the object? It would be very awkward for the client to make a method call, then attempt a second call and fail because the first call caused the object to destroy itself. Thus, COM+ must distinguish between when the object is destroyed for the purposes of the transactional model and when the object is destroyed because the client no longer needs it. To distinguish between these two types of destruction, COM+ introduced JITA. JITA refers to the stage in which the object needs to be destroyed for the sake of a service as *deactivation*. If a client makes another call to the object, the JITA service will "reactivate" the object by creating a new instance of it. Thus a client that is holding a reference to an object can continue using it. JITA refers to the phase in which a client is done using the object as *destruction*. After the destruction phase, the client code cannot just make a method call into the object; it must create a new instance. Thus, the JITA server helps COM+ figure out when a unit of work has been completed.

Every object involved in a transaction by definition runs in its own context (JITA forces an object into its own context). The context space has what has been called the "happy" bit. When the happy bit is set to **True**, the object's vote is to commit the transaction. When the happy bit is set to **False**, the vote is to abort the transaction. If any object is deactivated in an unhappy state, then the transaction is doomed. That does not mean that the COM+ plumbing tells the DTC to abort the transaction. In fact, the COM+ plumbing does not abort the physical transaction until the root object is deactivated. Deactivating the root object tells COM+ that the unit of work is complete.

Voting on the outcome of a transaction is done through the `IContextState` interface. The interface has a method called SetMyTransactionVote that sets the state of the happy bit. The function has one input parameter whose value can be either `TxAbort` or `TxCommit`. The following code example shows how to set the state of the happy bit in code:

```
Public Sub MakeDeposit(ByVal Amount As Currency)

    If Amount < 0 Then
        Dim ctxState As IContextState
        Set ctxState = GetObjectContext
        ctxState.SetMyTransactionVote(txAbort)
    Else
        ctxState.SetMyVoteTransactionVote(txCommit)
    End If

End Sub
```

The MakeDeposit method votes to abort the transaction if the amount for the deposit is less than 0. If an object does not vote on the outcome of the transaction, then its vote is to commit the transaction. Thus, it is not necessary to execute the code in the `Else` clause, but it is good practice.

The `IContextState` interface also has a method, GetMyTransactionVote, for reading the state of the happy bit.

Remember that the vote is not final until the object is deactivated, and that doesn't happen until you set the done bit to `True` and exit the method. Some developers take advantage of this fact to protect their code. They begin their code by voting to abort the transaction and to deactivate the object. Then the remaining code executes, and, at the end, the vote is changed back to committing the transaction. This is seen in the following code example:

```
Public Sub MakeDeposit(ByVal Amount As Currency)
    Dim ctxState As IContextState
    Set ctxState = GetObjectContext
    Call ctxState.SetMyTransactionVote(txAbort)
    Call ctxState.SetDeactivateOnReturn(True)

    If Amount < 0 Then
        Exit Sub
    Else
        'Do something useful
    End If
```

```
        Call ctxState.SetMyTransactionVote(txCommit)
    End Sub
```

Developers use this technique to essentially change the default state of the vote to aborting the transaction. The code is meant to protect us from any unforeseen errors. If an error occurs in the middle of the function, then by default the transaction will be aborted. This trick works, and it is useful because the vote does not take effect when you set the happy bit nor when you set the done bit—COM+ will not check these values until the method ends. Therefore, during the method, you can change these values back and forth until satisfied.

Methods for backward compatibility

COM+ has a few methods for voting and setting the done bit that were introduced in MTS and have been left for backward compatibility so that any existing code you have for MTS will port to Windows 2000. The methods are in the `ObjectContext` interface and are SetComplete, SetAbort, EnableCommit and DisableCommit. I have rewritten the previous code example to use the legacy methods, as shown:

```
Public Sub MakeDeposit(ByVal Amount As Currency)
    Call GetObjectContext.SetAbort

    If Amount < 0 Then
        Exit Sub
    Else
        'Do something useful
    End If

    Call GetObjectContext.SetComplete
End Sub
```

The code looks simpler with these methods, but be aware that in MTS, almost every major command was part of the `ObjectContext` interface and, with COM+, an effort has been made to break this interface into smaller interfaces. Therefore, use the old methods at your own risk. Table 9-1 shows how SetComplete, SetAbort, EnableCommit, and DisableCommit control the happy bit and the done bit. As you can see, SetComplete and SetAbort make final votes when the method completes, while EnableCommit and DisableCommit set passive votes.

Table 9-1. How ObjectContext methods set the happy and done bits

Method	Happy bit	Done bit
SetComplete	True	True
SetAbort	False	True
EnableCommit	True	Does not change
DisableCommit	False	Does not change

Coding guidelines

The basic idea in developing transactional applications is to divide the work among several components. Then each component involved in the transaction should perform its task and base its vote on whether it finished its task successfully or not.

For example, in a banking application, a customer may want to move money from one account to another. Generally, there is one component that takes on the role of administrator for the task. Let's suppose the component is called BankMgr and has a method called TransferFunds, as follows:

```
Public Sub TransaferFunds(ByVal Amount As Currency, _
        ByVal SrcAccount As Long, ByVal DstAccount As Long)
End Sub
```

The client code specifies the amount, the source account, and the destination account, then the function makes the transfer. That component may make use of another component that checks whether the account number is valid and the account has enough funds. The name of the second component may be AccountMgr, and it may have a method called CheckForFunds. Suppose the CheckForFunds function has the following code:

```
Public Sub CheckForFunds(ByVal AccountNumber As Long, _
        ByVal Amount As Currency)
    Dim ctxState As IContextState
    Set ctxState = GetObjectContext()
    Call ctxState.SetDeactivateOnReturn(True)

    If ValidAccountNumber(AccountNumber) = False Then
        Call ctxState.SetMyTransactionVote(txAbort)
        Exit Sub
    End IF

    If AvailableBalance(AccountNumber) < Amount Then
        Call ctxState.SetMyTransactionVote(txAbort)
        Exit Sub
    End If

End Sub
```

The previous code example first checks whether the account number is valid. If it is not, it votes to abort the transaction and exits. If the account number is valid, the function checks whether the available balance is greater than or equal to the amount. If it is less than the amount, then the code also votes to abort the transaction. The vote will be final when the method exits, because, if you notice at the very beginning of the routine, the code sets the done bit to **True**.

The preceding code is definitely legal code, but it is not optimized. If any object is deactivated in an unhappy state, the COM+ plumbing will vote to abort the transaction. There is really no point in continuing with the transaction. Therefore, the secondary objects should notify the root object that they have voted to abort the transaction. This is normally done by raising an error.

The following code example shows the optimized version of the CheckForFunds method:

```
Public Sub CheckForFunds(ByVal AccountNumber As Long, _
         ByVal Amount As Currency)
   Dim ctxState As IContextState
   Set ctxState = GetObjectContext()
   Call ctxState.SetDeactivateOnReturn(True)

   If ValidAccountNumber(AccountNumber) = False Then
       Call ctxState.SetMyTransactionVote(txAbort)
       Err.Raise vbObjectError + 1024, 'CheckForFunds', 'Invalid Account'
       Exit Sub
   End IF

   If AvailableBalance(AccountNumber) < Amount Then
       Call ctxState.SetMyTransactionVote(txAbort)
       Err.Raise vbObjectError + 1025, 'CheckForFunds','Not enough funds'
       Exit Sub
   End If

End Sub
```

The difference in this version is that it reports an error to notify the caller that it has set its vote to abort and that therefore the transaction is doomed. Let's look at the code for the root object:

```
Public Sub TransaferFunds(ByVal Amount As Currency, _
         ByVal SrcAccount As Long, ByVal DstAccount As Long)
   Dim ctxState As IContextState
   Set ctxState = GetObjectContext()
   Call ctxState.SetDeactivateOnReturn(True)

   Dim check As AcctMgr
   Set check = CreateObject("BankServer.AcctMgr")

   On Error Resume Next
   Call check.CheckForFunds(SrcAccount,Amount)

   If Err.Number <> 0 Then
       Call ctxState.SetMyTransactionVote(txAbort)
       On Error Goto 0
       Err.Raise vbObjectError + 1025, 'CheckForFunds', 'Transfer Failed'
       Exit Sub
   End If

   Call ctxState.SetMyTransactionVote(txCommit)
End Sub
```

The code in the root object uses the secondary object to check whether the source account has enough funds. If the secondary object votes to abort the transaction either because the account number is invalid or because the account does not have enough funds, the root object catches the error, also votes to deactivate and to abort the transaction, and exits immediately.

Avoid New

Notice that the previous code for creating the secondary component uses the *CreateObject* function instead of New. New in VB 6 is tricky because it works differently, depending on where the secondary component is. If the secondary component is in the same DLL as the root component, then New does not go through the SCM to activate the component. It instead uses an internal mechanism to create the component. Therefore, if I had used New, both components would share the same context, and the secondary component would not have a vote of its own. This is not the expected behavior. To guarantee that your COM+ components end up in their own context, use the *CreateObject* method. In VB.NET, it is safe to use New all the time.

In both the code for the secondary component and that for the root component, the components specify at the beginning that they wish to be deactivated when the code returns. This is a good practice for secondary components and essential for primary components. You should never return control to the client without resolving the outcome of the transaction. If you do, the client has influence over the duration of the transaction. Giving control back to the client usually means that the component has methods by which the client drives the steps necessary to complete the transaction. This is normally not considered a good approach, because it usually means that the client has code that must be maintained and that may mean making frequent changes to the client program to keep it up to date; if your clients are web clients, distributing custom applications to them is not easy. Besides, putting code on the client means making more round-trips across the network, which means slower applications.

From the client side

Let's talk about the client code. To run a method within a transaction, all that the client needs to do is make a method call. In our bank example, the client code may be as follows:

```
Dim Bank As BankMgr
Set Bank = CreateObject("BankServer.BankMgr")
On Error Resume Next
Call Bank.TransferFunds(500,1001,2001)
```

```
If Err.Number = vbObjectError + 1025 Then
    MsgBox "Transaction Failed"
Else
    MsgBox "Transaction Succeeded"
End If
```

Notice that the code for the root object raises an error when it votes to abort the transaction. This is the only way that the client knows that the transaction failed. The client program then traps the error and notifies the user.

Stateless components

Because transactional components, if coded correctly, set the done bit to **True** in each transactional method, the component's lifetime is tied to the duration of the method. When the method ends, the COM+ plumbing deactivates the component. This means that your transactional components are normally stateless. If you need to maintain state across method calls, you can add a nontransactional object as the entry point into the application.

For example, in the previous bank example, we could introduce a component called BankCenter and have this component maintain state between method calls. This component would have its transaction property marked as Not Supported. The default interface of this component would have the same methods as the BankMgr component; it would just create an instance of BankMgr (the transactional component) and forward the methods to it. BankMgr would then be stateless, but BankCenter would maintain state information.

Transaction programming scenarios

We will cover some important transaction programming scenarios briefly.

Imagine that a secondary object votes to abort the transaction and to deactivate, and the root object then calls a second method in the object that votes to commit the transaction. The COM+ plumbing will create a new instance of the secondary object (as usual with the JITA service). It will activate the secondary component, but it will not execute the method. Instead, it will fail the call with error &H8004E003, "You made a method call on a COM+ component that has a transaction that has already aborted or is in the process of aborting."

Imagine that, instead of aborting the transaction, the secondary component votes to commit the transaction and to deactivate, and then the root object calls on another method of the secondary component. This situation is a little different: COM+ will let you call on methods of secondary objects if the object has never voted to abort the transaction.

Another interesting scenario occurs when a secondary object tells COM+ to abort the transaction, yet the root object tells COM+ to commit the transaction. Any secondary object may vote to commit the transaction without taking into consideration the votes of other objects. However, the root object does not have that freedom. If a secondary object voted to abort the transaction and to deactivate, the root object cannot vote to commit the transaction. If it does, the COM+ infrastructure will return error &H08004E002, "The root transaction wanted to commit, but transaction aborted."

BYOT

You have to love Microsoft abbreviations like BYOT. BYOT stands for bring your own transaction, and it is a new service in COM+. The idea is that you may want to drive the DTC transaction yourself. There are a couple of reasons for this:

- Instead of guessing when the first interesting call occurs (and thus, when the timeout period begins), you may want to know exactly when the DTC communication begins—it begins when you start it with code.

- You can control DTC parameters such as the timeout period and especially the serialization level (which cannot be changed through properties) directly.

What is the difference between using BYOT and using the DTC directly, as shown earlier in this chapter? With BYOT, you can take the Transaction reference that the DTC gives you and tell COM+ to stuff it into context. Then, when you open an ADO connection, instead of having to use the `ITransactionJoin` interface that you saw earlier, the ADO connection will itself reach into context and join the transaction automatically. (If you talk to the DTC directly and don't put the transaction in context, then you have to manually join connections to a transaction, as shown earlier.) So the only thing you have to do manually is obtain an `ITransaction` pointer reference from the DTC and ask COM+ to store it into context space, then let the COM+ transaction stream mechanism take care of distributing the `ITransaction` pointer.

Beginning the DTC connection and obtaining an `ITransaction` pointer reference can be done using some of the code I showed earlier in the chapter (I'll show the code again later). Then, you create an instance of the BYOT component and ask for the `ICreateWithTransactionEx` interface. This interface has a method called CreateInstance that creates an instance of a component and starts a COM+ transaction stream. The object you create with the CreateInstance method becomes the root of the transaction. Unfortunately, the `ICreateWithTransactionEx` interface is not VB friendly, so I have provided a wrapper for VB. In VB code, you create the BYOTVB component and ask for `ICreateWithTransactionExVB`, then call the CreateInstance method. The CreateInstance method has the following syntax:

```
Public Function CreateInstance(ByVal ProgId As String, _
    ByVal Tx As IUnknown) As Object
```

The method's first parameter, *ProgId*, is the ProgID of the component you want to create (remember this is the project name, a dot, and the class name, in the case of VB COM components). The second parameter, *Tx*, is the transaction pointer that you obtain from the DTC. The method returns a reference to the object you want to create. I made the return parameter of the CreateInstance function an Object (which, as you should know from previous chapters, means `IDispatch`). I did this so that you can use the BYOTVB component from an ASP script.

The following code example shows how to use the BYOT service. This code example assumes that you are using the BankMgr and AcctMgr components from the previous code examples. Instead of the client creating the BankMgr component, the client will now create another component that will use the BYOT service to create the BankMgr component. The name of the new component, for the sake of the example, will be BankTransactions. This component has a method called TransferFunds in its default interface, just like the BankMgr component.

```
Public Sub TransferFunds(ByVal Amount As Currency, _
         ByVal SrcAccount As Long, ByVal DstAccount As Long)
   Dim ctxState As IContextState
   Set ctxState = GetObjectContext()
   Call ctxState.SetDeactivateOnReturn(True)

   Dim byotvb As ICreateWithTransactionExVB
   Set byotvb = CreateObject("DTCVB.BYOTVB")

   Dim pTxDisp As Unknown
   Set pTxDisp = DtcGetTransactionManager("Computer1","My DTC connection", _
            "ITransactionDispenser")

   Dim Tx As IUnknown
   Set Tx = DtcBeginTransaction(pTxDisp, ISOLATIONLEVEL_SERIALIZABLE,60, _
         "My distributed transaction")

   Dim bank As BankMgr
   Set bank = byotvb.CreateInstance("BankServer.BankMgr",Tx)
   Call bank.TransferFunds(Amount,SrcAccount,DstAccount)
End Sub
```

The code first creates an instance of the BYOTVB component in the DTCVB library and then does a *QI* for `ICreateWithTransactionExVB`. Then it makes a connection to the DTC, gets the `ITransactionDispenser` interface, and asks the DTC transaction dispenser to begin a new transaction. The transaction pointer is stored in the Tx variable. The last step is to call CreateInstance in the `ICreateWithTransactionExVB` interface. The code passes the ProgID of the BankMgr component and the `ITransaction` pointer stored in Tx. This function returns a pointer to the BankMgr component. Finally, the code forwards the call to the BankMgr's TransferFunds method.

For the stream to flow, the BankMgr component must have its Transaction property set to Transaction Required or Transaction Supported, and the secondary component must have its Transaction property marked to Required or Supported as well (as in the case of normal declarative transactions).

The client code is virtually the same, except for a minor change to create the BankTransactions component instead of BankMgr:

```
Dim Bank As BankMgr
Set Bank = CreateObject("BankServer.BankMgr")
On Error Resume Next
Call Bank.TransferFunds(500,1001,2001)
If Err.Number = vbObjectError + 1025 Then
    MsgBox "Transaction Failed"
Else
    MsgBox "Transaction Succeeded"
End If
```

All the technologies we've talked about so far involve using a resource manager that knows how to interact with OLE transactions. OLE transactions are the transactions you get from the DTC or the transactions you start manually with BeginTrans from the connection component. COM+ has a new service, Compensating Resource Managers, which enables you to involve other resources in the transaction.

Compensating Resource Managers

Compensating Resource Managers enable you to involve a commonly nontransactional resource—such as a registry key, for example—in a declarative transaction. The catch is that you have to do the job of rolling back any work done on the resource if the transaction fails. Let's see how the service works by writing some code that involves an Access local database in a distributed transaction with SQL Server.

The problem

One of the resources you might want to involve in a transaction is an Access database. There is an OLEDB provider for the Access database engine, Jet, that supports transactions. However, the Session object (wrapped through the ADO Connection object) does not support **ITransactionJoin**. What that means is that an Access database cannot participate in a DTC transaction. In fact, if you try to open a connection to an Access database using ADO in a transactional component, as shown in the following code, you will get an error:

```
Call Conn.Open("Provider=Microsoft.Jet.OLEDB.4.0;" & _
               "Data Source=C:\Writing\COM+\Chapter 08\crm\changes.mdb;" & _
               "Persist Security Info=False")
```

There is nothing wrong with this code per se; the problem is that ADO does not create the OLEDB provider directly. ADO uses the OLEDB Service Component Manager (another SCM). The OLEDB SCM is a component that adds functionality (or services) to OLEDB providers. It was introduced with OLEDB 2.0, and it is now required for clients to create their OLEDB providers through this component. One of the services that the OLEDB SCM provides is automatically joining an existing transaction. Thus, in ADO, when you open a connection, the OLEDB SCM will find out if your code is running within a transaction. It is not hard to find out if your code is running within a transaction—remember that ADO components are nonconfigured components and therefore run in the same context as the creator. The OLEDB SCM looks in context for an **ITransaction** pointer. If it finds a transaction, the OLEDB SCM *QI*s the Session object for **ITransactionJoin**. If the Session object supports this interface, the OLEDB SCM calls the JoinTransaction method in the interface, passing the **ITransaction** pointer from context. This is how the ADO connection autoenlists in the transaction.

The problem is that, in the case of Access, the Session object does not support **ITransactionJoin**, causing the *QI* to fail and ADO to return an error when you open the connection. A workaround is to tell the OLEDB SCM not to autoenlist by adding the following clause to the connection string:

```
Call Conn.Open("Provider=Microsoft.Jet.OLEDB.4.0;" & _
            "Data Source=C:\Writing\COM+\Chapter 08\crm\changes.mdb;" & _
            "Persist Security Info=False;OLE DB Services = 0")
```

The connect string now has a directive for the OLEDB SCM to turn off all services. There are more services than just autoenlisting in distributed transactions. For more information, consult MSDN.

The preceding code does not entirely fix the problem. The main problem is not that you get an error if you do not add the clause to the connect string. The real problem is that the Jet OLEDB provider cannot participate in the transaction. To illustrate the problem, let's talk about a possible scenario.

Suppose that you are writing an application for the Pubs SQL Server database. Let's say that you have a component named CAuthors and that this component has a method in its default interface to change an author's last name. The method, ModifyAuthor, has two parameters: the author's current last name and the author's new last name. Let's say also that you would like to keep a log of all the authors that were modified per day in a local Access database. Every time a client calls ModifyAuthor, if the change was successful, you are going to add a record to a table in the Access database with the author's ID, author's old last name, author's new last name, and the date and time when the change occurred. You should not write a record if the modification did not take place, only if the change was successful.

Assuming that the CAuthors component uses declarative transactions, it makes sense that the record should not be added if the transaction is aborted. We could put the code to write the log record to the Access table in the ModifyAuthor method of the CAuthors class. Since CAuthors is the only component in our example and therefore is the root of the transaction, it is easy to write the log record just before the code calls SetComplete, and not to write the record if the code is going to call SetAbort. However, what if the code calls SetComplete and you write the record to the Access database, but for some reason SQL Server is not able to complete the transaction? Remember that in a declarative transaction, it is not until the root object deactivates that the COM+ plumbing tells the DTC to commit or abort the transaction. When COM+ tells the DTC to commit the transaction, the DTC begins the two-phase commit. In phase 1, the preparatory phase, SQL Server may tell the DTC to abort the transaction because of internal problems. It is too late at this point for your object to get involved, because it is already deactivated when the two-phase commit protocol begins. Therefore, it would be impossible for you to roll back the changes made to the log.

The Compensating Resource Manager lets one of your components participate in the two-phase commit. In fact, it lets you add a wrapper to the Access code that simulates a DTC-compatible resource manager.

The solution

To involve the Access code in the two-phase commit protocol with the DTC, you first create a component that serves as the resource manager. This component must implement the `ICrmCompensatorVariants` interface. You are going to see this interface in detail later; just keep in mind that what distinguishes the RM component for the other components is that it implements this interface. Another requirement is that the component should have its transaction property set to Not Supported. For the sake of the example, let's call the RM component CAuthorChanged; this is the component that will talk to the Access database.

The first step is to tell COM+ that this component will be the compensating resource manager. This must be done from the root transactional component—in our example, that is the CAuthors class. To register the resource manager, you first create an instance of the COM+ component CRMClerk. The job of the clerk is to maintain a log with information about the transaction and to involve the resource manager component in the two-phase commit. The CRMClerk has a default interface named `ICrmLogControl`. You tell COM+ about your CRM by calling RegisterCompensator in the `ICrmLogControl` interface. You register the CRM only once, so a good place to put this code is in the Activate event of the `ObjectControl` interface (for the JITA service). The following code shows how to register the CRM:

```
Implements ObjectControl
Dim clerk As ICrmLogControl

Private Sub ObjectControl_Activate()
    'create clerk
    Set clerk = New CRMClerk
    Call clerk.RegisterCompensator("AuthorsServer.CAuthorChanged", _
        "Access Author Changed Records", 7)
End Sub
```

Notice, first, that the CAuthors component implements the `ObjectControl` interface. Notice also that there is a module-level declaration for the clerk variable to hold a pointer to the `ICrmLogControl` interface. The code in the Activate method creates the CRMClerk component. (You get the definition for this component when you add the COM+ 1.0 Services Type Library reference to your project.) The code then calls RegisterCompensator. The first parameter in the call is the ProgID of the component that will serve as the compensator. (The compensator component can be in the same DLL as the other components in the application.) The second parameter is a description. The third parameter tells COM+ what phases in the two-phase commit protocol you are interested in. The value 7, tells COM+ that you are interested in both phases. Consult the documentation for other values. The code to register the compensator may fail if the clerk is executing a recovery phase from a previous system failure (you will learn more about this later in this chapter, and we will need to modify the previous code example then to account for this).

The next piece of code is for the ModifyAuthors method in the CAuthors component. The code is going to open a connection to the Pubs SQL Server database and attempt to make the modification. It is not going to write the log record to the Access database directly; instead, it is going to write information about the transaction to the clerk's log file. The COM+ plumbing maintains a different log file per application that requests the CRM service. To turn on logging, you must turn on the Enable Compensating Resource Managers option on the Advanced tab of the COM+ application's Properties dialog box (see Figure 9-7).

The location of the log file is dictated by a setting in the properties of My Computer. Right-click on My Computer in the Component Services applet, choose Properties, and select the MSDTC tab. The path in the Location text box of the Log Information section of the dialog box tells the COM+ architecture where to store the log files (see Figure 9-8 for details).

The name of the log file is the GUID for the COM+ application. The code in ModifyAuthors writes records to the log file to tell the CRM component (CAuthorChanges) how to update the Access database. The following code example shows the code in the ModifyAuthors method:

```
Public Function ModifyAuthor(ByVal OldName As String, _
```

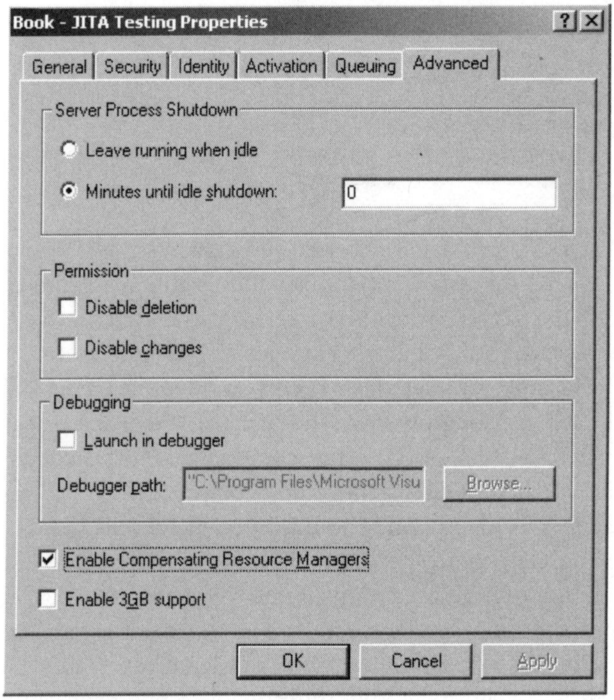

Figure 9-7. Enabling the Compensating Resource Manager service

```
      ByVal NewName As String) As Integer
'enlist a SQL OLEDB Connection in the
'transaction
Dim iChanged As Integer
Dim rs As Recordset

Dim SQLconn As Connection
Set SQLconn = New Connection
Call SQLconn.Open("Provider=SQLOLEDB.1;Integrated Security=SSPI;" & _
                "Persist Security Info=False;Initial Catalog=pubs;" & _
                "Data Source=JOSE")
Set rs = SQLconn.Execute("select * from authors where au_lname - ;" & _
                OldName & "';update authors set au_lname='" & _
                NewName & "' where au_lname = '" & OldName & "'")

If Not rs.EOF Then

    'write records to the clerk log
    While rs.EOF = False
        Dim changedrecords(0 To 2) As Variant
        changedrecords(0) = rs.Fields("au_id")
        changedrecords(1) = OldName
        changedrecords(2) = NewName
        Call clerk.WriteLogRecordVariants(changedrecords)
```

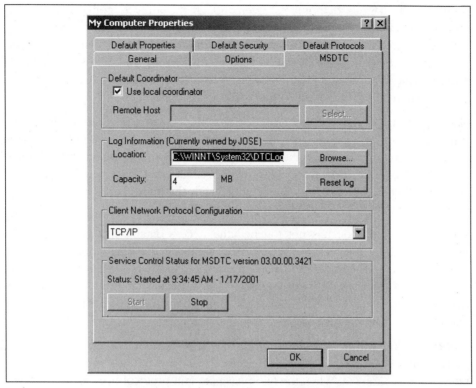

Figure 9-8. The location setting where the clerk log files are stored

```
        rs.MoveNext
        iChanged = iChanged + 1
    Wend

    'save log records
    Call clerk.ForceLog
End If

Call GetObjectContext.SetComplete
ModifyAuthor = iChanged
End Function
```

As you can see, the code first makes an ADO connection to the SQL Server Pubs database. It then uses the Connection object to execute two queries in one Execute method call. The queries are separated by a semicolon. The Execute statement asks for a list of all matching records, and it performs the update. After making the connection and making the changes to the records, the code writes records to the CRM log file. To write records from within VB, you use the WriteLogRecordVariants method of the ICrmLogControl interface. The WriteLogRecordVariants method has one parameter, an array of variants to add to the log file. The information in the array must be strings or numbers. Even though the array is going to have only strings or numbers, the method is very picky about always receiving an array of Variants. Therefore, the code first dimensions an array of three variants. Each array represents one record. In this case, a record contains the author's ID, the author's current name, and the author's new name. The code sets each entry in the array to the corresponding data and calls WriteLogRecordVariants.

The records are stored in memory until you tell COM+ to write them to disk. (You must write them to disk in order for the service to work.) You tell COM+ to write the records to disk by calling the ForceLog method of the `ICrmLogControl` interface. Notice that the code accounts for the possibility that there may be more than one record changed (two or more authors with the same last name). The code returns the number of records that were modified.

At this point, the code has not touched the Access database; it has just written information about the records that must be written if the transaction succeeds to the CRM log file. The code also calls SetComplete, so there is a good chance CRM will write the records to the Access table. That is all that the transactional component needs to do: create the CRM clerk, register the CRM component, and add information to the log.

The transaction will flow as usual, and once the root component is deactivated, COM+ will tell the DTC to commit the transaction, and the DTC will run the two-phase commit protocol. When the two-phase commit protocol begins, the clerk will create an instance of your CRM component. Remember from earlier that your component needs to implement the `ICrmCompensatorVariants` interface. This interface is simple to understand if you know about the two-phase commit protocol. The first event that the clerk calls in the interface is the SetLogControlVariants event, which has the following syntax:

```
Private Sub ICrmCompensatorVariants_SetLogControlVariants( _
        ByVal pLogControl As COMSVCSLib.ICrmLogControl)
```

This event is fired so that the clerk can give your component a reference to its default interface, `ICrmLogControl`. You must store this reference in a member variable. You get a reference to `ICrmLogControl` because you can log a new set of entries in the first phase of the two-phase commit protocol. The following code in CAuthorChange illustrates the use of the SetLogControlVariants event:

```
Dim Log As ICrmLogControl
Private Sub ICrmCompensatorVariants_SetLogControlVariants( _
        ByVal pLogControl As COMSVCSLib.ICrmLogControl)
    Set Log = pLogControl
End Sub
```

The other events in the interface can be grouped into three categories: prepare, commit, and abort. The first group of events has to do with phase 1 of the two-phase commit protocol. Depending on the outcome of phase 1, you will either get calls for the commit set of events or for the abort set of events. The events for each group have the following syntax:

```
' Prepare group of events
Private Sub ICrmCompensatorVariants_BeginPrepareVariants()
End Sub
Private Function ICrmCompensatorVariants_PrepareRecordVariants( _
        pLogRecord As Variant) As Boolean
End Function
Private Function ICrmCompensatorVariants_EndPrepareVariants() As Boolean
End Function

' Commit group of events
Private Sub ICrmCompensatorVariants_BeginAbortVariants(ByVal bRecovery As Boolean)
End Sub
Private Function ICrmCompensatorVariants_AbortRecordVariants( _
        pLogRecord As Variant) As Boolean
End Function
Private Sub ICrmCompensatorVariants_EndAbortVariants()
End Sub

' Abort group of events
Private Sub ICrmCompensatorVariants_BeginCommitVariants( _
        ByVal bRecovery As Boolean)
End Sub
Private Function ICrmCompensatorVariants_CommitRecordVariants( _
        pLogRecord As Variant) As Boolean
End Function
Private Sub ICrmCompensatorVariants_EndCommitVariants()
End Sub
```

Each group has a Begin... event, an action event, and an End... event, as in: BeginPrepareVariants, PrepareRecordVariants, and EndPrepareVariants. Let's take a look at the code for each event involved in the transaction beginning with the prepare events.

In the BeginPrepareVariants event, we are going to connect to the Access database as follows:

```
Private Sub ICrmCompensatorVariants_BeginPrepareVariants()
    Call TRACE("BeginPrepareVariants")
    On Error Resume Next
    Set ACCConn = New Connection
    Call ACCConn.Open("Provider=Microsoft.Jet.OLEDB.4.0;" & _
                "Data Source=C:\Writing\COM+\Chapter 08\crm\changes.mdb;" _
                & "Persist Security Info=False")
End Sub
```

In the EndPrepareVariants event, we are going to close the database connection as follows:

```
Private Function ICrmCompensatorVariants_EndPrepareVariants() As Boolean

    If ACCConn Is Nothing Then
        Exit Function
    End If

    Call ACCConn.Close
    Set ACCConn = Nothing
    ICrmCompensatorVariants_EndPrepareVariants = True
End Function
```

The reason we are not going to leave the connection open for phase 2 is that there is no guarantee that we will have the same object for both phases. It is likely that COM+ will destroy the object after phase 1 and create a new instance of the CRM for phase 2. COM+ will call BeginPrepareVariants first, then it will call PrepareRecordVariants for each entry in the log (each time you called Write-LogRecordVariants), and then it will call EndPrepareVariants.

Let's look at the PrepareRecordVariants event procedure:

```
Private Function ICrmCompensatorVariants_PrepareRecordVariants( _
        pLogRecord As Variant) As Boolean
    Dim au_id As String
    Dim OldName As String
    Dim NewName As String
    Dim sguid As String

    'read record information from array
    au_id = pLogRecord(0)
    OldName = pLogRecord(1)
    NewName = pLogRecord(2)
    sguid = CreateGUID()

    'insert record to Access table
    Call ACCConn.Execute("insert into authors (au_id,oldname,newname," & _
                    "lastchanged,changeguid) values('" & au_id & "','" & _
                    OldName & "','" & NewName & "',#" & Now & "#,'" & _
                    sguid & "')")

    'write rollback information to log
    Dim guidarr(0 To 0) As Variant
    guidarr(0) = sguid
    Call Log.WriteLogRecordVariants(guidarr)
    Call Log.ForceLog

    'remove current log entry
    ICrmCompensatorVariants_PrepareRecordVariants = True
End Function
```

The first part of the code retrieves the record information from the array of variants. The line in the code that calls the *CreateGUID* function requires some explanation. The code writes records to the database in the prepare phase. You may instead want to delay writing to the database until the commit phase. If you do, then you do not have to worry about rolling back the transaction. For the sake of illustration, I chose to write records to the database during the prepare phase. This means that if the transaction fails, I have to roll back the changes. In the code, I have assigned each record a unique identifier. The CRM service lets you write a new set of log entries to the CRM log file. So, the code assigns each record a GUID (obtained from the *CreateGUID* function that I've added to the RM helper library). The code then writes this GUID to the log file. (The lines in boldface show how to write information for the rollback operation to the log file.) If the transaction is aborted, the clerk will play back those new log entries in the Abort method, and I will simply delete the records with those GUIDs from the Access database. The following code shows how to handle the rollback notifications:

```
Private Sub ICrmCompensatorVariants_BeginAbortVariants(ByVal bRecovery As Boolean)
    On Error Resume Next
    Set ACCConn = New Connection
    Call ACCConn.Open("Provider=Microsoft.Jet.OLEDB.4.0;" & _
                "Data Source=C:\Writing\COM+\Chapter 08\crm\changes.mdb;" & _
                Persist Security Info=False")
End Sub

Private Function ICrmCompensatorVariants_AbortRecordVariants( _
        pLogRecord As Variant) As Boolean
    Call ACCConn.Execute("delete from authors where changeguid='" & _
                pLogRecord(0) & "'")
    ICrmCompensatorVariants_AbortRecordVariants = True
End Function

Private Sub ICrmCompensatorVariants_EndAbortVariants()
    Call ACCConn.Close
    Set ACCConn = Nothing
End Sub
```

Again, we open and close the database connection in the BeginAbortVariants and EndAbortVariants methods, respectively. The clerk calls AbortRecordVariants for each entry in the new log file. All the code does in the AbortRecordVariants is execute a delete query using the unique identifier that was stored in the log file in the prepare phase. The code example does not make use of the Commit events, since all the changes are committed in the prepare phase. However, we could have put the code to save the records in the commit phase, and then we wouldn't need to put any code in the prepare phase or in the abort phase.

There are two other things that deserve attention in the prepare phase. If you look back at the sample code for the Prepare events, you will notice that the PrepareRecordVariants event has a Boolean output parameter. The code sample returns

`True`, which means that it is OK for the clerk to remove the delivered record from the log file. If you return `False`, the clerk will keep the delivered record in the log. If you add more records, the clerk will play the latest records first and the old records last in the second phase. The EndPrepareVariants event also has a Boolean output parameter. With this parameter, you tell COM+ whether the first phase was successful. Remember that a resource manager may tell the DTC that phase 1 failed, and the DTC would then tell all the resource managers to abort the transaction. If you return `True` in the EndPrepareVariants event, then you are telling the DTC that everything is fine; if you return `False`, you are telling the DTC that phase 1 failed. Keep in mind that the default is `False`. You have to return `True` if you want the operation to succeed.

Recovery phase

It is possible for your resource manager to finish with phase 1 and then for the network to die or for your machine to crash. In that case, when you reboot your machine and restore the network, the first time someone creates a component in your machine, COM+ will create your resource manager first and continue with phase 2. This is why it is important to not assume that you are using the same instance of the object in both the first and the second phases.

One complication that results from the recovery phase is that a call to RegisterCompensator will fail with error &H8004d082. The solution is to continue calling the RegisterCompensator function in a loop until you no longer get an error, as follows:

```
Implements ObjectControl
Dim clerk As ICrmLogControl

Private Sub ObjectControl_Activate()
    'create clerk
    On Error Resume Next
    Set clerk = New CRMClerk
    While Err.Number <> x
        Call clerk.RegisterCompensator("AuthorsServer.CAuthorChanged", _
            "Access Author Changed Records", 7)
    Wend
End Sub
```

Summary

In this chapter, you learned how to create transactional components. You first learned what constitutes a transaction. You learned that transactions follow the ACID rules: Atomic, Consistent, Isolated, and Durable. Isolation controls how other transactions affect your transaction. Both SQL Server and Oracle let you control the degree of isolation for transactions.

You also learned the difference between *local transactions* and *distributed transactions*. Local transactions involve a single resource manager. Distributed transactions involve the Distributed Transaction Coordinator (DTC). The DTC dispenses a resource known as an `ITransaction` pointer. OLEDB libraries can join a DTC transaction if they support the `ITransactionJoin` interface.

COM+ has a service known as declarative transactions. In a declarative transaction, COM+ drives a DTC transaction. Your components are marked through declarative properties as transactional. The first component that is marked as Transaction Required or Transaction Requires New begins a new transaction stream and becomes the root of the transaction. The root of the transaction then creates secondary components. These components must be marked as Transaction Required or Transaction Supported to be part of the same transaction stream. Each component votes on the outcome of the transaction. When the root component is deactivated, the votes are collected. If no component voted to abort the transaction, the COM+ plumbing tells the DTC to begin the two-phase commit protocol. If at least one component voted to abort the transaction, then the COM+ plumbing tells the DTC to abort the transaction.

Certain aspects of the DTC transaction—like its isolation level—cannot be changed through declarative properties. COM+ has a service that enables you to initiate the DTC transaction manually. This service is called BYOT.

Through CRM you can involve non–distributed-transactional resources in a declarative transaction.

In the next chapter, you will learn all about COM+ security, especially how security flows from a web application into a COM+ application.

10

COM+ Security

Everyone thinks security is necessary, but no one really wants to implement it. Developers often view security in the same light as setup programs—as a necessary evil that is put off until everything else is done. This chapter will make the transition to security easier. First, you will learn some of the terms related to security. Then you will learn how to use the COM+ features for security. The last part of the chapter discusses web-based security with IIS.

Security Terminology

Before you can understand how COM+ security works, you must understand some security terms.

Windows NT and Windows 2000 are secure operating systems. In a secure operating system, resources such as files, printers, programs, and so on can be protected against unwanted access. Secure operating systems are also able to log each access attempt against one of the resources. To gain access to a resource, a *principal*—that is, a person or a computer attempting to access the resource—must be authenticated. The purpose of authentication is to prove to the operating system that the principal attempting to gain access to the resource is in fact who it claims to be. Principals prove their identity by presenting a set of credentials. The software that checks the credentials and certifies that the principal is in fact who it claims to be is known as the *authority*. The authority is a service in Windows NT or Windows 2000 that runs under *LSASS.EXE*.

Windows NT and Windows 2000 enable companies to set up a network using either a workgroup architecture or a domain architecture. When computers are set up in a workgroup, each machine authenticates users locally. When the authority responsible for authenticating users is the local machine, we refer to the software that authenticates the user as the local security authority. In a workgroup scenario, if Bob on machine A wants to use a file on machine B, machine B must have Bob listed as a user. The user ID in B must match the user ID in A. Furthermore, the passwords in both machines must be the same. The workgroup scenario is OK for companies with only a few machines, but what if the company grows to the point that it has a few hundred machines? Then it would be almost impossible for an administrator to ensure that every machine has a list with all the users in the company. What makes it even more difficult is the fact that a user may change her password on one machine. This would make it necessary for the user to go to each machine and ensure that the password is also changed on those as well. Because that would be an administration nightmare, a company can choose to promote one of its workstations to the role of domain controller. In a network with a domain controller, one machine does the job of authentication. Accounts are kept in a centralized security database on the domain machine. When a domain user logs into a workstation, the workstation trusts the domain controller machine to authenticate the user for the workstation.

Logon Sessions

Authenticating a principal results in a *logon session*. There are different types of logon sessions. The one that most users are familiar with is the interactive logon session. The interactive logon session is created as the result of logging on to the machine, when you use Ctrl-Alt-Del and enter your user ID and password. The program that displays the user ID and password dialog box for you to log in is called *Winlogon.exe*. This program runs under another logon session called the System logon session. The System logon session is a specialized logon session available from boot time and is part of what is called the Trusted Computing Base (or TCB). Programs that run in this logon session have complete control over the system.

Winlogon.exe calls an operating system function named *LogonUser*. You can call this function directly in a VB program if you know the name of the user and the user's password and if your program runs under an account that has the "Act as part of the operating system" privilege. You can adjust privileges by using the Local Security Policy program, which is available by selecting Programs → Administrative Tools from the Start menu. The following code shows you how to call *LogonUser* directly:

```
Const LOGON32_LOGON_INTERACTIVE = 2
Const LOGON32_PROVIDER_DEFAULT = 0

Private Declare Function LogonUser Lib "advapi32" Alias "LogonUserA" ( _
        ByVal lpszUsername As String, ByVal lpszDomain As String, _
        ByVal lpszPassword As String, ByVal dwLogonType As Long, _
        ByVal dwLogonProvider As Long, phToken As Long) As Long
```

```
Public Sub CreateLogonSession()

Dim lReturn As Long
Dim lToken As Long

lReturn = LogonUser("john", "josemojica.com", "mypassword", _
                LOGON32_LOGON_INTERACTIVE, LOGON32_PROVIDER_DEFAULT, _
                lToken)

End Sub
```

In this code, the call to *LogonUser* requests an interactive logon session. Notice that the first three parameters are the username, the domain name, and the password for the user. The fourth and fifth parameters are the type of logon session you would like to establish and the logon provider. The choices for provider are default, NT 3.5, NT 4, or NT 5. You should leave the logon provider set to 0, the default, to make the call generic. An interactive logon session is a logon session that has access to the interactive desktop. Only users that are logged on to the interactive logon session have access to the keyboard and mouse and can display forms and message boxes to the visible display.

When you access resources on another machine, the other machine must authenticate you and create a logon session for you. This type of session is a *network logon session*. If you run a COM+ server, the system creates a network session for you and a *batch logon session* for the COM+ server to run in. We will talk about the differences between these two types of logon sessions throughout this chapter.

The *LogonUser* function returns a handle to a token in its last parameter. This token handle points to a structure that contains information about the user that was logged in. The token has a security identifier or SID for the user on whose behalf the token was created. The token also contains information about all the groups to which the user belongs. So how is this token used?

The token associated with the logon session created as the result of calling the *LogonUser* function will be assigned to each process that runs within that session. Every process that runs within a session must have a process token assigned to it. The operating system has functions for us to extract the process token and find out the user for which the process is running. Remember that in Windows NT and Windows 2000, everything that is done against a secured resource must be attributed to a principal.

It is possible to extract the process token and find out the user using Visual Basic code alone and a whole bunch of API calls. I am going to spare you the agony of looking at the printed version of this code; however, if you are interested, I have included the code that does this in the downloadable software for this book.

Another issue in security is how tokens are managed in multithreaded applications. Processes have threads. In fact, you learned earlier that every process begins with one thread called the main thread. By default, threads (even the main thread) do not have their own tokens. If a thread does not have its own token, then all the work the thread does happens with the process token. Sometimes, it is convenient for a thread to temporarily use a different token while it is doing work. For example, when you create a new session for a user by calling the *LogonUser* function, the program that is executing the code is running in one logon session, while the *LogonUser* function creates another session. It is possible for the process to temporarily use the token from the second session. The process does this by using the *ImpersonateLoggedOnUser* function, as follows:

```
Private Declare Function ImpersonateLoggedOnUser Lib "advapi32" ( _
        ByVal hToken As Long) As Boolean

Public Sub CreateLogonSession()
    'code sample introduced earlier
    Dim lReturn As Long
    Dim lToken As Long

    lReturn = LogonUser("john", "josemojica.com", "mypassword", _
            LOGON32_LOGON_INTERACTIVE, LOGON32_PROVIDER_DEFAULT, lToken)
    Call ImpersonateLoggedOnUser(lToken)
End Sub
```

The preceding code enables the thread—most likely the main thread in this case, because it is a VB program—to adopt a different token. This means that if the code after the impersonate call tries to open a file or launch a program, for example, the security check would be done against the user to which the token belongs. Later on, you will see how systems like Internet Information Server (IIS) use this technique.

After doing some work, the thread may want to return to its original token; it can do so by calling the *RevertToSelf* function, as follows:

```
Private Declare Function RevertToSelf Lib "advapi32" () As Boolean

Public Sub CreateLogonSession()

    Dim lReturn As Long
    Dim lToken As Long
    lReturn = LogonUser("john", "josemojica.com", "mypassword", _
            LOGON32_LOGON_INTERACTIVE, LOGON32_PROVIDER_DEFAULT, lToken)

    Call ImpersonateLoggedOnUser(lToken)
    '...do some work here
    Call RevertToSelf()

End Sub
```

After issuing the *RevertToSelf* function, the thread will no longer be using its own token, and access to resources will be measured against the process token.

How can we use this technique of impersonation? Well, suppose that you were writing an application in VB using a Standard EXE project. When your application runs, it runs under a certain set of credentials. If you simply launch the compiled executable, the executable will run with the credentials of the interactive user. Suppose that your application needs to access a database that has been secured with a special account so that only your application can access it. In this case, it would be very convenient to create a temporary logon session as illustrated, temporarily impersonate the new set of credentials, access the database, then revert back to the original set of credentials.

RPC Security

To truly understand COM+ security, we must take a look back at the foundation of COM, RPC. You may recall from previous chapters that the COM remoting protocol, normally referred to as the DCOM wire protocol, is built on top of MSRPC. In truth, all DCOM calls are true MSRPC calls. MSRPC is the Windows implementation of the Remote Procedure Call (RPC) specification written by the Open Software Foundation (OSF). MSRPC is a protocol, and, like all other protocols, it is a set of rules for how to format byte streams from one program to another. RPC is a protocol that is built on top of other network protocols such as TCP, UDP, SPX, and so forth. The RPC protocol enhances the existing protocols by providing the rules for how to make method calls and transmit method parameters. Even today, all COM+ calls from one machine to another are true MSRPC calls.

Because all COM+ calls across the wire are really "object-oriented" MSRPC calls, COM+ security has as its foundation RPC security. If you learn a little about MSRPC security, then you will be very close to understanding COM+ security. With that in mind, let's discuss RPC security. I am not going to bore you will all the RPC commands that you must use to create an RPC server and an RPC client program. Instead, let's talk about RPC security at a higher level.

In the good old days, if you wanted a client program to talk to a server program, you would write RPC code. You would first define an interface (yes, interfaces were really used in RPC long before COM existed) in IDL. You would then run the IDL source code through a compiler that would generate proxy/stub code for the interface. Suppose that your interface were called ICHecking and your method were called MakeDeposit. MIDL would generate code for your client program that would take all the parameters for MakeDeposit and package them using a format known as Network Data Representation (NDR), then do the job of calling the appropriate RPC calls to send the buffer to the server side. The code that MIDL would generate for the server would listen for RPC requests, unpackage the buffer parameter, and make the actual call to MakeDeposit, wait for the call to complete, then take the output parameters and package them into a return buffer for the client. This was RPC.

The security model for RPC was much simpler, in my opinion, than the security model of COM+. By default, there was no security. Any client could make a method call to the server. The client did not even need to be authenticated, and because the client did not need to be authenticated, the system did not need to create a logon session for the client. By default, the call always went through, and the parameters were always sent in clear view. It was possible for anyone with a network sniffer to look at the parameters being sent and to even intercept parameters, modify them, and send different parameters to the server. It was also possible to fool the client into making calls to a "fake" server. This was the way things were by default. If you wanted to protect the information being sent between the two programs, a client program would call a function called *RpcBindingSetAuthInfoEx* just before making the call to the interface method.

In RPC security, the client dictates what security it wants before it makes the method call. The server does not really have much say over security before receiving the call. The job of the server is really to receive the call, then to programmatically determine whether the call's security level and user ID are adequate for the call to continue. If the security settings the client chooses are not sufficient for the server, the server can reject the call by raising an "Access denied" error. Thus, in RPC security, it is the client that chooses the level of security, and the server then rejects or approves the call.

The client's call to *RpcBindingSetAuthInfoEx* enabled the client to specify different aspects of security. Among them are the identity name of the server (such as *EarthComputer@SolarSystemDomain* or *SolarSystemDomain\EarthComputer)*, the level of encryption, the security provider (such as NTLM or Kerberos) doing the authentication, an alternate set of credentials to use to make the call, whether mutual authentication (the server verifies the client's identity, and the client verifies the server's identity) is needed, whether the server can impersonate the client (i.e., use the client's token to make method calls), and if we are not using another set of credentials, whether the call should use the process token or the thread token (and how often it should look for a new thread token).

Let's talk about the things that we can affect today with COM+ security in Visual Basic (in C++, you can still affect all these aspects of RPC and COM+ security). The first item of interest is the level of protection for the information or, in security terms, the level of authentication.

Authentication Level

The authentication level controls how secure the information that is sent from the client to the server and from the server to the client is. The client dictates the level of security for the input parameters and for the output parameters (the parameters sent from the server). The server just examines the settings and accepts the call or rejects the call based on whether it can live with the level of authentication.

I mentioned that, by default, the RPC call does not use any protection for the data; the parameters are sent in clear view. If you do not use any type of authentication, the client's credentials do not need to be verified, and the server does not create a logon session for the client. However, if we want to protect the parameters in some fashion, things change completely. The client must be authenticated on the server. That means that the client must have a set of credentials that must be verifiable on the server, and the server will create a network logon session for the client on the server's machine. For the server to verify the credentials, the client must have an account with the same user ID and password on the server machine if you are using a workstation model; if you are using the domain model, the credentials must be domain credentials, and the server machine must either be part of the domain or have a path of trust to the domain. After the server verifies the identity of the client, the end result is that the client and the server will each end up with a session key. The client uses the session key to lock the information, and the server uses the session key to unlock the information.

There are different levels of protection. The higher the level of protection, the longer the method call takes to complete (the more work must be done to protect and decipher the information); the lower the level, the less protection and the higher the performance. The levels of authentication are:

None
> The lowest level of authentication. It means that there is no authentication.

Connect
> Authentication is performed as follows: the server verifies the credentials of the client, and a network logon session for the client is created on the server's machine. A session key is exchanged as the result of authentication, but it is not used after that. The parameters for the call are not protected in any way. This level prevents someone without credentials from making a call into the server. Actually, what this really tells the server is that if it gets a call from the client, the client's identity was verified by the system on the first call.

Call
> None of the security providers implement this level, so the infrastructure automatically promotes it to packet.

Packet

Normally, the information for a method call is not sent to the server in one stream; rather, it is broken into smaller segments or packets. The size of the packets is dictated by the protocol that MSRPC is using, like TCP, UDP, SPX, and so on. The packet authentication level says that the headers for each packet (the target machine address, the source machine address, the sequence number of the packet, how much information there is in the packet, etc.) is signed with the session key. To sign some information means that the information is run through an algorithm that produces a message authentication code (or MAC). This code is the result of encrypting a numeric representation of the message (or hash) with the session key. This MAC is sent at the end of each message. A "bad guy" can look at the parameters being sent but cannot modify anything that would result in a change of the headers. If tampering occurs to the headers, then the server-side security provider will run the algorithm through the headers, decrypt the MAC with the session key, discover that the MAC in the message is not the MAC for the headers sent, and then reject the call before it arrives on the server.

Packet integrity

The entire set of packets is run through the algorithm, and a MAC for the entire payload, including the parameters, is produced and encrypted with the session key. At this level, the information in the parameters is not encrypted, but we can detect if there was any tampering with the parameters themselves. This means, for example, a "bad guy" can see how much your deposit was for but would not be able to modify the amount.

Packet privacy.

The highest level of security. All the information sent is encrypted with the session key.

Impersonation Level

If authentication is used, the result is that there will be a network logon session on the server's machine. MSRPC keeps track of all the network logon sessions created as the result of authentication done via RPC requests and makes the session information available to the server via an RPC binding handle. The network logon session has a token that the server may use to impersonate the client. For example, a client program accesses the BankServer RPC server through the ICheckingAccount interface in a call to MakeDeposit. MakeDeposit then has code to access a local SQL Server (notice that I said a local server). One approach for securing the application is that the database administrator may grant or deny access based on the credentials of the client. The MakeDeposit method then would impersonate the client's token using the code explained earlier and connect to the database, specifying in the connect string to use integrated security.

The question is, can the server use the token for impersonation? Well, it depends on the client: the client program may be running under Joe Smith, the window cleaner for the company, or it may be running as Bill Gates, the company's chief technology architect and major stockholder. Joe Smith may not care how his credentials are used, but you can guarantee that Bill Gates would care. Thus, in RPC, the client can specify in each method call what the server can do with his token. The impersonation levels are:

Anonymous
> Available in MSRPC only if the client and the server program are on the same machine; otherwise, this level is automatically promoted to identify. Anonymous means that the token does not have any information about the client.

Identify
> The server can examine the token and find out things like the user ID and the groups the user belongs to, but it cannot use the token to access any resources locally (much less remotely).

Impersonate
> Grants the server the right to use the token when accessing local resources. The token may not be used to make outgoing calls to another machine. Interestingly, at this level of impersonation, you cannot implement a three-tier architecture in which the server impersonates the client to access a database server in a different machine.

Delegate
> The highest level of trust. The delegate level enables the server to use the token as it sees fit. It can use the token to make calls to other machines, and in fact, the other machine may use the token again to make a call to yet another machine. The delegate level is available only if you use a security provider that enables you to delegate credentials. Unfortunately, the only SSP that enables you to delegate credentials is Kerberos. Kerberos is available only on Windows 2000 machines.

There's one more topic related to the subject of impersonation: identity tracking.

Identity Tracking

The RPC client calls *RpcBindingSetAuthInfoEx* once before making calls. One of the parameters in this function enables the developer to choose a set of credentials on whose behalf the call is being made. Alternatively, the developer may choose to pass null values for these parameters, in which case the RPC layer is going to choose the thread credentials. But as you know, the developer may want to impersonate a token for one call and revert to self for another. Identity tracking is a setting that a developer specifies in one of the parameters in *RpcBinding-SetAuthInfoEx* that tells the RPC layer when to look at the thread token. Without this feature, an RPC developer would have to call *RpcBindingSetAuthInfoEx* each time she changed the thread token; with identity tracking, the RPC layer can do this automatically.

In RPC, you can choose from the following three types of identity tracking:

Static
> The RPC layer looks at the thread token only when the client calls *RpcBindingSetAuthInfoEx*. After that, every call will be made under those credentials, even if the thread impersonates another set of credentials.

Dynamic
> Every time a client makes a method call, the RPC layer grabs whatever token the thread is impersonating. If the thread is not using impersonation, then it simply grabs the process token.

Ignore
> New to Windows 2000, the ignore level tells RPC to ignore the thread token completely and always use the process token when making the call.

You may wonder why this is important. It is particularly important because the default in Windows 2000 is to use the ignore option. What that means is that if you do not do anything about setting security options programmatically (as you normally would not do in Visual Basic), a call will normally run using the process' token.

COM/COM+ Security

How does RPC security relate to COM+ security? I made the statement earlier that every DCOM call is actually an RPC call. When you use remoting in COM+, as you learned in Chapter 5, the client talks to a server object through a proxy, and the object receives calls through the stub. Deep in the proxy/stub code is the code that makes RPC calls. As you learned in the previous section, for an RPC call to be secured, you must call the *RpcBindingSetAuthInfoEx* function. What COM+ provides are high-level API functions for setting the parameters of *RpcBindingSetAuthInfoEx*. The two most important functions (the ones we are going to discuss here) are *CoInitializeSecurity* and *CoSetProxyBlanket*.

In RPC, when the client wanted to make secured calls, it had to call *RpcBindingSetAuthInfoEx* for each binding handle; this is the equivalent in COM+ of making a similar call once for each interface in each object. The server had even more work to do because it had to evaluate each call and decide whether the security level of the call was sufficient, and then accept or reject the call based on its evaluation.

Because in COM+ the proxy/stub code wraps the RPC code, it is possible for COM+ to automate the process and minimize the work that the client and the server have to do. For example, on the client side, we can tell COM+ at program startup what level of authentication to use for all of its RPC calls. On the server side, COM+ enables us to tell it the minimum level of security that we accept at program startup. The proxy/stub code will then take care of rejecting calls that do not meet the requirement automatically. In addition to setting security information at startup, COM+ still gives us the choice of setting this information on a call-by-call basis.

CoInitializeSecurity

CoInitializeSecurity enables us to set default parameters that the proxy/stub code will use in deciding how to make calls from the client and whether to accept calls on the server. Both the server program and the client program can call this function. This function must be called before creating any COM+ components.

In the client program it is a good idea to call this function, if you care about security, in your **Sub Main** method. On the other hand, you will not be able to make this call directly in your server code. By the time your server code loads, the COM+ architecture has already made this call. However, you can control how the architecture makes this call through declarative settings. You will see later in this chapter how to set these security settings on the server side.

Let's focus on client security for the moment. The following code shows you how to declare the *CoInitializeSecurity* function in Visual Basic:

```
'Security Provider
Public Const RPC_C_AUTHN_NONE = 0
Public Const RPC_C_AUTHN_DCE_PRIVATE = 1
Public Const RPC_C_AUTHN_DCE_PUBLIC = 2
Public Const RPC_C_AUTHN_DEC_PUBLIC = 4
Public Const RPC_C_AUTHN_GSS_NEGOTIATE = 9
Public Const RPC_C_AUTHN_WINNT = 10
Public Const RPC_C_AUTHN_GSS_KERBEROS = 16
Public Const RPC_C_AUTHN_MSN = 17
Public Const RPC_C_AUTHN_DPA = 18
Public Const RPC_C_AUTHN_MQ = 100
Public Const RPC_C_AUTHN_DEFAULT = &HFFFFFFFF

'Authorization Service
Public Const RPC_C_AUTHZ_NONE = 0
Public Const RPC_C_AUTHZ_NAME = 1
Public Const RPC_C_AUTHZ_DCE = 2
Public Const RPC_C_AUTHZ_DEFAULT = &HFFFFFFFF

'Authentication Level
```

```
Public Const RPC_C_AUTHN_LEVEL_DEFAULT = 0
Public Const RPC_C_AUTHN_LEVEL_NONE = 1
Public Const RPC_C_AUTHN_LEVEL_CONNECT = 2
Public Const RPC_C_AUTHN_LEVEL_CALL = 3
Public Const RPC_C_AUTHN_LEVEL_PKT = 4
Public Const RPC_C_AUTHN_LEVEL_PKT_INTEGRITY = 5
Public Const RPC_C_AUTHN_LEVEL_PKT_PRIVACY = 6

'Impersonation Level
Public Const RPC_C_IMP_LEVEL_DEFAULT = 0
Public Const RPC_C_IMP_LEVEL_ANONYMOUS = 1
Public Const RPC_C_IMP_LEVEL_IDENTIFY = 2
Public Const RPC_C_IMP_LEVEL_IMPERSONATE = 3
Public Const RPC_C_IMP_LEVEL_DELEGATE = 4

'Identity Tracking
Public Const EOAC_NONE = &H0
Public Const EOAC_DEFAULT = &H800
Public Const EOAC_MUTUAL_AUTH = &H1
Public Const EOAC_STATIC_CLOAKING = &H20
Public Const EOAC_DYNAMIC_CLOAKING = &H40

Public Declare Function CoInitializeSecurity Lib "ole32.dll" ( _
            pSD As Any, _
            ByVal cAuthSvc As Long, _
            asAuthSvc As Long, _
            pReserved1 As Any, _
            ByVal dwAuthnlevel As Long, _
            ByVal dwImpLevel As Long, _
            ByVal pAuthInfo As Long, _
            ByVal dwCapabilities As Long, _
            pvReserved2 As Any _
            ) As Long
```

As you can see, there are a number of constants that can be used with this function. Also, there are a number of parameters that cannot be used directly through VB—they require the use of types that are not available in VB. The parameters that you will be able to set through this function are authentication level (*dwAuthnLevel*), impersonation level (*dwImpLevel*), and identity tracking (*dwCapabilities*). These should sound familiar from the discussion on RPC security. Notice that I have separated the constants into groups for each of the parameters in the call.

If you do not adjust the security settings, all calls by default will be made at authentication level 2, Connect. Let's suppose that you want all the calls for all your objects to be made by default at level 6, packet privacy. You can set the default using the *CoInitializeSecurity* function, as follows:

```
Sub Main()
    Dim lRetVal As Long
    Dim lngAuthn As Long
    lngAuthn = RPC_C_AUTHN_DEFAULT
```

```
        lRetVal = CoInitializeSecurity(ByVal 0, -1, _
            lngAuthn, ByVal 0, _
            RPC_C_AUTHN_LEVEL_PKT_PRIVACY, RPC_C_IMP_LEVEL_DEFAULT, _
            0, EOAC_DEFAULT, ByVal 0)
    Form1.Show
End Sub
```

Notice that there are a number of parameters passed as `ByVal 0`. These are parameters that are either reserved or not supported. Later in this chapter, you will learn how to verify on the server side that the call made was actually done at this level.

In addition to setting default security settings, the client can change the level of security on a call-by-call basis using the *CoSetProxyBlanket* function.

CoSetProxyBlanket

COM+ has an API function that internally does the job of calling the RPC *RpcBindingSetAuthInfoEx* function; it is called *CoSetProxyBlanket*. The word Blanket in the method refers to a security blanket—a little humor from the COM+ team. *CoSetProxyBlanket* enables you to set things such as the authentication level, impersonation level, and identity tracking programmatically.

First, you must declare the *CoSetProxyBlanket* function:

```
Private Declare Function CoSetProxyBlanket Lib "ole32.dll" ( _
  ByVal pProxy As Object, _
  ByVal dwAuthnSvc As Long, _
  ByVal dwAuthzSvc As Long, _
  ByVal pServerPrincName As Long, _
  ByVal dwAuthnlevel As Long, _
  ByVal dwImpLevel As Long, _
  ByVal pAuthInfo As Long, _
  ByVal dwCapabilities As Long) As Long
```

The *CoSetProxyBlanket* function uses the same constants as the *CoInitializeSecurity* function. You can call the *CoSetProxyBlanket* function as follows:

```
Public Sub MakeSecuredCall()
    Dim sec As securedclass
    Dim lRetVal As Long
    Set sec = CreateObject("complussecurity.securedclass")
    lRetVal = CoSetProxyBlanket(sec, _
                        RPC_C_AUTHN_DEFAULT, _
                        RPC_C_AUTHZ_DEFAULT, _
                        0, _
                        RPC_C_AUTHN_LEVEL_PKT_PRIVACY, _
                        RPC_C_IMP_LEVEL_DEFAULT, _
                        0, _
                        EOAC_DEFAULT)
    sec.methodA()
End Sub
```

The preceding code first creates an instance of a component called `complussecurity.securedclass`. Next, it immediately calls *CoSetProxyBlanket* before making a method call. Then it makes the method call. The previous code raises the authentication level to packet privacy.

As you can see from the code, there are a number of things you can set with the *CoSetProxyBlanket* function. The first parameter to this call is the proxy object. This call works only if you obtain a proxy as the result of *CreateObject* instead of a direct pointer to the object (i.e., when you are remoting). The second parameter is very interesting; it enables you to select the security provider for the call. This means that you can select whether you want to use NTLM security or Kerberos security. The default setting is to use a protocol called SPNEGO (secure, protected negotiation), which negotiates what security provider to use between the client and the server. A full discussion of the different security protocols is beyond the scope of this book. The fifth parameter is the authentication level. The sixth parameter controls impersonation. The last parameter controls identity tracking (although it can be used to tell the system other things, such as if you want mutual authentication for calls; consult the MSDN documentation for details).

Using Registry Keys

In addition to setting security programmatically on the client side, you can also adjust the client's authentication level through registry keys by associating the client's executable program with an app ID. To do this, you will need to use *GUIDGEN.EXE*. (*GUIDGEN.EXE* is discussed in Chapter 6.)

To see how this works, suppose that the GUID that *GUIDGEN.EXE* generates is `{6E445B90-5511-43c2-BBBA-7E6708FB24A7}`. The steps are as follows:

1. Create a key with the name of your executable under `HKEY_CLASSES_ROOT\AppId`.

2. Add an `AppId` string value entry whose value is the GUID generated by *GUIDGEN.EXE*. For example, if your client application program is BankClient, the keys you add to the registry are:

```
HKCR
    AppId
        BankClient.exe
            AppID = {6E445B90-5511-43c2-BBBA-7E6708FB24A7}
```

3. Create a subkey of `HKCR\AppId` named `{6E445B90-5511-43c2-BBBA-7E6708FB24A7}` (the application's GUID).

4. Add an `AuthenticationLevel` DWORD value entry and make it equal to the authentication level you wish to use. For our example, the key would look as follows:

```
HKCR
    AppId
        {6E445B90-5511-43c2-BBBA-7E6708FB24A7}
            AuthenticationLevel = 1
```

The possible values are:

1 = None

2 = Connect

3 = Call

4 = Packet

5 = Packet integrity

6 = Packet privacy

Unfortunately, you cannot control other things in VB client executables, such as the impersonation level and the identity tracking, as easily with registry keys. In COM+, the client selects the authentication level, but the server can tell the infrastructure the lowest level of authentication that it will accept. Let's turn our attention to server-side security.

Server-Side Authentication Level

A COM+ application can set the authentication level it requires through declarative properties. To do so, right-click on the application in the Component Services Manager and select Properties from the pop-up menu. Then click on the Security tab. There you will see a field called "Authentication level for calls." If you examine the options for the authentication level, you will notice that they are exactly the same as the RPC settings (see Figure 10-1 for details).

As we discussed in the previous section, the client can call *CoInitializeSecurity* to set the default authentication level, among other things. The server doesn't call *CoInitializeSecurity* directly; it sets the authentication level through declarative settings that tell COM+ the lowest level of security that the server requires. When a VB client creates an instance of a COM+ component, the COM+ architecture sees if the server requires a higher level than the client requested in *CoInitializeSecurity*. If the sever requires a higher level then the proxy that the COM+ architecture gives, the client program is automatically adjusted to the minimum authentication setting the server will accept, regardless of what the client specified in *CoInitializeSecurity*. Thus, if you do not specify an alternate authentication level with *CoSetProxyBlanket*, the client will make calls at the minimum level of the server.

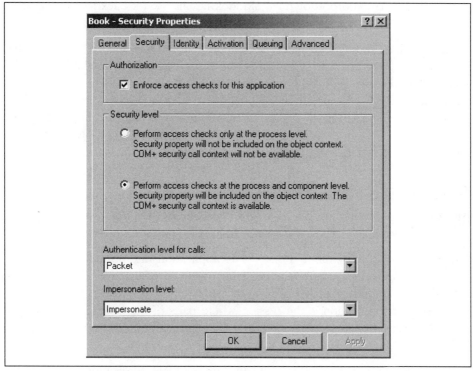

Figure 10-1. Security settings

What if you do make a call to *CoSetProxyBlanket* and request a lower authentication level than the minimum the server specified? In that case, the COM+ proxy/stub code will reject the call and return runtime error 70, "Permission Denied."

Server-Side Impersonation Level

The server does not have a say on the impersonation level that the client sets. In fact, there is no way to set the minimum impersonation level the server requires through declarative properties. Later on in this chapter, you will learn how to programmatically (without API functions) find out the impersonation level of the caller.

It is possible that your server program will at one point take the role of a client. For example, one of your components may get a call and, as the result of the call, create a secondary component in another application and make a method call. In this case, your server can set the impersonation level through declarative properties. If you look back at the dialog box in Figure 10-1, you will notice that below the authentication level, there is an "Impersonation level" setting. Keep in mind that this setting is available only when your server is acting as a client. The options in the Impersonation drop-down should look familiar. Refer back to the RPC security section in this chapter for information about each of the settings.

Something that's different between RPC security and COM+ security is that in RPC you have to launch the server manually to start listening for method calls. This means that the server will be running with the same credentials as the entity that started it, either a person double-clicking an icon or a service program perhaps running in the System logon session. In COM+, the SCM launches applications. So under what set of credentials does your COM+ application run when the first client creates an instance of a component?

COM+ Application Tokens

All COM+ applications run under a set of credentials just like any other application. However, COM+ applications differ from other applications in several ways.

One way in which they differ is that COM+ applications are normally launched by the Service Control Manager (SCM or "scum") instead of the interactive user. The SCM runs in its own special logon session known as the System logon session. The System logon session is the session where parts of the operating system that are fully trusted by the system run. Most services, including IIS, run in the System logon session. A program in the System logon session can do anything.

The SCM can do one of two things. It can run the COM+ application in the interactive logon session, or it can create a special logon session for the process. This type of logon session is called a batch logon session. If the SCM chooses this option for two COM+ applications, then each of these COM+ applications runs in its own batch logon session. The system administrator tells the SCM what session to run in by modifying the identity settings of the application. To do this, right-click on the COM+ application from the Component Services Administration program and choose Properties. Then select the Identity tab. You will see the dialog box in Figure 10-2.

These settings are available only for Server applications (applications that have the Activation property for the application set to Server). Library applications run in-process to another application; thus, the hosting application will already be running under a set of credentials.

If you look at the Identity properties in Figure 10-2, you will notice that there are two settings: Interactive user and This user. The Interactive user option tells the SCM to run the application as if the user currently using the machine had double-clicked on the icon for the application. Notice that there has to be a user logged in for this option to work. If no user is currently logged in, then the application fails to activate. This option is good when you are debugging your application for two reasons. First, your COM+ application enjoys the same rights that you have

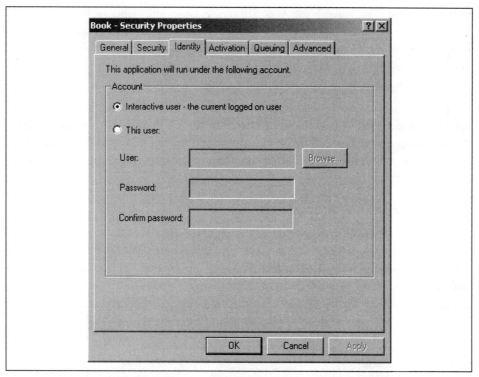

Figure 10-2. Identity settings of COM+ applications

(because it is running under your credentials). Second, it enables you to view message boxes and trace output. If your application were to run in its own batch session, as it would if you chose the "This user" option, you would not be able to see any message boxes you display or any trace messages. This happens because only the interactive session has access to the interactive desktop or *WinStation*. A WinStation is a security boundary for the Windows messaging system and drawing system. Each logon session (for the most part) runs in its own WinStation. The only WinStation that is visible is the interactive WinStation. The other WinStations have imaginary desktops. When you display a message box in an imaginary desktop, no one can see it, except that the message box does wait for someone to click its imaginary OK button. This means that your application will seem frozen. For this reason, VB added a feature to turn all message boxes into event log messages. You can turn on this feature by going to the VB project properties and selecting Unattended Execution in the project Properties dialog box.

If you choose the second option, "This user," your application runs under a specific set of credentials. This option enables you to set a user ID and a password to use. The SCM will then call *LogonUser*, as you learned previously, create a batch logon session, and run the server in it. Because this option will work regardless of whether a user is logged in, you should choose this option when you are deploying the application in a production server. Also, this option guarantees that every time the server runs, the application will run with a predictable set of rights and privileges, whereas with the Interactive user option, the rights and privileges could vary depending on who is currently using the server.

People always have one question at this point, "How does the administrator of the application keep other people from changing the credentials of the application?" To fully understand the answer to that question, you will have to first understand roles, which we will discuss later in the chapter; however, a short answer seems appropriate now.

Keeping others from modifying settings

Securing an application from changes is a two-step process. First, each COM+ application has two settings that prevent changes to and deletions from the application. The settings are under the Advanced tab of the application's Properties dialog box (seen in Figure 10-3) in the Permission frame.

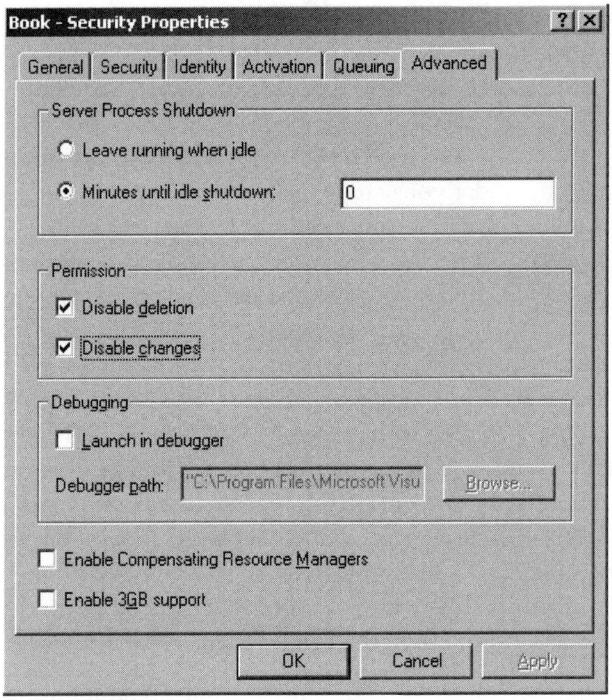

Figure 10-3. Permission settings

The two options are "Disable deletion" and "Disable changes." If you select these options, no one can delete or change the application. It is very easy to undo these two restrictions by simply unchecking these two properties. You may be thinking that this does not give you any protection, since anyone can just uncheck these two options. However, it turns out that you can restrict who can modify the values of these two options. You do so by changing the security settings of the COM+ System Application. The System Application is installed automatically by the operating system. If you expand the System Application branch in Component Services Explorer, you will see that there is a Roles subbranch. If you expand the Roles branch, you will see the Administrator role. Only members of the Administrator role can change the "Disable deletion" and "Disable changes" options. If you examine the Administrator role, you will see that, by default, this role contains the Administrators group. You can change this to any account, including a single-user account (it does not have to be a group). If you change this to a single account, only that user will be able to modify the two settings for all COM+ applications. Thus, to prevent changes to an application, first be sure that the application has the "Disable deletion" and "Disable changes" boxes checked, and second, be sure that you restrict the users in the Administrator role of the System Application.

Who Can Use Your Application

You now have information about what logon session your server application will run in and what process token it will receive. The next question is who can access the application. Accessing the application actually involves three separate issues: who can launch the application, who can create components, and who can make method calls. All three of these aspects of accessing your application have to do with role-based security.

Role-based security

MTS and COM+ introduced an enhancement to security known as role-based security. Recall from the earlier portion of this chapter that in RPC, all calls are forwarded to the server, and the server determines programmatically whether to let the call through. COM+ defined a system by which you can tell the infrastructure through declarative properties who should have access to the application and its methods. The system involves defining roles. Defining roles means that you define a group. This is not a domain group; its definition makes sense only in the context of COM+ and only on the server machine where you create the role. A role can include individual users and local or domain groups. Examples of roles are Bank Tellers, Bank Supervisors, Bank Customers, and so on. To create a role, expand the COM+ application branch to expose the Components and Roles folders. Right-click on the Roles subfolder and choose New → Role. You will see the dialog box in Figure 10-4.

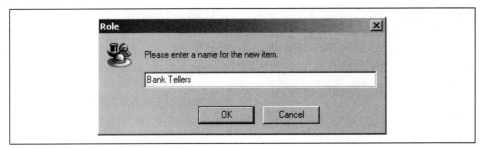

Figure 10-4. New Role dialog box

Enter the name of the role in the dialog box. Once you have created the role, you add users or groups to the role by expanding the role branch. Then, right-click on the Users folder and select New → User. You will see a dialog box resembling the one in Figure 10-5.

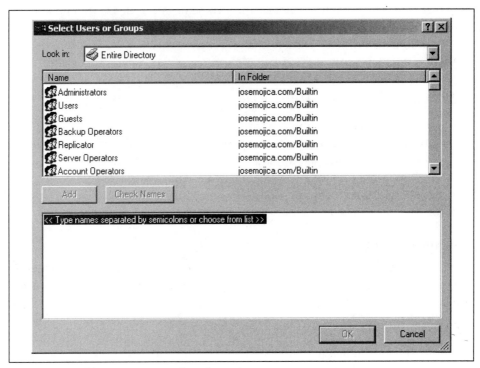

Figure 10-5. Adding new users to the role

Select the users or groups in this dialog box that will belong to the role and click OK. This is all you have to do to create roles. Now that you know how to create a role, let's talk about how the roles affect who can access the application.

Turning on security

The first thing you have to know is that by default the security for the application is turned off. Any user that can be authenticated in the machine has full access to the components and to their methods. What's more, anyone can launch the application, and anyone can create instances of the components.

To turn on security, you must access each COM+ application's properties. Right-click on the application and select Properties from the pop-up menu, then navigate to the Security tab (refer to Figure 10-1). To turn on security, you must check the "Enforce access checks for this application" option. Then you must choose one of the two "Security level" options in the same dialog box. The first option in the dialog box lets you select application only (or process) security. Application security controls who can launch your application and who can instantiate components, but it does not control who can access methods. The second option, process- and component-level security, also controls who can access each method. The only thing to remember about this option is that it forces each object to be in its own context (this is because the COM+ plumbing has to check security before it lets each method call through).

Launching access and creation access

Determining who can access the application and who can create an instance of a component in the application is easy. Anyone who is assigned to a role, no matter what the role is and what else they can do, will be able to launch the application or create an instance of a component. Now, one interesting bit of information is that if you decide to turn on security by selecting the "Enforce access checks for this application" option, but if you do not assign any users to a role, no one will be able to launch the application or create objects.

Method access

After the user launches the application and creates an instance of a component, can he make a method call? Remember anyone can make a method call if security is set to application security only, as long as the call is made with a sufficient authentication level. If you have security set to component-level security, then access checks are done any time a user outside of the application makes a method call through the context boundary for the object.

I showed you earlier how to turn on security checks at the component level, but there is another setting that enables you to turn on and off access checks for each component. To turn on and off access checks for individual components, right-click on the component and select Properties, then click on the Security tab (see Figure 10-6 for details).

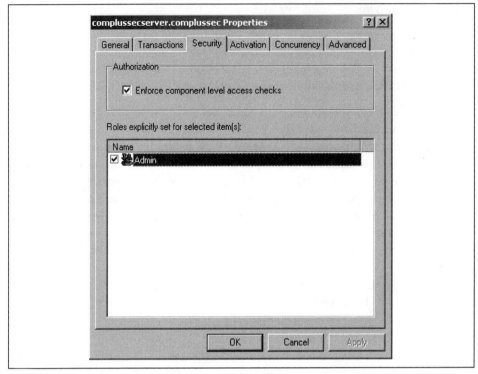

Figure 10-6. Security options at the component level

Once you turn on security for the application, set security checks at the component level, and make sure that each component has security at the component
level turned on as well, then the system will control access to each method based
on the roles you assign to each component, interface, or method. By default,
access is denied to everyone; you have to grant access to different roles (and,
therefore, to the members of that role). It is easy to understand who can gain
access if you keep in mind that what they are gaining access to is the method
itself.

There are three places where you can assign a role. You can assign a role at the
method level, the interface level, or the component level. If you expand the
branch for the component, you will see a list of interfaces for your component,
and if you expand each interface, you will see a list of methods. If you get the
properties for each one of these levels, you will see that each dialog box has a
Security tab and that each one of these Security tabs looks similar. See Figure 10-7
for details.

The bottom half of the screen shows a list of roles to choose from. Select roles to
which you would like to grant access. It is easier to think about access permissions if you keep in mind that ultimately what you are granting access to is a

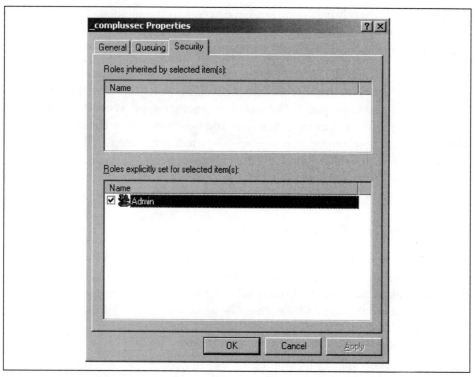

Figure 10-7. Security options for an interface

method. With that in mind, let's analyze the different options for granting access to a method:

- If you assign a role to a method, any user in the role can access that method.

- If a role is assigned to an interface, it can access any method in the interface.

- If a role is assigned to a component, it can access any method in any interface in the component.

- If a user is in two different roles, and one of the roles has access to the method but the other does not, the call will go through; as long as the user has access to the method through any one role at any level, that user will be able to make the method call.

What if a client program makes a call to one object, then that object creates a second object and makes a method call—does COM+ check access rights again? Access checks are done only when you cross application boundaries. Suppose, for example, that Bob is in the Bank Clients role and has access to a method called MakeDeposit in one component but does not have access to method Audit-Account in another component. If MakeDeposit makes a call to AuditAccount and the component that has the method is in the same COM+ application, then the call will go through even if Bob does not have access to the method. That is because the access check is done only when you cross the application boundary. But if Bob tried to make a direct method call into AuditAccount, the call would fail.

The fact that access checks are done when you cross application boundaries means that if you want to force an access check between MakeDeposit and Audit-Account, then you must put AuditAccount in another application. A good way to do this is to put the component that has AuditAccount into a library application. This leads us to another question—on whose behalf is the access check done? Is it the token of the client that originated the call, or is it the token for the application that made the direct call? Access checks are always performed against the direct caller, which leads us to the subject of server-side programmatic security.

Programmatic Security

Remember how in RPC security a server program is able to find out information about its caller programmatically? In COM+, you can also obtain information about the caller and, in fact, about all the callers that were involved in the call and even information about the tokens for each caller.

IsCallerInRole, IsSecurityEnabled, and IsUserInRole

The main interface related to security in Visual Basic is `SecurityCallContext`. The suffix CallContext in the interface name means that the interface gathers information for a causality. Causality is the idea that COM keeps track of a call chain: A calls B, B calls C, C calls D, and so on. Along with information such as the causality ID and error information, COM+ also keeps track of security-related information. For example, COM+ keeps track of the users that were involved in each method call and what groups they belong to. To obtain that information, you first call a function called *GetSecurityCallContext*, which returns a pointer to a `SecurityCallContext` interface. The `SecurityCallContext` interface has three methods (IsCallerInRole, IsSecurityEnabled, and IsUserInRole) and two properties (Count and Item). The syntax for the three methods is as follows:

```
Function IsCallerInRole(ByVal Role As String) As Boolean

Function IsSecurityEnabled() As Boolean

Function IsUserInRole(pUser As Variant, bsRole As String) As Boolean
```

Let's suppose that Bob is a member of the Bank Tellers role and has access to a method called CloseAccount. However, let's say that the account Bob wants to close has a million dollars in it. Bank policy says that you cannot close an account that has a large amount of money unless you are also a member of the Bank Supervisors role. The fact that anyone from Bank Tellers can close an account but only if the account has a small amount of money implies that we must test pro-grammatically whether Bob is also part of the Bank Supervisors. You can do this through the IsCallerInRole method, as shown in the following code:

```
Public Sub CloseAccount(ByVal AcctNo As Long)
    If GetAccountBalance(AcctNo) > 1000000 Then
        If GetSecurityCallContext.IsCallerInRole("Bank Supervisor") Then
            ...
        End If
    End If
End Sub
```

There is something not quite right with this code. It turns out that if security is turned off, the IsCallerInRole method always returns **True**. Therefore, to make sure that the results of the function are accurate, you can check whether security is enabled through the IsSecurityEnabled method. The following code shows the modified version of the *CloseAccount* function to protect against security being turned off:

```
Public Sub CloseAccount(ByVal AcctNo As Long)
    If GetAccountBalance(AcctNo) > 1000000 Then
        If GetSecurityCallContext.IsSecurityEnabled = True Then
            If GetObjectContext.IsCallerInRole("Bank Supervisor") Then
                ...
            End If
        End If
    End If
End Sub
```

The IsUserInRole method is an enhanced version of IsCallerInRole. The differ-ence is that IsUserInRole lets you specify any user ID in the form *userid@domain* or *\\domain\user*. This function also lets you specify a SID as a Variant array if you happen to know the SID for a user. However, I should warn you that IsUser-InRole is a lot more costly than IsCallerInRole—IsUserInRole goes to each com-puter involved in the call and collects information about the groups that the user is in. The following code shows you how to do this by testing whether the alex account is part of the BankSupervisor role:

```
Public Sub CloseAccount(ByVal AcctNo As Long)
    If GetAccountBalance(AcctNo) > 1000000 Then
        If GetSecurityCallContext.IsSecurityEnabled = True Then
            'check if the account is part of the role
            If GetSecurityCallContext.IsUserInRole("alex@josemojica.com", _
                                            "Bank Supervisor") Then
                'generate an error
            End If
        End If
    End If
End Sub
```

SecurityCallContext collections

The `SecurityCallContext` interface gives you access to some security-related properties (some of which return collections) through the Item property. In fact, if you use the interface's Count property, you can access five subproperties through the Item property: DirectCaller, OriginalCaller, MinAuthenticationLevel, Num-Callers, and Callers.

The DirectCaller item returns a pointer to the `SecurityIdentity` interface that represents the last caller (the direct caller) in the chain of calls leading to the current method. For example, if A calls B and B calls C and C calls MakeDeposit, the direct caller is C.

The OriginalCaller item also returns an instance of the `SecurityIdentity` interface, but it represents the caller that originated the call chain. In the previous example, A would be the OriginalCaller.

The `SecurityIdentity` interface points to a collection with the following items:

SID
    The security identifier for the client

AccountName
    The domain–user ID combination

AuthenticationService
    Describes whether you are using Kerberos, NTLM, SPENGO, and so forth

ImpersonationLevel
    The degree of impersonation rights the caller is granting

AuthenticationLevel
    How secure the information that was sent was when the call was made (see the "Authentication Level" section earlier for details).

The following code shows how to get the OriginalCaller (use the same code to get the DirectCaller, replacing the OriginalCaller string with the DirectCaller string):

```
Public Sub MakeDeposit(ByVal Amount As Currency)
    Dim sCaller As String
    sCaller = GetSecurityCallContext.Item("OriginalCaller").Item("AccountName")
    If GetSecurityCallContext.IsUserInRole(sCaller,"Bank Customers") Then
        ...
    End If
End Sub
```

This code gets the user ID of the original caller and uses it to find out if the user is a member of the Bank Customers role.

The MinAuthenticationLevel item in the SecurityCallContext collection is a handy property that takes all the AuthenticationLevels in the chain and returns a Long that reports the lowest level that was used in the chain. For example, A might have used packet privacy, but B might have used Connect, so this property would report Connect as the lowest level in the chain. See the "Authentication Level" section in this chapter for a complete list of values for this property.

The NumCallers item in the SecurityCallContext collection returns a Long indicating the number of callers involved in the call. You can use this function in conjunction with the Callers item to enumerate through each caller in the chain. Callers returns a pointer to the **SecurityCallers** interface. This interface represents the collection of all the callers in the chain. The methods for this interface are Count and Item. The Item property in **SecurityCallers** enables you to specify the ordinal number of the caller information you wish to obtain and returns a pointer to a **SecurityIdentity** interface. This is the same interface returned by the DirectCaller and OriginalCaller items. Then you can obtain information, such as the SID, AccountName, and so on. The following code shows how to enumerate through all the users in the chain:

```
Public Sub MakeDeposit(ByVal Amount As Currency)
    Dim lCallerCount As Long
    Dim Callers As SecurityCallers
    Set Callers = GetSecurityCallContext.Item("Callers")

    For lCallerCount = 0 To GetSecurityCallContext.Item("NumCallers")-1
        Dim SID As Variant
        SID = SecurityCallers.Item(lCallerCount).Item("SID")
    Next

End Sub
```

Internet-Based Security

Today most clients accessing our COM+ application do not use custom VB client applications. Instead, they use the browser as their client program. This last section discusses how IIS security integrates into COM+ security. I am not going to spend a lot of time defining how to create web applications and ASPs or how to configure your server. However, for the sake of discussion, I would like to give you a brief overview of what a web application is and how it integrates with COM+.

Web Application Overview

In Windows 2000, the Microsoft web server is Internet Information Services 5.0 (IIS 5.0). IIS runs as a service in a process called *InetInfo.EXE. InetInfo.EXE* gives the developer the ability to create extensions and filters known as ISAPI extensions and ISAPI filters. Whenever a client sends an HTTP request to the server, it normally sends the request through TCP/IP port 80. IIS listens for HTTP requests through port 80 and has the job of sending an HTTP response. By writing filters and extensions, you can read the information in the HTTP request and customize the response to the client. The most famous ISAPI extension is *ASP.DLL*, which wraps the low-level functionality of ISAPI into scripting friendly interfaces.

IIS enables you to define a number of web applications for a particular server. To define an application, you create what is called a *virtual directory* (consult the IIS documentation for details on how to create a virtual directory). Each virtual directory is a different application with its own list of ISAPI extensions and its own security settings. Whenever IIS gets a request for a document in your application, it does one of two things. If the request is for a pure HTML document, it handles it by itself. It reads the document and returns the document to the client as the response. If, on the other hand, the request is for another document type, IIS checks the list of ISAPI extensions for the application. When you assign an ISAPI extension to the application, you tell IIS to use a particular ISAPI DLL whenever it gets a request for a document with a particular file extension. In the case of ASPs, each application you create automatically has *ASP.DLL* associated with the *.asp* extension. Whenever IIS gets a request for a document with an *.asp* extension, it knows that the *ASP.DLL* ISAPI extension should handle the request.

Whenever IIS discovers that the document should be handled by one of the extensions in the list, IIS hands the request to a specialized COM object known as the Web Application Manager (WAM) object. The WAM is a configured component (it runs within a COM+ application). The job of the WAM is to load the appropriate ISAPI extension into memory and ask it to do its work based on the request. Because the WAM is a configured component, that means that *ASP.DLL* and therefore your ASP pages will run within a COM+ application. In other words, if you do nothing with COM+ manually, you are still using COM+ with your web application because the WAM object always runs within COM+.

Application protection

What COM+ application is the WAM object in? Well, it is possible for the WAM for your application to run in one of three different configurations, which is determined by a setting in your virtual application known as Application Protection. Let's create a simple web application and see how the Application Protection property affects the configuration of the WAM object.

To create a web application, use the Internet Services Manager. You can find this program in Start → Programs → Administrative Tools. (If you are using the Professional version of Windows 2000, then you have to install IIS using the Add/Remove Windows Components feature in the Add/Remove Programs applet in Control Panel.) You should see the dialog box in Figure 10-8.

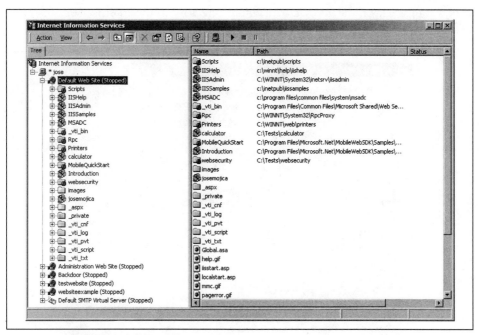

Figure 10-8. Internet Services Manager

Before creating a virtual directory, create a folder somewhere in your drive to store the ASP documents. Then from the Internet Services Manager, right-click on the Default Web Site branch and choose New → Virtual Directory. You will see a wizard that will guide you through the process. Enter an alias for the application; call it *websecurity*. Then when the wizard asks for the content directory, enter the path of the folder you created before starting the process. The next dialog box will ask you to set the access permissions; leave the permissions settings with the default values (Read and Run Scripts) and click Next. After you have completed the wizard, you should see an entry for the *websecurity* virtual directory in the Default Web Site branch. You can then create ASP documents and place them in the virtual directory. For example you could create a text document called *hello. asp* with the following code:

```
<@Language = VBScript >
<% For i = 1 To 10 %>
Hello World!
<% Next %>
```

This document just sends the string "Hello World!" 10 times as part of the response. To run the application, the client would specify the following URL: *http://webservermachine/websecurity/hello.asp* or *http://localhost/websecurity/hello. asp*. That ASP document is being managed by the *ASP.DLL* ISAPI extension. But in what application is the extension running?

If you right-click on the *websecurity* virtual directory in the Internet Services Manager and choose Properties, you will see the dialog box in Figure 10-9.

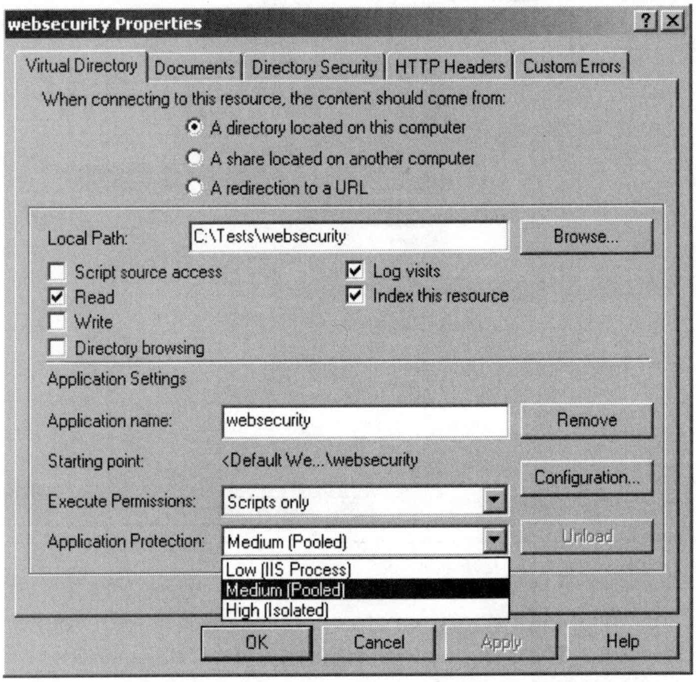

Figure 10-9. The virtual directory properties

If you examine the field called Application Protection, you will notice three options: Low, Medium, and High. To understand the options, take a look at the Component Services Manager in Figure 10-10.

Notice that there is an IIS In-Process Applications application. IIS installed this application automatically when it was installed. If you look at the application's components, you will see the WAM component, which IIS uses to run your ASPs when you select the Low application protection option. If you examine the Activation settings for the IIS In-Process Applications application, you will notice that it is configured to be a library application. The significance of this is that this application runs in the same process as *INetInfo.EXE*. That means that scripts running with this application level run under the process token for INetInfo. INetInfo runs with the SYSTEM token—it has full power over the machine. This is why this level of protection is called low; if there is an attack from hackers, they can potentially gain access to the SYSTEM account.

If you look back at the Component Services Manager, you will see another application called IIS Out-Of-Process Pooled Applications. This application also has a

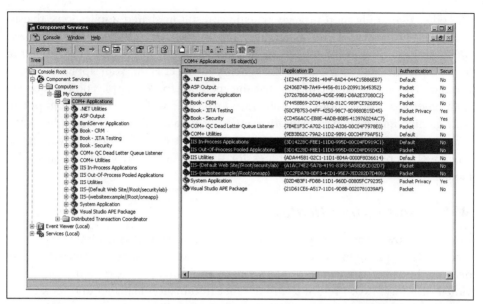

Figure 10-10. COM+ Component Services Manager highlighting the IIS applications

WAM component. IIS uses the WAM component in that application if you select the Medium level of application protection. The difference is that this application is configured as a server application and therefore runs in its own process. Thus, it runs under its own set of credentials. Notice that this is the default for IIS applications. Looking through the properties for this COM+ application, you will notice a few interesting things. First, access security is turned off by default. Second, if you look at the Identity tab, you will notice that it is configured to run as a certain user. In fact, the username is `IWAM_ComputerName`. This is an account that IIS creates. The reason IIS applications use this account is that the account has very low access privileges, thus if a hacker is able to take over the web app, she will not be able to do very much.

A side effect of having a user account assigned to the application is that it is harder to debug your COM+ components because the COM+ application will be running under its own WinStation, and you will not be able to see things like message boxes or trace messages. You can temporarily change this to the Interactive user while you are developing so that you can see this information. Interestingly, you can also change the identity to another account; you do not have to use the default `IWAM_ComputerName`.

The third option is application protection High. When you select this option, IIS creates a COM+ application with a WAM component just for your web application. In our case, the application name is `IIS-{Default Web Site//Root/websecurity}`.

The other two application protection settings result in shared applications; that is, all the applications that run as medium run in the same instance of *DllHost.exe* (the surrogate process for COM+ applications). All the low-level applications run in the same instance of *INetInfo.EXE*. When you select High, your application runs isolated. The advantage of this is that the memory for the application is isolated from other web applications. This shields a malicious web application from potentially gaining information in memory from other web applications. It also helps the server isolate problems—if one web app crashes, it does not bring down all the other web apps. The security settings for this configuration are identical to the medium-level application.

Web Client Authentication

Now you know what token your ASP application is using. It is determined by how you set the application protection property. The next question is what set of credentials the client is using. For this we have to examine the properties of the IIS virtual directory. If you return to the Internet Information Manager and look at the property dialog box for your virtual directory, you will notice a Directory Security tab, which is shown in Figure 10-11.

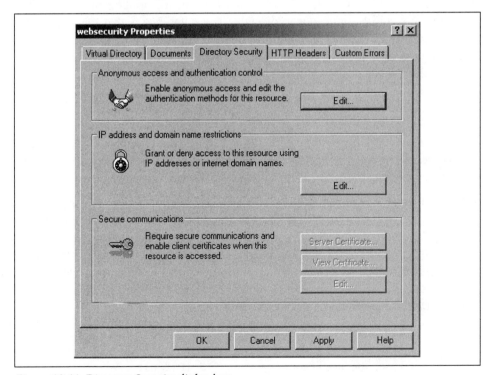

Figure 10-11. Directory Security dialog box

Click the Edit button on the Anonymous Access and Authentication Control section to reveal the Authentication options dialog box (see Figure 10-12). The available authentication options are Anonymous access, Basic authentication, Digest authentication, and Integrated Windows authentication. The default is Anonymous access. Let's take a look at each of these options.

Figure 10-12. Authentication Methods dialog box

Anonymous access

Anonymous access means that the client does not need an account on the machine. In fact, this option makes sense for clients that do not have Windows or even for servers that handle commercial web sites with a lot of users. Think about Amazon.com, for example. They cannot create an account on their server for every user. What they do instead is create their own form of security by assigning you a password when you register with them. They keep these passwords in a database such as Oracle or SQL Server. However, even if you use a custom system to track security, COM+ still needs to attribute the actions of the user to an account in the operating system. IIS uses a specific account to log in anonymous web clients. If you click Edit in the "Anonymous access" section, you will see the dialog box in Figure 10-13.

This account is set by default to be `IUSR_MachineName`, although you can use an alternate account if you wish. If the "Anonymous access" option is selected, all users accessing the web application will use this set of credentials. Let's say that your ASP application is running in medium-level application protection and then

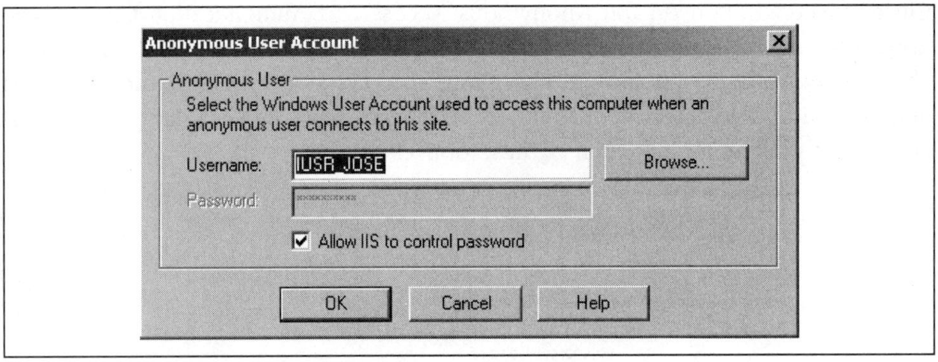

Figure 10-13. Anonymous user account

instantiates a COM+ component. Here is an example of what the ASP script may
look like:

```
<%
Dim O
Set O = Server.CreateObject("bankserver.cchecking")
Call O.MakeDeposit(5000)
Response.Write("Done!")
%>
```

Let's suppose that the **Bankserver.CChecking** component is a configured component in a server application on the same machine. What we have is InetInfo
making a call into the WAM that runs in *DllHost.EXE* making a call (in essence) to
your component that runs in another *DllHost.EXE*. How many callers do we end
up with and what are their credentials? Well, it turns out that we have only one
caller in this scenario, and its account name is IUSR_*MachineName*. Let's talk
about what happens.

When the client accesses the application with an HTTP request, IIS creates a logon
session for the client and uses IUSR_*MachineName*. Then it hands the request to a
WAM object. The WAM object is running in its own *DllHost.EXE*. The process
token for this instance of *DllHost.EXE* is running as IWAM_*MachineName*. However, when the WAM talks to your ASPs, it impersonates IUSR_*MachineName*.
COM+ applications are marked to use dynamic cloaking by default; this means
that when you make a method call to a component outside of the application,
COM+ is going to use the credentials the thread is impersonating, which is IUSR_
MachineName, as if the server itself were making the call. Therefore, when your
component gets the call, if the identity of your application is set to the interactive
user, the direct caller is going to be IUSR_*MachineName*. If your component, however, makes a call into another application, then the user for that application will
be the Interactive user (or whatever user you have set as the identity for your

application). This makes it easier for you to restrict or grant access to your application for anonymous users. All you have to do is turn on security for your application, then assign `IUSR_MachineName` to a role like Web Users and assign the role to different parts of your application.

If you do not want to have anonymous access in your web application, then you can select Basic authentication, Digest authentication, or Integrated Windows authentication.

Basic authentication and Digest authentication

Basic authentication and Digest authentication involve presenting the client with a dialog box and having the client enter his user ID and password. In Basic authentication the user ID and password are transmitted as part of the HTTP request. The user ID and password are sent as clear text (they are actually sent as base 64 encoded, but anyone can decode the information without needing a key). In Digest authentication, the credentials are not sent across the wire; the protocol can authenticate the user the same way that other protocols like NTLM can without passing the password from one machine to the other. However, Digest authentication is not recommended, because it requires the passwords to be stored using reversible encryption, which is a weaker form of protection. Also, with Digest authentication, you must have the web server on the same machine as the domain controller.

In both of these approaches, the web server uses these credentials to log on the user and create an interactive logon session by default, although it is possible through the IIS Metabase to adjust what type of logon session to create. Consult the MSDN documentation for information on how to use the IIS Metabase. Because these options create an interactive logon session by default, the session will have network credentials, which means that you will be able to use the token to make another jump across the network.

Integrated Windows authentication

Integrated Windows authentication is a proprietary form of authentication that works only with IE clients. It treats the client as if it were accessing the file with Windows Explorer (without IE). It involves authenticating the user normally. The drawback with this type of security is that the logon session it creates is a network logon session. In a network logon session, the session does not have information for making another hop across the network. The programs can impersonate the token, but only for local access. If they try to make a call to another machine, the call will most likely fail. However, if your ASPs make a call to a local server application and then that application makes a call into another object in another machine, the call will most likely succeed. In this case, the credentials being used will be the credentials of the intermediary application.

Summary

The first half of this chapter reviews the terminology that relates to security. All applications run under a certain set of credentials, and this set of credentials is known as the process token. You can use this token to extract information—such as the account name and the groups the account belongs to—about the account used to start the process. By default, threads in a process do not have their own tokens. A thread may decide to use an alternate token; this is called impersonation. The thread will then do some work, and the system will reject or grant access to resources based on the new set of credentials.

COM+ security is built on top of RPC security. In RPC security as well as in COM+ security, the client is the one that dictates the security settings, and the server grants or rejects calls programmatically. COM+ simplifies the process of rejecting and granting access to functions in several ways. For one thing, COM+ enables you to set the minimum level of authentication through declarative properties. Then you can further restrict access into your application by creating roles. By default, security is turned off for your application. If you turn it on, you can tell COM+ if you wish to check security only at the application level or at the application level and the component level. If a user is assigned to a role, even if the role is not assigned to a component, interface, or method, the user will be able to launch the application and create instances of the components. To grant the user access to methods, you must then assign the role to a component, an interface, or the method itself.

COM+ collects information about the callers that were involved in making the call. You can obtain information about the callers through the *GetSecurityCallContext* function. This function returns a pointer to the `SecurityCallContext` interface. You can use this interface to retrieve information about the original caller, the direct caller, and every caller involved in the call.

The last portion of the chapter was about web security. You learned that anonymous users run under the credentials of the `IUSR_MachineName` account by default. You also learned that IIS hands requests for ASP pages to a WAM object. The WAM uses impersonation when it invokes your ASP page. You also learned that if you do not want to use anonymous authentication, you can use Basic authentication, Digest authentication, or Integrated Windows authentication. These other types of security require that you have an account in the domain for each user. Therefore, these options may not be feasible for a large web application.

In the next chapter, you are going to get an introduction to the .NET architecture and in particular some of the more exciting features in VB.NET.

11

Introduction to .NET

At the time I started writing this chapter, .NET had entered its Beta 1 cycle. Even though this product is only in Beta 1 (and if you have read the documentation shipped with the .NET SDK, you will see that there is at least a Beta 2 planned), I know that with the Microsoft marketing muscle, many of you may be feeling in some ways as if you are already behind for not having already converted all your applications to use .NET. The reality is that .NET is a brand new architecture; it is not the next version of COM+. What's more, all the Microsoft compilers that were written before have to be rewritten to emit code compatible with the new architecture. In many cases, the language constructs themselves have also been rewritten. Visual Basic, for example, has gone through many syntactical changes—so many that some may argue it is not the same language.

In this chapter, you are first going to get an introduction to the .NET architecture, then you are going to get an overview of some of the new features in VB.NET, and after you have an understanding of how to use the features, you will learn about how to mix .NET components with COM+ components. Because I am currently using beta software, the information in this chapter is subject to change. There is no way that I can pretend that this chapter will give all the information necessary to be a .NET developer, but it is my hope that you will learn enough to satisfy your curiosity.

The .NET Architecture

Why are we talking about .NET and not the next version of COM or COM+? .NET in fact is a brand new architecture with few things related to the current architecture. So what is wrong with COM and why is Microsoft going in a different direction? Well, before we can point out the benefits of .NET over COM/COM+, let's talk about the architecture itself.

First, how do you get .NET? .NET comes in two main parts. One of the parts is the .NET SDK. The .NET SDK team builds what was previously known as the Universal Runtime (URT) and is now called the Common Language Runtime (CLR). It is a runtime environment that includes a loader for .NET code, a verifier, certain utilities, and a number of .NET DLLs that compose what is called the .NET Common Type System. The SDK also includes four command-line compilers: one for VB.NET, one for a new language called C# (C-Sharp), a new version of the C++ compiler and linker that produces what is called managed C++ (or MC++), and one for the Intermediate Language (IL), which you will learn about shortly. A number of other language compilers are also being developed by third parties to emit .NET-compatible code, such as Cobol.NET, Component Pascal, Eiffel, and others.

The second part of .NET is called Visual Studio.NET. Visual Studio.NET is composed of the IDE that you use to write code, several programming tools, and online documentation. Visual Studio.NET uses the .NET SDK compilers to compile your program. In reality, if you like using *NotePad.exe*, you do not need Visual Studio.NET; you could write your VB programs in Notepad and then run the command-line compiler.

One important thing to understand about .NET is that it is a lot more than its name implies. At first glance, it may seem like a technology geared toward writing Internet applications. Although this is true in some sense, it is a lot more than that. .NET is primarily an architecture for writing applications that are object-oriented in nature, and both hardware and operating system agnostic. You may have heard similar claims from another language—Java. Under the covers, .NET is very different from Java, but conceptually the two architectures have the same goal.

IL

The heart of .NET is the Intermediate Language (IL). IL is a hardware-independent object-oriented form of assembly language. The following code shows a "hello world" program written in IL:

```
.assembly hello {}
.assembly extern mscorlib {}
.method static public void main() il managed {
    .entrypoint
    .maxstack 1
    ldstr    "Hello World"
    call        void [mscorlib]System.Console::WriteLine(class System.String)
    ret
}
```

A line-by-line discussion of the preceding code is beyond the scope of this book; however, we will discuss some of the most interesting parts of the code shortly.

Notice for now that the code resembles assembly language but uses a different set of commands, and it does look like a much higher-level language than pure *.asm*.

You could take the previous code and save it as a text file with Notepad, giving it the extension .IL (*helloworld.il*, for example). If you have the .NET SDK installed, you could run the IL compiler from the command line by entering the following command:

```
ILASM helloworld.il
```

The output of that command would be the executable *helloworld.exe*. You could then run the program and witness "Hello World" appear on your console.

IL-generated code is processor and operating system independent. The IL source code must be changed to native code before it is run. IL programs are not interpreted; they are instead converted to native code using one of three compilers provided in the .NET SDK.

The default compiler is the Just-in-Time (JIT) compiler. The JIT compiler takes IL and first compiles the entry-point function and any code that the function needs; then as the code executes, any other code that that code needs is also compiled; and so on. Sometimes some of the earlier compiled code may be thrown out from memory to make room for other code, then recompiled when needed.

Another option for compilation is to use the EconoJIT compiler, which is due to come out in a future release of the Platform SDK. The EconoJIT compiler does the same job as the JIT compiler, but it produces less efficient code. Sometimes developers feel that having code compiled at runtime may decrease the performance of the program considerably. Although this may be the case, depending on how the compiler is written, it is more likely that your code may see better performance when it is JIT compiled than when it is compiled in a traditional way. The reason for this is that the JIT compiler can take into consideration your hardware and optimize the code to function well with it. If you think about it, when code is precompiled from the factory, it follows a "one size fits all" approach; it is often optimized to run on a machine that has an Intel processor. If you ran your program on a machine with an AMD processor, a JIT compiler would be able to use the AMD extensions as needed. This is the way that the JIT compiler is supposed to work, and it produces high-quality machine code at the price of load time. The EconoJIT compiler, on the other hand, compiles faster at the cost of execution performance.

The third type of compilation is called OptJIT. The OptJIT compiler is due to come out in a future release, but the idea is that some third-party vendors will emit a subset of IL called Optimized IL (OptIL). OptIL is IL with instructions embedded into it that tell the OptJIT compiler how to optimize its output for certain tasks. For example, the third-party language may be optimized to do mathematical calculations and would like the generated code to do mathematical calculations in a certain fashion. The third-party OptIL output would embed information in the IL that would tell the OptJIT compiler how to optimize calculation code when it generates the machine code.

The operating system that you are using does not know how to take IL, run it through the JIT compiler, and run the results directly. Later versions of Windows (probably beyond Windows XP) will be IL ready. This means that the operating system may be able to see a text file with IL in it and run it as is. However, Windows 2000 cannot do this, so IL must be embedded into an executable or a DLL. The ILASM compiler can take the IL and build a PE file around it. PE stands for portable executable and is the format that .EXE files and .DLL files use. The PE wrapper that the ILASM compiler generates has code to invoke the runtime loader found in *mswks.dll* and other files shipped with the .NET SDK. The PE file has the IL embedded in it. The IL may be embedded as "text," although some formatting of the text is done to make it easier to parse, or it may be prejitted (turned into native code). Microsoft will ship some files that have IL already changed to native code or prejitted. The runtime is able to run compiled IL code or text IL code.

Most of the time, you will not be writing IL code from scratch. Instead, you will use your language of choice. A number of language compilers have been rewritten to generate IL instead of native code. Visual Basic is one of these languages. In addition Microsoft has created a brand new language called C# (C-Sharp). C# is a C++-like language that in many ways also resembles Visual Basic. It eliminates a number of features from C++ that, although they provided a lot of "power," also produced a lot of confusion. For example, C# does not have pointers. It also does not have macros or templates. The successor to VB 6 is VB.NET. VB.NET is a completely new version of Visual Basic. Many things have changed, and later in this chapter you will learn about some of the new features.

Assemblies

Along with a new form of assembly language and a new set of compilers, Microsoft has also redefined what it means to be an application. If you think about the current operating system boundaries, there are two main entities: processes and threads. Threads give us an order of execution. You may recall from Chapter 5 that a program may launch another thread in order to do two tasks seemingly simultaneously. A process determines primarily a memory boundary. Two processes do not share memory. Their memory is isolated, and although it is possible to share memory using low-level functions, that is not the standard. However, more than a memory boundary, the process also serves as a security boundary. In Chapter 10, you learned that each process in the operating system runs under a certain set of credentials.

Microsoft has redefined what it means to be a process. In fact, the new world does not address processes per se; the new world uses assemblies. You're probably wondering whether assemblies are DLLs or EXEs. The answer is that assemblies are neither (it is almost better to forget that EXEs and DLLs ever existed). In many ways, processes are better matched to a new boundary in the .NET architecture known as AppDomains.

As you already know, the runtime runs IL. A developer may declare one file or a number of files containing IL as being part of an assembly. An assembly is the smallest unit that can be versioned; it determines the boundary for which classes are made public or private; it is also a unit that can be secured. Because IL files are packaged in EXEs and DLLs, an assembly can be a single EXE, a single DLL, or a combination of EXEs and DLLs. An assembly may also contain other files, such as resource files and even help files. Figure 11-1 shows the relationship between EXEs, DLLs, and assemblies.

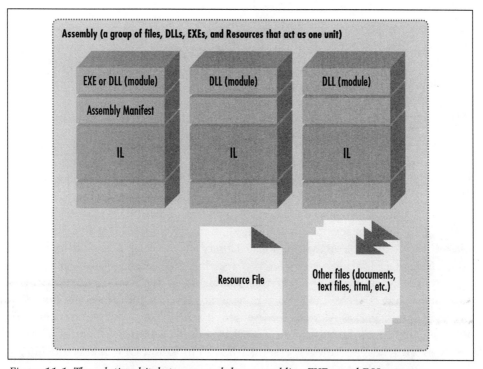

Figure 11-1. The relationship between modules, assemblies, EXEs, and DLLs

Each image file containing valid IL is called a module. To be an assembly, one of the files in the group must have an assembly manifest. The assembly manifest is created with an assembly definition. If you look at the "hello world" example presented earlier, the code begins with the directive `.assembly hello`. Without the `.assembly` directive, the assembler would produce only a module. Having the `.assembly` directive does two things: it declares an assembly with the name hello, and it creates the assembly manifest.

A manifest is metadata, which is a fancy word for descriptive text. You can think of the manifest as the type library for the assembly. It defines properties of the assembly such as the version number of the assembly and the culture (or locale) that the assembly was built for. The manifest also lists all the modules, all the files, and all the external assemblies on which the assembly depends. For example, if your assembly requires data access, you will need to reference the Microsoft.Data assembly. In the earlier IL example, the second line of code, `.assembly extern mscorlib`, tells the loader that the assembly uses a system assembly known as mscorlib. The reason the code needs to reference this assembly is because it uses a class called System.Console. This class has a method called WriteLine that the IL code uses to output "Hello World" to the console.

As you may suspect, Microsoft provides a number of prebuilt assemblies that you may use. These assemblies contain a series of public classes, interfaces, and attributes (you will learn about attributes shortly). These sets of classes, interfaces, and attributes constitute the .NET Common Type System.

The Common Type System

If you think about the type system in Visual Basic 6, you may separate the types into two main groups: objects and intrinsic types. We can say that intrinsic types include things like integers, strings, doubles, and so on, while object types refer to classes you define. C++ has its own type system. It also includes some native types like int, double, short, and long, and it includes object types—classes that you define. C++ also has several class libraries, among them the Microsoft Foundation Classes (MFC) and the Active Template Library. If you look at a third-generation language like Delphi, for example, you see that that language also has its own type system. A common problem was making these type systems communicate with one another. COM+ handled this by letting each compiler decide how they were going to map types to a few C++ types. If you wanted your component to be VB compatible, you had to figure out what subset of all the C++ types mapped neatly to VB types, and the VB compiler had to look at a C++ interface definition and translate it as best it could to VB.

To resolve most of the issues of compatibility between languages, Microsoft is also introducing a common type system. I say most, because it turns out that every type that can be represented in the type system is not necessarily available to every language. Instead Microsoft defines the Common Language Subset (or CLS) to be a subset of the type system that every language should support. However, for the most part, having a common type system means that every language that produces IL knows how to use types declared in any other language. Three things make the type system particularly interesting:

- Every object has the same root object: System.Object.

- Classes are self-describing. Through a set of classes that define reflection, a developer can find out from a running object all the information about the class that was used to generate that object.

- Microsoft decided to distinguish between reference types and value types. A *reference type* is a reference to an object that is allocated on the heap. A *value type* is an object allocated on the stack. The concept of value types is nothing new; after all, in VB 6 we have things like Integers, Doubles, Singles, and UDTs. These are all examples of value types.

What makes value types in the new type system different is that they also derive ultimately from System.Object. In other words, even value types are classes with methods, fields, and interface implementations. For example, when you dim a variable as type Integer, VB turns that declaration into a variable of type System. Int32. System.Int32 is a class.

What distinguishes a value type from other classes is that value types are derived from a class called System.ValueType. Sometimes it may be necessary to take a value type and cast it to a variable of type System.Object (think of System.Object as the VB 6 Variant type or the VB 6 Object type). However, System.Object declarations are reference types, and the runtime treats them differently from value types. To allow this conversion, the runtime supports an operation known as *boxing*. Boxing means that the system duplicates the data stored in the value type and creates a copy of the object on the heap. The reverse procedure, in which a value type is created from a reference type and the data is replicated once again, is called *unboxing*. You are going to see an example later on in the chapter.

To make it possible for every object, including value types, to derive from System. Object, the CLR uses inheritance. There are two types of inheritance in the system: class inheritance and interface inheritance. You can inherit from only a single class, and, in fact, every class must inherit from at least one class, System.Object. On the other hand, you can implement any number of interfaces. That stated, let me complicate things by saying that interfaces are also classes derived from System.Object. However, they are a special type of class marked as abstract, and every member in the interface is really a pointer to a function (the concept of vtables to vptrs is still the same).

Why .NET and Not COM+ 2.0?

The first question that people often have is why Microsoft had to come up with a different component technology. Why not improve COM+? Let's talk about some of the limitations in COM and how .NET addresses them.

One problem with COM+ was the lack of a common type system. We have talked a little about this problem. To summarize, each language involved in COM had its own type system, and the best the compilers could do was match a type from one language to another by the amount of memory that the type consumed and the semantics of the type. With .NET, we have a common type system, each language creates types that follow the rules of the type system, and every type is a subtype of System.Object.

Another problem with COM was how to advertise the types that the server exposed. C++ developers relied primarily on header files that described the set of interfaces exposed by the server. VB relied on type libraries. Often an interface would originate from one of the Microsoft groups in C++ syntax. Then a developer would have to write a type library for Visual Basic that had VB-friendly syntax. .NET uses a better approach. Assemblies expose types, and an assembly can be referenced directly when building a new assembly. Thus, if you create a program (an assembly) that relies on a database class, for example, when you compile your assembly, you will tell the compiler to reference the database assembly. Visual Studio.NET will give you an easy way to tell the compiler what assemblies you need. In fact, there is almost no difference visually between referencing a type library in VB 6 and referencing an assembly. Later on you will see how to expose a class in an assembly and how to reference the assembly in another assembly.

A third problem with COM was that the architecture did not have perfect knowledge of the types in your process. For example, there was nothing in COM that told the operating system what COM servers your client program was dependent on at load time. The type library told COM about what types your server exposed, but the client relied on *CreateObject* or **New**. So there was no way for the OS to know at load time if your EXE needed a server that wasn't available in the system. The OS didn't know until it executed the line of code that tried to create a type in the server whether that server was available. With .NET, the manifest contains a list of not only the types that your server exposes, but also the types that the server needs. The CLR loader verifies that it can find all the assemblies that your assembly is dependent on before running your program.

Another related problem concerned versioning. How many versions of ADO could you use on one computer at a time with COM+? Only one. When you registered ADO on the machine, there was a single registry key, `InProcServer32`, that told the system where ADO was located. If you had another version on the system, there was no way to use it side-by-side with the first one. You would have to register the new version, and that would override the `InProcServer32` key to point exclusively to the new version, and every program would use the new version. One problem resulting from this approach was that there was no guarantee that existing client programs could use the new version of ADO. Nothing in your client process told the OS what version of ADO your program was dependent on and whether you could use a new version or not.

In contrast, .NET has an improved versioning scheme. When you build a client assembly, the manifest tells the loader the version of each assembly that you are dependent on. In addition, .NET recognizes *shared assemblies* and *private assemblies*. Private assemblies are used with just your applications. Something like ADO.NET would be a shared assembly—an assembly that many assemblies count on. Shared or public assemblies are signed with a private and public encryption key. The process of signing the code produces an originator. Once your assembly has an originator, you may put it in the global access cache (GAC). The GAC physically lives under the *WINNT\Assembly* directory and stores a copy of all shared assemblies. The CLR loader looks at the list of assemblies you are referencing, and if it does not find a private assembly that is a later version than the version the client was compiled against, then it will try to find the assembly in the GAC. The GAC can store multiple versions of the same assembly. For example, you may have ADO.NET Version 1, 2, and 3 in the GAC. When you build an assembly, the manifest will contain a reference not only to the assembly name, but also to the assembly's version number. It could happen that your application requires one version of the shared assembly and another assembly requires another version, and it could happen that the same process may be running both versions at the same time. Therefore, .NET now gives you the capability of having side-by-side versions of shared components. Later in this chapter, I will show you how to sign your code with a key and add it to the GAC.

Yet another problem resulting from the lack of perfect knowledge of the types you used internally was knowing when to release an object from memory. You can tell if a programmer has done COM+ at the C++ level if you ask about circular references. As VB developers, we do not have to deal with things like reference counting and circular references directly, but C++ COM+ developers do. A common problem with COM components is that object A may be holding a reference to object B, and, because B needs to make a callback call into A, it may be holding a reference to object A. B will never be released from memory as long as A is holding a reference to it, and A will never be released because B is holding a reference to it. This is known as a *circular reference*.

.NET does not use reference counting to determine when an object's memory should be reclaimed. Instead the system implements garbage collection. Managed code can no longer ask for a chunk of memory directly. To take advantage of garbage collection and other services, your code creates an instance of a type or of an array of types, and the memory needed is allocated by the runtime in a managed heap. When there is no more memory to hand out, the system will release memory for objects no longer in use. The garbage collection system differs from reference counting in the way that memory is cleaned up—no longer is memory reclaimed as long as there are no references to the object. Instead, the system waits to release memory until there is need for more memory. There are also commands for telling the garbage collector to collect memory immediately.

You should now have a basic understanding of the .NET architecture and how .NET improves on the existing COM+ architecture. Shortly, you are going to learn about how to have COM+ components using .NET components and vice versa. But before talking about interoperability and about the new features in VB.NET, let's talk about how to compile and version .NET assemblies.

Developing Assemblies

There are two ways to create VB.NET applications. One way is to use the next version of Visual Studio, Visual Studio.NET. Visual Studio.NET is a development environment built on top of the .NET SDK. The .NET SDK is packaged separately from the Visual Studio.NET environment. The SDK includes a C# command-line compiler, a VB.NET command-line compiler, and the DLLs and EXEs necessary to run your .NET applications.

I have decided that in order to make the information in this chapter last, I am not going to use the Visual Studio.NET designer. One reason is that the product has not been released yet. Another reason is that the product is not yet stable. A third reason is that, for the first time, Visual Basic has a true command-line compiler that can be used in conjunction with NMAKE and MakeFiles. You may be familiar with MakeFiles if you have ever worked with C++. MakeFiles are text files that tell *NMAKE.EXE* how to build your program. For all these reasons, I have decided to use the second most widely used development environment in the Windows platform, *Notepad.EXE*. So for the next set of examples, you will need three things: the .NET SDK downloadable from Microsoft, *Notepad.EXE*, and a command prompt. Let's start with a simple Hello World application to get a taste for how to use the command-line compiler.

Run *Notepad.EXE* and enter the following text:

```
Public class HelloSupport
    Shared Public Function GetGreeting(ByVal sName As String) As String
        return "Hello " + sName
    End Function
End Class
```

This code declares a class called HelloSupport. At first it seems strange to create a class for just one function, but in VB.NET every function is exposed through a class. Even when you declare a module with functions, the module becomes a class when it is compiled, and all of the functions in the class become shared, very much like in the preceding example.

So what is **Shared**, anyway? Classes in VB.NET have two types of methods: instance methods and shared (or static) methods. VB 6 class methods were instance methods: you had to create an instance of the class to use them, and the method performed a task on the data for that instance only. Shared methods are new to VB.NET. They can be executed without creating an instance of the class. The only limitation is that if your class has both shared methods and instance methods, you cannot call the instance methods from within the shared methods. You can call shared methods only from within shared methods. If you need to call the instance method, then you have to create an instance of your class and make the method call just as any other function outside the class would. You also cannot use any of the member fields in the class from shared methods unless the fields are also marked as shared. In a module, the VB.NET compiler turns all functions to shared.

The GetGreeting function returns a string that says "Hello *x*", where *x* is the string that the calling program passed to it. Save the preceding file as *hellogreeting.vb*. Then run the VB command-line compiler, *VBC.EXE*. If you installed the SDK, the path to the *VBC.EXE* compiler should be reflected in the environment so that you can run it from any folder. Open a command window and switch to the directory where you saved the files, then enter the following command:

```
vbc /t:library hellogreeting.vb
```

This command creates a DLL file with the name *hellogreeting.dll*. If you look at the command line, you will notice that the first option is the **/t** switch, which tells the compiler the target type. VB.NET is able to produce Windows applications, console applications, DLLs, and modules that can be linked with other modules to produce a multimodule assembly. They can be packaged as EXEs or as DLLs. An assembly is the smallest unit of code that can be versioned.

The keyword **library** produces a DLL. If you are unsure about the syntax, you can enter **vbc** /? for a list of command-line switches. Now it's time to create an executable that can use the function in the DLL. Create a new file in Notepad and enter the following text:

```
class Helloworld

    Shared Sub Main()
        Dim sName As String = "World"
        Dim sGreeting As String = HelloSupport.GetGreeting(sName)
        System.Console.WriteLine(sGreeting)
    End Sub

End Class
```

Save the file as *helloworld.vb*. To compile the program, use the following command line:

```
vbc /t:exe helloworld.vb /r:hellogreeting.dll
```

The preceding code declares a class called Helloworld. The class has a procedure called Sub Main. The Sub Main function is the equivalent of Sub Main in VB 6. The only difference is that the function must be declared as a shared (or a static) subroutine. If you are a hard-core VB 6 (or earlier) developer, you will appreciate the fact that you can now declare variables and assign them a value all in the same line, which is what I have done in the first line of code inside Sub Main. The function declares two variables: sName holds the name that the GetGreeting function will use for the greeting, and sGreeting holds the response from the GetGreeting function. Notice that to use the GetGreeting function, you have to qualify it with the name of the class. Because the GetGreeting function was declared as a shared function, you do not have to create an instance of the class to use it. The code in Sub Main then prints the greeting to the console using the System.Console.WriteLine function.

System.Console.WriteLine is a new function in the CLR. The function is part of the System assembly. Microsoft has defined a set of classes that gives support for the operating system functionality. Not only are these classes a replacement for using the WIN32 API functions directly, but also for other COM libraries that Microsoft ships, such as MSXML and ADO. The runtime has assemblies that Microsoft has included for XML, for HTTP communication, for data access, for threading, for IIS programming—for practically anything you can think of. There is still a way to call WIN32 APIs directly using the Interop classes; however, jumping outside of the runtime is a costly operation, and you are discouraged from doing so.

To build the executable, you must specify the name of the DLL (and the path to the DLL) that your executable needs to resolve all functions. The result of running the previous command-line command is the *Helloworld.exe* image. If you run *helloworld.exe*, you should see the phrase "Hello World" displayed in the command prompt.

Microsoft ships a disassembler with the SDK called *ILDASM.EXE*. Let's run *ILDASM. EXE* on the resulting executable to see how the *helloworld.exe* assembly references the *hellogreeting.dll* assembly. Run the following command from the command prompt:

```
ILDASM.EXE HelloWorld.EXE
```

You should see the window in Figure 11-2.

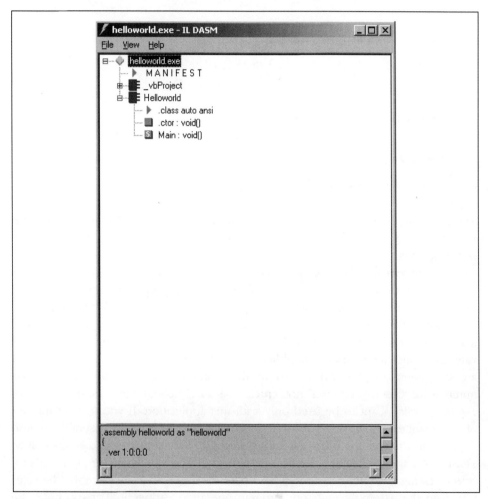

Figure 11-2. ILDASM program

Once you open ILDASM, double-click on the MANIFEST branch, and you should see the following code:

```
.assembly extern mscorlib
{
  .originator = (03 68 91 16 D3 A4 AE 33 )                    // .h.....3
```

```
  .hash = (52 44 F8 C9 55 1F 54 3F 97 D7 AB AD E2 DF 1D E0    // RD..U.T?........
          F2 9D 4F BC )                                       // ..O.
  .ver 1:0:2204:21
}
.assembly extern Microsoft.VisualBasic
{
  .originator = (03 68 91 16 D3 A4 AE 33 )                          // .h.....3
  .hash = (5B 42 1F D2 5E 1A 42 83 F5 90 B2 29 9F 35 A1 BE    // [B..^.B....).5..
          E5 5E 0D E4 )                                       // .^..
  .ver 1:0:0:0
}
.assembly extern hellogreeting
{
  .hash = (12 09 10 58 91 53 C7 13 7D 3D 53 87 A4 62 79 4F    // ...X.S..}=S..byO
          14 63 47 99 )                                       // .cG.
  .ver 1:0:0:0
}
.assembly helloworld as "helloworld"
{
  .hash algorithm 0x00008004
  .ver 1:0:0:0
}
.module helloworld.exe
// MVID: {4C781D06-B3E4-4376-A19D-E068C05D7A39}
```

The manifest shows a list of assemblies that your assembly is dependent on. That
is nothing new; after all, before COM, DLLs had a list of imported types that you
could see with the *depends.exe* program. However, even with the *depends.exe*
tool, the system had no idea what DLLs you were loading dynamically in code.
For example, the OS knew that your VB program was dependent on *MSVBVM60.
DLL* (the VB runtime), but it had no knowledge of any other DLLs you might have
been using through `Declare` statements, not to mention any COM DLLs you
loaded with *CreateObject*. What is also interesting is the difference between private assemblies and public assemblies. If you notice, the manifest shows that you
are dependent on Version 1.0.0.0 of the hellogreeting assembly. The version
number for this assembly is not crucial because hellogreeting is not a public
assembly; it is meant to be used only with this application. If you look at the rest
of the manifest, however, you will notice that the helloworld assembly is also
dependent on the mscorlib assembly and the Microsoft.VisualBasic assembly.
These latter assemblies are public assemblies; the creator went through the process of creating a public assembly, and because it is a shared assembly, the rules
for using the assembly with our program are more stringent. For example, we
have to tell the runtime whether our assembly can use a newer version of
Microsoft Visual Basic or whether it must have the same assembly it was built
with.

Versioning Assemblies

To illustrate the concept of versioning in the CLR, let's turn the hellogreeting assembly into a shared assembly, install it to the GAC, then build a second version of the assembly and create a configuration file to control which version of hellogreeting the helloworld assembly will use.

The first step is to digitally sign the code with a public/private digital key. It is impossible for us to discuss the encryption algorithm in this chapter, but the basic idea is that with a public/private key, encryption is done with the private portion of the key and decryption is done with the public portion. The various compilers first run an algorithm over the manifest information and produce what is called a hash. Then they use the public/private key file (from now on referred to as a private key file) and run an encryption algorithm through this hash to encrypt it. The signature is then embedded into the image. Also, the manifest for the signed assembly includes an originator field. This field advertises the public key to the world. Anyone can therefore use this public key to decrypt the encrypted manifest hash, run the hash over the manifest once again, and detect if there was any tampering to the manifest itself. In addition, any client programs referencing the assembly have a token of the public key known as the public token. This token is the result of a one-way hash algorithm run through the public key. Anyone can run the same algorithm. This step is done to verify that the assembly the runtime has found is really the assembly that the client program was compiled against.

To generate the private key, you run *sn.exe*, the strong name utility that ships with the .NET SDK. Enter the following command in a command-prompt window:

```
sn.exe -k "widgetsusa.snk"
```

The name of the file—even its extension—is something you make up entirely, although tools like VS.NET look for the .SNK extension. I'm using the name of a fictional company, since a company would likely use its name for the filename and use this key to sign every shared assembly it produces.

Once you have generated the private key file, now you can sign your assembly with that code. Modify the *hellogreeting.vb* source code as follows:

```
<Assembly: AssemblyKeyFile("widgetsusa.snk")>
<Assembly: AssemblyVersion("1.0.0.0")>

Imports System.Runtime.CompilerServices

Public class HelloSupport
    Shared Public Function GetGreeting(ByVal sName As String) As String
        return "Hello " + sName
    End Function
End Class
```

Notice that there are three new lines of code at the beginning. The first line of code uses an **assembly** attribute. Attributes are specified with angle brackets and are classes derived from System.Attribute. They are special classes that provide tools with configuration information. They can be specified at the assembly level, the module level, the class level, and even at the method level. The first attribute specifies the name of the private key file. The second attribute specifies the version number of the assembly. Notice that the third line in the code asks the compiler to use another assembly called System.Runtime.CompilerServices. We need to include a reference to that assembly, because that is where the AssemblyKeyFile and AssemblyVersion attributes are declared. The compiler will look for these attributes and, if it finds the AssemblyKeyFile attribute, it will run a cryptographic algorithm on the manifest for the code using the private/public key file stored in the file you specified. The visible effect of signing your code is that you will now see an originator (or public key) in the assembly's manifest. The **AssemblyVersion** attribute is very important. The version number follows the following format:

```
major.minor.build.revision
```

You will see how it is used shortly. Once you have modified the code, you must build the assembly again. At the time of this writing there was a problem with the VB.NET compiler; it would ignore the **AssemblyVersion** attribute. This should be fixed in Beta 2. For now, there is a workaround: the VB.NET compiler lets you specify the version number as a command-line parameter. Compile the hellogreeting assembly as follows:

```
vbc /t:library hellogreeting.vb /version:1.0.0.0
```

Because we have changed the version number of the assembly and assigned the assembly a strong name, you must rebuild the client program. Rebuilding is necessary so that the client program's manifest will contain information about the strong name and version of the hellogreeting assembly.

If you look at the manifest of the client program once again with ILDASM, you will notice that two things have changed for the external reference to the hellogreeting entry:

```
.assembly extern hellogreeting
{
  .originator = (A9 FE 7C 65 17 60 13 3E )                          // ..|e.`.>
  .hash = (4E 89 F0 45 B1 1E 0F 4B 31 65 BB 75 9D A8 71 6E   // N..E...K1e.u..qn
          64 0A 93 27 )                                             // d..'
  .ver 1:0:0:0
}
```

As you can see, the client program has a dependency on an assembly named hellogreeting. Furthermore, it expects the assembly to come from a certain originator (this is the public key token that was generated from the hash of the public key at the time the client program was compiled), and it expects a certain version number, 1.0.0.0. You will see how important the version number is shortly.

Once the assembly has been signed, it can be moved to the GAC. You do this with another program, *Gacutil.exe*. *Gacutil.exe* has a very simple set of commands. You can see the complete list by using /? as the command-line switch. The command-line switch to add an assembly to the GAC is –i. Enter the following command at the command prompt:

```
Gacutil -i hellogreeting.dll
```

Adding the assembly to the GAC turns the assembly into a public shared assembly. If you use Windows Explorer, you should be able to see the list of shared assemblies under *WINNT**Assembly*, as depicted in Figure 11-3.

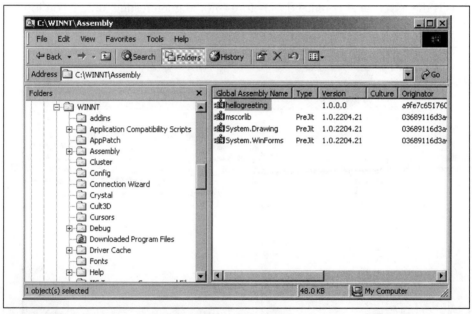

Figure 11-3. Global Assembly cache

You can now delete *hellogreeting.dll* and run *helloworld.exe*. The program runs without the DLL being in the same directory, because a copy has been moved to the GAC.

Suppose that we change the greeting to "New Hello" + sName, as follows:

```
<Assembly: AssemblyKeyFile("widgetsusa.snk")>
<Assembly: AssemblyVersion("1.0.0.1")>
```

```
Imports System.Runtime.CompilerServices

Public class HelloSupport
    Shared Public Function GetGreeting(ByVal sName As String) As String
        return "New Hello " + sName
    End Function
End Class
```

Next, rebuild with the same version number as before. If you run the program again, you will notice that the client program still outputs "Hello World"—it uses the assembly in the cache. What if we recompile with the version number of 1.0.0.1? Then the story changes. The client program uses the local assembly instead of the one in the GAC. We can move the new version to the GAC as follows:

```
gacutil -i hellogreeting.dll
```

This is the exact same command as before—nothing interesting, unless you look at the assembly list in *WINNT\Assembly* once again (see Figure 11-4).

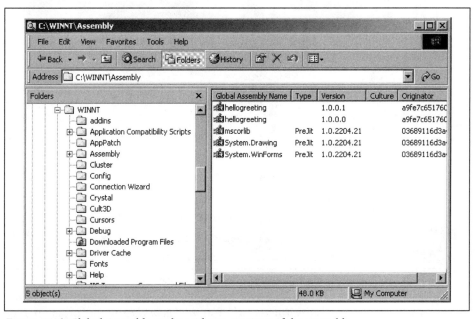

Figure 11-4. Global Assembly cache with two versions of the assembly

You can see that there are two versions of the assembly in the cache. If you run the client program again, it would use the latest version. However, let's make another change to the code:

```
<Assembly: AssemblyKeyFile("widgetsusa.snk")>
<Assembly: AssemblyVersion("2.0.0.0")>
```

```
Imports System.Runtime.CompilerServices

Public class HelloSupport
    Shared Public Function GetGreeting(ByVal sName As String) As String
        return "New Hello 2.0.0.0" + sName
    End Function
End Class
```

This time, build the assembly as Version 2.0.0.0. Once you build the DLL, if you run the client once again, the client will use the version of the DLL in your local directory. The change occurs when you move this version to the GAC and delete the local copy. The GAC, according to our examples, so far contains three versions of the DLL. The latest version is 2.0.0.0. If you run the client program this time, you should see that the client program continues to use Version 1.0.0.1. What has happened is that the CLR is conscious of the difference between a major/minor release and a build/revision release. If your version number differs only by build/revision number, then by default the CLR assumes you can use a later version. On the other hand, if your version number differs by major/minor numbers, then the CLR assumes that you are better off with your previous version—it only gives you the version that matches the major/minor numbers exactly.

In either case, by default, if you have a private copy in your directory, the CLR assumes that you put it there because that's the one you want to use. You can control the process of locating a certain assembly with a configuration file. The following code shows an application configuration file:

```
<BindingPolicy>
    <BindingRedir Name="hellogreeting"
                  Originator="a9fe7c651760133e"
                  Version="*" VersionNew="2.0.0.0"
                  UseLatestBuildRevision="yes"/>
</BindingPolicy>
```

You would save the code in a file with the same name as the executable but with the extension .CFG and in the same directory as the executable.

Notice that the syntax of the application configuration file is XML. The <BindingPolicy> tag has a <BindingRedir> subtag. This subtag has a Name attribute. The Name attribute points to the name of the assembly that needs to be resolved, in this case the DLL file. The next attribute is Originator; this is a public key token. The easiest way to obtain this number is from the GAC. If you look back at Figure 11-4, you will see the Originator field. The third attribute is Version, the version number. This attribute lets you redirect any requests for a certain revision number. In this case, we are redirecting any requests. The next attribute is VersionNew; this is the version number we would like to use. Finally, there is a UseLatestBuildRevision attribute, which is set to yes in our example.

This attribute says that if there is a later build differing only by build/revision, then that one should be used. Therefore, if the GAC contained 2.0.1.0, it would use that one.

What if you wanted to use Version 1.0.0.0? After all, that is exactly the version that the client program was built in. By default, the resolver uses the assembly with the latest build revision. You could do that two ways. The first way is to change the `VersionNew` attribute to 1.0.0.0 and set the `UseLatestBuildRevision` attribute to no, as shown in the following configuration file:

```
<BindingPolicy>
    <BindingRedir Name="hellogreeting"
                  Originator="a9fe7c651760133e"
                  Version="*" VersionNew="1.0.0.0"
                  UseLatestBuildRevision="no"/>
</BindingPolicy>
```

The second way is to use what is called safe mode. Safe mode uses a different subtag named `<AppBindingMode>`, as illustrated in the following code:

```
<BindingPolicy>
    <BindingMode>
        <AppBindingMode Mode="safe"/>
    </BindingMode>
</BindingPolicy>
```

This code shows the `<AppBindingMode>` subtag's `Mode` attribute set to safe; by default, it is set to normal. When you use safe mode, the resolver tries to locate an assembly with the exact same version number as the one used to compile the client program. Thus, running helloworld would produce the original output, "HelloWorld." If you were to set the mode equal to normal or just delete the configuration file, you would obtain the second output, "New Hello World." To obtain the Version 2.0.0.0 output, you would have to use the redirection technique shown earlier and redirect any assembly (or any 1.0.0.0 assemblies in our case) to Version 2.0.0.0.

At this point, you should have a good feel for how to build assemblies and how to turn private assemblies into shared assemblies. Now let's discuss some of the more exciting language features in VB.NET.

VB.NET Features

Now that you know the basics of running the VB compiler and the difference between private assemblies and shared assemblies, let's discuss some of the new features in VB.NET. In many ways, VB.NET is a different language. The language has been extended to have a number of object-oriented features that it did not have before, such as method inheritance, method overloading, and exception handling.

Inheritance

In Chapter 2, you learned the difference between interface inheritance and code inheritance. VB 6 enabled you to do only one type of inheritance—interface inheritance. VB.NET adds support for the second type of inheritance, code inheritance. The way it works is that you first create a base class. In our ongoing example of a banking application, let's suppose that your design accounted for two main classes: a Checking class and a Savings class. It is likely that these two classes have functionality in common. In fact, a better design may be to create a base class named Account from which these two classes are derived. The following code shows an application that declares three classes: Account, Checking, and Savings. The Checking and Savings classes inherit all their functionality from the Account class:

```
Public class Account
    Dim m_Balance As Decimal
    Public Sub MakeDeposit(ByVal Amount As Decimal)
        m_Balance += Amount
    End Sub

    Public ReadOnly Property Balance() As Decimal
        Get
            return m_Balance
        End Get
    End Property
End Class

Public Class Checking
Inherits Account
End Class

Public Class Savings
Inherits Account
End Class

Public Class App

    Shared Sub Main()
        Dim Acct As Account = new Checking
        Call Acct.MakeDeposit(5000)
        System.Console.WriteLine(Acct.Balance)
    End Sub

End Class
```

The Account class has a member variable, called m_Balance, that stores a Decimal (Decimal replaces the VB 6 Currency type). The class has a MakeDeposit method that accepts an amount in its parameter and adds the amount to the balance. The class also has a Balance property that reports the internal balance. The code then declares two subclasses, Checking and Savings, that inherit all their functionality from the Account class. The rest of the code declares the class that will host the Sub Main function. In Sub Main we are declaring a class of type Account and assigning an instance of the class Checking. Why can we assign an instance of Checking to a variable of type Account? Because inheritance establishes an "IS A" relationship between the base class and the derived class. For all purposes, a Checking class "IS AN" Account. The opposite is not true; Account classes are not Checking classes.

The fact that Checking is derived from Account means that we can send an instance of Checking to a function that receives an Account as its parameter. Consider the following code:

```
Module GenFunctions
    Public sub ReportBalance(ByVal AnyAccount As Account)
        System.Console.WriteLine(AnyAccount.Balance)
    End Sub
End Module
```

The preceding code defines a module. Even though it seems as if the module provides a way to export standalone functions without having to declare a class, in reality, VB changes the module to a class and makes any functions inside of it shared. The previous code declares a function called *ReportBalance* that reports the balance of any class derived from Account. As expected, you can send the function an instance of the Checking class or an instance of the Savings class. In fact, the following code should work as expected:

```
Public Class App
    Shared Sub Main()
        Dim check As Checking = new Checking
        check.MakeDeposit(500)
        Dim sav As Savings = new Savings
        sav.MakeDeposit(100)
        Call ReportBalance(check)
        Call ReportBalance(sav)
    End Sub
End Class
```

Suppose that there is a request for the Savings class to work differently. The MakeDeposit method should add $10 to every deposit (this is a very good Savings account). That means that we have to change the functionality of the MakeDeposit method. The following code shows how you might do this. First you have to modify the MakeDeposit method in the Account class as follows:

```
Public class Account
    Dim m_Balance As Decimal
    Public Overridable Sub MakeDeposit(ByVal Amount As Decimal)
        m_Balance += Amount
    End Sub
```

Notice that there is a change in the MakeDeposit method—it has the keyword `Overridable`. It is necessary for the developer writing the Account class to have foresight and add the word `Overridable` to any methods that may be modified in subclasses. The code for the Savings class has also been modified as follows:

```
Public Class Savings
Inherits Account
    Public Overrides Sub MakeDeposit(ByVal Amount As Decimal)
        Amount += 10
        MyBase.MakeDeposit(Amount)
    End Sub
End Class
```

In the Savings class we add the MakeDeposit method with the attribute `Overrides`. The code adds 10 to Amount, then forwards the call to the base implementation of MakeDeposit. This is done with the MyBase object. MyBase is a new global object that references your most direct base class. The runtime supports only single inheritance. All classes must derive from at most one class, and all classes must derive from System.Object. If you do not specify a class to derive from in code, then the compiler automatically makes System.Object the base class.

Suppose that we add to the Account class a withdrawal method that subtracts a certain amount from the balance:

```
Public Overridable Sub MakeWithdrawal(ByVal Amount As Decimal)
    If m_Balance - Amount >= 0 Then
        m_Balance -= Amount
    End If
End Sub
```

In the preceding example, MakeWithdrawal subtracts the amount from the balance only if the resulting balance is greater than or equal to 0. What if the MakeWithdrawal method in the Checking account needs to work differently? Suppose that the Checking account allows a client to overdraw the account up to $1,000. If you were to write the following code, you would get an error:

```
Public Class Checking
Inherits Account
    Public Overrides Sub MakeWithdrawal(ByVal Amount As Decimal)
        If m_Balance - Amount >= -1000 Then
            m_Balance -= Amount
        End If
    End Sub
End Class
```

The code is attempting to access the m_Balance variable, which is marked as `Private` in the Account class. The problem is that m_Balance must be private to the client but public to the derived class. For this reason, VB.NET has a third category named `Protected`. You must change the declaration of the m_Balance variable as follows:

```
Public class Account
    Protected m_Balance As Decimal
```

You can specify that it is illegal to write a derived class from your class with the `NotInheritable` attribute. `NotInheritable` results in what the runtime refers to as a *sealed class*. For example, we could have said that the Checking class cannot be inherited as follows:

```
Public NotInheritable Class Checking
```

On the other hand, we may want to prevent a developer from creating instances of the Account class directly. It may be our rule that a developer must create instances of a derived class. This is done with the `MustInherit` attribute, as in the following:

```
Public MustInherit Class Account
```

This doesn't prevent a client from declaring a variable of type Account, only from creating instances of the Account, as in `var = new Account`. It is possible also to force a developer into not only creating derived classes, but also overriding certain methods. For example, we could have stated that every derived class must override the MakeWithdrawal method. Of course, that change produces a number of changes. If a developer must always override the MakeWithdrawal method in the Account class, then the MakeWithdrawal method should not have any code in the Account class, and the compiler should issue an error if there is code. In addition, since everyone must override the method, a client cannot just create an instance of the class. Therefore, the class must also be marked with the `MustInherit` attribute. Suppose that we marked every method with the `MustOverride` method; we would have the equivalent of an interface.

An interface is a class in which every method must be implemented in a concrete class. There is a shorthand for defining interfaces in VB.NET using the keyword `Interface` instead of the `Class` keyword. The `IAccount` interface can be defined in VB.NET as follows:

```
Public Interface IAccount
    Overloads Sub MakeDeposit(ByVal Amount As Decimal)
    Overloads Sub MakeDeposit(ByVal Source As Account)
    ReadOnly Property Balance() As Decimal
End Interface
```

The preceding definition shows the new way of defining interfaces in Visual Basic. Notice that the methods in the interface do not have an `End Sub` statement (or its equivalent). Also notice that there is no `Public` attribute—that is because all the methods must be public in an interface. Another interesting thing is that there is method overloading in an interface (a feature you will learn about shortly). This code is roughly equivalent to the following:

```
Public MustInherit Class IAccountClone
    Overloads MustOverride Sub MakeDeposit(ByVal Amount As Decimal)
    Overloads MustOverride Sub MakeDeposit(ByVal Source As Account)
    ReadOnly MustOverride Property Balance() As Decimal
End Class
```

The only difference is that interfaces do not have a constructor—code that is executed when an instance of a class is instantiated. The fact that they do not have constructors means that they cannot be subclassed except by an entity that would also not have a constructor. This means you cannot inherit from an interface unless you are an interface. Classes can produce subclasses, and interfaces can produce subinterfaces (if that were a term). For example, interfaces can derive from other interfaces, as in the following example:

```
Public Interface IAccount2
Inherits IAccount
    Sub CloseAccount
End Interface
```

You are still required to implement the entire interface. If you implement the preceding interface in a class, the class will support both the `IAccount` and `IAccount2` interface. Let's take a look at how implementing an interface has changed slightly:

```
Public Interface ISaveToDisk
Public Sub Save()
End Interface

Public Class Checking
Implements ISaveToDisk
Public Sub Bark() Implements ISaveToDisk.Save
End Sub
End Class
```

Notice that you now have to specify in each method implementation what method in the interface you are implementing. You do this by declaring the method, then adding `Implements` `Interface.Method` at the end of the method declaration.

Method Overloading

A new feature in VB is the ability to do method overloading. Method overloading involves having several implementations of the same method, each method with a different set of parameters. For example, you may want to add to the Account class a second MakeDeposit method that takes as a parameter an instance of a second Account object. The idea is that the client can transfer money from one account to another by just calling the MakeDeposit method in the Account receiving the money and passing the Account where the money will come from as the parameter. As in C++, you cannot overload a method if the only difference is the return value—at least one of the parameters must be different, or the number of parameters must be different. The following code shows the two MakeDeposit methods:

```
Public Overridable Overloads Sub MakeDeposit(ByVal Amount As Decimal)
    m_Balance += Amount
End Sub
Public Overridable Overloads Sub MakeDeposit(ByVal Source As Account)
    m_Balance += Source.Balance
    Source.m_Balance = 0
End Sub
```

You do not have to override every form of the overloaded method in a derived class.

Value Versus Reference Type

By default, to use a class, you must declare a variable of the type of class you wish to use and create a new instance of the class. In VB 6 there was a difference between a UDT and a class. The same is true for VB.NET. In VB.NET you can define a UDT using the keyword **Structure**, as in the following:

```
Public Structure MyPoint
Public x As Long
Public y As Long
End Structure
```

Structures are classes that are derived from a class called System.ValueType. Ordinarily, when you create a class that is *not* derived from System.ValueType, the variable that holds the instance of the object really contains a pointer to a vptr that points to the location in memory where your data is stored. You must create an instance of the class with the **New** operator. If your class is derived from System.ValueType, the runtime treats your class differently. With a structure, you do not have to call **New**—when you **Dim** a variable of the structure type, the system allocates space for the structure automatically and the variable points to the storage directly. If you send in an instance of a structure as a parameter (marked as **ByVal**), the contents of the structure are put on the stack, and the receiving procedure gets a copy of the structure. If you pass a class instance to a function as a parameter (also marked as **ByVal**), then you are passing the pointer to the class' storage, and the receiving side gets a copy of the pointer. In the case of the structure, any changes made to the members of the structure do not change the original values in the caller's structure. In the case of the class reference, if you change the value of a class variable, the changes affect the caller's instance of the class, since both the caller and the function share the same instance of the class. Other examples of classes that derive from System.ValueType are the Integer, Decimal, and Boolean classes—any basic datatype. (Yes, Integer, Decimal, and Boolean are actually classes in the runtime that are ultimately derived from System.Object.)

Structures have more functionality than Types had in VB 6. Structures can now have methods and can implement interfaces. Perhaps the most interesting new feature of structures is Boxing. Boxing creates a clone of your structure whenever a reference type is needed. Consider the following code:

```
Public Interface IAccount
    Sub MakeDeposit(ByVal Amount As Decimal)
    ReadOnly Property Balance() As Decimal
End Interface

Public Structure AccountInfo
Implements IAccount
    Public m_Balance As Decimal
    Public Sub MakeDeposit(ByVal Amount As Decimal) Implements _
                                    IAccount.MakeDeposit
        m_Balance += Amount
    End Sub
    Public ReadOnly Property Balance() As Decimal Implements _
                                    IAccount.Balance
        Get
            return m_Balance
        End Get
    End Property
End Structure

module modMain
    Sub Main()
        Dim Acct As AccountInfo
        Acct.MakeDeposit(500)
        Dim AcctBoxed1 As IAccount
        AcctBoxed1 = Acct
        AcctBoxed1.MakeDeposit(300)
        Dim AcctBoxed2 As IAccount
        AcctBoxed2 = AcctBoxed1
        AcctBoxed2.MakeDeposit(300)
        System.Console.WriteLine("Acct.Balance=" & Acct.Balance)
        System.Console.WriteLine("AcctBoxed1.Balance=" & AcctBoxed1.Balance)
    End Sub
end module
```

This code defines an interface called **IAccount**. There should be no surprises in the interface definition if you have been following along in this book. The interface, as usual, has a MakeDeposit method and a Balance property. I am implementing the interface in a structure called AccountInfo. This structure has a member called m_Balance to store the balance. It also implements both the MakeDeposit method and the Balance property.

The code example begins by allocating an instance of the AccountInfo structure. Remember that you do not have to call **New** to allocate a structure's memory. The code then calls the MakeDeposit method to increase the Balance to 500. Next, the code declares a variable named AcctBoxed1 of type IAccount. The code then uses the AcctBoxed1 variable to make another deposit for $300. This is where it gets tricky. In the runtime, an interface is a reference type; it is not a value type, like the AccountInfo structure. So when you assign the reference type to the value type, the system creates a copy of the structure and assigns the pointer of the copy to the reference type variable. In the preceding example, after setting AcctBoxed1 to Acct, there will be two copies of the data members in memory. The second copy has a starting balance of 500 because that's what the structure had before the copy was made. However, when you call the MakeDeposit method through the structure, the values of the original remain at 500, while the balance of the copy increases to 800. The code then creates a second reference type, AcctBoxed2 from AcctBoxed1. Because both are reference types, AcctBoxed2 is set to point to the same memory as AcctBoxed1. Therefore, after calling MakeDeposit for the third time, the original balance in Acct1 is still at $500, but the balance of the reference type is now at $1,100. In fact, when you output the values in the last two lines of code, the value for Acct.Balance will be reported as 500, and the value for AcctBoxed1.Balance will be 1100.

Delegates

VB 6 had a limitation with function pointers. It was possible to get the address of a function in memory with the **AddressOf** operator. The **AddressOf** operator returned a Long with the location in memory of the function, but something that I always envied C++ for was that you couldn't take that Long value and turn it back into a function. For example, C++ lets you define what is called a function pointer declaration. You can define a function signature (function name, parameters, and return value) and use the definition as a datatype. With this datatype, you can declare a variable to hold the address to a function with the same signature. Then you can make a method call through the variable. In VB 6 you couldn't do this.

VB.NET now lets you create function pointer datatypes; they are called *delegates*. Delegates are classes derived from System.Delegate. The following example shows how to define a delegate. Suppose that you want to create a general function for our banking server that reports the balance but that, instead of accepting Account or Checking or Savings, will accept any class that has a subroutine to report the balance. To do this, we can define a delegate with the signature for the Report-Balance function as follows:

```
Delegate Sub ReportBalanceSig()
```

The delegate declaration defines a datatype that can be set to the **AddressOf** any function with the same signature. Let's suppose that the BankServer application has the following classes:

```
Public Class Checking
    Public Sub CheckingBalance()
        System.Console.WriteLine("CheckingBalance")
    End Sub
End Class
Public Class Savings
    Public Sub SavingsBalance()
        System.Console.WriteLine("SavingsBalance")
    End Sub
End Class
```

Notice that the two classes, Checking and Savings, each has a method to report the balance, CheckingBalance and SavingsBalance, respectively. These two methods serve the same purpose but do not have the same name and are not implementing any interface. They do, however, have the same signature. Let's now define the ReportBalance function and the client code in a module:

```
module modMain
    Sub ReportBalance(ByVal Func As ReportBalanceSig)
        Func
    End Sub
    Sub Main()
        Dim Check As Checking = new Checking
        Dim Sav As Savings = new Savings
        ReportBalance(AddressOf Check.CheckingBalance)
        ReportBalance(AddressOf Sav.SavingsBalance)
    End Sub
End module
```

The first function in modMain, *ReportBalance*, accepts as a parameter a function of type *ReportBalanceSig*. It does not matter what the function is called; it just needs to have the same signature as the delegate. Notice that the code in *ReportBalance* simply calls the routine that was sent in. (It looks a little awkward because calling the function can be done by just writing the name of the variable holding the function pointer.) The second function in the module is Sub Main. In Sub Main we create an instance of the Checking class and then an instance of the Savings class. Then, the function calls *ReportBalance*, passing the address of the *CheckingBalance* function, followed by a second call to the *ReportBalance* function passing the address of the *SavingsBalance* function.

Constructors and Finalizers

There is no more Class_Initialize or Class_Terminate. Every class not derived from System.ValueType and not defined as a structure or an interface has a default constructor. The default constructor has the name New and takes no parameters; it is called when the developer uses the **New** operator. For example, the following code shows how to write code for the default constructor in the Checking class:

```
Public Class Checking
    Private m_Balance As Decimal

    Public Sub New
        m_Balance = 0
    End Sub

    Public Function ReportBalance() As Decimal
        return m_Balance
    End Function
End Class


module modMain
    Sub Main()
        Dim Acct As Checking = New Checking
    End Sub
end module
```

In this code example, the runtime calls the New method in the class when the developer creates an instance of the class. In this case, this happens in Sub Main.

A more interesting feature is that you can now add parameterized constructors. For example, it may make more sense to require the developer using the Checking class to create the class with an initial balance as follows:

```
Public Class Checking
    Private m_Balance As Decimal

    Public Sub New(ByVal InitialBal As Decimal)
        m_Balance = InitialBal
    End Sub

    Public Function ReportBalance() As Decimal
        return m_Balance
    End Function
End Class


module modMain
    Sub Main()
        Dim Acct As Checking = New Checking(500)
    End Sub
end module
```

In this code, there is a definition for a parameterized constructor. This is done by adding a New function that receives a parameter, in this case the initial balance. As soon as you add a parameterized constructor, the compiler no longer adds the default constructor. This means that the developer cannot just say New Checking without passing a parameter. As you can see in the code for Sub Main, the code creates an instance of Checking passing in the initial balance of $500.

As with other functions, you may overload the constructor. In fact, if you wish to have both the parameterized constructor and the default constructor, you could rewrite the class as follows:

```
Public Class Checking
    Private m_Balance As Decimal

    Public Overloads Sub New
        m_Balance = 0
    End Sub

    Public Overloads Sub New(ByVal InitialBal As Decimal)
        m_Balance = InitialBal
    End Sub
```

There are things to watch for when your class derives from a base class. Constructors are not inherited. If the base class has a default constructor, the system will call the base constructor first before calling your constructor. However, if the base class does not have a default constructor, then you must call a constructor for the base class in your constructor, and the call must be the first call in your constructor. The following code shows you how to do this:

```
Public Class Account 'base class
    'this class only has a parameterized constructor
    Public Sub New(ByVal InitialBal As Decimal)

    End Sub
End Class

Public Class Checking 'derived class
Inherits Account
    Public Sub New(ByVal InitialBal As Decimal)
        'call the base class' constructor
        MyBase.New(InitialBal)
    End Sub
End Class

module modMain
    Sub Main()
        Dim Acct As Account = new Checking(500)
    End Sub
end module
```

The Account class does not have a default constructor. Therefore, the runtime cannot call the base constructor for your class automatically. You must add a constructor to the derived class, then call the base constructor for your class programmatically. You can refer to your direct base class by using the MyBase object. Notice that you must call the base constructor first before doing anything else in the derived constructor.

Just as you can write constructors for your classes, you can also write *finalizers*. Finalizers are a little different from destructors because they do not necessarily happen when a client releases your object. When the client creates an instance of your class, the object becomes part of the global managed heap. When all clients release their instances of your object, your object becomes marked for garbage collection. The garbage collector will call your finalizer when it is time to destroy your object, and that may happen any time after all clients have released their references to your object but not sooner. To add a finalizer to the class, you must write a Finalize subroutine. (Interestingly, Finalize is an overridable method in System.Object.) The following code shows how to add a Finalize method:

```
Public Class Checking

    Protected Overrides Sub Finalize()
        'do cleanup code here
    End Sub

End Class
```

Exception Handlers

Error catching in VB 6 was done with the Err object and either **On Error Resume Next** or **On Error Goto**. If you found this aspect of programming very limiting, you will be glad to know that VB.NET supports exception handling. With exception handling, you write **try...catch** blocks. The **try** part of a **try...catch** block contains the code that you want to execute. Outside of the **try** block, you write handlers for different kinds of exceptions. Exceptions are classes derived from System.Exception. Because every exception is generated from System.Exeception, you can also write a general exception handler to handle any exception you may get. The System.Exception class has properties that provide very rich error information. Part of the **try...catch** block is the **finally** block. The **finally** block executes at the end of the function whether an exception occurs or not. This block lets you do cleanup for the function. The following code shows how to add a **try...catch...finally** block:

```
Public Interface IAccount
End Interface
Public Interface ISaveToDisk
End Interface
```

```
Public Class Checking
Implements IAccount
End Class
module modMain
    Sub Main()
        Dim Acct As IAccount = new Checking
        Try
        Dim Sav As ISaveToDisk = CType(Acct,ISaveToDisk)
        Catch e As System.InvalidCastException
            System.Console.Writeline("The cast failed")
        Catch e As System.Exception
            System.Console.WriteLine(e)
        finally
            System.Console.WriteLine("cleanup code here")
        End Try
    End Sub
End module
```

This code defines two interfaces, **IAccount** and **ISaveToDisk**. The code also defines a class called Checking. The Checking class implements only **IAccount**. The code in Sub Main creates an instance of the Checking class by asking for the **IAccount** interface, then tries to convert the type to **ISaveToDisk** using the new VB.NET command CType. Since the class does not support the second interface, the system generates an exception: System.InvalidCastException. The code places the cast attempt code within a **Try** block. Notice that there are different exception handlers after the code inside the **Try** block. The first exception handler handles System.InvalidCastExceptions only. If the code generates this exception (and the previous code will), the line System.Console.WriteLine ("The cast failed") is executed followed by the code in the **Finally** block. After the handler for System.InvalidCastException, the code has a general exception handler. This is done with a catch section that either has the word Catch by itself or by catching the System.Exception class.

In VB 6, generating an error was done with Err.Raise. In VB.NET you can create your own exception class derived from System.ApplicationException. System.ApplicationException is derived from System.Exception. Then use the **Throw** command to generate the exception. The following code shows you how to define your own exception class and generate it:

```
Public class MyException
            Inherits System.ApplicationException
    Sub New()
       MyBase.New("My Error Description")
    End Sub
End class
Module modMain
    Sub Main()
        Dim e As MyException = new MyException
        Throw e
    End Sub
End Module
```

Mixing COM+ and .NET

Many of you are feeling the urge to experiment with .NET components and like the new features in Visual Basic. Most likely, you have already made an investment in COM and would like to know how to use your existing COM components in VB 6 with the new .NET components. Microsoft is very aware of this need and has built in capabilities for mixing the two.

As you know from the previous sections in this chapter, code that runs in the CLR is managed code. It is in IL, and it is run by the common language runtime. The runtime has its own techniques for allocating objects and managing things like thread allocations and so forth. In the VB 6 world, code was unmanaged. The compiler translated your code to native code that the processor could run. Thus, if we are going to mix these two worlds, we must create intermediary components that enable us to travel to and from managed space into unmanaged space. Let's address the idea of using VB.NET components from your Visual Basic 6 code first.

Using VB.NET Components with VB 6

Microsoft provides a tool called *tlbexp.exe* with the .NET SDK that enables you to create a type library (.TLB) file from an assembly manifest but does not register it. A type library (especially an unregistered one) does not really provide the functionality of a COM server. If we were to try to use a managed DLL as a COM server, the managed DLL would have to have the functionality of an in-process COM server. For example, it would have to have the four entry points to any COM DLL: *DllRegisterServer, DllUnregisterServer, DllGetClassObject,* and *DllCanUnloadNow.* It would also have to add the necessary keys to the registry for the SCM to load the DLL. Remember that the SCM must find the CLSID followed by the `InprocServer32` key pointing to the DLL.

Unfortunately for COM developers, CLR assembly DLLs do not have COM entry points, nor are they self-registering. However, Microsoft has made the CLR execution engine (*MSCorEE.dll*) a full COM server. It can load your assembly at runtime and provide you with a proxy to your .NET classes. Microsoft provides another tool called *RegAsm.exe*, also included with the .NET SDK, that enables you to register your .NET assemblies. Let's look at the process. Consider the following VB. NET code:

```
Public Class Inventory
    Private m_Quantity As Integer

    Public Sub AddWidgetToInventory(ByVal Amount As Integer)
        m_Quantity += Amount
    End Sub
```

```
Public ReadOnly Property Quantity() As Integer
    Get
        Return m_Quantity
    End Get
End Property

End Class
```

This code declares a single class named Inventory. The Inventory class has a private member named m_Quantity; it stores the number of widgets in inventory. The class also has a public method for adding widgets to inventory, cleverly named AddWidgetToInventory, as well as one property for retrieving the quantity. You can save the preceding code as *inventory.vb* and compile it as a DLL with the following command:

```
vbc /t:library inventory.vb
```

Let's suppose that we would like to use the Inventory class in a VB 6 client program. The best way to do this is to use the *RegAsm.exe* tool. From a command prompt, locate the *inventory.dll* .NET assembly and enter the following command:

```
Regasm inventory.dll /tlb:inventory.tlb
```

I mentioned earlier that Microsoft has another tool called *tlbexp.exe* that creates a type library. However, that tool does not automatically register the type library, nor does it add registry keys for a client program to be able to create an instance of your .NET classes. *RegAsm* does all of these. It adds registry keys so that your classes can be instantiated from COM and, if you use the `/tlb` command-line switch, it also creates a type library for all public classes in the assembly and registers the type library. After you run the *RegAsm.exe* tool, you should be able to use your .NET assemblies from VB 6.

RegAsm plays a trick with the registry. If you look at the registry, you should see that RegAsm has added COM registry keys (see Figure 11-5).

First of all, in Figure 11-5, the CLSID key with the visible subkeys contains the class identifier of our assembly. In fact, your CLSID should be the same as mine, even if you typed the program from scratch. If this doesn't sound strange to you, then you may need to read Chapter 3 again. In VB 6, if two people compile the same program on different machines, VB generates different GUIDs by default unless there is an existing type library that both machines could reference using project compatibility and binary compatibility. VB 6 uses *CoCreateGUID* to generate a unique number, and, because it was guaranteed to be unique, it would be different from machine to machine (it would actually be different on the same machine if you compiled twice with no compatibility).

VB.NET does not use GUIDs in the same way as VB 6. They are present just for compatibility with COM, but internally they are never used. What's different about

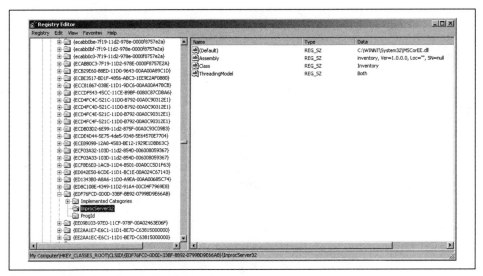

Figure 11-5. Registry keys added by RegAsm

VB.NET is that it assigns a CLSID to each class, but it uses a different algorithm that is based on the combination of the name of the assembly (in our case, inventory) and the name of the class (in our case, also inventory). Therefore, if we name the class and the assembly the same thing, we are going to end up with the same CLSID. This has the potential of two companies having a conflict if they name their assemblies and classes the same. There is a solution to this—the developer can assign the class a specific GUID using the GuidAttribute class in System. Runtime.InteropServices.

Notice from Figure 11-5 that the `InprocServer32` key has a number of values. First, notice that the path to the COM server points to *MSCorEE.dll. MSCorEE.dll* is the DLL that is responsible for loading your assembly into managed space. However, it also serves as a COM entry point. When a COM client requests a class through *DLLGetClassObject*, MSCorEE looks at the other values in `Inproc-Server32`, in particular the `Assembly` value entry. This value tells MSCorEE the name and location of your assembly, the version, localization information (such as `EN_US`), and the originator. You should know from reading the earlier sections how to assign an originator to the assembly by compiling it with a private key.

There is a little inconvenience with using *RegAsm.exe*. If you notice, there is no exact path to your assembly. You could manually set this path in the registry (as seen in Figure 11-6), although this capability may be removed in later versions of the SDK.

Another solution, in fact the optimal one, is to sign the assembly with a private key and add it to the global assembly cache. Once the assembly is in the GAC,

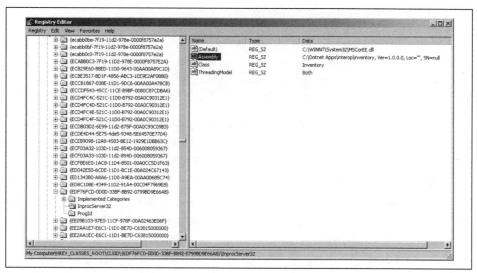

Figure 11-6. Adding the exact path to the assembly in the registry

you do not have to specify a path to use the assembly. To use the assembly from VB 6, all you have to do is create a program as usual and find the assembly name in the Project References dialog box.

Using VB.NET for versioning VB 6 components

A good use for *RegAsm.exe* and VB.NET is to serve as a replacement for IDL. If you are hesitant to use IDL to version your components because it is yet a new syntax to learn and it is like C++, then you may want to define your interfaces and manage your GUIDs in VB.NET and use it for versioning purposes. Let's look at a short example of how to define your interfaces in VB.NET and manage the GUIDs using attributes. Examine the following VB.NET code:

```
<Assembly: System.Runtime.InteropServices.Guid("3C53B8E3-81FC-4645-B65F-
ACABE77A79D0")>

Imports System.Runtime.InteropServices

Interface <Guid("1393732E-8D27-431a-A180-8EDA0E4499E2"), _
          InterfaceType(ComInterfaceType.InterfaceIsIUnknown)> IAccount
    Sub MakeDeposit(ByVal Amount As Currency)
    ReadOnly Property Balance() As Currency
End Interface
```

The code is in VB syntax. What makes this code different from regular VB is the use of attributes throughout the code. These attributes are used by the various tools, like tlbexp, to dictate how the tool ought to do its job. In this case, attributes are used to control how the type library is generated. Notice that the library name is the name of the assembly. The LIBID for this library is the GUID specified with the `Guid` attribute at the Assembly level. The `Guid` attribute is part of System. Runtime.InteropServices. Actually, all the attributes used in the VB.NET code are part of the same assembly. The interface also uses the `Guid` attribute to assign an IID to the interface. In addition to the `Guid` attribute, it uses the `InterfaceType` attribute to tell tlbexp that the interface should be derived from `IUnknown` (the default is to make it a dual interface).

Once you compile the preceding code as a DLL, you can run the tool *tlbexp.exe* to generate the type library. Suppose you named your DLL *bankinterfaces.dll*; you can generate a type library entering the following command in console mode:

```
tlbexp.exe bankinterfaces.dll
```

By default, the tlbexp tool uses the root filename of the DLL to name the type library; thus, the resulting file would be *bankinterfaces.tlb*. The resulting type library source is as follows:

```
// Generated .IDL file (by the OLE/COM Object Viewer)
//
// typelib filename: bankinterfaces.tlb

[
  uuid(3C53B8E3-81FC-4645-B65F-ACABE77A79D0),
  version(1.0)
]
library BankInterfaces
{
    // TLib :      // TLib : OLE Automation : {00020430-0000-0000-C000-
000000000046}
    importlib("stdole2.tlb");

    // Forward declare all types defined in this typelib
    interface IAccount;

    [
      odl,
      uuid(1393732E-8D27-431A-A180-8EDA0E4499E2),
      oleautomation,
      custom({0F21F359-AB84-41E8-9A78-36D110E6D2F9}, "BankInterfaces.IAccount")

    ]
    interface IAccount : IUnknown {
        HRESULT _stdcall MakeDeposit([in] CURRENCY Amount);
        [propget]
        HRESULT _stdcall Balance([out, retval] CURRENCY* pRetVal);
    };
};
```

Tlbexp.exe creates a type library but does not register it, but in Chapter 6, you learned that you could use *regtlib.exe* to register the type library. After you register the type library, you could use it like any other type library in Visual Basic.

First, add it to your project through the Project References dialog box, then implement it in a concrete class. The interface methods resulting from the preceding VB. NET code would look like the following in VB 6:

```
Option Explicit

Implements IAccount

Private Property Get IAccount_Balance() As Currency
End Property

Private Sub IAccount_MakeDeposit(ByVal Amount As Currency)
End Sub
```

Using VB 6 Components with VB.NET

Going from .NET to VB 6, you needed to create a type library; going from VB 6 to .NET, you must generate an assembly. In the previous section, you learned about *tlbexp.exe*. In this section, you'll learn about *tlbimp.exe*. *Tlbimp.exe* creates an assembly from the definition of a type library. Consider the following VB 6 code:

```
Option Explicit

Private m_Balance As Currency

Public Sub MakeDeposit(ByVal Amount As Currency)
    m_Balance = m_Balance + Amount
End Sub

Public Function Balance() As Currency
    Balance = m_Balance
End Function
```

This is the usual Checking class. Let's say for the sake of argument that this code represents a class in *BankServer.DLL*. You can create an assembly that contains the definitions in your type library using *tlbimp*. To do so, you would enter the following command in a command-prompt window in the same directory as your DLL:

```
tlbimp BankServer.dll /out:BankServerAsm.dll
```

It is very straightforward; you run the tool, and it will create an assembly you can reference from your .NET program. For example, you may write a client program as follows:

```
module mainmod
    public Sub Main
        Dim Acct As New BankServer.Checking
        Acct.MakeDeposit(new System.Currency(5000))
        System.Console.WriteLine(Acct.Balance)
    End Sub
End module
```

To compile the client, you would have to reference the *BankServerAsm.DLL* assembly as follows:

```
vbc /t:exe bankclient.vb /r:BankServerAsm.dll
```

The COM DLL and the .NET assembly do not have to be in the same directory. If at some point you need to debug your Visual Basic code, you can easily do this by running the VB 6 COM code in the VB 6 IDE. You can put breakpoints in the VB 6 code and run the .NET code. The code should stop at your breakpoints. The only requirement to make this work is that you must set the project to binary compatibility with the DLL you used for creating the assembly.

Using COM+ Services

I hesitate to write this section because many things are going to change down the road with respect to using .NET assemblies in COM+ applications. However, for the sake of completion, let's talk about how to add a .NET class to a COM+ application as of Beta 1.

In the future, the MTS (now COM+) team will migrate all the COM+ services to work seamlessly with all the .NET architecture. For now, we must use a few COM interop tricks. In essence, the interaction occurs through the same mechanism explained earlier, by which you must make your .NET class look like a COM class by adding information to the registry and using *MSCorEE.dll* as the COM server wrapper for your assembly. However, we must also add information to the COM+ catalog. Microsoft provides another tool called *RegSvcs.exe* that does the job of RegAsm with the `/tlb` command-line switch, plus adds information about the class to the catalog. In addition, *RegSvcs.exe* is able to interpret certain attributes from the assembly, which enables you to set the declarative attributes in COM+.

For Beta 1, if you want a .NET class to work with COM+ services, you must derive the class from System.ServicedComponent. Because RegSvcs is going to generate COM information for the registry, you should also manage the IIDs and CLSIDs with attributes. For example, the following VB.NET code shows an interface named `IAccount` implemented in a Checking class:

```
<Assembly: System.Runtime.InteropServices.GuidAttribute("1D1D3D4C-52BE-46de-9100-
8F5AEB8207C0")>
<Assembly: System.Runtime.CompilerServices.
AssemblyKeyFileAttribute("complusservices.key")>
<Assembly: Microsoft.ComServices.Description("Book - Dotnet")>
<Assembly: Microsoft.ComServices.ApplicationName("Book - Dotnet")>
<Assembly: Microsoft.ComServices.ApplicationID("7319F24B-6DEA-4479-8027-
1E8E1816C626")>
<Assembly: Microsoft.ComServices.ApplicationActivation(Microsoft.ComServices.
ActivationOption.Server)>
```

```
Imports System.Runtime.InteropServices
Imports Microsoft.ComServices

Interface <guidattribute("874A6DD2-E141-41fd-A379-E066E8E23921")> IAccount
    Sub MakeDeposit(ByVal Amount As Integer)
    ReadOnly Property Balance() As Integer
End Interface

Public Class <guidattribute("FB03ABE6-982D-436e-919C-CA1D8BE1B71A"), _
             Transaction(TransactionOption.Required)> _
          Checking
    Inherits ServicedComponent
    Implements IAccount

    Private m_Balance As Integer

    Private Sub MakeDepositImpl(ByVal Amount As Integer) _
             Implements IAccount.MakeDeposit
        m_Balance += Amount
    End Sub

    Private ReadOnly Property BalanceImpl() As Integer Implements IAccount.Balance
        Get
            Return m_Balance
        End Get
    End Property

End Class
```

The top portion of the code uses a number of **Assembly** attributes. The first is **GuidAttribute**, which is used at the assembly level to control the LIBID for the type library that is generated. The second one is **AssemblyKeyFile**, which you should also be familiar with. One of the requirements to use your assembly in COM+ is that it be a public assembly. As you know, that means that you must assign an originator to the assembly. Thus, this attribute points to a private key file. The other four attributes have to do with COM+ application properties. If you remember from Chapter 7, you can create COM+ applications programmatically using the catalog COM components. When you create a COM+ application, you can specify various attributes, such as the Application ID (this is a GUID that represents the true name of the application). You can also specify the Application Name and give the application a description. Also, you can specify things like the Activation property (Server or Library).

All these properties can be set easily in VB.NET through attributes. The advantage of doing this is that when you run the RegSvcs tool on your VB.NET DLL, the tool will automatically create the COM+ application for you and add your components to it. All the COM+ attributes—not only the ones at the application level, but also the ones at the class interface and method levels—have been replicated as attributes. They are contained in the Microsoft.ComServices namespace.

The sample code also uses the **Transaction** attribute at the class level to specify that this class requires transactions.

Something that might look strange is that the Checking class implements the **IAccount** interface and makes the implementation methods private. In addition, it also gives each method a different name. This has nothing to do with the fact that I am going to use this interface in COM+. If you make the implementation methods public, that means that there are two ways of calling the method: through the interface and through a class reference directly. If you make the implementation methods private, the only way to reach the methods is through the interface. Notice also that you do not need to name the implementation methods the same as the interface methods; you must only match the signatures and use the Implements directive at the end of the method. It is interesting that both of these aspects of implementing interfaces in VB.NET (making methods private and giving them different names) are just like implementing interfaces in VB 6—except that somehow it seems clearer in VB.NET.

To compile the code, you use the standard **vbc** command at the command prompt. Because the code uses a security key file, you have to create one with *sn. exe*. Also, because the code uses the Microsoft.ComServices assembly, you must reference this assembly in the command line. The following code shows how to compile the code in a command-prompt window:

```
vbc /t:library bankserver.vb /version:1.0.0.0 /r:Microsoft.ComServices.dll
```

The next step is to add the assembly to the GAC. To review, that is done with the *gacutil.exe* tool. Once the assembly is in the GAC, you can run the *RegSvcs.exe* tool as follows:

```
RegSvcs /fc bankserver.dll
```

The **/fc** switch tells the tool to find an application or create one. The name of the application is defined by the **ApplicationName** attribute in the preceding source code. Optionally, you can enter an application name in the command line after the assembly name. Figure 11-7 shows the end result of running the RegSvcs tool.

Using the components is just like using any COM+ component. In fact, the following code should present no surprises:

```
Dim acct As IAccount
Set acct = CreateObject("bankserver.Checking")
Call acct.MakeDeposit(500)
MsgBox acct.Balance
```

One thing that may take you by surprise, however, is that as of Beta 1, unless you add an attribute to your class to turn on a specific declarative attribute, the attribute will be turned off by default. One nice thing about creating COM+ components with .NET is that the resulting component uses a different threading

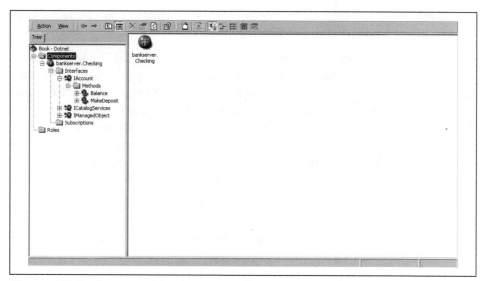

Figure 11-7. BankServer .NET application in Component Services administration program

model than VB 6 components. If you recall, VB 6 components use the apartment-threading model. VB.NET COM components are marked as using the both-threading model. That means that VB.NET components run in the MTA by default instead of in the STA. Also, VB.NET COM components can be pooled. Pooling VB. NET COM components is beyond the scope of this chapter, but be aware that living in the MTA means that you must handle synchronization issues in your methods.

Summary

In this chapter, you have learned the basics of the .NET architecture. You learned some of the limitations in COM and why Microsoft has created the new architecture. A number of languages are being written to support the new architecture. These languages compile to a processor-independent form of assembly language known as Intermediate Language (IL). Two of the main languages for .NET are VB. NET and C#. Both of these compilers generate IL. When you run a program written in IL, a Just-in-Time compiler converts the code into native machine code.

VB.NET has a number of enhancements over VB 6. Among them are: code inheritance, method overloading, enhanced user-defined types, function pointers, parameterized constructors, and true exception handling.

.NET components follow a different versioning scheme than COM+. When you build an assembly that references another assembly, the client assembly's manifest contains the version number of the referenced assembly. The runtime matches the major and minor numbers in the version for the assembly. You can redirect the runtime to use a different version with a configuration file.

To use an assembly from a VB 6 program, you use a tool called *RegAsm.exe*. Alternatively, you can use the *tlbexp.exe* tool to create a type library. However, *RegAsm.exe* does the job of adding keys to the registry to make the public classes in the assembly creatable from COM. It also builds a type library and registers it. In addition to providing you with a way to use .NET components from COM, you can use this functionality for versioning your existing COM components. To use COM components from .NET, you can use the *tlbimp.exe* tool to create an assembly from your type library.

You can also add a .NET component to a COM+ application. In fact, it makes good sense to mix COM with .NET components, because .NET components do not have the same threading restrictions as COM+ components. To use an assembly in COM+, you must first sign it and add it to the cache. Then you must run the tool RegSvcs to register the classes in the assembly, create a type library, and add it to the catalog. There are attributes in the Microsoft.ComServices assembly that enable you to specify the declarative attributes of the COM+ application.

Index

We'd like to hear your suggestions for improving our indexes. Send email to *index@oreilly.com*.

About the Author

Jose Mojica is an instructor and researcher at DevelopMentor, a company that's gained an international reputation for its experience with COM and COM+. He teaches various courses that focus on enterprise development in COM+, IIS, .NET, and Visual Basic. Before joining DevelopMentor, Jose was a consultant at IBM, writing DCOM servers that performed speech recognition and creating ActiveX controls in ATL for the ViaVoice SDK. He has worked with Visual Basic since Version 1.0. Jose is the author of *Building ActiveX Controls with Visual Basic 5.0* and coauthor of *Programming Internet Controls* and *Distributed Applications with Microsoft Visual C++ 6.0 MCSD Training Kit.*

Colophon

Our look is the result of reader comments, our own experimentation, and feedback from distribution channels. Distinctive covers complement our distinctive approach to technical topics, breathing personality and life into potentially dry subjects.

The fish on the cover of *COM+ Programming with Visual Basic* are minnows. Although the term "minnow" is commonly used to describe any number of small freshwater fish, minnow is actually the name for a family of fish, most of which are dull in color and only a few inches in length. Some species of minnow, however, grow to a foot in length, and the males turn bright red or orange just before the spring spawning season. The family includes various types of chubs, daces, shriners, minnows, and carp, all of which have scaleless heads, toothless jaws (but teeth on a bone in the throat), pelvic fins (rather than fins extending from their sides), and a single dorsal fin in common.

Minnows are extremely plentiful in North American freshwaters, forming the basis of fish fauna in most ponds, lakes, streams, and rivers. Many of the smaller minnow species perform key roles in the food chain; these "primary consumers" feed on bottom ooze, algae, and aquatic plants and in turn serve as protein-rich meals for larger fish and fish-eating birds.

While the minnow family has been evolutionarily successful, diversifying into many species that densely occupy a variety of habitats and perform key functions in the food chain, it has been challenged recently by the human practice of diverting and polluting waters. In fact, in 1994, the U.S. Fish and Wildlife Service Division of Endangered Species identified the Rio Grande silvery minnow *Hybognathus amarus* as endangered due to "dewatering, channelization and regulation of river flow to provide water for irrigation; diminished water quality caused by municipal, industrial, and agricultural discharges; and competition or predation by introduced non-native fish species." Apparently, this particular species now occupies only "five percent of its known historic range."

Catherine Morris was the production editor and proofreader, and Norma Emory was the copyeditor for *COM+ Programming with Visual Basic*. Linley Dolby, Nicole Arigo, and Claire Cloutier provided quality control. Pamela Murray wrote the index.

Pam Spremulli designed the cover of this book, based on a series design by Edie Freedman. The cover image is a 19th-century engraving from the Dover Pictorial Archive. Emma Colby produced the cover layout with QuarkXPress 4.1 using Adobe's ITC Garamond font.

David Futato designed the interior layout based on a series design by Nancy Priest. Anne-Marie Vaduva converted the files from Microsoft Word to FrameMaker 5.5.6 using tools created by Mike Sierra. The text and heading fonts are ITC Garamond Light and Garamond Book; the code font is Constant Willison. The illustrations that appear in the book were produced by Robert Romano and Jessamyn Read using Macromedia FreeHand 9 and Adobe Photoshop 6. This colophon was written by Sarah Jane Shangraw.

Whenever possible, our books use a durable and flexible lay-flat binding. If the page count exceeds this binding's limit, perfect binding is used.

More Titles from O'Reilly

Visual Basic Programming

Visual Basic Shell Programming

By J. P. Hamilton
1st Edition July 2000
392 pages, ISBN 1-56592-670-6

Visual Basic Shell Programming ventures where none have gone before by showing how to develop shell extensions that more closely integrate an application with the Windows shell, while at the same time providing an advanced tutorial-style treatment of COM programming with Visual Basic. Each major type of shell extension gets attention, including customized context menu handlers, per instance icons, and customized property sheets.

VB & VBA in a Nutshell: The Language

By Paul Lomax
1st Edition October 1998
656 pages, ISBN 1-56592-358-8

For Visual Basic and VBA programmers, this book boils down the essentials of the VB and VBA languages into a single volume, including undocumented and little-documented areas essential to everyday programming. The convenient alphabetical reference to all functions, procedures, statements, and keywords allows programmers to use this book both as a standard reference guide and as a tool for troubleshooting and identifying programming problems.

Writing Word Macros

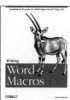

By Steven Roman
2nd Edition October 1999
410 pages, ISBN 1-56592-725-7

This no-nonsense book delves into VBA programming and tells how you can use VBA to automate all the tedious, repetitive jobs you never thought you could do in Microsoft Word. It takes the reader step-by-step through writing VBA macros and programs.

CDO & MAPI Programming with Visual Basic

By Dave Grundgeiger
1st Edition October 2000
384 pages, ISBN 1-56592-665-X

CDO and MAPI Programming with Visual Basic dives deep into Microsoft's Collaboration Data Objects (CDO) and the Messaging Application Programming Interface (MAPI), then moves into succinct explanations of the types of useful messaging applications that can be written in Visual Basic.

VBScript in a Nutshell

By Paul Lomax, Matt Childs, & Ron Petrusha
1st Edition May 2000
512 pages, ISBN 1-56592-720-6

Whether you're using VBScript to create client-side scripts, ASP applications, WSH scripts, or programmable Outlook forms, *VBScript in a Nutshell* is the only book you'll need by your side – a complete and easy-to-use language reference.

Access Database Design & Programming, 2nd Edition

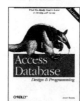

By Steven Roman
2nd Edition July 1999
432 pages, ISBN 1-56592-626-9

This second edition of the bestselling *Access Database Design & Programming* covers Access' new VBA Integrated Development Environment used by Word, Excel, and PowerPoint; the VBA language itself; Microsoft's latest data access technology, Active Data Objects (ADO); plus Open Database Connectivity (ODBC).

O'REILLY®

TO ORDER: **800-998-9938** • **order@oreilly.com** • **http://www.oreilly.com/**
OUR PRODUCTS ARE AVAILABLE AT A BOOKSTORE OR SOFTWARE STORE NEAR YOU.
FOR INFORMATION: **800-998-9938** • **707-829-0515** • **info@oreilly.com**

Visual Basic Programming

ASP in a Nutshell, 2nd Edition

By A. Keyton Weissinger
2nd Edition July 2000
492 pages, ISBN 1-56592-843-1

ASP in a Nutshell, 2nd Edition, provides
the high-quality reference documentation
that web application developers really need
to create effective Active Server Pages. It
focuses on how features are used in a real
application and highlights little-known or
undocumented features.

Developing ASP Components, 2nd Edition

By Shelley Powers
2nd Edition March 2001
832 pages, ISBN 1-56592-750-8

Microsoft's Active Server Pages
(ASP) continue to grow in popularity
with web developers – especially as web
applications replace web pages. *Developing
ASP Components, 2nd Edition*, provides
developers with the information and real
world examples they need to create custom ASP components.

ADO: ActiveX Data Objects

By Jason T. Roff
1st Edition May 2001 (est.)
450 pages (est.), ISBN 1-56592-415-0

The architecture of ADO, Microsoft's newest
form of database communication, is simple,
concise, and efficient. This indispensable
reference takes a comprehensive look at
every object, collection, method, and property
of ADO for developers who want to get a leg
up on this exciting new technology.

Subclassing & Hooking with Visual Basic

By Stephen Teilhet
1st Edition June 2001 (est.)
722 pages (est.), ISBN 0-596-00118-5

Subclassing and the Windows hooking
mechanism ("hooks") allow developers
to manipulate, modify, or even discard
messages bound for other objects within the
operating system, in the process changing the
way in which the system behaves. This book
opens up a wealth of possibilities to the Visual Basic developer –
possibilities that ordinarily are completely unavailable, or at least
not easy to implement.

Win32 API Programming with Visual Basic

By Steve Roman
1st Edition November 1999
534 pages, Includes CD-ROM
ISBN 1-56592-631-5

This book provides the missing documentation
for VB programmers who want to harness the
power of accessing the Win32 API within
Visual Basic. It shows how to create powerful
and unique applications without needing a
background in Visual C++ or Win32 API programming.

O'REILLY®

TO ORDER: **800-998-9938** • **order@oreilly.com** • **http://www.oreilly.com/**
OUR PRODUCTS ARE AVAILABLE AT A BOOKSTORE OR SOFTWARE STORE NEAR YOU.
FOR INFORMATION: **800-998-9938** • **707-829-0515** • **info@oreilly.com**

How to stay in touch with O'Reilly

1. Visit Our Award-Winning Web Site

http://www.oreilly.com/

★"Top 100 Sites on the Web" —*PC Magazine*
★"Top 5% Web sites" —*Point Communications*
★"3-Star site" —*The McKinley Group*

Our web site contains a library of comprehensive product information (including book excerpts and tables of contents), downloadable software, background articles, interviews with technology leaders, links to relevant sites, book cover art, and more. File us in your Bookmarks or Hotlist!

2. Join Our Email Mailing Lists

New Product Releases

To receive automatic email with brief descriptions of all new O'Reilly products as they are released, send email to:
ora-news-subscribe@lists.oreilly.com
Put the following information in the first line of your message (*not* in the Subject field):
subscribe ora-news

O'Reilly Events

If you'd also like us to send information about trade show events, special promotions, and other O'Reilly events, send email to:
ora-news-subscribe@lists.oreilly.com
Put the following information in the first line of your message (*not* in the Subject field):
subscribe ora-events

3. Get Examples from Our Books via FTP

There are two ways to access an archive of example files from our books:

Regular FTP

- ftp to:
  ftp.oreilly.com
  (login: anonymous
  password: your email address)
- Point your web browser to:
  ftp://ftp.oreilly.com/

FTPMAIL

- Send an email message to:
  ftpmail@online.oreilly.com
  (Write "help" in the message body)

4. Contact Us via Email

order@oreilly.com
To place a book or software order online. Good for North American and international customers.

subscriptions@oreilly.com
To place an order for any of our newsletters or periodicals.

books@oreilly.com
General questions about any of our books.

software@oreilly.com
For general questions and product information about our software. Check out O'Reilly Software Online at **http://software.oreilly.com/** for software and technical support information. Registered O'Reilly software users send your questions to: **website-support@oreilly.com**

cs@oreilly.com
For answers to problems regarding your order or our products.

booktech@oreilly.com
For book content technical questions or corrections.

proposals@oreilly.com
To submit new book or software proposals to our editors and product managers.

international@oreilly.com
For information about our international distributors or translation queries. For a list of our distributors outside of North America check out:
http://www.oreilly.com/distributors.html

5. Work with Us

Check out our website for current employment opportunites:
http://jobs.oreilly.com/

O'Reilly & Associates, Inc.
101 Morris Street, Sebastopol, CA 95472 USA
TEL   707-829-0515 or 800-998-9938
       (6am to 5pm PST)
FAX   707-829-0104

O'REILLY®

International Distributors

http://international.oreilly.com/distributors.html

UK, EUROPE, MIDDLE EAST AND AFRICA (EXCEPT FRANCE, GERMANY, AUSTRIA, SWITZERLAND, LUXEMBOURG, AND LIECHTENSTEIN)

INQUIRIES
O'Reilly UK Limited
4 Castle Street
Farnham
Surrey, GU9 7HS
United Kingdom
Telephone: 44-1252-711776
Fax: 44-1252-734211
Email: information@oreilly.co.uk

ORDERS
Wiley Distribution Services Ltd.
1 Oldlands Way
Bognor Regis
West Sussex PO22 9SA
United Kingdom
Telephone: 44-1243-843294
UK Freephone: 0800-243207
Fax: 44-1243-843302 (Europe/EU orders)
or 44-1243-843274 (Middle East/Africa)
Email: cs-books@wiley.co.uk

FRANCE

INQUIRIES & ORDERS
Éditions O'Reilly
18 rue Séguier
75006 Paris, France
Tel: 1-40-51-71-89
Fax: 1-40-51-72-26
Email: france@oreilly.fr

GERMANY, SWITZERLAND, AUSTRIA, LUXEMBOURG, AND LIECHTENSTEIN

INQUIRIES & ORDERS
O'Reilly Verlag
Balthasarstr. 81
D-50670 Köln, Germany
Telephone: 49-221-973160-91
Fax: 49-221-973160-8
Email: anfragen@oreilly.de (inquiries)
Email: order@oreilly.de (orders)

CANADA (FRENCH LANGUAGE BOOKS)

Les Éditions Flammarion ltée
375, Avenue Laurier Ouest
Montréal (Québec) H2V 2K3
Tel: 00-1-514-277-8807
Fax: 00-1-514-278-2085
Email: info@flammarion.qc.ca

HONG KONG

City Discount Subscription Service, Ltd.
Unit A, 6th Floor, Yan's Tower
27 Wong Chuk Hang Road
Aberdeen, Hong Kong
Tel: 852-2580-3539
Fax: 852-2580-6463
Email: citydis@ppn.com.hk

KOREA

Hanbit Media, Inc.
Chungmu Bldg. 210
Yonnam-dong 568-33
Mapo-gu
Seoul, Korea
Tel: 822-325-0397
Fax: 822-325-9697
Email: hant93@chollian.dacom.co.kr

PHILIPPINES

Global Publishing
G/F Benavides Garden
1186 Benavides Street
Manila, Philippines
Tel: 632-254-8949/632-252-2582
Fax: 632-734-5060/632-252-2733
Email: globalp@pacific.net.ph

TAIWAN

O'Reilly Taiwan
1st Floor, No. 21, Lane 295
Section 1, Fu-Shing South Road
Taipei, 106 Taiwan
Tel: 886-2-27099669
Fax: 886-2-27038802
Email: mori@oreilly.com

INDIA

Shroff Publishers & Distributors Pvt. Ltd.
12, "Roseland", 2nd Floor
180, Waterfield Road, Bandra (West)
Mumbai 400 050
Tel: 91-22-641-1800/643-9910
Fax: 91-22-643-2422
Email: spd@vsnl.com

CHINA

O'Reilly Beijing
SIGMA Building, Suite B809
No. 49 Zhichun Road
Haidian District
Beijing, China PR 100080
Tel: 86-10-8809-7475
Fax: 86-10-8809-7463
Email: beijing@oreilly.com

JAPAN

O'Reilly Japan, Inc.
Yotsuya Y's Building
7 Banch 6, Honshio-cho
Shinjuku-ku
Tokyo 160-0003 Japan
Tel: 81-3-3356-5227
Fax: 81-3-3356-5261
Email: japan@oreilly.com

SINGAPORE, INDONESIA, MALAYSIA AND THAILAND

TransQuest Publishers Pte Ltd
30 Old Toh Tuck Road #05-02
Sembawang Kimtrans Logistics Centre
Singapore 597654
Tel: 65-4623112
Fax: 65-4625761
Email: wendiw@transquest.com.sg

ALL OTHER ASIAN COUNTRIES

O'Reilly & Associates, Inc.
101 Morris Street
Sebastopol, CA 95472 USA
Tel: 707-829-0515
Fax: 707-829-0104
Email: order@oreilly.com

AUSTRALIA

Woodslane Pty., Ltd.
7/5 Vuko Place
Warriewood NSW 2102
Australia
Tel: 61-2-9970-5111
Fax: 61-2-9970-5002
Email: info@woodslane.com.au

NEW ZEALAND

Woodslane New Zealand, Ltd.
21 Cooks Street (P.O. Box 575)
Waganui, New Zealand
Tel: 64-6-347-6543
Fax: 64-6-345-4840
Email: info@woodslane.com.au

ARGENTINA

Distribuidora Cuspide
Suipacha 764
1008 Buenos Aires
Argentina
Phone: 5411-4322-8868
Fax: 5411-4322-3456
Email: libros@cuspide.com

O'REILLY®